Y0-BYK-742

Economic and Social Survey of Asia and the Pacific 2009

Addressing
Triple Threats to
Development

United Nations

New York, 2009

ECONOMIC AND SOCIAL COMMISSION FOR ASIA AND THE PACIFIC

ECONOMIC AND SOCIAL SURVEY OF ASIA AND THE PACIFIC 2009

Addressing Triple Threats to Development

United Nations publication
Sales No. E.09.II.F.11
Copyright © United Nations 2009
All rights reserved
Manufactured in Thailand
ISBN: 978-92-1-120577-0
ISSN: 0252-5704
ST/ESCAP/2522

FOREWORD

We are living through a period of tremendous turmoil and uncertainty. The current global economic downturn is not the only crisis. Volatility in food and fuel prices has raised levels of poverty, hunger and malnutrition in many countries. The overarching menace of climate change, meanwhile, threatens to undermine all our work for development.

These crises are interrelated. All have profound social and political implications. Each needs solutions that take the others into account. The *Economic and Social Survey of Asia and the Pacific 2009* analyses how these multiple threats have affected the region, and considers ways in which the region can address them. The *Survey's* central thrust is that the convergence of the crises and the fundamental changes they have brought to the macroeconomic landscape present a unique opportunity for the region to make growth more fair and inclusive. Furthermore, by implementing reforms in unison, the region can make a major contribution to reshaping the global economic architecture.

We face unprecedented threats to development. Our immediate task is to help the poor and vulnerable get through these hard times, the devastating effects of which are still unfolding. Over the long term, we must find a more equitable and sustainable path for all the world's people. The recommendations in this publication are meant to inspire policy-makers to be bold and collaborative. In that spirit, I commend this *Survey* to a wide global audience.

BAN Ki-moon
Secretary-General of the United Nations

March 2009

PREFACE

In 2008, three global crises converged to threaten development in the Asia-Pacific region, bringing to the fore particularly testing challenges for policymakers – a Great Recession in developed countries, food and fuel price volatility and climate change calamities. The *Economic and Social Survey of Asia and the Pacific 2009* analyses these threats and outlines ways in which economies in the region can move forward in unison from crisis resilience to crisis resistance. It concludes that some countries in the region are in a stronger position to help not only themselves but also others to smooth the impact of the crises and strengthen regional solidarity. The converging crises could be turned into an opportunity to jump-start a regional reorientation towards a more inclusive and sustainable development path.

Asia and the Pacific as a crisis-prone region...

During the first part of the year, crude oil prices soared to historical record levels and food commodity prices increased to the highest levels in over 20 years, causing alarm across the developing countries of the Asia-Pacific region because of the disproportionate impact of these increases on the poor. The impact was particularly severe in this region, where the price of main staple food, rice, increased by a staggering 150% in only four months. As the second half of the year unfolded and commodity prices started to retreat from their peaks, financial turbulence that had remained largely confined to the United States subprime market took a dramatic turn for the worse, turning into a full-fledged global financial crisis and setting in motion the most severe economic downturn of the world economy in post-war history. By early September, it was clear that, for the second time in a decade, the region would be hit by a financial crisis and that the crisis would be particularly damaging in view of the region's heavy reliance on exports to industrial countries for growth. A total of 24 million people are in danger of losing their jobs, with women and youth – who make up a large share of the manufacturing workforce – disproportionately affected, and this is aggravated by an increase in the number of undernourished to 583 million in 2007 (from 542 million in 2003-2005). A worsening of the state of poverty and hunger in the region is now impossible to avoid.

In 2008, yet a third global crisis loomed on the horizon – a stealthier but potentially more virulent one than the first two: climate change calamities. Natural disasters, often associated with climate change stresses and lower tolerance to increased heat in lower latitudes of this region, struck with intensity in 2008. The number of deaths in Asia and the Pacific in 2008 reached 232,500 persons, accounting for a staggering 97.5% of such fatalities worldwide. One of the deadliest storms ever to occur in the North Indian Ocean Basin, Cyclone Nargis, made landfall in Myanmar's Ayeyarwady Delta on 2 May 2008 and left a heart-wrenching trail of death and destruction – 84,500 people dead and 53,000 missing. Australia's "big dry", the worst drought in more than 100 years, entered its seventh year with fires – believed to be the worst in its history – causing widespread devastation and hundreds of deaths in the south-eastern part of the country. Natural disasters tore apart communities at the opposite ends of the development spectrum, just as the origin of financial crises showed that they no longer fit into easy developed- versus developing-country classifications.

...yet, its developing countries show remarkable resilience to the financial crisis

Developing countries in the region have shown that they are better prepared for a financial crisis. Over the past decade, their regulatory reforms in the financial sector, combined with cautious macroeconomic management policies, have improved current account balances, fiscal deficits and other macroeconomic shortcomings and built a protective shield of foreign exchange reserves. To a large extent, therefore, the region possesses the resilience to withstand the worst of the deleveraging process that caused the global financial system to spiral downwards, leaving no financial institution unaffected.

Export growth in 2008 remained strong until the third quarter, buoyed by weakening currencies and relatively robust external demand. The developing countries of the region managed to maintain an average growth rate of 5.8%, as compared with –0.4% in Asia-Pacific developed economies. The region continued on its long-term development path, which is predicated on an outward-oriented and export-led development paradigm that enabled it to attain astounding progress and remarkable transformations over the past two decades. In 2009, the region's developing countries are expected to grow at 3.6%, which – compared with growth of –2.0% in the world's major developed countries – further highlights the region's resilience to the crises. This comparatively high growth, coupled with the large aggregate size of the region's economies, could result in the Asia-Pacific region being the locus of any global growth that may take place in 2009.

Of course, not all countries exhibited this resilience. Some countries have been more exposed than others to short-term financial flows, and their currencies have suffered from the retreat of those flows from the region in the last quarter of 2008. Other countries have substantially less fiscal space to implement necessary expansionary fiscal policies. Nevertheless, major developing countries in the region were in a stronger position, which presents them with an opportunity to renew partnerships among themselves and with developed countries to bridge equity divides and contribute to strengthened regional solidarity.

...but major vulnerabilities remain

Resilience notwithstanding, this is no time for complacency. The crisis-prone nature of the region has brought to the fore vulnerabilities that need to be carefully tracked and for which forward planning and policy action will be essential.

Paradoxically, some of the region's vulnerabilities are the very reasons for its success. The fact that the region is more integrated through finance, trade, investment, technology, transport and knowledge with the rest of the world than with itself has allowed it to benefit for decades from export-led growth. But these linkages are also channels through which global instabilities and economic recession are transmitted to the region.

Trade – once the engine of growth in the region – moved from double-digit growth to double-digit declines in some economies during the fourth quarter of 2008, and fresh evidence indicates that the worst is yet to come. As the economic outlook continues to darken at the global level, the tried and true recourse that mitigated the economic crisis in 1998 – boosting exports – has lost its effectiveness. Although intraregional trade has grown dynamically over the last decade, its cushioning effects are stymied by the fact that it consisted largely of trade in parts and components in the manufacturing sector that are, in turn, linked to demand for final consumer products in recession-hit developed countries. Economies with enterprises that are most directly linked through vertically integrated production networks supplying the United States and European Union markets – such as China, the Republic of Korea, Singapore, Thailand, and Hong Kong, China – are those experiencing the strongest downward pressure on economic growth. Another worrisome signal on the trade front is the growing protectionist pressure in recession-hit countries, where domestic sourcing of inputs is given preferential treatment over imports – often as conditionalities imposed on bailout packages – could distort market-entry conditions for exports from Asia-Pacific countries. Furthermore, declining – or at best sluggish – exports will keep exchange rates in the region under pressure, with a marked possibility of further devaluations both among currencies within the region and vis-à-vis the currencies of main trading partners outside the region, in an effort to enhance export competitiveness. If conducted in an uncoordinated manner, devaluation could lead to unnecessary losses in foreign exchange earnings across the region and increased debt burdens.

An area of immediate concern for the region is the significant share of foreign portfolio capital in external financial liabilities in some economies of the region. At a time of generalized international risk aversion in which flights to safety have low-threshold triggers, defending excessive currency depreciation due to the exit of short-term portfolio capital can reduce the amount of reserves available to cover external short-term debt repayments and current account deficits. It is clear that access to a greater pool of reserves than is normally adequate is now needed to reassure investors and it can in turn serve to reduce the extent of net capital outflows.

A further concern is that, when economic growth resumes its long-term trend, it could cause a return of the sharp increases in commodity prices experienced in recent years. This is highly likely because imbalances between fast-rising demand and sluggish supply responses have yet to be resolved. The risk of recurring commodity price rises may be exacerbated by the massive liquidity created for stimulus programmes, which may find its way into commodity futures markets once again, adding volatility to the expected increasing price trend. Furthermore, the current low agricultural prices are reducing incentives for farmers to invest for the long-term, perpetuating the neglect of agriculture and making it more difficult to reverse. Further compounding the risks to future agricultural production are the changes in temperatures and rain patterns that climate change will bring. For all these reasons, threats to food security resembling those of recent years loom large and will intensify in the medium to long term.

A major concern in the region is that the coverage of basic social protection programmes is very low: only 30% of the elderly receive pensions; and only 20% of the unemployed and underemployed have access to labour market programmes, such as unemployment benefits, training or public works programmes, including work-for-food programmes. In addition, only 20% of the population has access to health-care assistance. In fact, Asia and the Pacific has the highest out-of-pocket health-care expenditures in the world.

While progress was made in the aftermath of the 1997 financial crisis, this issue moved off the radar of policymakers, as resumed economic growth generated new jobs and business opportunities, lifting millions out of poverty. At the same time, inequality worsened in all countries.

The vulnerabilities facing the region underline the risk that the convergence of the three crises – a triple threat – could bring compounding effects that would superimpose new layers of crises. With the list of distressed institutions and people growing – be it ailing banks, strategic industries, the growing ranks of the unemployed in urban areas or farmers unprepared for commodity price shocks – it is certain that any complacency on the part of policymakers will see the increased ranks of the poor put substantial pressure on social cohesiveness. Increased poverty amid great inequality will be a combustible combination. As the late Indira Gandhi prophetically warned four decades ago, at the twenty-third session of the General Assembly:

> "The chasm between the rich and poor nations, which is already a source of tension and bitterness in the world, is not decreasing but growing…It is natural that we in the developing countries should be more aware of the peril than those who live in the affluent countries. The peril is on our doorstep, but it is not too far from theirs".

There is thus a significant risk that developed country recession may evolve into a deeper and wider regional crisis that will bring with it political instability, widespread social unrest, further downward pressures on economic growth, rising unemployment, and a new cycle of crises, both within and among countries.

…and yet, the triple crisis could be turned into an opportunity to address policy gaps and reorient the development paradigm

While the Asia-Pacific region emerges with economic performance indicators that are showing resilience, its increasing vulnerability to crises brings to the fore a number of policy challenges. Impacts of the crises varied among subregions, as did coping mechanisms, and even though there are a number countries that could take action alone to overcome the worst of the crisis, the global scope common to all three crises underlines the need for policy coordination: Cooperation among countries to enhance mutually reinforcing synergies in policy interventions, evolving long-term planning perspectives, identifying best practices, exchanging ideas about which policies work best in different contexts – all are clearly needed. Working together, as a region, towards the common goal of improving the livelihoods of their people in difficult circumstances will also motivate individual countries to persist in the implementation of new and challenging policy agendas, which would be difficult to do in isolation.

At a time when the convergence of three crises threatens development in the Asia-Pacific region, there is a need for comprehensive responses that balance economic, social and environmental considerations, for partial responses will only provide a temporary respite until a new major crisis hits the region. The *Survey* proposes a number of crisis-specific and comprehensive policy actions, which are highlighted below, in which regional cooperation can be boosted.

Asia-Pacific role in reforming the multilateral system of economic governance

The reform of the global financial architecture is currently under intense debate and should remain at the top of the international policy agenda for some time to come. Commensurate with its rising contribution to global economic prosperity, the Asia-Pacific region should have an increasingly influential voice in shaping the future multilateral system of governance. Rules reducing frictions in trade, albeit imperfect, have been in the making for 70 years. In contrast, financial regulation has remained to a large extent nationalized despite the integrated nature of financial markets and the increasing frequency and costs of crises. To cite but one example: international coordination of monetary, financial and fiscal policies could prevent excessive liquidity build-up in international financial markets, which might otherwise find an outlet in speculation on commodity markets.

A world finance mechanism, either through reform of the current architecture, or through the creation of a new organization that balances efficient decision-making with global representation, through a variable geometry configuration of decision-making and consensus building, is certainly needed. The time to act is now, and through a more effective use of existing regional platforms, Governments and their partners in Asia-Pacific countries can debate the policy options, sharpen their focus and build political consensus around the multilateral reforms needed. It is clear that, in the coming years, much more work will be needed towards creating a more stable, inclusive and sustainable system of economic governance at the multilateral level.

On the trade front, there is a need to ensure that WTO rules and principles, including a conclusion of the Doha Round of negotiations, are upheld in the service of development. With export opportunities for the region rapidly declining and protectionist pressures rising as recession-hit economies scramble to support ailing domestic industries, a strengthening of the multilateral trading system is called for, as this system can offer the most stable, predictable and transparent environment in which to conduct global and regional trade for development.

Prioritization of regional macroeconomic cooperation

At the regional level, a largely neglected debate concerns the formulation of effective and coordinated macroeconomic policies to move the region from crisis-resilience to crisis-resistance. Coordinated monetary and fiscal responses have greater credibility and help shore up confidence while enhancing regional and global multiplier effects. Furthermore, coordinated responses will enable countries to institute measures to "insulate themselves from regulatory and macroeconomic failures in systemically significant countries", as recommended by the Commission of Experts of the President of the United Nations General Assembly on Reforms of the International Monetary and Financial System in January 2009. Exchange rate coordination would benefit from the establishment of more coordinated and durable regional arrangements, as would the closely related challenge of managing vulnerability to reversals in short-term capital flows.

Of equal concern for Asia and the Pacific is the need to establish a regional contingency plan to respond quickly to the liquidity and capitalization problems of domestic banks. However, this would require the accelerated establishment of a regional surveillance system that focuses on emerging risks.

The curtailment of trade has been exacerbated by the lack of trade credit. Somewhat anomalously for this trade-oriented region, it is the only one that does not have a regional institution specifically dedicated to export credit and export credit guarantees. A regional trade financing facility would enable risk pooling across countries and scale economies, and would be more credible than isolated national initiatives, thus offering countries with special needs, in particular, greater access to international finance. There should be an accelerated process of analysis and dialogue in order to establish such a facility. The announcement by the Government of Japan that a $1 billion fund would be set up through the Japan Bank for International Cooperation (JBIC) in collaboration inter alia, with ADB is an important step in the right direction.

Addressing food security and sustainable agriculture

In order to reduce the likelihood that commodity price crises will occur in the future, it is important to promote energy efficiency and investment in renewable sources of energy. Securing energy supplies and speeding up the transition to a low-carbon energy system calls for decisive action by governments at the national and local levels to encourage households and businesses to economize their use of fuel and energy suppliers to invest in developing and commercializing low-carbon technologies. Appropriate financial incentives and regulatory frameworks are needed to support both goals.

The state of deprivation of smallholder farmers needs to be addressed in order to improve the food supply response, reduce poverty and make growth more inclusive. To achieve these objectives in a sustainable manner, increased public investments, particularly through the fiscal stimulus packages being designed or already under implementation, are needed. Of key concern is the need to alleviate conditions for small farmers throughout the supply chain – at the farm level and in production infrastructure, access to markets and processing.

Biofuels have proven to be double edged. Biofuel guidelines and safeguards that minimize adverse impacts on global food security and the environment will be needed at the global level. A regional preparatory and policy coordination process would be important to ensure that region-specific challenges are adequately addressed at the global level.

Building the social foundations for more resilient societies

The rapid economic growth that the region has experienced over the last few decades is creating the means to make definitive progress in eradicating poverty and hunger, but reaching such goals calls for the implementation of effective social protection systems. As the current crisis weaves its way through the fabric of society, social protection should build strong social foundations that will make societies more crisis resilient. Furthermore, by providing a basic level of income support, protection schemes make individuals feel more secure and less inclined to increase their savings to protect themselves from possible income losses in times of crisis, thereby contributing to domestic demand and macroeconomic stability. The provision of social protection thus makes for good economics. These systems however, should be put in place as part of an overall long term strategy of building resilient social foundations rather than being ad hoc crisis-driven initiatives. The objective of enhancing social protection as a means of strengthening the social foundation for a more inclusive society should thus be included as part of a framework for a new future development paradigm for the region.

Mitigating and adapting to climate change

Although policy attention is focused on fighting the economic crisis and political commitment on climate change may be fading, there is not necessarily a contradiction between these two policy objectives. The Global Green New Deal promoted by the Secretary-General is based on the premise that investing in the green economy can both generate millions of jobs and start addressing the challenges associated with reducing carbon dependency, protecting ecosystems and preserving water resources. Initiatives such as this require a drastic change in the "grow first and clean up later" attitude towards climate change, and that must be done through behavioural change because, if the burdens of climate change mitigation and adaptation are foisted on future generations, the cost will be prohibitively high. Cooperation among developing countries in the region to develop more practical and affordable climate-friendly technologies in energy efficiency, renewable energy and carbon capture and storage is another area with untapped potential.

Evolving appropriate financial incentives and regulatory frameworks on a regional cooperative basis would help to secure energy supplies and speed up the transition to a low-carbon energy system to encourage (a) households and businesses to economize their use of fuel and (b) energy suppliers to invest in developing and commercializing low-carbon technologies. Further development and implementation of the ESCAP framework on renewable and sustainable energy should be given priority, while the region should, play a more influential role in the multilateral process of climate change negotiations.

Boosting regional cooperation through an Asia-Pacific framework for inclusive and sustainable growth and development

The recommendations highlighted above have complex and, in many ways, novel linkages with each other. The scale of the economic crisis and related challenges is such that Governments will be required – and many have already started – to put in place public expenditure programmes on a much larger scale and with a much longer reach than in the past. However, boosting public expenditure to jump-start battered economies is only part of the response; it is more important for Governments to use this opportunity to jump-start a reorientation of the development paradigm towards more inclusive and sustainable economic growth.

Serving as a knowledge-based hub, ESCAP can be a forum for exploring policy options and forging a consensus on regional cooperation and policy coordination. Building on the work of the secretariat of ESCAP – notably, its leadership in promoting low-carbon green growth, the 2008 theme study on energy security and sustainable development in Asia and the Pacific and the Bali Outcome Document and subsequent policy analyses – a consultative process involving key policy- and decision makers could be started, in partnership with interested stakeholders, with the goal of devising a framework that will guide future policy planning towards a regional development paradigm that rebalances economic, social and environmental systems. A new priority needs to be given to government as a planner of development while also ensuring that comprehensiveness is the key principle that guides this framework, for partial frameworks can create potential inconsistencies by which the pursuit of one goal is detrimental to another. The consensus reached at the regional level can then provide a building block for a truly inclusive multilateral system of economic governance.

In conclusion, the costs and risks inherent in market failures and the decades-long neglect of the traditional capabilities of government have proven too brutal. The convergence of crises could be turned into an opportunity to move the regional policy agenda towards a more stable, inclusive and sustainable process of economic growth that will preserve the progress of the past and enable it to continue into the future. The time to act is now, and in unison, for the peace and security of all the peoples of the United Nations.

Noeleen Heyzer
Under-Secretary-General of the United Nations and
Executive Secretary, United Nations Economic and
Social Commission for Asia and the Pacific

ACKNOWLEDGEMENTS

This report was prepared under the substantive direction and guidance of Noeleen Heyzer, Under-Secretary-General of the United Nations and Executive Secretary of the Economic and Social Commission for Asia and the Pacific (ESCAP), and under the overall supervision of Shigeru Mochida, Deputy Executive Secretary of ESCAP and Officer-in-Charge of the Macroeconomic Policy and Development Division. The core team, led by Tiziana Bonapace, included Amarakoon Bandara, Shuvojit Banerjee, Somchai Congtavinsutti, Eugene Gherman, Aynul Hasan, Alberto Isgut, Nobuko Kajiura, Muhammad H. Malik and Amy Wong.

Many others provided substantive contributions and gave helpful comments and advice. ESCAP staff who contributed substantively include: Christopher Kuonqui, Sangmin Nam and Le Huu Ti of the Environment and Development Division; Shahid Din and Cihat Basocak of the Information and Communications Technology and Disaster Risk Reduction Division; Beverly Jones and Marco Roncarati of the Social Development Division; Andres Montes of the Statistics Division; Mia Mikic of the Trade and Investment Division; John Moon and Madan Regmi of the Transport Division; and Siliga Kofe and Hirohito Toda of the ESCAP Pacific Operations Centre. The statistical annex was prepared by the Statistics Division, with Eric Hermouet acting as the focal point (tables 10-18), and Somchai Congtavinsutti (tables 1-9), of the Macroeconomic Policy and Development Division. Kinlay Dorjee, of the FAO Regional Office for Asia and the Pacific, Bangkok and Phu Huynh, of the International Labour Organization, Bangkok, also made substantive contributions.

Valuable advice and extensive comments were received from Jorge Carrillo, Jeffrey Crawford, Yann Duval, Matthew Hengesbaugh, Kyungkoo Kang, Raj Kumar, Aneta Nikolova, Marit Nilses, Syed Nuruzzaman, Simon Olsen, Hiren Sarkar, David Smith, Srinivas Tata, J.L. Vignuda, Ryuji Yamakawa and Zhendai Yang (ESCAP); Pingfan Hong, Matthias Kempf, Hung-Yi Li, Ingo Pitterle, and Rob Vos (Department of Economic and Social Affairs, United Nations, New York); Suzanne Hinsz and Mahesh Patel (United Nations Children's Fund); Garimella Giridhar (United Nations Population Fund, Thailand); Pilar Fajarnes (United Nations Conference on Trade and Development); Yilmaz Akyüz (Third World Network); Ramkishen Rajan (George Mason University); Scott Irwin (University of Illinois).

The following consultants provided country reports: Mushtaq Ahmad, Sonam Chuki, Tarun Das, Ron Duncan, Mohammad Kordbache, Panom Lathouly, Hang Chuon Naron and Prakash Kumar Shrestha.

The report benefitted from an external peer review, which incorporated comments and suggestions from a group of prominent Asian policymakers, scholars and development practitioners, namely: Myrna Clara B. Asuncion, Assistant Director, National Planning and Policy Staff, National Economic and Development Authority, Philippines; Juergen Bischoff, Director, GTZ-ASEM, India; Stephen Y.L. Cheung, Professor (Chair) of Finance, City University of Hong Kong; Tarun Das, Professor (Public Policy), Institute for Integrated Learning in Management, India; Ashfaque H. Khan, Special Secretary Finance/Director General (Debt Office), Ministry of Finance, Pakistan; Opart Panya, Assistant Professor, Faculty of Environment and Resource Studies, Mahidol University, Thailand; Prabowo, Director, Strategic Asia, Indonesia; Ramkishen S. Rajan, Associate Professor, School of Public Policy, George Mason University Arlington, United States of America; Marsel Salikhov, Head of Economic Research, Institute of Energy and Finance, Russian Federation.

Sarah Comer, Tommy Kostka, Aphitchaya Nguanbanchong, Kiatkanid Pongpanich and Amornrut Supornsinchai of the Macroeconomic Policy and Development Division, ESCAP provided research assistance.

The manuscript was edited by Bruce Ross-Larson and Peter Whitten of Communications Development Incorporated, Orestes Plasencia and Suzanne Starcevic, Editorial Unit of ESCAP and Peter Stalker. The layout and printing were provided by TR Enterprise, and Parottawat Dechsupha contributed to the design of the cover page.

Woranut Sompitayanurak, supported by Metinee Hunkosol, Anong Pattanathanes and Sutinee Yeamkitpibul of the Macroeconomic Policy and Development Division, ESCAP, proofread the manuscript and undertook all administrative processing necessary for the issuance of the publication.

Hak-Fan Lau, Ari Gaitanis, Bentley Jenson, Thawadi Pachariyangkun and Chavalit Boonthanom of the United Nations Information Service, coordinated the launch and dissemination of the report.

CONTENTS

CONTENTS *(continued)*

CONTENTS *(continued)*

BOXES

TABLES

FIGURES

FIGURES *(continued)*

FIGURES *(continued)*

FIGURES *(continued)*

EXPLANATORY NOTES

Staff analysis in the *Survey 2009* is based on data and information available up to the end of January 2009.

The term "ESCAP region" is used in the present issue of the *Survey* to include Afghanistan; American Samoa; Armenia; Australia; Azerbaijan; Bangladesh; Bhutan; Brunei Darussalam; Cambodia; China; Cook Islands; Democratic People's Republic of Korea; Fiji; French Polynesia; Georgia; Guam; Hong Kong, China; India; Indonesia; Iran (Islamic Republic of); Japan; Kazakhstan; Kiribati; Kyrgyzstan; Lao People's Democratic Republic; Macao, China; Malaysia; Maldives; Marshall Islands; Micronesia (Federated States of); Mongolia; Myanmar; Nauru; Nepal; New Caledonia; New Zealand; Niue; Northern Mariana Islands; Pakistan; Palau; Papua New Guinea; Philippines; Republic of Korea; Russian Federation; Samoa; Singapore; Solomon Islands; Sri Lanka; Tajikistan; Thailand; Timor-Leste; Tonga; Turkey; Turkmenistan; Tuvalu; Uzbekistan; Vanuatu; and Viet Nam. The term "developing ESCAP region" excludes Australia, Japan and New Zealand. Non-regional members of ESCAP are France, the Netherlands, the United Kingdom of Great Britain and Northern Ireland and the United States of America.

The term "Central Asian countries" in this issue of the *Survey* refers to Armenia, Azerbaijan, Georgia, Kazakhstan, Kyrgyzstan, Tajikistan, Turkmenistan and Uzbekistan.

The term "East and North-East Asia" in this issue of the *Survey* refers to China; Hong Kong, China; Mongolia; and the Republic of Korea.

The designations employed and the presentation of the material in this publication do not imply the expression of any opinion whatsoever on the part of the Secretariat of the United Nations concerning the legal status of any country, territory, city or area, or of its authorities, or concerning the delimitation of its frontiers or boundaries.

Mention of firm names and commercial products does not imply the endorsement of the United Nations.

The abbreviated title *Survey* in footnotes refers to the *Economic and Social Survey of Asia and the Pacific* for the year indicated.

Many figures used in the *Survey* are on a fiscal year basis and are assigned to the calendar year which covers the major part or second half of the fiscal year.

Growth rates are on an annual basis, except where indicated otherwise.

Reference to "tons" indicates metric tons.

Values are in United States dollars unless specified otherwise.

The term "billion" signifies a thousand million. The term "trillion" signifies a million million.

In the tables, two dots (..) indicate that data are not available or are not separately reported, a dash (–) indicates that the amount is nil or negligible, and a blank indicates that the item is not applicable.

In dates, a hyphen (-) is used to signify the full period involved, including the beginning and end years, and a stroke (/) indicates a crop year, fiscal year or plan year. The fiscal years, currencies and 2008 exchange rates of the economies in the ESCAP region are listed in the following table:

Country or area in the ESCAP region	Fiscal year	Currency and abbreviation	Rate of exchange for $1 as at December 2008
Afghanistan	21 March to 20 March	afghani (Af)	52.12
American Samoa	..	United States dollar ($)	1.00
Armenia	1 January to 31 December	dram	305.10[a]
Australia	1 July to 30 June	Australian dollar ($A)	1.44
Azerbaijan	1 January to 31 December	Azeri manat (AZM)	0.81[a]
Bangladesh	1 July to 30 June	taka (Tk)	68.94
Bhutan	1 July to 30 June	ngultrum (Nu)	49.25[a]
Brunei Darussalam	1 January to 31 December	Brunei dollar (B$)	1.48
Cambodia	1 January to 31 December	riel (CR)	4 081.00
China	1 January to 31 December	yuan renminbi (Y)	6.84
Cook Islands	1 April to 31 March	New Zealand dollar ($NZ)	1.72
Democratic People's Republic of Korea	..	won (W)	139.00
Fiji	1 January to 31 December	Fiji dollar (F$)	1.83[a]
French Polynesia	..	French Pacific Community franc (FCFP)	85.73

Country or area in the ESCAP region	Fiscal year	Currency and abbreviation	Rate of exchange for $1 as at December 2008
Georgia	1 January to 31 December	lari (L)	1.67
Guam	1 October to 30 September	United States dollar ($)	1.00
Hong Kong, China	1 April to 31 March	Hong Kong dollar (HK$)	7.75
India	1 April to 31 March	Indian rupee (Rs)	48.45
Indonesia	1 April to 31 March	Indonesian rupiah (Rp)	10 950.00
Iran (Islamic Republic of)	21 March to 20 March	Iranian rial (Rls)	10 009.00[a]
Japan	1 April to 31 March	yen (¥)	90.28
Kazakhstan	1 January to 31 December	tenge (T)	120.77
Kiribati	1 January to 31 December	Australian dollar ($A)	1.44
Kyrgyzstan	1 January to 31 December	som (som)	38.21[b]
Lao People's Democratic Republic	1 October to 30 September	new kip (NK)	8 609.20[c]
Macao, China	1 July to 30 June	pataca (P)	7.98[a]
Malaysia	1 January to 31 December	ringgit (M$)	3.46
Maldives	1 January to 31 December	rufiyaa (Rf)	12.80
Marshall Islands	1 October to 30 September	United States dollar ($)	1.00
Micronesia (Federated States of)	1 October to 30 September	United States dollar ($)	1.00
Mongolia	1 January to 31 December	tugrik (Tug)	1 267.51
Myanmar	1 April to 31 March	kyat (K)	5.74
Nauru	1 July to 30 June	Australian dollar ($A)	1.44
Nepal	16 July to 15 July	Nepalese rupee (NRs)	79.60[b]
New Caledonia	..	French Pacific Community franc (FCFP)	85.73
New Zealand	1 April to 31 March	New Zealand dollar ($NZ)	1.72
Niue	1 April to 31 March	New Zealand dollar ($NZ)	1.72
Northern Mariana Islands	1 October to 30 September	United States dollar ($)	1.00
Pakistan	1 July to 30 June	Pakistan rupee (PRs)	79.11
Palau	1 October to 30 September	United States dollar ($)	1.00
Papua New Guinea	1 January to 31 December	kina (K)	2.68
Philippines	1 January to 31 December	Philippine peso (P)	47.49
Republic of Korea	1 January to 31 December	won (W)	1 262.00
Russian Federation	1 January to 31 December	ruble (R)	29.38
Samoa	1 July to 30 June	tala (WS$)	2.73[b]
Singapore	1 April to 31 March	Singapore dollar (S$)	1.44
Solomon Islands	1 January to 31 December	Solomon Islands dollar (SI$)	8.01
Sri Lanka	1 January to 31 December	Sri Lanka rupee (SL Rs)	113.33
Tajikistan	1 January to 31 December	somoni	3.45
Thailand	1 October to 30 September	baht (B)	34.98
Timor-Leste	1 July to 30 June	United States dollar ($)	1.00
Tonga	1 July to 30 June	pa'anga (T$)	2.07
Turkey	1 January to 31 December	Turkish lira (LT)	1.23
Turkmenistan	1 January to 31 December	Turkmen manat (M)	14 250.00[b]
Tuvalu	1 January to 31 December	Australian dollar ($A)	1.44
Uzbekistan	1 January to 31 December	som (som)	1 328.00[b]
Vanuatu	1 January to 31 December	vatu (VT)	112.62
Viet Nam	1 January to 31 December	dong (D)	16 977.00

Sources: United Nations, *Monthly Bulletin of Statistics* website, http://unstats.un.org/unsd/mbs/Default.aspx, 10 February 2009; CEIC Data Company Limited; and national sources.

[a] November 2008.
[b] October 2008.
[c] August 2008.

ABBREVIATIONS

ADB	Asian Development Bank
APCAEM	Asian and Pacific Centre for Agricultural Engineering and Machinery
ASEAN	Association of Southeast Asian Nations
BRT	bus rapid transit
CAPSA	Centre for Alleviation of Poverty through Secondary Crops Development in Asia and the Pacific
CDM	clean development mechanism
CD-ROM	compact disk read-only memory
CH_4	methane
c.i.f.	cost, insurance, freight
CNG	compressed natural gas
CO_2	carbon dioxide
CO_2e	equivalent carbon dioxide
CO_2-eq	carbon dioxide equivalent
CPI	consumer price index
CRED	Centre for Research on the Epidemiology of Disasters
CSR	corporate social responsibility
EIU	Economist Intelligence Unit
EM-DAT	Emergency Events Database
EU ETS	European Union Emission Trading Scheme
FAO	Food and Agriculture Organization of the United Nations
FDI	foreign direct investment
f.o.b.	free on broad
GDP	gross domestic product
GHG	greenhouse gas
IEA	International Energy Agency
IES	Integrated Environmental Strategies

ABBREVIATIONS *(continued)*

IGES	Institute for Global Environmental Strategies
ILO	International Labour Organization
IMF	International Monetary Fund
IPCC	Intergovernmental Panel on Climate Change
LIBOR	London Interbank Offer Rate
LPG	liquefied petroleum gas
M2	broad money supply
MDG	Millennium Development Goal
NGO	non-governmental organization
N_2O	nitrous oxide
NPL	non-performing loan
OECD	Organization for Economic Cooperation and Development
OFDA	Office of Foreign Disaster Assistance (United States)
ppm	parts per million
PPP	purchasing power parity
PRSPs	poverty reduction strategy papers
PTA	preferential trade agreement
R&D	research and development
REDAT	Regional Disaster Information Management System
SAARC	South Asian Association for Regional Cooperation
Sida	Swedish International Development Cooperation Agency
SME	medium-sized enterprise
TCG	Tripartite Core Group (ASEAN-United Nations-Myanmar)
UNCTAD	United Nations Conference on Trade and Development
UNDP	United Nations Development Programme
UNEP	United Nations Environment Programme

ABBREVIATIONS *(continued)*

UNFCCC	United Nations Framework Convention on Climate Change
USAID	United States Agency for International Development
VAT	value added tax
WFP	World Food Programme
WHO	World Health Organization
WMO	World Meteorological Organization
WTO	World Trade Organization
WWF	World Wildlife Fund

SOURCES OF QUOTATIONS

(a) Page 2: an excerpt from a statement entitled "Let us work together to promote economic development" delivered by President Hu Jintao at the APEC CEO Summit, held in Lima, Peru, on 21 November 2008 (source: http://www.fmprc.gov.cn/eng/wjdt/zyjh/t524324.htm).

(b) Page 40: an excerpt from the message of Prime Minister Manmohan Singh to the General Assembly of the United Nations on 26 September 2008 (source: http://www.un.int/india/2008/ind1452.pdf).

(c) Page 70: an excerpt from a statement delivered by President Lee Myung-bak as he presided over the first session of the Green Growth Commission of the Republic of Korea, published on 27 February 2009 (source: http://www.futuregov.net/articles/2009/feb/27/green-growth-commission-launched-korea/).

(d) Page 92: an excerpt from an exclusive interview with Prime Minister Lee Hsien Loong in the *Bangkok Post*, published 27 February 2009 (source: http://www.bangkokpost.com/news/asian/136919/exclusive-interview-with-singapore-prime-minister-lee-hsien-loong).

(e) Page 154: an excerpt from the message of Prime Minister Kevin Rudd to the General Assembly of the United Nations on 26 September 2008 (source: http://www.un.org/ga/63/generaldebate/pdf/australia_en.pdf).

(f) Page 172: an excerpt from a keynote speech delivered by President H. Susilo Bambang Yudhoyono at the APEC CEO Summit, held in Lima, Peru, on 21 November 2008 (source: http://www.presidenri.go.id/index.php/eng/pidato/2008/11/22/1035.html).

"The international community should earnestly draw lessons from the ongoing financial crisis and...undertake necessary reform of the international financial system...with a view to establishing a new international financial order that is fair, just, inclusive and orderly and fostering an institutional environment conducive to sound global economic development.

Hu Jintao
President of China

CHAPTER 1. THE RETURN OF THE FINANCIAL CRISIS: MANAGING, VULNERABILITIES AND DEEPENING REGIONAL COOPERATION

Asia-Pacific economies have been hit once again by a financial crisis. On 15 September 2008, the American investment bank Lehman Brothers collapsed, triggering an extraordinary downward spiral in confidence and financial turmoil. It was also the day when the crisis truly hit Asia-Pacific shores, spreading beyond its equity markets and posing the greatest threat to the region's development since the Asian financial crisis of 1997.

Many of the policy failures blamed on the region in 1997 were seen once again in the United States and Europe, albeit to varying degrees – lax supervision of financial systems, excessive credit creation and the build-up of asset bubbles. This time, the Asia-Pacific region is better prepared for currency and balance-of-payment crises than it was a decade ago, having improved current account balances and built up a protective shield of foreign-exchange reserves. Notwithstanding this resilience, the improvements have not been enough to prevent severe domestic impacts.

The crisis has worked its way through the Asia-Pacific region and has had deep repercussions on financial systems and real economies. Policymakers are now faced with the task of identifying vulnerabilities and finding ways in which the region's sources of resilience, built up from its experience with the 1997 crisis, can resist shocks in the future.

The global credit crunch has been far greater than at the peak of the 1997 crisis

---

Despite the downward pressures on equity markets, corporate profits and aggregate domestic demand, the financial markets have shown an inherent resilience and relative stability in the current crisis, especially when compared with previous crises. However, the region's integration with the global economy through finance, trade and investment has revealed potential vulnerabilities that will need to be tracked closely during the crisis. No country can address this threat to development on its own. What is needed are policies that enhance regional coordination and will enable the Asia-Pacific region to be crisis-resistant.

Impact of the crisis on Asia-Pacific

Decline in domestic demand and exports

Half a year after the eruption of the global financial crisis, the region is feeling several effects. The financial sector is under stress, and while the likelihood of a global financial meltdown has been skirted through aggressive policies, the decimation of financial wealth has exerted significant downward pressures on aggregate demand and the growth prospects of the region, with the attendant social consequences still unfolding.

Equity market declines impact domestic demand

Equity markets in developing countries around the world have suffered large declines in value since mid-September 2008, reflecting a global credit crunch and a worldwide flight to safety among investors. The global credit crunch, measured by the price of credit, has been far greater than at the peak of the 1997 crisis (figure 1.1), with the result that global investors have been forced to pull their funds out of emerging markets to fund internal operations. The dramatic in-

Figure 1.1. Spread of 3-month LIBOR to 3-month United States Treasury bill rate, 1995-2008

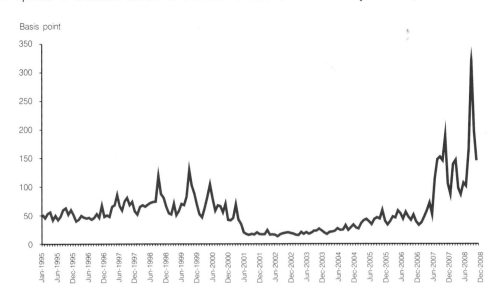

Sources: CEIC Data Company Ltd., and British Banker's Association.

crease in the price of credit in late 2008 stemmed from the unwillingness of banks to lend, as seen from the markup of credit prices as compared with the risk-free interest rate proxied by that of United States Treasury bills.

This led to sharp declines (figure 1.2) in the region's equity markets. In the past, foreign and domestic investors had, thanks to high global liquidity, acquired an increasing presence in local equity markets, which in turn led to a large run-up in prices. Nevertheless, when compared with emerging markets in other parts of the world (figure 1.3), the losses in Asia and the Pacific were less, reflecting lower investor concerns about the prospects for Asia and the Pacific as a whole. Bond market declines in Asia, while substantial, were also lower than those in Eastern Europe and Latin America, as evidenced by corporate bond spreads, reflecting varying perceptions of sovereign risk (World Bank, 2008a).

Furthermore, as of end-December 2008, equity markets had fallen less than in the 1997 crisis (figure 1.4), although the current crisis may still not have reached its nadir and there may be a further fall for equity markets. A comparison of the movement from peak to trough in 1997/98 with the present path of equity market decline reveals a similar trend. Thailand, Singapore, Indonesia and Taiwan Province of China, all of which were affected by the 1997 crisis, have experienced faster falls in their markets in the current crisis than in 1997/98 (figure 1.5). This is due to the sheer

magnitude of the current crisis, but also the higher exposure of these Asia-Pacific economies to foreign investors in relation to other economies of the region.

These declines are expected to cause a number of effects that will dampen domestic demand, especially declining personal consumption and corporate investments. Although equity market investments constitute a small portion of household wealth, and equity financing makes up a relatively small portion of corporate investment in Asia and the Pacific as compared with developed countries, the declines will affect the more advanced economies of the region, such as the Republic of Korea, Singapore and Hong Kong, China. In these economies, about 36% of financing is equity-based, with the remainder coming from bonds and bank credit.[1]

Declines in property markets to further dampen domestic demand

Another dampening effect on domestic demand will come from the downturn in property prices. While equities were the first asset class to experience large declines in late 2008, property markets followed suit and can be expected to continue to fall, both as a consequence and a cause of the unfolding crisis. As

---

[1]   Based on data for China, Indonesia, Malaysia, the Philippines, the Republic of Korea and Thailand (Asia Bonds Online, 2008).

Figure 1.2. Equity markets for selected developing ESCAP economies, 2006-2008

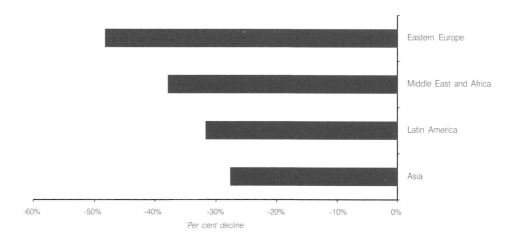

China (Shanghai Stock Exchange) Hong Kong, China (Hang Seng Index)
India (Sensex) Republic of Korea (KOSPI)
Philippines (Philippine Stock Exchange) Russian Federation (RTS Exchange Index)
Singapore (SGX Strait Times) Thailand (SET index)

Source: ESCAP calculations based on data from CEIC Data Company Limited.

Figure 1.3. Performance of regional emerging markets equities indices, 15 September 2008 – 9 January 2009

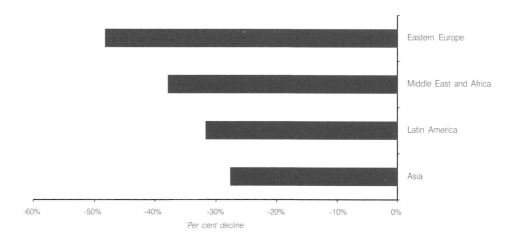

Source: ESCAP calculations based on data from MSCI Barra.

Figure 1.4. Peak-to-trough equity market fall, decline from peak to trough in 1997/98 and peak to end-December 2008 in 2007/08

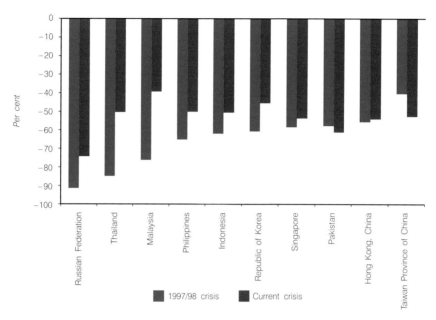

Source: ESCAP calculations based on data from CEIC Data Company Limited.

Notes: Declines for 1997/98 crisis measure major stock market index falling from the peak to the trough during that period. Declines for recent crisis measure the corresponding movement from the recent peak to December 2008.

with equity markets, foreign capital had also played an important role in property markets in some countries and contributed to large property price rises. At the time of its bankruptcy, Lehman Brothers had $1 billion invested in real estate in Thailand and a similar amount in Hong Kong, China (Financial Times, 2008). House price rises fuelled by rapidly expanding domestic credit have been important for India, China and Viet Nam.

> ## The degree of bank lending to the property sector is a significant concern

The reduction in house prices will have an effect on real estate investments, which have played a particularly important role in the growth of domestic demand in a number of countries – most notably in China, where the property sector accounts for about a quarter of all investment. The degree of bank lending to the property sector, both the construction industry and homeowners, is a significant concern. The impact from lending to institutional property developers is greater because home mortgages are less important in the

region than in developed countries. Home loans represented only 12% of GDP in China and 5% in India, whereas in the United States the ratio is 105% (Reuters, 2008). There is a danger of a significant increase in non-performing loans held by banks due to the inability of real estate companies to repay their loans.

Private consumption will also be affected by the fall in property prices, particularly in more advanced economies in the region, where property assets account for a more significant portion of household wealth, such as in the Republic of Korea, Singapore and Hong Kong, China. In less advanced economies, the consumption of the middle-income population, for whom property asset holdings have grown rapidly in recent years – notably in China and India – will also be curtailed.

Reduced bank lending: the most significant factor curtailing corporate activity and domestic demand

Restrained bank lending is currently the greatest obstacle to the region's ability to grow out of the crisis. The concern here is the effect it is having on corporate investment because an ailing corporate sector in a climate of slowing domestic growth could add a new layer of financial stress to the crisis-hit banking

Figure 1.5. Path of equity market decline from peak to trough in 1997/98 as compared with equity market decline from peak to end-December 2008 in 2007/08

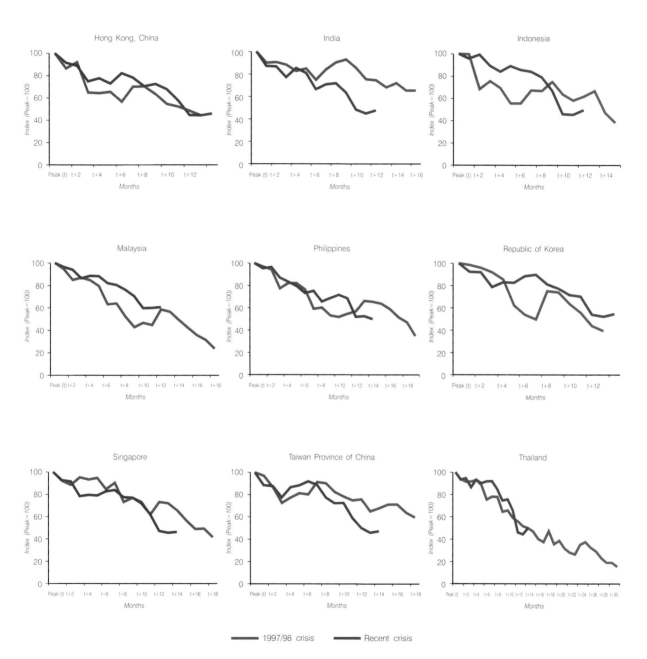

Source: ESCAP calculations based on data from CEIC Data Company Limited.

Notes: Declines for 1997/98 crisis measure major stock market index falling from the peak to the trough during that period. Declines for recent crisis measure the corresponding movement from the recent peak to December 2008.

sector. As access to funds becomes more difficult, an increase in non-performing loans will lead to greater risk aversion, restraints on new lending and possibly higher costs for new borrowers. Increased borrowing costs may in turn lead to further pressures for corporate defaults. The ability to repay corporate loans is especially a risk in export manufacturing sectors across the region, as well as real estate sectors. There is the risk of a vicious cycle, for eventually even previously healthy companies may face liquidity or even solvency problems, resulting, in turn, in a negative effect on the balance sheets of banks and a curtailment in aggregate demand.

Small and medium-sized enterprises may be particularly vulnerable due to their generally higher risk profile and their smaller pool of internal funds

---

Small and medium-sized enterprises (SMEs) may be particularly vulnerable because they are less likely to attract funding due to their generally higher risk profile and their smaller pool of internal funds to see them through the credit crunch. The most immediate concern is the rollover of short-term debt positions, and the most affected SME sectors are export-oriented enterprises, such as textiles, footwear and toys. The drying up of trade financing has further exacerbated the situation of SMEs.

It is also expected that bank lending will be curtailed by a more difficult climate for financing from abroad and consequently higher borrowing costs from foreign banks. Some countries are expected to be hit harder than others. There may be some reorientation of fund-raising from foreign to domestic sources, resulting in less credit being available, with negative impacts on overall corporate investments and household expenditures.

There has also been a marked reduction in bond issuance, with spreads on Asian emerging market bonds more than doubling in late 2008. Those countries where the corporate sector has used bond issuances to raise money will be most affected. In India, convertible bond issuance by corporations, one of the preferred instruments for raising capital in 2007, stood at $578 million by November 2008, down 91% from $6.6 billion in 2007 (Economic Times, 21 November 2008).

These difficulties notwithstanding, it is important to recognize that, overall, banks in the region appear strong enough to maintain solvency, for the level of non-performing loans is currently below the interna-

tional threshold of 8% across major economies in the region (figure 1.6). This provides an important buffer that will reduce the systemic risk of increases in non-performing loans in the coming months.

Figure 1.6. Non-performing loan rates in selected developing ESCAP economies, Q2 2008

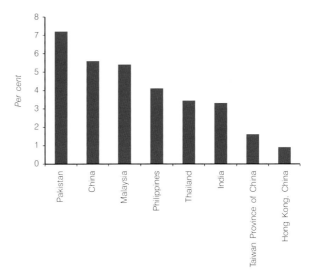

Source: CEIC Data Company Limited.

Note: Data for India and Pakistan refer to 2006 and Q4 2007 respectively.

Exports and foreign direct investment, particularly those linked to export production, to be hit by global slowdown

In the latter part of 2008, export performance in the region exhibited a swift downturn attributable to the curtailment of external demand, both demand globally and from within the region (figures 1.7 and 1.8).

Among selected export-oriented economies, quarterly export growth (year-on-year) for Singapore reversed from over 20% in the first three quarters of 2008 to a decline of 14% in the fourth quarter (figure 1.9). The shrinkage of exports in the Republic of Korea and Thailand was equally pronounced, falling from an average of over 20% growth in the first three quarters of 2008 to a decline of nearly 10% in the last quarter of the year. Taiwan Province of China experienced a turnaround from double-digit growth of nearly 15% in the first three quarters of 2008 to a fall of nearly 25% in the fourth quarter. A sharp deceleration of exports was

Figure 1.7. Export and import growth of selected ESCAP members and associate members to and from the world, August-November 2008

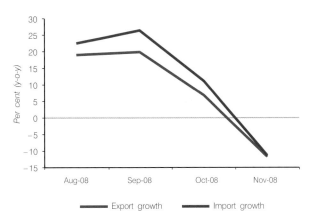

Export growth   Import growth

Source: ESCAP, "Regional trade and investment: Trends, issues and ESCAP responses", note by the secretariat prepared for the sixty-fifth session of the Commission, April 2009 (E/ESCAP/65/2).

Note: ESCAP economies include: Armenia, Australia, China, Georgia, India, Japan, Kazakhstan, Malaysia, New Zealand, Pakistan, Philippines, Republic of Korea, Russian Federation, Singapore, Sri Lanka, Thailand, Turkey, Hong Kong, China and Macao, China.

Figure 1.8. Export and import growth of selected ESCAP members and associate members to and from Asia, August-November 2008

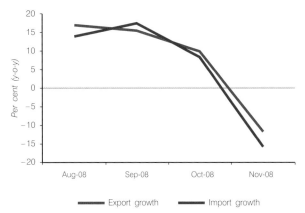

Export growth   Import growth

Source: ESCAP, "Regional trade and investment: Trends, issues and ESCAP responses", note by the secretariat prepared for the sixty-fifth session of the Commission, April 2009 (E/ESCAP/65/2).

Note: Economies for which data available: China, Japan, Malaysia, New Zealand, Republic of Korea, Singapore, Hong Kong, China and Macao, China.

Figure 1.9. Export performance of selected export-oriented developing ESCAP economies by quarter, 2008

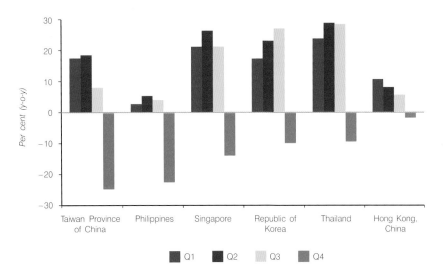

Q1   Q2   Q3   Q4

Sources: CEIC Data Company Limited and Bank of Thailand (for Thailand).

Note: Exports performance derived from growth rate in United States dollar.

observed in direct exports from the region to the final destinations of the United States and the European Union. Concurrently, exports to China from the economies in the region also registered sharp declines.

Owing to the sharp deterioration in exports and much weaker domestic demand, the economic growth of some of these export-oriented economies also weakened noticeably in the last quarter of 2008. The highest significant negative growth was registered for Taiwan Province of China at about 8% in the fourth quarter of 2008 (figure 1.10). Thailand shrank by 4.3%, while Singapore, the Republic of Korea and Hong Kong, China, are estimated to have fallen by 3.7%, 3.4% and 2.5% respectively. The performance of the Philippines remained largely stable as a result of continued inflows of remittances to render support for consumption demand.

Most countries in the Asia-Pacific region have relied on open trade and investment and export-led growth for their development. As a result, the region enjoyed prolonged periods of high export and GDP growth except for two interruptions: the Asian financial crisis of 1997-1998 and the dot-com crisis of 2001 (figure 1.11). On both occasions, the growth rates of exports became negative, and GDP growth decelerated. With export growth decelerating significantly in 2008 and expected to continue to do so in 2009, it is not surprising that the GDP growth rate also decelerated substantially in 2008 and is forecast to continue decelerating in 2009.

It is possible that the current drop in exports will be associated with less of a decline in GDP growth than in 1997. The impact of the 2001 dot-com crisis on GDP growth was substantially less than the crisis of 1997, as the 2001 crisis, like the present one, originated in industrial countries outside Asia. The dot-com crisis was shallower and shorter than the current crisis, but, during that time, other components of aggregate demand were able to pick up the slack, although exports dropped by similar amounts.

---

*Foreign direct investment is
expected to slow down markedly*

As foreign direct investment (FDI) is long term, it is often thought to be a more stable source of inflows during a crisis. It has increased dramatically over the past decade after the sharp fall following the 1997 crisis, even recently returned to pre-1997 values in South-East Asia, but is now expected to slow down markedly. This scaling down is already reflected in estimates of declining FDI contribution to GDP in 2008 (figure 1.12) The drop is primarily due to the origin of the current crisis, the developed world – where most of the region's FDI comes from – as opposed to the 1997 crisis, which started within the Asia-Pacific region. Foreign investors are concerned about their ability to finance direct investment while their profits are

Figure 1.10. Real GDP growth of selected export-oriented developing ESCAP economies by quarter, 2008

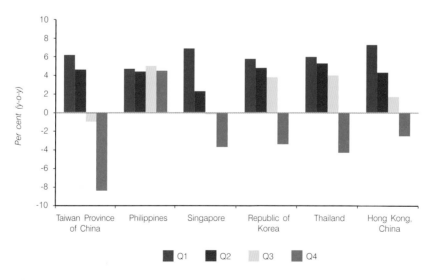

Sources: CEIC Data Company Limited; Ministry of Trade and Industry, Singapore *Press Release*, 21 January 2009 (for Singapore) and Taiwan Province of China, Directorate-General of Budget, Accounting and Statistics, November 2008 (for Taiwan Province of China).

Figure 1.11. Value of export and nominal GDP growth for ESCAP developing economies

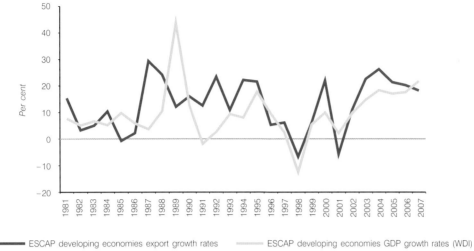

Sources: ESCAP calculations based on IMF, *Direction of Trade Statistics* (CD-ROM) (Washington, D.C., September 2008); and World Bank, *World Development Indicators* online (accessed October 2008).

Figure 1.12. Inward direct investment as a share of GDP in selected developing ESCAP economies

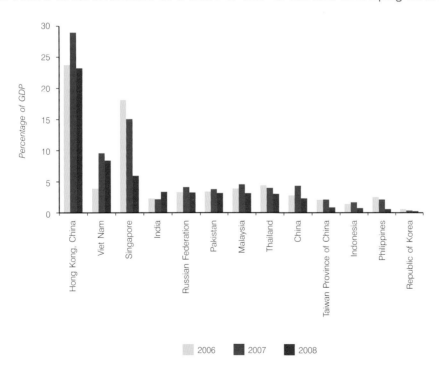

Sources: UNCTAD, *World Investment Report: Transnational Corporations and the Infrastructure Challenge* (United Nations publication, Sales No. E.08.II.D.23); EIU, *Country Forecasts* (London, 2008); and IMF, *World Economic Outlook Databases* (Washington, D.C, 2008).

Note: Inward direct investment for 2008 are estimates.

declining at home and there is less funding available from their financial institutions. Furthermore, the worsening perceptions of investors regarding the depth and length of the economic contraction will cause them to defer pipeline investment decisions.

Still, the multi-year planning horizon inherent in FDI decisions is expected eventually to tap into positive growth prospects and override shorter-term concerns. There will likely be some reorientation, however, towards FDI that is market- and labour-seeking, in order to tap into the region's competitive resources, its positive long-term growth prospects and buoyant domestic demand. This change will come at the expense of more traditional forms of intrafirm FDI directed to export production, notably in China, where such export-oriented investment accounts for a sizeable part of total investment. Similarly, intraregional FDI, which became particularly pronounced between and within East Asian economies and South-East Asian economies, may also decline. The decline will be all the more significant for investments that supported regional production networks supplying parts and components for consumer products destined for developed country markets.

Domestic demand under pressure but holds the key to stabilizing economic growth prospects

In some major economies of the region, domestic demand has played an important role in recent growth, and it will need to play a supportive role in the face of declining exports. In the immediate future, domestic demand will most likely not prove robust, as has already been seen in the declines in absolute terms, which have come in tandem with a fall in net exports (figure 1.13). Nevertheless, domestic demand contributed a greater share of growth in 2008 for the many economies that had an even greater decrease in net exports, but it will face additional pressure from credit constraints as well as the effects of higher unemployment, uncertainty and very low wage increases in 2009. It is nevertheless expected that the lower dependence on banking credit for the household sector will alleviate some of the pressures of constrained availability and increased price of credit on domestic consumption.

Figure 1.13. Contributions of domestic demand to GDP growth for selected developing ESCAP economies

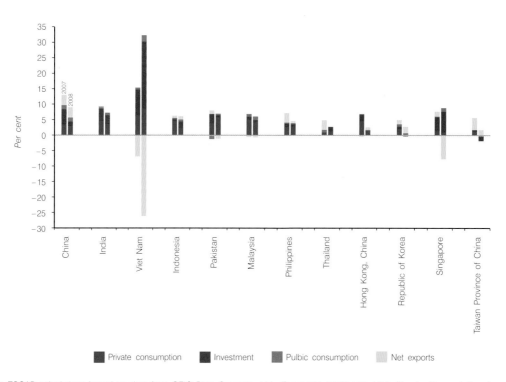

Sources: ESCAP calculations based on data from CEIC Data Company Ltd.; Economist Intelligence Unit, *Country Forecast* (London, 2008).

Note: Figures for 2008 are estimates.

Negative impact on livelihoods and vulnerable groups

The labour market and the vulnerable to be under great strain

As the crisis is still unfolding, its impact on people's income levels and their welfare is difficult to estimate. Preliminary estimates indicate in 2009 that unemployment in Asia-Pacific could increase by between 7 to 23 million workers (ILO, 2009). In 2008, the greatest employment impact was felt in the export manufacturing sector, including garments, electronics and autos, which constitutes a large part of many East and South-East Asian economies. The crisis is also expected to hit such sectors as construction, tourism, finance, services and real estate. The countries experiencing the greatest impact will be those with slowing economies and rapid labour force growth, such as Cambodia, Pakistan and the Philippines (ILO, 2008a). Wage growth is slowing across the region – the average wage growth in real terms in 2009 is unlikely to exceed 1.8% – and an outright wage reduction in countries with low economic growth seems inevitable (ILO, 2008b). Wage growth has already been reduced through agreements between governments and social partners in some cases, such as in Singapore, or through a cap on minimum wage increases, as in Indonesia. Apart from an increase in formal unemployment, there will be a rise in informal employment. Notably, it is expected that migrants will return to rural areas, where they will remain underemployed, while wage competition in urban areas may cause an increased neglect of labour standards, as well as an increase in income inequality between top executives and employees.

The people most at risk from the crisis are the poor, women who are labourers in the manufacturing sector, the youngest and oldest populations and socially excluded groups

---

Mere unemployment figures tend to mask the full extent of the problem. Hundreds of millions more will bear a disproportionate cost of the crisis. As the 1997 crisis showed, when people are affected by sudden shocks, the ones most at risk are the poor, women who are labourers in the manufacturing sector, the youngest and oldest populations and socially excluded groups. Not only do these groups have fewer resources with which to cushion the impact of shocks, such as real assets and savings, but they also have less influence on economic and political decision-making. The negative impacts last much longer than the crisis itself: although economic growth resumed relatively quickly after the 1997 crisis, in some countries it took up to 10 years to recover lost ground in the struggle against poverty (ILO, 2008c). During the high-growth period following the 1997 crisis, relatively robust employment growth was achieved, but a number of important distributional inequities emerged (ILO, 2008d). Employment growth varied considerably within each subregion, large numbers of women remained excluded from the world of work and labour's share of income declined in three quarters of 83 countries surveyed by the International Labour Organization (ILO, 2008b).

Communities or groups that have been excluded from productive resources, decent work and social security are likely to be highly vulnerable to the negative impact of the global financial crisis and to volatility in food and fuel prices. Such groups include: indigenous communities; ethnic minorities; persons with disabilities; populations displaced due to conflict, large development projects, environmental degradation or disasters; stateless people; and migrants. In particular, many refugees and internally displaced populations depend on food assistance for their survival and generally do not have access to land for farming, employment or income generation.

During a crisis, low-skilled immigrants, especially the untrained, are among the first to be laid off because they are concentrated in vulnerable sectors, such as construction or tourism, and often hold temporary jobs. The very poor and the socially excluded as well as non-citizens are especially at risk of being exploited due to an inability to earn enough to obtain basic necessities for themselves and their families and due to their lack of access to social protection.

In countries where the population dependency ratio is high (i.e., where a large proportion of the population is below 15 or above 64 and therefore not normally in the labour force), many families may find it hard to meet the basic needs of the members of their households, particularly children. Most of the countries or territories in the region where at least 15% of the population is over 60 years of age are higher-income economies with social protection schemes in place.[2] But even

---

[2] Australia, Georgia, Japan, New Zealand, Russian Federation, Singapore and Hong Kong, China, as of 2007.

there, however, families may require greater financial assistance and care in response to rising costs. Families, and especially women, may experience the additional pressure of job insecurity on top of unpaid work, straining the capacities of households to cope.

Another major challenge during a crisis is youth unemployment, which is expected to increase from its already high levels in some countries – in 2007, for example, 25.1% in Indonesia, 25.0% in Sri Lanka and 14.9% in the Philippines (ILO, 2008a). Youth unemployment also shows gender variations. Indonesia showed a dramatic increase of 17 percentage points in the unemployment rate of young women between 1996 and 2006 (from 17.0% to 33.9%). Employment prospects for young Indonesian men, however, were only slightly better than those of young women: the male youth unemployment rate in 2006 was 27.1% (ILO, 2007; ILO, 2008d). In the Pacific, where economic growth has not kept pace with high rates of population growth, large youth populations combined with school dropouts make youth employment a major concern for this subregion.

The financial crisis could exacerbate the child labour situation in the Asia-Pacific region, for children may have to go to work to supplement household income. As of 2004, by ILO estimates, 122 million children were economically active in the region. Children are also at risk of being withdrawn from school or not enrolled. Where families have to pay school fees for their children, economic hardship often leaves them with no option but to keep their children out of school. When families have to cut back on the quantity and quality of food, poorer nutrition in children can have permanent effects on intellectual capacity and cause chronic poor health, which, along with lower educational completion rates, could undermine human capital development and set back economic and social development for decades.

Women to be affected in specific ways

It is expected that men and women will be affected somewhat differently by the current financial crisis. In the Asia-Pacific region, especially with the growth of exports, many women have entered the labour market, but many of them work in export processing zones, where they may not have labour rights, or in industries which sometimes offer very low wages, poor working conditions and no job security. Many women also work in the informal sector, which is precarious and offers no social protection. Although in many cases women have taken up paid work because male household members lost their jobs, women and girls

may be seen as a burden on the family because their work may not be valued as highly as that of male household members.

In difficult times, families often rely on women to care for the sick, older persons and those who cannot fend for themselves, making it difficult for women to earn an income outside the home. Culturally, women and girls are often expected to contribute financially to the family regardless of how that money is earned. When there are few opportunities for wage work, girls and women may end up being trafficked through the promise of a job or being lured or forced into prostitution and other forms of extreme exploitation. Men may migrate out of rural areas, leaving women as household heads and often among the most poor. In general, households in which only women earn an income and those with many dependents are the poorest.

There are also important subregional variations. In South Asia, the proportions of both male and female workers in vulnerable employment, either unpaid contributing family workers or own-account workers, are the highest in the world. Even though the proportion of total female workers in vulnerable employment decreased slightly more than that of men (3.9 percentage points for women and 2.4 percentage points for men), women continue to carry a higher risk of finding themselves in a vulnerable employment situation: more than 8 out of 10 working women, compared with more than 7 out of 10 working men, are vulnerable. In South-East Asia and the Pacific, although the overall unemployment rates are comparatively low and have stabilized in recent years, there is a worrisome trend of rising unemployment rates for women, which the financial crisis could further exacerbate. In 2007, unemployment rates were 6.9% for women, compared with 5.6% for men (ILO, 2008e). Ten years earlier, the rate for women was 4.2%, only 0.3 percentage points higher than the rate for men.

Lack of social protection exacerbates impact of crisis

Most developing countries of the region do not provide adequate social protection for their citizens – leaving millions to resort to limited, often harmful, coping mechanisms, such as reducing meals, eating less nutritious foods, taking children out of school, selling livestock and other assets or borrowing money to feed their families. In the case of sudden spikes in the price of food, the poor have to spend an even larger proportion of their income on food and will probably buy less food or food that is less nutritious. Chapters 2 and 5 examine this issue in more detail.

Remittances expected to slow but will have stabilizing effect

After several years of strong growth, remittance flows to developing countries have begun to slow markedly, leading to heightened concerns about the impact of the financial crisis. Empirical data on the impact are not yet available, but anecdotal evidence suggests that the slowdown will deepen further, and for 2009 growth is expected to be negative, falling to −0.9% (World Bank, 2008b).

Many countries of the region have experienced a surge in labour migration in recent years, with a concomitant increase in remittances. In 2006 alone, over one million migrant workers left the Philippines. Annual labour migration from Bangladesh, mainly to the countries of the Gulf Cooperation Council (GCC) and Malaysia, surged from 252,000 in 2005 to over 800,000 in 2007 (World Bank, 2008b). In 2007, the remittances sent by migrants to countries in the ESCAP region exceeded $121 billion, up from $110 billion in 2006 and more than twice the level reached in 2000. In 2008, 5 countries in the region – Bangladesh, China, India, Pakistan and the Philippines – were listed among the global top 10 economies receiving remittances (figure 1.14). Remittances make up an important share of GDP for a number of other economies, particularly smaller ones, such as Kyrgyzstan and Nepal and some of the Pacific island countries (World Bank, 2008b). With regard to source countries, remittance flows from the

GCC countries to East and South Asia have grown particularly fast (World Bank, 2008b).

Despite the global economic slowdown, the contribution of remittances to the external position of developing countries is expected to increase relatively in 2009-2010 because other private flows and official aid are expected to decrease much more than remittances. Furthermore, while the intake of additional migrants may slow, the stock of migrants from these countries remains large.

On the negative side, as unemployment increases in developed countries, governments are likely to cut back on the intake of new migrant workers, or perhaps even require migrants to return upon completion of their contracts, especially in the information technology and tourism sectors. In the GCC countries, a slowdown following the decline in oil prices has led to a slowdown in the construction and tourism-related industries, resulting in lower demand for migrant workers and the likelihood of cutbacks on migrant workers' wages or their benefits.

Other sectors exhibit a more positive outlook. In developed countries, there may be increased reliance on outsourcing as they struggle to reduce their costs, which could benefit some countries and industries in Asia and the Pacific. Similarly, demand in developed countries for caregivers and medical service professionals is expected to remain stable, particularly in countries with rapidly ageing populations. The work done by unskilled migrant workers may also be less sensitive to downturns since they often fill jobs that are considered undesirable in the local market but are nevertheless necessary.

Overall, remittance flows are generally more stable than other capital flows, and they also tend to be countercyclical, i.e., increasing during economic downturns or after a natural disaster in the migrants' home countries. Furthermore, remittances depend not only on flows of migrants but also on the stock of migrants abroad. Even if the flow of migrants declines due to the financial crisis, remittances may not be affected substantially, as the stock of migrants remains large.

Remittances have traditionally been an important source of external funding in the Pacific islands in view of the small size of the economies. While remittances will be under pressure, they are expected to show resilience to economic changes. In 2000-2001, despite a slowing of economic growth in Australia, New Zealand and the United States, remittances to the Pacific islands increased. In 2005 and 2006, remittances again remained strong. In addition, there is some hope that seasonal worker schemes between Pacific island countries and Australia and New Zealand will provide a new source of remittances (ADB, 2008, p. 19).

Figure 1.14. Top 10 remittance-recipient developing economies in Asia and the Pacific, 2008 estimate

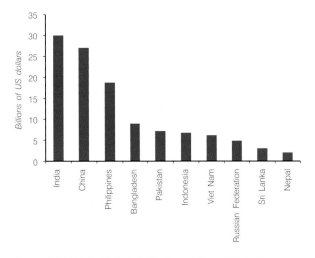

Source: World Bank, *Outlook for Remittance Flows 2008-2010.*

Growth outlook for 2009

Growth down across the board

The outlook for Asia-Pacific economies has darkened since the last quarter of 2008, as the economic setback deepens and there is more financial turbulence than was anticipated. A credit crunch, along with financial deleveraging, has choked off economic activities. The export sector is expected to be hardest hit by the shrinkage of import demand, so economic prospects in the region hinge more on domestic demand, but investment and consumer confidence has been shaken by more entrenched economic difficulties, poor expectations of corporate profits, a slowdown in remittances and mounting concerns about job security and household income. Nevertheless, fiscal stimulus programmes should be able to render some support, particularly if domestic demand in Asia's largest emerging economies – China, India and Indonesia – can remain buoyant. Further intra-regional trade flows may be triggered, adding some shock-absorbing effects to the region's economy.

The backdrop for 2009 forecasts

It is expected that monetary policies around the world will remain loose for most of 2009. The downward adjustment of food and energy prices will be conducive to a looser monetary environment. Specifically, the United States Federal Reserve Bank target rate is expected to remain at a very low level in 2009. In 2008, the Federal Reserve cut its target rate seven times. As of 31 January 2009, 400 basis points had been slashed, from 4.25% at the beginning of 2008 to 0.25%. At the current level, further cuts would not be very effective, and the Federal Reserve may opt for direct injections of liquidity into the financial system. A gradual tightening may only occur towards the end of 2009, when the United States economy is expected to be on a path of stable recovery. Similarly, the European Central Bank is expected to hold the main refinancing rate at the currently low level of 2.0% for most of 2009. A gradual policy normalization is expected to take place near the end of 2009, when the global economy is stabilized. The Bank of Japan lowered its uncollateralized overnight call rate marginally to 0.3% in October 2008 and further to 0.1% in December 2008. It is expected that the Bank will only revert to monetary tightening towards the end of 2009.

As for the key exchange rates, the United States dollar has shown significant volatility, including a strengthening against the euro, but overall downward pressures on the dollar will remain as the unwinding of the country's fiscal and trade deficits becomes inevitable. The dollar averaged $1.32 against the euro in the fourth quarter of 2008, and expectations are that it will edge up to about $1.40 in 2009. The Japanese yen appreciated notably towards the end of 2008 and averaged at ¥96 in the fourth quarter of 2008. This trend is expected to continue in the first half of 2009, before the yen falls back again in the second half of the year.

Oil prices have fallen considerably since their peak monthly average of about $135 per barrel in mid-2008. It is expected that prices will average about $45 per barrel in 2009. Economic contraction is expected in the United States, the European Union and Japan in 2009.

Against this backdrop, the forecast for developing economies in the Asia-Pacific region is a slowdown in growth to 3.6% in 2009 from an estimated 5.8% in 2008 (figure 1.15). For the region as a whole, performance for the first half of 2008 showed resilience. Exports grew at 24%, thus remaining strong and riding on the back of weakening currencies and relatively robust external demand, but the full effect of a slowdown in developed

Figure 1.15. Real GDP growth of selected developing ESCAP and developed economies, 2003-2009

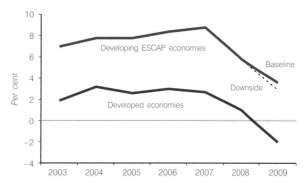

Sources: ESCAP calculations based on national sources; IMF, International Financial Statistics (CD-ROM) (Washington, D.C., November 2008); ADB, Key Indicators for Asia and the Pacific 2008 (Manila, 2008); website of the Interstate Statistical Committee of the Commonwealth of Independent States, www.cisstat.com, 22 October 2008 and 3 February 2009; and ESCAP estimates. Figures for developed economies are taken from IMF, World Economic Outlook Update (Washington, D.C., January 2009).

Note: GDP growth to 2008 and 2009 are estimates and forecasts respectively.

country markets on exports will surface in 2009. Economies that are highly dependent on exports, such as those of East and North-East Asia and South-East Asia, will inevitably be more vulnerable (figure 1.16). The extent of deceleration will depend on the extent to which domestic demand, stimulated by expansionary fiscal policy, can offset the setback in exports.

Still, it is important not to lose sight of the fact that aggregate growth in Asia and the Pacific will remain higher than in other global regions. While difficulties in the region will be important at the domestic level due to the enormous social consequences of even moderate decreases in growth rates, the region is relatively strong compared with the rest of the world (figure 1.15). Comparatively high growth coupled with the large aggregate size of the region's economy will make Asia and the Pacific the locus of global growth in 2009. The region is forecast to account about 115% of global GDP growth in 2009.[3]

Significant downside risks from protracted recession

The possibility of a deeper economic setback in the United States and consequently in the European Union and Japan cannot be ruled out, given the highly fluid financial conditions and the uncertain impact of expansionary monetary policy and fiscal rescue programmes. Failure to jump-start the economy and trigger economic growth is the biggest downside risk for the regional forecast.

A major baseline assumption is that the United States economy will contract by 1.0% in 2009, following estimated growth of 1.3% in 2008. If a more pronounced setback in the United States occurs, growth in the economy would fall by another 2 percentage points, from −1% to −3%. The more severe deceleration in growth is based mainly on steeper reductions in in-

Figure 1.16. Rates of economic growth of selected developing and developed ESCAP economies, 2007-2009

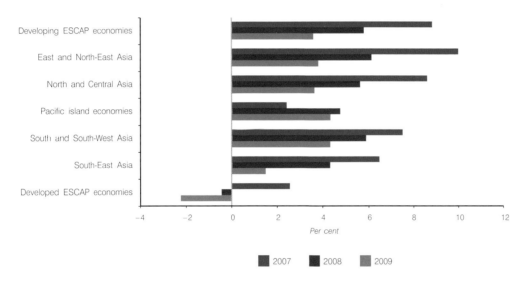

Sources: ESCAP calculations based on national sources; IMF, *International Financial Statistics* (CD-ROM) (Washington, D.C., November 2008); ADB, Key *Indicators for Asia and the Pacific 2008* (Manila, 2008); website of the Interstate Statistical Committee of the Commonwealth of Independent States, www.cisstat.com, 22 October 2008 and 3 February 2009; and ESCAP estimates.

Notes: Rates of real GDP growth for 2008 are estimates, and those for 2009 are forecasts. The term "developing economies" of the region comprise 38 developing economies (including the Central Asian countries), and the calculations are based on the weighted average of GDP figures in 2004 United States dollars (at 2000 prices).

---

[3] Calculations based on the share of developing ESCAP economies in world GDP being about 16% in 2008, an IMF forecast of global growth of 0.5% in 2009 and an ESCAP forecast of growth in developing ESCAP economies of 3.6%.

vestment and consumption, with a significant increase in bankruptcies and layoffs, job insecurity for those who are still employed, a further fall in asset prices and a tighter policy on lending to households. If there is a deeper United States downturn, economic growth in Japan and the Euro zone will also fall into more negative territory.

Under this more severe scenario, the Republic of Korea, Singapore, Hong Kong, China, and Taiwan Province of China would most feel the pinch. On top of slower export growth due to curtailment in global demand, their deeper integration with the financial sectors of the developed economies would induce a more negative impact on their investment and consumption sectors. China would also face slower growth in absolute terms, but given the high growth path and the introduction of a strong fiscal stimulus plan in late 2008, China is expected to achieve relatively robust growth even under the downside scenario. Other economies would inevitably be hit by a severe downturn in the developed economies. As commodity prices ease further amidst weaker global demand, however, inflationary pressure will also ease, giving many countries policy space for expansionary policies that can cushion the negative impact.

Indicators of resilience and potential vulnerabilities

For the third time in a decade, economic growth will be curtailed as the Asia-Pacific region falls victim to financial crisis and widespread contagion. The shocks and contagion effects triggered have brought to the fore certain country-specific vulnerabilities, particularly in external finance, trade and investment. At the same time, the region possesses sources of resilience in 2009 that it did not have in 1997. For policymakers, the challenge lies in moving the region forward from crisis resilience towards crisis resistance.

Sources of resilience

Post-1997 policy changes: building resilience through balance and stability

Rising current account deficits constituted one of the major factors that triggered the 1997 Asian crisis. By the end of 1996, national deficits ranged from 3.5% of GDP in Indonesia to 8% in Thailand (ESCAP, 1998). Since then, most economies of the region, with the exception of India, Pakistan and Viet Nam, have significantly improved their current account balances (figure 1.17), even if current account balances have declined in some of these countries in recent years.[4]

A crucial aspect of the 1997 crisis was that current account deficits went hand in hand with United States dollar-pegged exchange rates, which were rising significantly. Eventually, the rise of currency values combined with the drops in current account balances proved unsustainable. Speculators attacked, starting with the Thai baht. Despite central bank attempts to defend their currencies, countries did not possess adequate foreign exchange reserves to signal that they could sustain their defence. In contrast, most economies in the region today, while moving away from official currency pegs and a commitment to defend particular exchange rates, still maintain a de facto regime of adjustable pegs. This time, however, they have built up very high foreign reserves (figure 1.18), and they have shown their willingness to use reserves to defend currency values and maintain stability. Nevertheless, there is significant variation in holdings of

reserves across the region; thus, there are varying degrees of buffer in the event a currency comes under pressure.

In another major change in policy, most countries have reduced their exposure to external short-term debt, which was a key factor in the 1997 financial crisis. In 1997, given the inability to roll over such short-term debt due to risk aversion and unwillingness to lend on the part of banks, countries had no choice but to buy foreign currency to finance repayments, which exerted further pressure on currencies. This time around, the level of external short-term debt is healthier in most of the countries affected by the 1997 crisis and is not excessive for other major economies in the region (figure 1.19), though concerns remain for some countries.

Vulnerabilities on the watch list

These positive developments notwithstanding, there are a number of potential vulnerabilities that will need to be at the top of the watch list and tracked carefully.

Heightened exposure to short-term portfolio capital

The spark that has led to immediate macroeconomic difficulties for some economies of the region has been, once again, exposure to short-term portfolio capital. The growing share of foreign portfolio capital in external financial liabilities has been a significant feature of many major developing economies across the region (figure 1.20). At a time of international and country-specific risk aversion, defending the exit of short-term portfolio capital to prevent excessive currency depreciation can reduce the amount of reserves available to cover external short-term debt repayments and current account deficits. This is an ongoing concern for many countries.

An analysis of the portfolio investments held by foreigners as a percentage of reserves (figure 1.21) provides a snapshot of the possible vulnerabilities that currencies would face in the event of an outflow of short-term portfolio capital. Reserve cover for foreign portfolio investments is seen to have decreased substantially across much of the region over this decade,

---

[4]   The countries that suffered the worst effects of the 1997 Asian crisis were the Republic of Korea, Thailand, Indonesia, the Philippines and Malaysia.

Figure 1.17. Current account balance as a percentage of GDP in selected developing ESCAP economies, 1996 and 2008

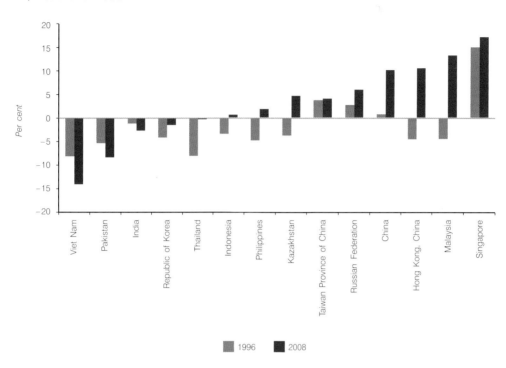

■ 1996   ■ 2008

Sources: IMF, *International Financial Statistics* (CD-ROM) (Washington, D.C., 2008) and *World Economic Outlook Database* (Washington, D.C., October 2008); and national source.

Notes: Figures for 2008 are estimates. Current account balance for Hong Kong, China refers to 1997

Figure 1.18. Foreign reserves as a percentage of GDP of selected developing ESCAP economies

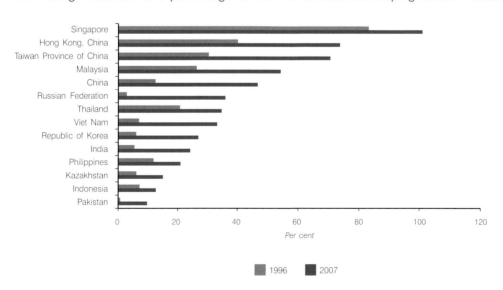

■ 1996   ■ 2007

Sources: IMF, *International Financial Statistics* (CD-ROM) (Washington, D.C., 2008) and *World Economic Outlook Databases* (Washington, D.C., October 2008).

Note: Figures refer to foreign reserves, excluding gold.

Figure 1.19. Short-term external debt as a percentage of GDP in selected developing ESCAP economies

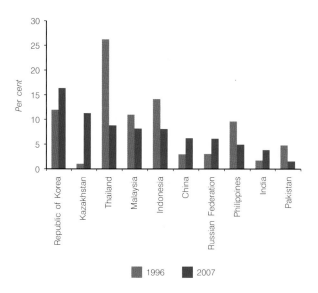

1996 2007

Sources: ESCAP calculations on the basis of World Bank, *Global Development Finance Database* (accessed on 22 December 2008); and ADB, *Key Indicators for Asia and the Pacific 2008* (Manila, 2008).

Note: Short-term external debt is defined as debt that has an original maturity of one year or less.

Figure 1.20. Stock of foreign portfolio investment as a percentage of total external foreign liabilities, 2002-2007

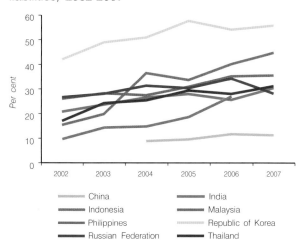

China | India
Indonesia | Malaysia
Philippines | Republic of Korea
Russian Federation | Thailand

Source: IMF, *International Financial Statistics* (CD-ROM) (Washington, D.C., 2008).

Notes: Derived from international investment position (IIP) of respective economies, including the categories of stock of portfolio investment and financial derivatives investment, excluding direct investments and other investments.

Figure 1.21. Stock of foreign portfolio investments as a percentage of reserves for selected emerging Asian countries, 2001 and 2007

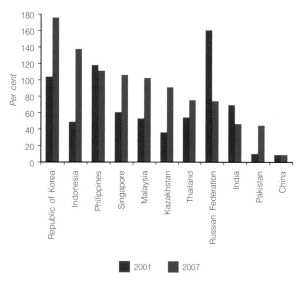

2001 2007

Source: IMF, *International Financial Statistics* (CD-ROM) (Washington, D.C., 2008).

Notes: Derived from international investment position (IIP) of respective economies, including the categories of stock of portfolio investment and financial derivatives investment, excluding direct investments and other investments.

with cover being less than 100% for some countries of the region. At a time of unprecedented financial instability, in which flights to safety have low threshold triggers, or in which declining equity values can trigger margin calls for highly leveraged investors, reserves may easily come under strain. Such outflows of foreign portfolio capital may be further compounded by a similar exit of capital by domestic residents, to the extent that residents are free to make portfolio investments abroad. It is clear that access to a greater pool of reserves than normally adequate assumes an even more important role in reassuring investors, and it can, in turn, serve to reduce the extent of net capital outflows.

Excessive currency volatility

Closely linked to the problem of capital-flow vulnerability is the fact that countries are now faced with a new climate of lower currency values as currencies in some countries tumble (figure 1.22). The fall began in 2007, with portfolio capital exiting regional markets as the subprime crisis took hold in the United States and Europe.

With the exception of India and the Republic of Korea, the falls in currency value are of a lower magnitude than the drops seen in the 1997 crisis. Nevertheless, currencies remain vulnerable (figure 1.23).

Figure 1.22. Exchange rate movements of selected developing ESCAP economies, 2007-2008

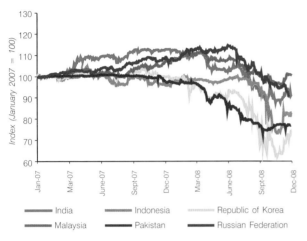

Source: CEIC Data Company Limited

Figure 1.23. Change in nominal effective exchange rate from peak to trough in 1997-98 and 2007-08

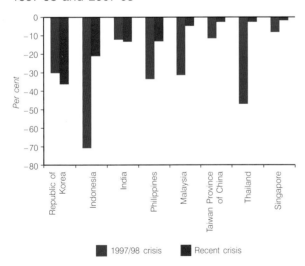

Source: ESCAP calculations based on data from Bank of International Settlements.

Notes: Declines for 1997-98 crisis measure the nominal effective exhange rate movement from the peak to trough during that period. Declines for the recent crisis measure the corresponding movement from the recent peak to November 2008.

Figure 1.24 shows an increasing drawdown of foreign exchange reserves as countries come under increased pressure to defend currencies. Pakistan has faced the most pressing difficulty in maintaining its currency value, requiring IMF support to bolster dwindling reserves as the currency fell to an all-time low in October 2008. The Republic of Korea and Singapore each agreed to a precautionary $30 billion currency swap facility with the United States Federal Reserve Bank to support their reserves.

Exchange rates in the region may remain under pressure for some time because the global recession will mute the contributions of portfolio inflows, FDI inflows and export earnings. Furthermore, in a climate of sluggish exports and intracountry variation in exchange rate movements, there is a risk of further competitive devaluations between countries in the region, resulting in a beggar-thy-neighbour cycle of competitive relations to the detriment of all in the region.

China has recently shifted the central peg downward, devaluing the yuan for the first time in over a decade. In December 2008, the greatest depreciation in the currency took place since the fixed rate to the dollar was removed in 2005. Economies in the region will be under pressure to devalue against the dollar in line with the yuan to maintain the competitiveness of their exports to the United States. Furthermore, countries may continue to devalue against the yuan and the yen (table 1.1) to maintain their competitiveness in exporting to China and Japan. Such extraregional and

Figure 1.24. Foreign reserves in selected developing ESCAP economies, December 2007 to December 2008

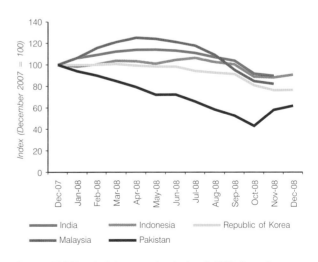

Source: ESCAP calculations on the basis of CEIC Data Company Limited.

Table 1.1. Rate of change of average exchange rates for January-June 2008 as compared to July-December 2008

Currencies	Rates of changes (%)									
	US$	Yen	Euro	Yuan	Rupiah	Ringgit	Peso	Won	S$	NT$
Yen	3.3									
Euro	−9.3	−11.6								
Yuan	2.6	−0.3	13.7							
Rupiah	−9.3	−11.4	−0.2	−11.6						
Ringgit	−7.0	−9.5	2.8	−9.4	3.4					
Peso	−10.6	−13.0	−1.2	−12.9	−0.6	−3.9				
Won	−17.5	−19.2	−9.4	−19.6	−9.1	−11.5	−7.9			
S$	−3.7	−6.2	6.5	−6.1	7.1	3.6	7.6	17.9		
NT$	−3.5	−6.0	6.8	−5.9	7.4	3.8	7.9	18.2	0.2	
Baht	−5.9	−8.5	4.1	−8.3	4.8	1.2	5.2	15.4	−2.3	−2.6

Source: ESCAP calculations based on data from CEIC Data Company Limited.

Note: (−/+) = depreciation/appreciation against currencies in the row.

intraregional devaluations, if conducted in an uncoordinated manner, can lead to unnecessary losses in national export earnings.

Banking sector vulnerabilities on the radar

The current crisis has also highlighted concerns about the banking sector. Although most economies in the region possess adequate reserve cover for their external short-term debt at the national level, banking sectors may run the risk of being overly dependent on foreign sources for their lending. It is important to ensure that the banking sector is healthy without the need of government assistance, for such assistance can itself create a generalized loss of confidence in the sector. Non-performing loans (NPLs) are currently below the international threshold of 8% across major economies in the region (figure 1.6), creating less immediate solvency risk and providing a buffer for possible increases in NPLs in coming months.

There are concerns about liquidity shortages, however. Banking loans in some countries are notable for substantially exceeding domestic deposits (figure 1.25), requiring banks to rely on significant wholesale funding. To the degree that such wholesale funding comes from external sources and is comprised of short-term loans, the global credit crunch may result in banks coming under stress in funding their activities. Currency mismatch of such funding exposes banks to exchange rate risk while maturity mismatch can lead to roll-over and interest rate risk. In response to such concerns, the Republic of Korea recently unveiled a $100 billion package to guarantee short-term foreign bank loans.

Figure 1.25. Loan-to-deposit ratio of selected developing Asian economies, November 2008

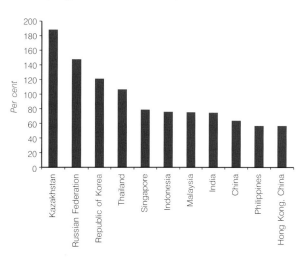

Sources: ESCAP staff estimation based on data from CEIC Data Company Limited; ADB Central and West Asia Department Report No. 2 (for Kazakhstan); and statistics by the Central Bank of the Russian Federation (for Russian Federation).

Notes: Data for the Philippines and Kazakhstan refer to February 2008 and March 2008 respectively. Data for India and Republic of Korea refer to September 2008. Data for Indonesia and Thailand refer to October 2008. Data for India refer to credit-to-deposit ratio of scheduled commercial banks. Data for Thailand refer to consolidated loan-to-deposit ratio.

External public sector repayment pressures also under scrutiny

Another potential vulnerability for a few countries in the region is public external debt and repayment pressures (figure 1.26). While short-term public debt levels are generally low, high levels of total external public debt can create long-term pressure on currencies in these countries.

Figure 1.26. External public debt as a share of GDP of selected Asian economies, Q2 2008

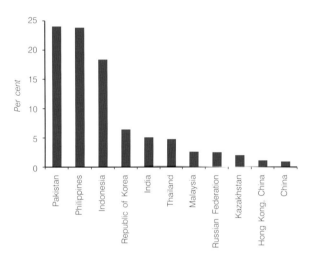

Sources: World Bank, *Quarterly External Debt Statistics* and CEIC Data Company Limited.

Notes: Public debt refers to debts of public sector (government and monetary authority) and publicly guaranteed private debts. For the Philippines, public debt refers to public sector debt and debts of central bank and government banks. For China, figures refer to foreign debts held by the State Council. For Kazakhstan figures related to GDP are as of Q4 2007.

Increased trade dependence as a source of vulnerability

Increasing trade dependence has characterized the economic growth in developed and developing countries alike. In the United States, the original locomotive of growth, GDP doubled (in current dollars) while its dependence on imports jumped from 12.3% to 16.3% of GDP between 1995 and today. This translated into large increases in exports for developing countries in the Asia-Pacific region, with the share of merchandise exports in GDP in Asian developing countries increasing by almost 8 percentage points to reach 37.5% in

2007, while their GDP increased almost threefold (figure 1.27). This increased trade dependence has now become a heightened source of vulnerability, raising serious concerns about the extent to which the financial crisis can be mitigated in this region.

ESCAP forecasts of the impact of the United States recession[5] on growth in merchandise exports from Asian economies indicate, in real terms, declines in India from an estimated 13.7% in 2008 to −1.3% in 2009, in Indonesia from 12.0% to −1.3%, in Thailand from 4.8% to −5.3%, and in the Republic of Korea from 6.5% to −3.6%. Under this scenario, the trend in the import demand of the United States declines from −2.9% in 2008 to −4.6% in 2009.

Small export-oriented economies in the region have already been hit hard. These countries were the most affected by the dot-com downturn in 2000-2001. Based on the changes in export growth and GDP growth that Asian economies underwent at that time, it is possible to derive an indicator of export sensitivity to recession: the higher the ratio of drop in the GDP rate per 10-percentage-point drop in exports, the more vulnerable an economy is, all other factors being constant.[6] In the cases of Malaysia, Singapore and Hong Kong, China, during the 2000-2001 crisis, the drop of 10 percentage points in exports was associated with a drop of 3 to 4.5 percentage points in GDP growth. In contrast, for the large economies of China, India and Indonesia, the same fall in exports caused their GDP to contract by less than half a percentage point (figure 1.28). Nevertheless, it is important to bear in mind that, this time, the likely impact of recession on exports in the region may differ in some respects as compared with the 2000-2001 downturn, as the current crisis is much more severe and complex. Furthermore, comparison with the previous downturn is less direct, as China and India today are much more integrated into the global economy than they were in 2001.

These vulnerability indices, when combined with increased intraregional trade flows and the intensification of the "factory Asia" phenomenon, would suggest that the economies and companies that are most directly linked through production networks supplying the United States and European Union markets could be the most vulnerable to the recession in those markets – specifically Malaysia, the Republic of Korea, Singapore, Thailand, Hong Kong, China, and Taiwan Province of China. These economies all have very high export

---

[5]   Set as a 2 percentage point reduction of the baseline growth rate.

[6]   Methodology from DBS Group research (2008, table 4).

Figure 1.27. Total trade as a percentage of GDP: ESCAP subregions (developing economies only)

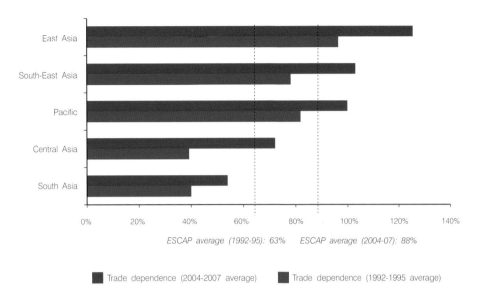

ESCAP average (1992-95): 63%   ESCAP average (2004-07): 88%

■ Trade dependence (2004-2007 average)   ■ Trade dependence (1992-1995 average)

Source: IMF, *Direction of Trade Statistics* (CD-ROM) (Washington, D.C., 2008).

Notes: South-East Asia: Brunei Darussalam, Cambodia, Indonesia, Lao People's Democratic Republic, Malaysia, Philippines, Thailand, Viet Nam. East Asia: China; Hong Kong, China; Republic of Korea; Macao, China; Mongolia. South Asia: Afghanistan, Bangladesh, India, Maldives, Nepal, Pakistan, Sri Lanka. Central Asia: Armenia, Azerbaijan, Georgia, Kazakhstan, Kyrgyzstan, Tajikistan, Turkmenistan, Uzbekistan. Pacific island economies: Fiji, Papua New Guinea, Samoa, Solomon Islands, Tonga, Vanuatu.

Figure 1.28. Vulnerability index of selected Asian export-led growers

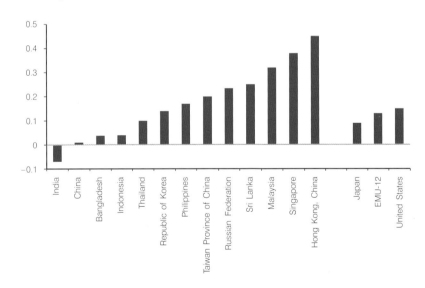

Sources: ESCAP calculations on the basis of DBS Research Group (2008) methodology using *World Development Indicator* data for GDP growth rates and data from IMF, *Direction of Trade Statistics* for export growth rates.

Notes: The vulnerability index is calculated as a ratio of the percentage point difference in GDP growth between 2000 and 2001 and the percentage point difference in export growth over 2000-2001. It shows the changes in GDP growth rates associated with a 1-percentage-point change in export growth rates. The higher the number, the more vulnerable an economy is; for example, a 1-percentage-point decrease in the exports of Malaysia is associated with the 0.32 percentage point difference in its GDP over the two years, while in China the same change in exports was related to a 0.01-percentage-point drop in GDP. In the case of India only, the export and GDP changes had different signs (while exports fell, GDP still grew).

shares vis-à-vis developed markets, these exports contribute much of their GDP and the economies have a high share of indirect exposure, mostly through China, to developed country markets now in recession.

At the same time, figure 1.29 shows that Asia's developing economies as a group have reoriented their trade away from the United States and Japanese markets and towards China, India and the European Union. The share of developing Asia's exports absorbed by the United States declined by 6%, while that of China increased by almost 5% between 1995 and 2007. This raised some expectations about possibilities that the region may be decoupling from the United States, and that new growth locomotives may be emerging in the region that will stymie the full brunt of the crisis. However, sharp contraction of trade, both global and intraregional, as well as the transmission of the economic slowdown have led to the conclusion that Asia remains firmly linked to the other parts of the global economy.

First, it is important to note that, while this reorientation has taken place, developing countries still rely greatly on exports to the United States, the European Union and Japan to generate economic growth. Expressed as an export-to-GDP ratio, export dependence on the United States and European Union markets is either

unchanged or increasing, signaling that a channel for the transmission of recession is still open (figure 1.29).

Second, Asian exports are increasingly dependent on the European Union, which has also been significantly affected by the economic crisis. The European Union now plays a bigger role than in 1995, in both export share and export dependence, with the result that recession in the European Union will magnify the adverse impacts of a reduction in United States aggregate demand.

Third, although rapid increases in intraregional and intra-industry trade among Asia's developing economies may signify a decoupling potential, it has grown quite asymmetrically. China, largely through the hub of Hong Kong, China, has become a dominant importer of intermediate products, parts and components that are produced in the Asia-Pacific region. In 2007, both China and India sourced about 30% of their total merchandise imports from Asia's developing economies (table 1.2). Furthermore, it is estimated that one third of the total Chinese imports of intermediate goods used for final Chinese exports, come from the region (Akyüz, 2008a).

Figure 1.30 shows that the commodity structure of Chinese imports from ASEAN countries, India and the Republic of Korea (accounting for 24% of total im-

Figure 1.29. ESCAP developing countries: export share and export dependence index differences, 1995-2007

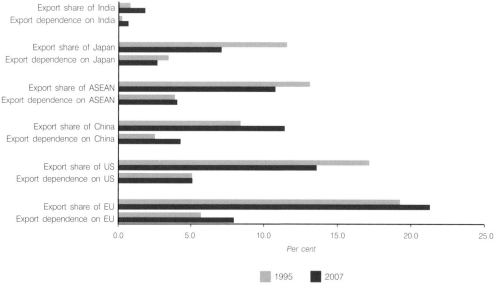

Source: ESCAP calculations based on IMF, *Direction of Trade Statistics* data.

Notes: Export share is defined as exports of ESCAP developing countries destined for a particular market as a percentage of the total exports of ESCAP developing countries. Export dependence is defined as exports of ESCAP developing countries destined for a particular market as a percentage of the GDP of ESCAP developing countries.

Table 1.2. Share of Chinese and Indian imports from the ESCAP region and its subregions (2007)

	Total ESCAP	Developing ESCAP economies	Developed ESCAP economies	East and North-East Asia	South-East Asia	South and South-West Asia	North and Central Asia	Pacific island economies
China	46.6	29.8	16.9	12.4	11.3	3.2	2.8	0.1
India	35.6	29.4	6.3	15.4	10.8	1.4	1.7	0.1

Source: Calculated based on IMF, *Direction of Trade Statistics*, 2007.

Figure 1.30. Commodity structure of Chinese imports from ASEAN economies, India and the Republic of Korea[a]

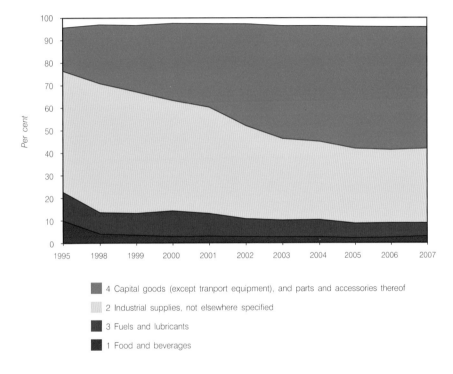

Source: ESCAP calculations based on COMTRADE data.

[a] Based on Classification by Broad Economic Categories of goods.

ports) has changed over the last decade in favour of capital goods and industrial supplies, which now comprise 87% of total imports from these countries. A significant contraction of Chinese exports to the United States and the European Union, slower economic growth in China and the associated contraction of imports of parts and components from the rest of Asia has been spreading throughout the regional supply chain.

Fourth, the potential of intraregional trade among developing countries is stymied by high tariffs. Figure 1.31 shows that developing countries have plenty of

scope to raise tariffs without running afoul of WTO rules due to the wide differences between applied and bound tariffs.

In times of economic difficulties, the spectre of rising protectionism is more than an abstract risk. Developed countries may find it opportune to use contingency protection and other forms of non-tariff barriers during an economic recession.

Fifth, international trade, by its very nature, requires financing. The time lag and resultant payment gap between the time when a good is exported and the

Figure 1.31. Differences between applied and bound tariffs, selected ESCAP members

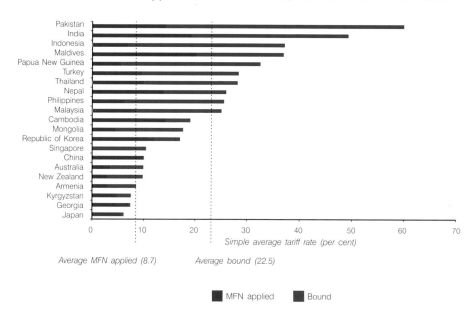

Source: WTO, Trade profiles 2007.

time it is received by the importer is typically resolved through the issuance of a letter of credit by banks. Trade finance supports credits of up to 90% of world merchandise trade (in 2007 amounting to about $14 trillion) and is considered one of the most secure forms of financing. The current financial crisis has dried up financing, and the gap was estimated by the World Trade Organization in November 2008 to be approaching $25 billion. In fact, some exporters are already unable to obtain financing of any type, even if they are prepared to pay a steep price. As expected, this imbalance between supply and demand has given rise to a number of small hedge funds and other financiers operating at interest rates that may be as high as 10% above LIBOR. While these credits are still taken by some exporters desperate not to default on their contracts, this also means that their profitability and competitiveness are under threat.

It is clear that this trade financing gap is exacerbating an already difficult environment of declining demand. While this is a global problem, there are some conditions unique to the Asia-Pacific region that compound the difficulties. Somewhat surprisingly for a trade-oriented region, Asia and the Pacific is the only region in the world that does not have a separate institution dedicated to export credits and export credit guarantees. Even though international organizations, notably regional development banks and the International Financial Corporation of the World Bank, have set up trade finance facilitation programmes, (TFFPs) their

success has varied across regions, with Asia and the Pacific having received far less support than other regions. Unfortunately, recent experience has demonstrated that TFFPs have not been able to solve the problem of tightening trade finance in times of financial instabilities.

China and the United States announced a finance facility of $20 billion that will create up to $38 billion in annual trade finance (United States, 2008). The drawback is that the facility is ad hoc and crisis-driven, making it much more difficult to trigger the desired effects. Furthermore, the financing is not available to everyone in the region, particularly enterprises that are small, or enterprises in vulnerable countries for which trade is a vital lifeline – players, in other words, that lack the leverage to access finance in international markets. A regional mechanism pooling funds and risks across all countries could go far towards financing this gap and facilitating intraregional trade across all countries of the region.

In conclusion, intraregional trade can provide a cushion against the contraction of exports to developed countries, but it will depend on strengthening aggregate demand through domestic sources of growth and restructuring the patterns of consumption, investments and government expenditure in this direction. A regional mechanism would also help to bridge current financing gaps that have frozen trade flows.

Much will hinge on the ability of the traditionally fast-growing economies, especially China and India, to readjust the mix of consumption, investment and exports. Importantly, it will also depend on an explicit policy choice directed to fulfil the role of the locomotive of growth in the Asia-Pacific region. Trade data show that, during first half of 2008, while Chinese exports to the United States were still growing, exports of major suppliers of parts and components to China also grew (figure 1.32). However, since the change in trend from mid-2008, it is clear that, based on current policies, there will be no replacement of the United States engine of growth from within Asia, as the prospects for the fast-growing economies to provide demand for exports from other Asian countries is not evident. That is not to say that there is no potential to at least fill some of the void caused by the recession in developed country markets. Most countries of the ASEAN+3 grouping, as well as India, have announced fiscal stimulus packages. Concerted action is required to ensure that such stimuli supports regional growth by preventing protectionist moves in the areas of goods and services trade, investment and mobility of labour. Such coordinated moves might position these countries as potential locomotives of growth – not in a decoupled manner but in a complementary role that supports the faltering locomotives. This regional positioning, inextricably linked to the global economy, underlines the importance of multilateral liberalization and the strengthening of disciplines that will keep trading relations open, equitable and fair. Thus, the conclusion of the Doha Round is indispensable (box 1.1).

Figure 1.32. Export growth of selected Asian economies grouping to China and China to the United States, 2006-2008

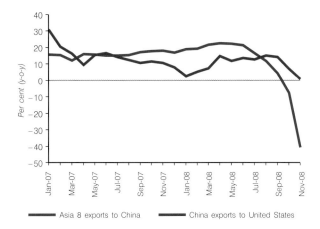

Source: ESCAP, "Regional trade and investment: Trends, issues and ESCAP responses", note by the secretariat prepared for the sixty-fifth session of the Commission, April 2009 (E/ESCAP/65/2).

Note: Asia 8 comprises Indonesia, Malaysia, Philippines, Republic of Korea, Singapore, Thailand, Hong Kong, China and Taiwan Province of China. Export growth derived from 3-month moving average (US$).

Box 1.1. In a time of crisis, a rule-based multilateral trading system is more important than ever

Given the level of trade dependence and integration in the Asia-Pacific region, one of the essential tasks ahead is to strengthen the rules of the world trading system to prevent backsliding on trade liberalization commitments. An open, rule-based, predictable and non-discriminatory trading system is a prerequisite for the continued prosperity and development of the region. This was recognized by world leaders who agreed to develop such a system as part of the Millennium Development Goals (MDG 8, Target 8a).

While estimates of the static economic gains from the ongoing round of negotiations at the World Trade Organization (WTO) are small, the potential losses from increased protectionism are expected to be large. Indeed, the estimated gains from the Doha Round are expected to be small because the negotiations are based on bound tariff rates as opposed to applied tariff rates. Because countries have unilaterally realized the potential benefits of trade liberalization, most currently apply much lower tariffs compared with the maximum tariffs – the bound tariffs – they could apply under the existing WTO agreements.

The scope to engage in new trade protectionism through tariff increases remains very high, and the current trade rules do not provide WTO member countries with adequate insurance against this increasing threat to development.

In the context of a difficult and recessionary global environment, a significant benefit from successfully concluding the Doha negotiations would be a clear signal that protectionism and the possibility of a trade war, as happened during the 1930s when the United States raised tariffs by 60%, will not be permitted by the rules. This would send out confidence-building signals that would enhance investor confidence and in turn contribute to a speedier recovery of the global economy, on which ESCAP member countries are dependent.

While there may be scope to improve the Doha Round package on the negotiating table, particularly in its development prospects, an agreement on the package can be expected to lead to some reduction in agricultural subsidies and tariff walls on industrial and agricultural goods, as well as to some new rules on trade facilitation and transparency on preferential trade agreements (PTAs). A conclusion of the Round would not overly affect the policy space of least developed countries as they do not have to provide reciprocity in liberalization, but it would improve the prospects for the WTO Aid for Trade initiative and reduce the distorting and discriminatory effects of PTAs. Finally, it would introduce some initial rules on export restrictions in agriculture products, an issue the recent food crisis has brought to the fore and a crucially important issue for net food-importing developing countries.

Reprioritization of the Doha Round's conclusion is a centrepiece of international policy. In these economically distressed times, there is a need not only for confidence-building measures that will boost economic growth but also for renewed motivations for multilateral cooperation that will bring coherence on other fundamental issues, such as financial regulations, food security needs and the mitigation of climate change.

From crisis-resilience to crisis-resistance: Next steps

Global and regional cooperation in financial issues are at an infant stage

As attention turns from immediate crisis-fighting measures to building resistance to future crises, reform of the global financial architecture is under intense debate. The G20 leaders have imparted a political momentum that will ensure that this issue remains at the top of the international agenda for some time to come.[7]

Even though there are a number of actions that each country could take independently, it is highly unlikely that any one country can ride out this crisis on its own. The attention turns, therefore, to building coordinated actions for a greater common regional prosperity. The crisis response to managing financial vulnerability in the region should be focused on regional policy measures while also maintaining an active role in the design of the evolving multilateral financial architecture.

A largely neglected debate concerns the formulation of effective and coordinated macroeconomic policies at the regional level to reduce economic vulnerability. Countries need to strengthen their policy coordination in the financial, monetary and trade areas. The importance of such policies was highlighted by the Commission of Experts of the President of the United Nations General Assembly on Reforms of the International Monetary and Financial System in January 2009. The Commission recommends that countries "insulate themselves from regulatory and macroeconomic failures in systemically significant countries" (United Nations, 2009).

Through its strengthened analytical and normative role, the ESCAP secretariat will be at the forefront in intensifying the debate and working towards consensus-building among the members and associate members of the Commission on needed policy actions. There is work to be done at both the global and regional levels (figure 1.33).

Global level

Reform of global financial architecture

A host of proposals have emerged for new models of finance, but very few decisions have been made. At this juncture, five principles should guide the future debate and policy actions at the multilateral and regional levels.

First, because the Asia-Pacific region is highly integrated globally, policy actions to regulate the new models of international finance must be global, but multilateral policies will need to evolve within a cooperative framework of economic governance that is multipolar in character. The new multilateral financial system will have to be designed with the participation of new national Government stakeholders who reflect the evolving balance of global economic influence, including the major countries of the Asia-Pacific region, such as through the G20.[8]

Second, because by their very nature financial markets are prone to boom and bust excesses, there is a need for sound regulations. These regulations should serve as a means of safeguarding the best of open economies and societies and avoiding outright economic protectionism.

Third, enhanced accountability should form the centrepiece of reforms at the global level. The financial innovations of past decades greatly increased the problem of moral hazard, as the old "buy and hold" model of bank lending evolved into "originate to distribute", in which banks originated loans and then repackaged and sold them to international investors, distributing risks throughout sectors and across the globe. Under this mechanism, banks had less incentive to monitor their borrowers as well as downstream investors. Banks switched from relying on soft information and long-term relationships with borrowers to model-based pricing. A mechanism is needed to require all originators and arrangers to keep a certain portion of the underlying assets and the structured products, as an incentive to examine and monitor more carefully, and then be held accountable for, the

---

[7] See G20 (2008a).

[8] See G20 (2008b).

Figure 1.33. Moving from crisis-resistance to crisis-resilience

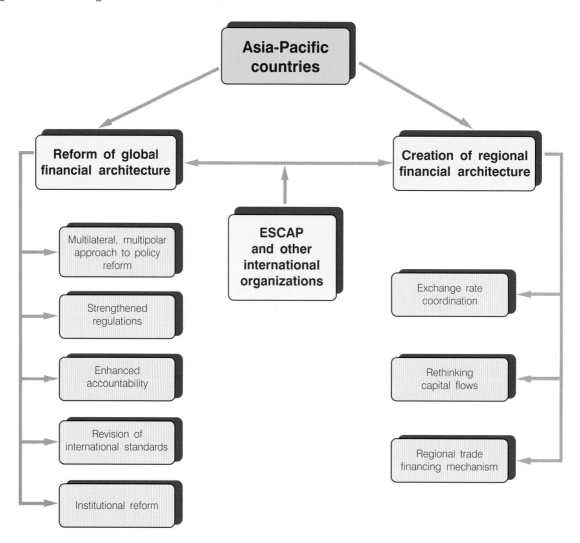

quality of their credits and securitized products. Banks should also be required to explain the complex structured products they design to investors in sufficient detail, including information on underlying assets and their risk profiles. Rating firms that evaluated new financial instruments that were illiquid and did not have clear market values must also be held responsible. Conflicts of interest played a role as ratings agencies received fees from the institutions whose products were being rated. Action will therefore need to be taken to standardize the valuation and risk-assessment methodologies used by credit-rating agencies.

Fourth, international standards need to be revised to bring about greater stability, while at the same time ensuring that market-driven principles are not overly diluted. The Basel Framework's pillar 2 – which requires banks and their management to explicitly assess their risk processes and evaluate their own risks, including a greater role for the central bank – should also be strengthened. While pillar 2 is an improvement on the laundry list of generic risks contained in pillar 1, many developing countries in Asia and the Pacific have yet to fully incorporate these provisions in their banking systems. A key constraint in this approach, not limited to developing countries, is the lack of technical and managerial expertise required for understanding the complexity of financial risks. Furthermore, there has been criticism that pillar 2 does not have adequate countercyclical standards for capital adequacy. For example, the availability of data on the leverage ratios of institutions would allow countercyclical regulations through leverage limits. In boom times, leverage limits should be lowered to prevent financial institutions taking on increasingly risky structures, while during a bust, the limits should be raised to aid recovery.

The region must take its rightful place at the table to reform global financial regulation

---

Fifth, while the principles underlying a policy to tackle the weaknesses of global financial regulation are fairly clear, the institutional structure that will devise and implement new regulations is less so. It is here where the region must take its rightful place at the table. Existing international institutions already engaged in financial regulation suffer from a lack of global membership; decision-making is done primarily by developed country representatives. The Financial Stability Forum, which sits at the centre of the current global financial regulatory system, does not include China or India. Of the 13 members of the Basel Committee, 10 are from Europe; Japan is the only Asian member. The Board of Directors of IMF comprises only a small group of developed countries. The Bank for International Settlements and the Basel Committee may be better placed than IMF to play the role of global regulator, but this would require fundamental reform to broaden their membership and increase the binding nature of their decisions. The question is whether such an increase in representation is even conducive to decision-making – the member-driven approach of WTO and its decades-long process of trade negotiations being a case in point.

These questions raise the potential for a world finance mechanism, either through a reform of the current one or a newly-created one, that balances efficient decision-making with global representation, through a variable geometric configuration of decision-making and consensus building. Rules reducing friction in trade are negotiated and administered in WTO. Financial regulation and liquidity support has remained essentially local, despite the fact that financial crises are occurring with increasing frequency at higher costs. A world finance mechanism that is member-driven and modeled on principles of consistent supervision with comprehensive non-discriminatory coverage of all systemically significant financial institutions is certainly worth examining.

Making trade work by locking in further liberalization through the conclusion of the Doha Round

The Asia-Pacific region is inextricably tied to trade and investment with the rest of the world and will therefore rely on the rapid resumption of global economic growth for its continued prosperity. The task

at hand is to narrow the channels along which the developed-country recession will be transmitted back to the region. The following policy actions are proposed:

- First, do no harm (Schott, 2008). In other words, both developed and developing countries should not resort to protectionist policies focused on narrowly defined nationalistic interests that would harm trading partners. Especially during this recessionary climate, new efforts are needed to push towards the conclusion of the negotiations under the Doha Development Agenda, both as a confidence booster and as a bulwark against possible slippage into protectionism. For example, the Doha Round could reduce gaps between applied and bound tariffs so there is less discretion in implementing tariff increases without running afoul of WTO rules. Similarly excessive use of contingency protection, or the indiscriminate use of product standards as covert forms of protectionism, could be tempered through tighter disciplines concluded under the Doha Round.[9]

- Second, "aid for trade" should be promoted and channeled, particularly into building the supply-side responses of developing countries so that developing countries are able to make more effective use of market access that will arise in the future. Tackling bottlenecks in transit, transport and trade facilitation is an important area of work.

Regional level

Exchange rate coordination

The region should consider establishing coordinated and durable regional currency arrangements. Uncoordinated national management of currencies can lead to beggar-thy-neighbour competition. The economic conditions of European countries at the time they entered into exchange rate cooperation – in 1979 through the European Exchange Rate Mechanism (ERM) of intracountry currency bands – has been pointed to as both an example of the way forward for Asia and the Pacific and as a path far different from the current state of the region's integration. The

---

[9] Strengthened multilateral rules and principles are needed not only in trade but also to improve the tracking and regulation of international financial flows. The region should not miss the opportunity to contribute to new ideas and solutions that would put forward the interests of developing countries and remove asymmetries in the global financial system.

structural diversity of the core developing economies in Asia – the original ASEAN members, China, the Republic of Korea and, increasingly, India – is not much greater than that of the European Union in 1979. East Asia enjoys greater macroeconomic convergence in inflation, interest rates, balance of payments, public deficits and debt than was the case in Europe not only in 1979 but also in the 1990s during the run-up to the common currency of the European Monetary Union (EMU). Furthermore, the conditions for currency cooperation in the European case can be seen to be endogenous, as economies have become far less diverse over time under ERM (Akyüz, 2008b).

The region should consider establishing coordinated and durable regional currency arrangements

---

Nevertheless, the European experience serves only as a guide and cannot be replicated in Asia and the Pacific. Specifically, the ERM concept of fixing currencies internally but floating externally is problematic. Asia's trade continues to be dependent on trade with countries outside the region, is more vulnerable to volatility in international capital flows and has no obvious anchor currency within the region, as Europe did. Asia therefore requires a system that provides both internal and external stability through a collectively managed currency float relative to the currencies of major developed country trading partners, based on agreement on a common basket, central rates and bands, and rules for intervention and changes in central rates. Such an approach has the potential to produce relatively stable intraregional currency values due to the similarity of trade baskets across the East Asian subgroup of countries. Countries are already managing their currencies independently in relation to their trade-weighted currency baskets. Regional cooperation could formally multilateralize these de facto national systems of exchange rate management. In undertaking such an approach, the European experience is worthy of study so that policymakers in this region can avoid the missteps of European economies and evolve a system that is best suited to the particular characteristics of Asia and the Pacific. In this regard, critical supporting mechanisms for an effective intraregional exchange rate arrangement include a common capital account regime, intraregional credit mechanisms and rules for interest rate and currency adjustments.

Rethinking capital flows

The challenge of managing vulnerability to reversals in short-term capital flows is difficult. Most countries in the region have chosen not to control the flows themselves but to amass sufficient reserves to defend currencies in the event of such outflows.

There is some evidence that short-term financial inflows do not provide countries with significant benefits even in good times, while clearly increasing vulnerability in bad times. Some have argued that financial globalization has not shown evidence of generating increased investment or higher growth in emerging markets (Rodrik and Subramaniam, 2008). Others assert that increased openness to capital flows has generally proven important for countries aiming to upgrade from lower- to middle-income status (Fischer, 1998; Summers, 2000). These divergent views point to the need for a renewed discussion at the regional level on the role of short-term capital flows, for exposure to these flows remains a significant vulnerability for this region.

In broad terms, the post-1997 solution was not to manage the flows themselves but to amass sufficient reserves to defend currencies in the event of such outflows. The present crisis has highlighted the fact that, despite a widespread perception that reserve accumulation has been sufficient in the region, such reserves may be inadequate for some countries in view of the huge inflows of short-term capital in recent years as a by-product of financial globalization. Furthermore, the build-up of national reserves is not an ideal solution because of the large cost for Governments. Currency sterilization during the process of reserves build-up while experiencing capital inflows requires the issuance of domestic bonds. Because foreign exchange reserves have been invested mainly in low-yield United States Government bonds, countries face fiscal costs from the interest rate differential between the two sets of bonds. It has been estimated that India, which has comparatively high interest rates, faced a cost in fiscal year 2007 of 2% of GDP (ABN AMRO India, 2007). Another cost is the loss in the capital value of foreign reserve holdings if the value of the dollar were to decline sharply. For example, China would suffer a capital loss on its reserves of about $67 billion if there were a 5% depreciation in the United States dollar.[10] A combination of two approaches should be considered in order to address

---

[10] The calculation is based on foreign exchange reserves of $1.9 trillion in September 2008, with roughly 70% held in United States dollars, according to estimates.

the challenge of vulnerability to short-term capital flows: management of the quantum of such flows through, for example, deposit requirements on capital inflows and financial transaction taxes, and regional cooperation to increase the potential availability of funds in the event of a currency crisis as well as to reduce the amount of precautionary funds needed by each country.

The imposition of capital controls is, however, a highly complex policy option. A problem with introducing ad hoc countercyclical capital-control measures is that they can trigger an adverse reaction from financial markets, leading to sharp falls in stock prices. The adverse market reaction to the introduction of countercyclical restrictions could be most dramatic in countries with large stocks of foreign debt, weak current account positions and a high degree of dependence on foreign capital. A possible solution is to have a permanent system of control in place, with instruments being adjusted according to cyclical conditions (Akyüz, 2008c).

Regional trade financing mechanism

It is important to keep trade flowing for the region and to understand the exacerbating effects when trade financing dries up. During a global recession, intraregional trade takes on additional importance. A regional trade financing mechanism would facilitate the provision of export credits and export credit guarantees to companies and banks from Asia-Pacific countries. At a time when the engine of trade risks a shutdown, ways of making trade work for the region must be found by the region itself (see also ESCAP, 1995). A regional trade financing mechanism will not only keep trade going but, more important, will contribute to export diversification and encourage SMEs involved in non-traditional production to develop new products and services with greater financing flexibilities.

A regional facility has several advantages compared with public financing institutions at the national level. It can:

- Pool risk and spread it across countries

- Pool capital and spread it across countries

- Promote co-financing schemes between private banks and public-sector institutions

- Encourage intraregional trade and decoupling from the recessionary markets

- Utilize economies of scale

- Increase credibility and better market outreach and access to better-quality international finance

Creation of regional financial architecture with its own institutional setup

The institutional arrangements to support this evolving regional financial and economic architecture will need attention. Political will and bold decision-making is important because the region will need to establish comprehensive and quick-response foreign exchange support for all economies vulnerable to a crisis. International programmes, such as the IMF short-term liquidity facility and the Federal Reserve swap facility extended to the Republic of Korea and Singapore, are insufficient and selective. The ASEAN+3 agreement to accelerate the implementation of the foreign exchange reserves pool is an important first step in a regional approach. However, the membership and size of the pool should be expanded, as should its purpose, so that the potential use of funds goes beyond balance of payments support to include liquidity and solvency problems. Furthermore, in the event of contagion, size matters, as multi-country requests for assistance would curtail its functioning and lead to a potentially devastating loss of confidence in the very reason for its existence. The importance of expanding arrangements such as the ASEAN+3 reserves facility was highlighted by the Commission of Experts of the President of the United Nations General Assembly on Reforms of the International Monetary and Financial System in January 2009 (United Nations, 2009). In fact, the ASEAN+3 has recently reached an agreement to increase the reserve fund from $80 billion to $120 billion, in order to restore confidence, strengthen financial stability and promote a sustainable economic growth in the region (ASEAN, 2009).

While support of foreign exchange reserves is an important short-term protective measure, it nevertheless does not address the fundamental causes of external vulnerability for economies in the region. A reserves support arrangement does not prevent the build-up of unsustainable current account balances and unrealistic exchange rates, currency and maturity mismatches in the private sector or asset and credit bubbles. An expanded reserve fund will thus require regional monitoring and supervision to provide early warning and determine conditions warranting disbursement of funds. Similarly, exchange rate coordination will require regional supporting mechanisms, including a common policy on capital account openness, credit mechanisms, and rules for interest rate and currency adjustments. The most efficient manner to combine these various regional actions related to financial and monetary cooperation would be through the establishment of an Asian monetary fund.

The rationale for the establishment of an appropriate regional institution is not new. It was supported by ESCAP during the 1997 financial crisis (see ESCAP, 1998, for example) but did not gain traction due to differences among member economies. A decade later, the issue should be revisited, as such an institution, if properly designed, would support and strengthen the evolving global financial architecture. The issue should not be imbued with undue political significance. The logic for a new regional institution does not stem from the desire to merely enhance the regional operations of existing global institutions, but rather from the inherent managerial challenge faced by any global institution that can provide sufficient regional emphasis only by spreading itself too thin, as well as the lack of representation of the region in the decision-making processes of such institutions.

The presence of an existing international institution, such as IMF, should not be a constraint to the establishment of a complementary regional institution. The ability of international and regional institutions to work in an integrated manner has already been shown to be effective in the development banking sphere through the operations of the World Bank at the global level combined with regional banks, such as the Asian Development Bank and the Inter-American Development Bank. Similarly, existing regional institutions are also unsuited to the new responsibilities. While possessing regional representation, the work and experience of such institutions are in very different fields, such as development banking, which is far removed and may even be in conflict with the role of a regional macroeconomic, financial and monetary coordinator.

References

ABN AMRO India (2007). "Does sterilization cost affect monetary instrument choice?", *The Knowledge Series* (New Delhi, 2007).

ADB, (2008). *Navigating the Global Storm: A Policy Brief on the Global Financial Crisis*, p. 19 (Manila).

Akyüz, Yilmaz (2008a). "The current global financial turmoil & Asian developing countries", ESCAP Series on Inclusive & Sustainable Development: 2.

_____ (2008b). "Global financial crisis and implications for Asia", presentation at ESCAP High-level Regional Policy Dialogue on "The food-fuel crisis and climate change", Bali, Indonesia, 9-10 December 2008.

_____ (2008c). "Financial instability and countercyclical policy", Background paper for United Nations World Economic and Social Survey (United Nations Department of Economic and Social Affairs).

Asia Bonds Online (2008). http://asianbondsonline.adb.org/regional/regional.php.

ASEAN (2009) "Joint Media Statement – Action Plan to Restore Economic and Financial Stability of the Asian Region", Report from the Finance Ministers of the ASEAN+3 to Heads of States/Governments, http://www.aseansec.org/22158.htm.

DBS Research Group (2008). "Asia: who's vulnerable?", Topical Reports, 15 August 2008, available at www.dbsvresearch.com/research/DBS research.nsf(vwAllDocs)A5E5BBA5BCFFAD1E 482574A90006049D/$FILE/asia_2008aug15. pdf.

Economic Times (2008). "Market sees convertible bond issues decline 91%", 21 November 2008.

ESCAP (1995). *Economic and Social Survey of Asia and the Pacific 1995* (United Nations publication, Sales No. E.95.II.F.10).

_____ (1998). *Economic and Social Survey of Asia and the Pacific 1998* (United Nations publication, Sales No. E.98.II.F.59).

Financial Times (2008). "Lehman's Asia risk is revealed", 26 November 2008.

Fischer, Stanley (1998). "Capital account liberalization and the role of the IMF", in "Should the IMF pursue capital-account convertibility?", *Essays in International Finance,* Department of Economics, vol. 207, pp. 1-10 (Princeton, NJ: Princeton University Press).

G20 (2008a). G-20 Communiqué, Meeting of Ministers and Governors, São Paulo, Brazil, 8-9 November 2008.

G20 (2008b). "Declaration of the Summit on Financial and the World Economy", The G20 Leaders Summit on Financial Markets and the World Economy, 15 November 2008, Washington, D.C.

ILO (2007). *Labour and Social Trends in Asia and the Pacific 2007* (Bangkok, 2007).

_____ (2008a). November 2008, Room paper on the likely impact of the financial and economic crisis and possible responses.

_____ (2008b). *Global Wage Report 2008/2009.*

_____ (2008c). "Shaping a fair globalization: Perspectives and prospects for a decent work agenda" (Working Party of the Social Dimension of Globalization, Governing Body document WP/SDG).

_____ (2008d) *World of Work 2008* (Geneva).

_____ (2008e). *Global Employment Trends for Women 2008.*

_____ (2009). *Global Employment Trends 2009* (Geneva).

Reuters (2008). "Asia's banks, economies still vulnerable to property downturn", 10 October 2008.

Rodrik, D. and Arvind Subramaniam (2008). "Why did financial globalization disappoint?", http://ksg home.harvard.edu/~drodrik/Why_Did_FG_Disappoint_March_24_2008.pdf.

Schott, Jeffrey J. (2008). "First, Do No Harm", www. petersoninstitutte.org/realtime/?p=210.

Summers, Lawrence H. (2000). "International financial crises: Causes, prevention, and cures", *American Economic Review*, vol. 90, No. 2, pp. 1-16.

United Nations (2009). "The Commission of experts of the President of the United Nations General Assembly on Reforms of the International Monetary and Financial System: Recommendations for Immediate Action", Statement following first meeting, 4-6 January 2009 http://www. un.org/ga/president/63/commission/financial_ commission.shtml.

United States (2008). "United States and China announce $20 billion in finance facilities that will create up to $38 billion in annual trade finance to assist global trade", United States Department of Treasury, http://www.treas.gov/ press/releases/hp1318.htm.

World Bank (2008a). "Global market conditions and implications for trade", presentation at IFC 2nd Annual GTFP Bank Partners Meeting, 22-23 October.

_____ (2008b). *Outlook for Remittance Flows 2008-2010* (Washington, D.C.).

"

I believe that the pursuit of ecologically sustainable development need not be in contradiction to achieving our growth objectives. As Mahatma Gandhi said, "The Earth has enough resources to meet people's needs, but will never have enough to satisfy people's greed".

"

Manmohan Singh
Prime Minister of India

CHAPTER 2. FOOD AND FUEL PRICE SHOCKS

Between 2002 and 2008, the price of crude oil soared, reaching an all-time record of $147 per barrel in July 2008, then fell precipitously as the international financial crisis deepened and economic activity slowed across the globe. In the last day of 2008, crude oil was trading at $36 per barrel. Food commodity prices followed a similar, though more moderate, trend. Their increase caused alarm around the world, for it threatened the food security of millions. It is estimated that higher food prices in Asia and the Pacific pushed up the number of undernourished people in the region from 542 million in 2003-2005 to 583 million in 2007 (FAO, 2008a). The additional food price increases in the first half of 2008 and the marked slowdown in economic activity in the second half are likely to have increased the number of undernourished even more, making it less likely that the Millennium Development Goal of halving the 1990 proportion of undernourished people by 2015 will be attained.

Higher food prices in Asia and the Pacific pushed up the number of undernourished people in the region from 542 million in 2003-2005 to 583 million in 2007

This chapter describes the evolution of crude oil and food commodity prices, evaluates the reasons for their sharp increase up to mid-2008, assesses their economic and social impacts and proposes policy responses. Three main conclusions emerge from the analysis. First, sustainable development requires a long-run balance between demand and supply in both the crude oil market and in food commodity markets. A major cause of soaring prices has been a sluggish supply response to fast-growing demand. While the recessionary impact of the global financial crisis has led to sharp drops in fuel and food prices, pressure on these prices will resume in the medium run, once the global economy recovers from the recession. In the absence of long-run policies to address these imbalances in fuel and food markets, episodes of soaring commodity prices can recur, pushing up domestic inflation rates, hurting the poor and putting pressure on budget deficits.

Second, given the interconnections between energy, food and financial markets, a comprehensive policy approach is needed. Since 2000, for instance, crude oil and food prices have become increasingly linked. Thus, policies aimed at moderating the demand for crude oil, such as promoting energy efficiency, are conducive to improved energy security *and* food security, as well as the mitigation of climate change. Also, an excessive degree of liquidity in international financial markets led to a growing presence of financial investors in commodity markets, and excessive speculation played a role in exacerbating commodity price booms and busts. Thus policies to promote the stability of international financial markets will also contribute to the stability of international commodity markets.

Third, in the absence of social protection programmes, food price increases leave the poor with limited, often harmful coping mechanisms – such as reducing the number of meals, eating less nutritiously, selling livestock and other assets, or taking children out of school. Some of these coping mechanisms may alleviate hunger temporarily, but they may also lead to malnutrition, harm livelihoods, and put children's prospects at risk. The coverage of basic social protection programmes is very low in developing countries of the Asia-Pacific region. Only 20% of the population has access to health care assistance; 30% of the elderly receive pensions; and 20% of the unemployed and underemployed have access to labour market programmes such as unemployment benefits, training, or public works programmes, including food for work programmes. Addressing these deficiencies is as important as taking measures to reduce the likelihood of a future food price crisis.

Evolution of fuel and food prices

Food and oil prices exhibited downward trends throughout the 1980s and 1990s (figure 2.1). Between 1981 and 1999, food prices dropped at an average rate of 2.3% per year; the price of crude oil dropped much faster, at an average rate of 5.9% per year between 1980 and 1998. When prices are adjusted for inflation, the decreases are steeper (figure 2.2).

Both downward trends reverted sharply in the 2000s.

The price of crude oil began to rise in 1999, after reaching a low of $13 per barrel in 1998. Between 1998 and 2007, the price of crude oil increased at an annual average rate of 21%, reaching $72 per barrel in 2007. It accelerated even more in the first half of 2008, reaching historic daily highs of more than $140

Figure 2.1. Food price index and Brent crude oil price, 1980-2008

Source: ESCAP, based on data from IMF, www.imf.org/external/np/res/commod/externaldata.csv.

Notes: The food price index in this figure is the IMF commodity food price index (2005 = 100). It includes price indices for cereal, vegetable oils, meat, seafood, sugar, bananas and oranges.

Figure 2.2. Food price index and Brent crude oil price, adjusted by inflation, 1980-2008

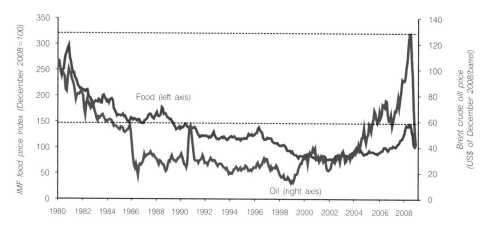

Source: ESCAP, based on data from IMF, www.imf.org/external/np/res/commod/externaldata.csv.

Note: Food price index and crude oil prices are deflated by the United States CPI-U, city average, all items, NSA, December 2008=100.

per barrel in July 2008. The price of food has also increased sharply since 2000, although not as fast as the price of crude oil. While food prices did not reach record levels in real terms (after adjusting for inflation), at their peak in June 2008, they were the highest in almost 20 years (figure 2.2). The high prices proved unsustainable. By the end of 2008, the price of Brent crude oil plummeted to less than $40 per barrel, 70% below its July peak. The food price index also dropped, though less dramatically.

In recent years, the rise and fall of the prices of different food commodities have not been synchronized. During 2006, sugar experienced a spike, but other food commodities remained fairly constant until the last quarter of the year (figure 2.3). In 2007, dairy prices soared, reaching their peak in November. The same year, cereals and vegetable oils started a vertiginous ascent that peaked in April 2008, pulling up the overall food price index.[1] In all, cereal prices increased 92% from April 2007 to their peak in April 2008, compared with an increase of 29% between April 2006 and April 2007.

Of the three main cereals, rice experienced the steepest price increase in the shortest time: 150% from January to May 2008 (figure 2.4). Wheat experienced a price increase of 134%, but it was stretched out over a year, from March 2007 to March 2008, and maize prices increased 95% between August 2007 and June 2008. Of the three cereals, wheat experienced the sharpest drop from its peak, followed by maize and rice. As of December 2008, their prices dropped 55%, 46% and 40%, respectively, from their peaks.

From a historical perspective, the recent run on food commodity prices was not unique (see box 2.1). Nevertheless, this episode was among the five largest price runs in the last 100 years.

---

[1] In order to avoid cluttering, the picture does not include vegetable oil prices, which follow a trend very similar to that of cereal prices. To construct the overall food price index, the Food and Agriculture Organization of the United Nations weights each commodity group by its share in world exports. Given the high weight of cereals, this commodity group has a high correlation with the overall food price index (r = 0.97, calculated over the period January 1992 to September 2008).

Figure 2.3. FAO food price index and its components, 2006-2008

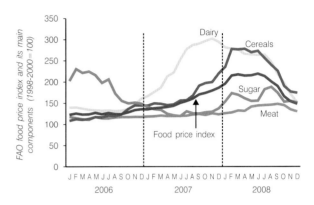

Source: ESCAP, based on data from FAO, www.fao.org/worldfood situation/FoodPricesIndex/en/.

Figure 2.4. Price indexes of selected cereals, 2007-2008

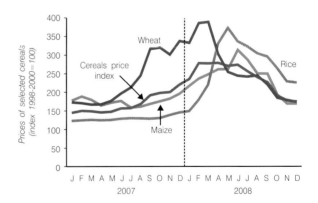

Source: ESCAP, based on data from FAO, www.fao.org/worldfood situation/FoodPricesIndex/en/ and www.fao.org/es/esc/prices/Prices Servlet.jsp? lang=en.

Note: Prices of individual commodities shown are for U.S. No. 2, yellow maize, U.S. Gulf (Friday); white rice, Thai 100% B second grade, f.o.b. Bangkok (Friday); and U.S. No. 2, soft red winter wheat, U.S. Gulf (Tuesday).

Box 2.1. Food commodity prices in the last 100 years

The 110% increase in food commodity prices from 2002 to 2008 was among the five largest price runs in the last 100 years (see figure below). The largest run occurred between 1968 and 1974, when commodity prices increased 236% in only seven years. In the next largest run, encompassing the second World War and the early post-war years, prices increased 229% in nine years. In both the run of 1914-1918 during World War I and in the rebound of 1932-1937 during the Great Depression, prices increased about 125%.

The largest price drawdown came at the beginning of the Great Depression, between 1929 and 1932, when prices dropped 58%. The fastest episode of dropping prices occurred in 1921: they plummeted 54% in only one year.

Food commodity prices over the last 100 years

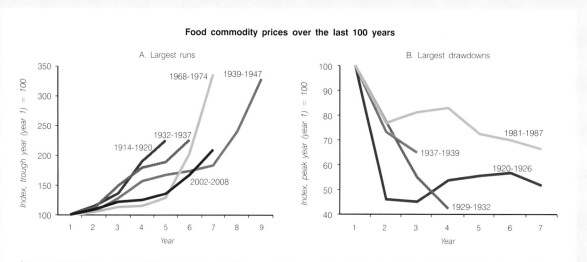

Sources: ESCAP, based on the Grilli-Yang index of agricultural food commodities in Stephan Pfaffenzeller, Paul Newbold and Anthony Rayner, "A short note on updating the Grilli and Yang commodity price index", *World Bank Economic Review* 21(1) (2007), pp.151-163, and data from FAO, www.fao.org/worldfoodsituation/FoodPricesIndex/en/.

Underlying reasons for the volatility of fuel and food prices

Fuel and food commodity markets are characterized by low short-term demand and supply price elasticities.[2] Market prices may thus be volatile and react sharply to news about events affecting present or future demand or supply.

Fuel

While world demand for petroleum has grown steadily for the last 10 years, production has often lagged behind (figure 2.5).[3] Between 1998 and 2006, world petroleum consumption increased at an average annual rate of 1.73%. The growth in consumption was even faster in the ESCAP region, at 2.81%. But world petroleum production grew at an annual average growth rate of only 1.40%. Given this situation of excess demand and the low short-term demand and supply price elasticities that characterized commodity markets, the speed at which crude oil prices rose was not surprising.

The major reason for the rapid increase in world petroleum consumption in the 2000s was accelerated world economic growth. The average annual world growth rate increased to 4.9% in 2003-2007 from an annual average of 3.2% in 1990-2002 (IMF, various issues). There is a positive association between economic growth and growth in petroleum consumption, as shown in figure 2.6. An increase in world income of 1% over the period 1982-2007 was associated with a 0.79% increase in the demand for petroleum. This estimate of the income elasticity of crude oil demand lies between Gately and Huntington's (2002) estimates for developed countries (0.55), on one hand, and the fast-growing developing countries (1.17) and oil-exporting countries (1.11) on the other (see also Hamilton, 2008).

Both developing countries and oil-exporting countries played a significant role in the increase in world petroleum demand in recent years. China, India and oil-exporting countries such as the Islamic Republic of Iran and the Russian Federation were among the 10 countries that most contributed to the increase in

Figure 2.5. Production and consumption of petroleum, 1997-2007

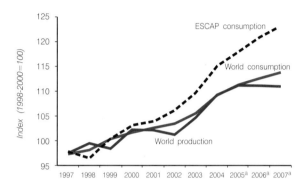

Sources: ESCAP, based on data from the United States Energy Information Administration, www.eia.doe.gov/iea/pet.html and www.eia.doc.gov/emeu/international/RecentTotalOilSupplyBarrelsperDay.xls.

[a] Preliminary consumption estimate.

Figure 2.6. World consumption of petroleum and world GDP growth rates, 1982-2007

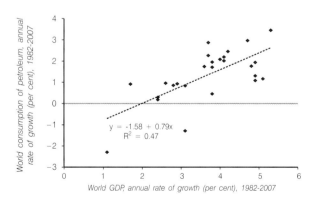

Sources: ESCAP, based on data from the IMF, www.imf.org/external/pubs/ft/weo/2005/02/data/index.htm and the United States Energy Information Administration, www.eia.doe.gov/emeuinternational/RecentPetroleumConsumptionBarrelsperDay.xls.

---

[2]   This section draws partly on ESCAP (2009).

[3]   Petroleum includes crude oil, natural gas, and other liquids. Over 1998-2006, crude oil represented 87.6% of total petroleum production.

Figure 2.7. Share of increase in world petroleum consumption: top 10 countries

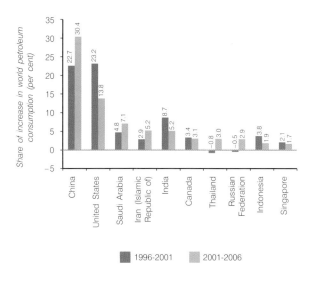

Source: ESCAP, based on data from the United States Energy Information Administration, www.eia.doe.gov/emeu/international/Recent PetroleumConsumptionBarrelsperDay.xls.

Figure 2.8. World grain stocks in days of consumption, 1978-2008

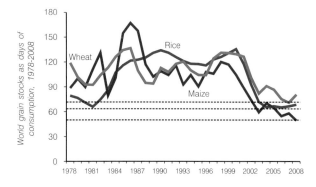

Source: ESCAP, based on data from United States Department of Agriculture, Grains: World Markets and Trade, April 2008 and October 2008.

Note: Calculated as (ending stocks/consumption)* 365. Consumption includes all possible uses of the commodity within each country: food, feed, seed, industrial processing and waste.

world petroleum consumption between 2001 and 2006 (figure 2.7). Seven of the 10 countries shown in the figure are developing countries from the fast-growing ESCAP region. Those seven countries contributed just over 50% of the world's increase in petroleum consumption between 2001 and 2006, up from 39% between 1996 and 2001. In contrast, the contribution of the OECD countries fell to 21% between 2001 and 2006, from 34% between 1996 and 2001.

As mentioned above, crude oil production has often lagged behind consumption in recent years (figure 2.5). As a result, the world's spare capacity of crude oil – unused production capacity that can be called upon in case of disruption – dropped from 5 million barrels per day in 2002 to 1 million barrels in 2005. Although it increased to 2.5 million barrels per day in 2007, spare capacity is still tight by historical standards. A major reason for the sluggish supply response has been the increased difficulty and costs of extracting oil from new fields. Costs more than doubled between 2005 and 2008, due mainly to an acute shortage of inputs such as engineers, scientists and equipment, while buoyant world economic growth has driven up the price of critical inputs such as steel and cement (Yergin, 2008).

Food

The causes of higher food prices are somewhat similar to those underlying the increase in the price of crude oil. The stocks of wheat, maize and rice, measured in consumption days, have dropped to the lowest levels in 30 years (figure 2.8).[4] The biggest drop has been for maize (59%), followed by rice (51%) and wheat (46%). Although wheat inventories recovered part of the lost ground thanks to a record harvest in 2008, that year they were still 31% lower than in 1999.

Declining inventories can be explained by a combination of fast-growing demand and stalling production. Unlike crude oil, the rate of consumption growth for cereals such as maize, rice, and wheat are less related to the world's rate of GDP growth. In data for the period 1981-2006, the correlation coefficient is slightly negative for rice (−0.21), close to zero for wheat (0.03) and positive but small (0.28) for maize. This phenomenon reflects Engel's Law, by which the share of income allocated to food and other basic necessities decreases as income grows.

---

[4] The stock of rice was as low as 65.8 consumption days in 1981, but it recovered quickly the following year. The current low is only slightly less, but it has lasted four years, from 2004 to 2007.

However, the consumption of maize trended up markedly since 2002 (figure 2.9). Unlike rice and wheat, about two thirds of global maize production is used for animal feed. Because food expenditures include larger shares of meat and dairy as income grows, the income elasticity of maize is higher than that of wheat or rice. Furthermore, in recent years a rapidly increasing share of world maize production has been used for the production of ethanol – as much as 70% of the increase in global maize production between 2004 and 2007 (Mitchell, 2008). The production of ethanol was boosted by the inability of crude oil production to catch up with the increase in petroleum demand and by generous government subsidies and use mandates in many countries.[5] As a result, the United States, the leading world producer of ethanol from maize, is estimated to have used 81 million tons of maize in the 2007/08 crop year to produce ethanol. With Canada, China and the European Union contributing an additional 5 million tons, the total use of maize for ethanol was 86 million tons in 2007, or about 11% of global maize production (Mitchell, 2008).

This additional demand for maize has pushed its price up and will continue to do so in future. A study conducted by the International Food Policy Research

Figure 2.9. Trends in world consumption of maize, rice and wheat, 1978-2008

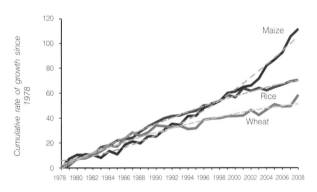

Source: ESCAP, based on data from United States Department of Agriculture, *Grains: World Markets and Trade*, April 2008 and October 2008.

---

[5] For instance, the United States has a tax credit of $0.51 per gallon to blenders of ethanol and passed legislation in 2005 mandating 7.5 billion gallons of renewable fuels by 2012. The EU directive on biofuels that entered into effect in October 2001 stipulated that EU countries should replace 5.75% of all transport fossil fuels with biofuels by 2010.

Institute (IFPRI) found that current investments in biofuel production capacity will increase the price of maize 26% above its baseline forecast by 2020, while doubling this production capacity would increase the price of maize 72% above the baseline (von Braun, 2008). Moreover, using more land and water to produce biofuels will put pressure on the production of other food crops. Trostle estimates the land use for biofuel crops in the major producing countries – United States, the EU-27, Brazil, China, Argentina and Canada – at 47.8 million acres (19.3 million hectares), or 3.4% of their arable land (Trostle 2008). But if all major countries and regions meet their stated biofuel targets for 2020, the total requirement for land could increase to as much as 166 million hectares (United Kingdom Renewable Fuels Agency, 2008), representing 29.2% of their arable land.

In addition, the dramatic increase in the price of crude oil up to June 2008 pushed up the costs of applying fertilizers, operating agricultural machineries, and transporting food to urban areas and across countries. Thus, the high costs of energy translate into higher costs of cultivation and therefore higher prices of output. The impact of high oil prices on agriculture is magnified because agriculture has become more energy-intensive in the past decade, with irrigation and fertilizers as critical inputs. Irrigation, especially groundwater exploitation, requires energy in the form of diesel or electricity to run pumps. As petroleum or natural gas is used to manufacture most fertilizers, their prices have also increased dramatically. Between January 2007 and June 2008, the price of a ton of fertilizer increased from $277 to over $450 for nitrogen-based fertilizers, from $172 to over $500 for potash-based fertilizers and from $250 to $1,230 for diammonium phosphate (Dap) (Vidal, 2008).

Short- and long-term supply factors also contributed to the increase in food prices. In the short-term, episodes of bad weather affected important grain-producing countries. Australia experienced its worst multi-year drought in a century since 2002, resulting in very low grain yields and plummeting exports. Ukraine and the Russian Federation have experienced two years of drought since 2005. In 2007, floods in Northern Europe, a hot and dry summer in Canada, frost in Argentina and the United States, and drought in South-Eastern Europe, North-Western Africa, and Turkey caused a second consecutive drop in global average yields for grains and oilseeds (Trostle, 2008).

A second short-term factor was the imposition of export restrictions, between the end of 2007 and the first half of 2008, to isolate domestic markets from the effects of higher international prices. Cambodia, India and Viet Nam temporarily banned rice exports.[6] Malaysia and Indonesia imposed export taxes on palm oil. Kazakhstan banned exports of oilseeds and vegetable oils. The Russian Federation raised export taxes on wheat. China first eliminated rebates on value added taxes on exported grains and grain products and later imposed an export tax on those products (Trostle, 2008). All these restrictions contributed to pushing up international grain prices even more, especially in the case of rice.

Falling prices and governments' neglect of agriculture resulted in lower yield growth rates and made millions of farmers migrate to the cities in search of better opportunities

---

The main long-term supply factor has been a marked decline in the growth rate of yield associated with the neglect of investment in agriculture over the last 20 years (ESCAP, 2008a). Following the "Green Revolution", yields grew at an average annual rate of 2.7% from 1970 to 1990. But as a consequence of a prolonged period of declining real prices (see figure 2.2), incentives for investment in agriculture declined, causing the average annual rate of growth in yield to drop to 1.2% between 1990 and 2005 (Hossain, 2007). The reduction in private investment was compounded by a drop in agriculture's share of official development assistance from 18% in 1979 to 3.5% in 2004 (World Bank, 2007). In addition, public agricultural spending has often subsidized private goods, such as fertilizers and credit – leading to socially regressive transfers which are "substantially less productive than investments in core public goods such as agricultural research, rural infrastructure, education, and health" (World Bank, 2007, p. 41).

Similarly, the global average annual growth rate of cultivated land area has also dropped significantly, from 0.7% between 1970 and 1990 to 0.2% between 1990 and 2005 (Hossain, 2007). The prolonged decline in agricultural prices also played a role, as rapid economic growth and urbanization created incentives for rural workers to migrate to cities in search of better incomes. The process of urban development also created incentives for the conversion of agricultural lands to alternative uses (Webb, 2008).

Weak incentives for farmers to keep up production have been particularly noteworthy in the late 1990s, following a drop of more than 50% in cereal prices between May 1996 and August 2000.[7] As a result, the world production of maize, rice, wheat and coarse grains lagged significantly behind consumption for four or more consecutive years in the early 2000s.[8] These episodes, which resulted in the large drops in cereals stocks shown in figure 2.8, were unusual. In the past 30 years, production of maize and wheat did occasionally drop substantially below consumption, usually as the result of major crop failures in important production areas, but the recovery was rapid.

Integration of food, fuel and financial markets

An additional factor that contributed to the soaring fuel and food prices is the integration of fuel and food markets with financial markets. In recent years, commodities have become more attractive to institutional investors, such as index funds, which try to replicate the performance of major commodity price indexes, and hedge funds. Some of them were attracted to commodities as a way to diversify traditional portfolios of stocks and bonds; others believed that commodity markets were experiencing a long-term trend that would drive prices higher for years to come. As a result, the stock of futures commodity contracts doubled from $200 billion in December 2005 to $400 billion in March 2008 (IFPRI, 2008). The extent to which this influx of funds into futures commodity markets and a resulting increase in speculation led to a commodity price bubble has been the subject of much debate (see box 2.2). Nevertheless, most observers agree that the growing presence of financial investors in commodity markets has contributed to increased volatility because it causes prices to react quickly, and often overreact, to new market information.

Fluctuations in the value of the United States dollar, in which currency commodity contracts are denominated, have also influenced the volatility of commodity prices through several possible channels.[9] First, depreciation of the dollar makes commodities cheaper for consum-

---

[6]   In the case of India, the ban applied to exports of rice other than basmati.

[7]   The FAO cereals index dropped from a peak of 168.0 to a trough of 78.5 during that period.

[8]   The period of drop in stocks varied somewhat across grains. For maize and wheat it was 2000-2003; for rice it was 2001-2004; for coarse grains, it was the five-year period 1999-2003.

[9]   See Abbott, Hurt and Tyner (2008) for a detailed analysis of the relationship between the United States dollar exchange rate and commodity prices.

Box 2.2. Are speculators to blame?

In principle, there is nothing wrong with speculation in futures markets. Technically, futures market speculators are market participants who seek to make a profit by predicting market moves and buying "on paper" a commodity for which they have no practical use. In that sense, speculators play two useful roles: providing liquidity and facilitating the process of price discovery. They provide liquidity by being willing to take risks as counterparts in futures contracts with farmers willing to guarantee the price they will get from selling their crop from a future harvest. By increasing the number of market participants, speculators enable these markets to work more efficiently, facilitating the incorporation of all the available information that can affect the future demand or supply of a commodity in the market price.

But market participants sometimes accentuate the impact of news on market prices, making them more volatile. In the case of crude oil and, to a lesser extent, that of food commodities, some of the new institutional investors participating in these markets, such as index funds, bought futures according to specified investment targets and disregarded the market price. Others, such as hedge funds, tended to bet only that commodity prices would rise. If enough market participants bet that commodity prices will continue going up, would they create a self-fulfilling prophecy – at least until the market turns? The answer to this question has been hotly debated. To better understand the gist of it, consider the following old Wall Street story:

> On a slow afternoon, trader A decided to open a market for a can of sardines. Bidding started at $1. B bought it for $2 and sold it to C for $3. D and E decided to get into the act, with the result that E became the owner for $5. E decided to open the can and discovered the sardines had gone bad. He went back to A to get his money back, protesting that the sardines were rotten. Trader A smiled broadly and said, "You don't understand. Those were trading sardines, not eating sardines" (Smith, 2008).

Commodities futures markets trade paper, not physical goods. Some argue that for futures market speculation to influence commodities cash (spot) prices, future prices should induce hoarding by sellers. In other words, unless future prices affect demand and supply for physical goods, cash prices should not be influenced. But with food inventories at historical lows (figure 2.8), he sees no evidence of hoarding in the data (Krugman, 2008).

However, hoarding behaviour may not be readily reflected in the inventory data because more hidden forms of hoarding may have taken place. For instance, in situations where the price of a commodity increases sharply and abruptly, with expectations that increases will continue, as was the case of rice in the first four months of 2008, illegal hoarding activities by large warehouses were detected in India and the Philippines (IFPRI, 2008), while farmers in Thailand and other rice-producing countries held onto stock waiting for higher prices and even defaulting on contracts in certain cases. Consumers are also prone to panic hoarding. Moreover, in the case of oil, an expectation of fast-increasing prices creates an incentive to hold oil underground, so no increase in inventories should be observed (Davidson, 2008). Thus the possibility of futures speculation influencing cash prices cannot be ruled out.

In any event, most analysts agree that while speculation is not a driver of commodity prices it is a factor that accelerates and amplifies price movements driven by fundamental supply and demand factors (Burkhard, 2008; IMF, 2006, pp. 15-18). Thus the growing presence of financial investors in commodity markets may have increased volatility by causing prices to react quickly, and often overreact, to new market information (UNCTAD, 2007).

ers located in Europe, creating an incentive to buy more, leading in turn to an increase in their dollar price. Second, if oil exporters have enough pricing power and want to keep their purchasing power over European imports, they have an incentive to increase oil prices when the dollar depreciates. Third, a falling United States dollar reduces the returns on dollar-denominated financial assets in foreign currencies, increasing the attractiveness of oil and other commodities as alternative assets for foreign investors (Crespo Cuaresma and Breitenfellner, 2008). Figure 2.10 shows a tight correlation between the Brent crude oil price and the dollar-euro exchange rate, especially between November 2006 and November 2008.[10]

In sum, the reasons for the soaring food and fuel prices up to June 2008 are complex and involve some novel aspects, such as the closer links between food and fuel markets, and financial aspects also played an important role. Therefore, devising policy responses to prevent similar episodes in the future will require the joint consideration of the food, fuel and financial crises.

Figure 2.10. Relationship between crude oil price and dollar/euro exchange rate, 2006-2008

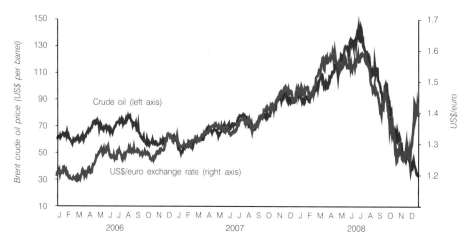

Source: Pacific exchange rate service, http://fx.sauder.ubc.ca/data.html.

---

[10] However, in December 2008, the euro recovered as the price of oil continued to fall.

Economic and social impacts

An increase in fuel and food commodity prices has a direct impact on a country's trade balance, inflation, poverty and fiscal balance. Several conclusions emerge from table 2.1, which shows estimates of the impact of commodity price increases on the trade balance (exports minus imports).[11] First, the impact was not trivial. The higher commodity prices cost India, China and the Republic of Korea about $10 billion each year between 2004 and 2007. To put these numbers in perspective, the table also expresses them as a percentage of each country's total merchandise imports. From that perspective, the annual costs during 2003-2007 represented 5% or more of imports for Mongolia, the Republic of Korea, Armenia, Georgia, Kyrgyzstan, India, Pakistan and Japan.

Second, for the limited number of countries for which estimates are available, the cost increased substantially during 2008, exceeding 7% of imports for Armenia, Kyrgyzstan, Fiji, New Caledonia, India, Maldives and Pakistan. Third, some countries in the region, most of them oil exporters, benefited from the increase in crude oil prices. In particular, the annual price impact for the Russian Federation and the Islamic Republic of Iran during 2004-2007 was very high, amounting to nearly 30% of their imports. The impact was also important for Kazakhstan, where it increased from 21% of the country's imports during 2004-2007 to 30% in 2008. The price impact was favourable, though to a lesser extent, for Indonesia, Malaysia and Viet Nam. Of course, high dependence on commodity exports is a double-edged sword that exposes countries to high volatility in the barter terms of trade and current account positions. While in 2008 the GDP growth of commodity exporters, such as Malaysia and Indonesia, was lower but not too different from the year before, the prospects for 2009 are more somber, for these countries are doubly exposed to deteriorating global demand and declining terms of trade.

The estimates in table 2.1 group together the impact of higher food and fuel prices on the trade balance. Figure 2.11 shows the differential impact of each commodity group. For the majority of countries in the Asia-Pacific region, most of the impact is attributable to the increase in fuel prices. Only in New Zealand was the impact of food prices rather high, representing 4.6% of the country's imports during 2004-2007.[12] This finding reflects the facts that (i) crude oil prices increased roughly three times faster than food prices between 2003 and 2007 (120% against 40%) and (ii) the average value of trade in crude oil for the countries considered is eight times higher than their trade in food commodities.

While the price of crude oil increased sharply in 2004 and 2005, concerns about inflation in the Asia-Pacific region became widespread following the large food price increases that occurred during the second half of 2007 and the first half of 2008.[13] Table 2.2 shows the impact of the increase in food commodity prices between 2006 and 2008 on domestic food prices for selected Asia-Pacific countries. The impact varies across countries for many reasons. First, the composition of food commodity trade differs among countries, and commodities with a higher share on a country's trade are likely to have a larger impact. To reflect this variation, column 1 of table 2.2 shows the rate of change of country-specific food commodity price indexes. The data shows that Bangladesh, India, Indonesia, Malaysia and Viet Nam experienced increases in food commodity prices of about 80% during the period analysed, compared with only 52% for the Republic of Korea and 41% for Hong Kong, China. The reason is that cereals and oils, whose prices increased the most during the period considered, represent over 80% of the food commodity trade of the first group of

---

[11] The estimation is as follows. The change in value of a trade flow X between year t and year $t - 1$ can be approximated as $X_t - X_{t-1} \approx Q_{t-1}(P_t - P_{t-1}) + P_{t-1}(Q_t - Q_{t-1})$, where Q is the quantity and P is the price. The first term represents the price effect and can be expressed as $X_{t-1}(P_t - P_{t-1})/P_{t-1}$. The FAO food prices indices for cereals, edible oils, sugar, meat and dairy products are used, as well as the Brent crude oil price, along with import and export data to estimate the price effect for each of these six commodities for each country in the Asia-Pacific region for which data are available between 2003 and 2006. The numbers shown in table 2.1 and figure 2.11 represent the price effect for exports minus the price effect for imports.

---

[12] Food represents close to one third of the country's exports. In particular, New Zealand is a leading world exporter of dairy products, whose prices have increased significantly in recent years.

[13] ESCAP (2007) estimated the impact of a 10% increase in crude oil prices on domestic inflation rates in selected countries. The impact was highest for Malaysia, the Philippines, Thailand and India (between 0.6% and 0.75%), but relatively low for China (0.1%).

Table 2.1. Impact of commodity price increases on the trade balance

	In dollars (millions)			As share of imports (per cent)		
	2003	average 2004-2007	2008	2003	average 2004-2007	2008
Developing ESCAP economies						
East and North-East Asia						
China	−1 904	−9 811	..	−0.6	−1.6	..
Hong Kong, China	−783	−1 783	..	−0.4	−0.6	..
Mongolia	..	−66	..	..	−5.8	..
Republic of Korea	−4 311	−11 749	..	−2.8	−4.8	..
North and Central Asia						
Armenia	−32	−74	..	−3.4	−4.6	..
Georgia	−27	−116	−393	−3.4	−5.1	−7.5
Kazakhstan	751	3 280	9 892	11.4	21.1	30.2
Kyrgyzstan	−16	−51	−208	−2.7	−4.6	−8.6
Russian Federation	8 241	28 635	..	17.8	31.0	..
Pacific Island economies						
Fiji	−5	−55	−141	−0.6	−3.9	−7.9
New Caledonia	−28	−65	−129	−2.6	−3.7	−5.3
South and South-West Asia						
India	−2 801	−7 734	−16 606	−4.6	−5.9	−7.6
Iran (Islamic Republic of)	3 624	9 798	..	17.8	28.4	..
Maldives	−12	−27	−78	−3.1	−3.9	−7.1
Pakistan	..	−972	−2 418	..	−4.5	−7.4
Turkey	−1 344	−3 402	..	−2.6	−3.2	..
South-East Asia						
Indonesia	1 480	2 056	4 763	4.7	4.2	6.4
Malaysia	1 226	2 807	6 730	1.6	2.6	4.6
Philippines	−534	−1 416	−3 244	−1.3	−2.9	−5.6
Singapore	−910	−1 766	..	−0.8	−0.9	..
Thailand	−767	−2 498	..	−1.2	−2.4	..
Viet Nam	204	646	..	1.0	1.9	..
Developed ESCAP economies						
Australia	2 009	3 443	..	2.9	3.1	..
Japan	−11 086	−28 931	..	−3.3	−6	..
New Zealand	506	595	..	3.4	2.6	..

Source: ESCAP, based on data from the United Nations COMTRADE database.

Notes: The economies selected had trade data available for each year between 2003 and 2006. Impacts for 2008 are estimates.

Figure 2.11. Impact of fuel and food prices on the trade balance, 2004-2007

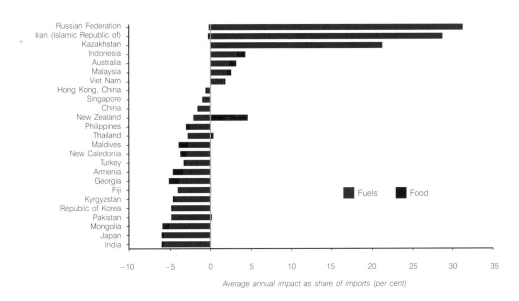

Average annual impact as share of imports (per cent)

Source: ESCAP, based on data from the United Nations COMTRADE database.

countries.[14] Instead, the commodity trade shares of meat, whose price increased much less during the period, and sugar, which decreased in price, is high for the Republic of Korea and Hong Kong, China.

A second source of variation in the impact of food commodity prices on domestic food prices is the exchange rate. The currencies of the Philippines, Thailand, China and Singapore appreciated 10% or more against the United States dollar in the period considered, softening the impact of the increase in international food commodity prices on domestic food prices. The opposite was true for countries such as Pakistan and the Republic of Korea, whose currencies depreciated 15% or more against the United States dollar.

Additional sources of variation are: (1) the share of food commodities in the total cost of production of processed foods, including distribution and commercialization costs; (2) government interventions in the form of import tariffs and quotas, taxes, and subsidies for food products, all of which vary across countries; and (3) differences in inflationary processes for

reasons other than food inflation. As a result, food commodity inflation does not pass through exactly into domestic food inflation. Indeed, column 4 of table 2.2 shows that, on average for the countries and period considered, the pass-through rate was only 39%.

Although domestic food inflation rates were, on average, considerably lower than food commodity inflation rates, the increase in the former was nevertheless important. As shown in figure 2.12, the association between increases in domestic food inflation and economy-wide headline inflation was positive and strong during the period considered. This is not surprising, given the weight of food in the consumer price index (CPI), which ranges between 16% for the Republic of Korea and 59% for Bangladesh, with an average value of 38% (column 5 of table 2.2). For the countries shown in figure 2.12, a 1% increase in the food inflation rate was associated, on average, with an increase of 0.63% in the headline inflation rate.

Obviously, the impact of food commodity inflation on domestic food inflation and headline inflation reverted in the second half of 2008 as commodity prices fell rapidly. With economic growth expected to be negative for the OECD countries in 2009, commodity prices are expected to remain low. The lower prices have had a significant impact on inflation rates across the region. In China, for instance, the year-on-year CPI inflation rate dropped from 8.6% in April 2008 to 1.2% in December,

[14] For Viet Nam, the share of cereals and oils is a little lower (74%), but the share of dairy products, which also increased substantially during the period, is rather high (19%).

53

Table 2.2. Impact of food commodity inflation on domestic food inflation

Average food pass-through rates, January–December 2006 to January–December 2008

	Food commodity inflation rate (US$) (1)	Food commodity inflation rate (domestic currency) (2)	Domestic food inflation rate (3)	Pass-through rate (4)=100*(3)/(2)	Memo item: Weight of food in consumer price index (5)
Bangladesh	81	80	22	28	59
China	70	49	28	58	33
Hong Kong, China	41	42	15	37	26
India	80	76	20	26	47
Indonesia	79	86	30	35	46
Malaysia	85	67	12	18	31
Pakistan	77	104	41	40	40
Philippines	74	49	17	34	47
Republic of Korea	52	72	8	11	16
Singapore	61	42	10	25	23
Sri Lanka	57	63	57	91	47
Thailand	55	35	16	46	33
Viet Nam	82	87	52	60	48
Average	69	66	25	39	38

Sources: ESCAP, based on data from the United Nations COMTRADE database, national statistical office websites, and IMF, *International Financial Statistics.*

Notes: The calculation for India is for the period January-November 2006 to January-November 2008. The numbers in columns (1) to (3) are 24-month growth rates expressed in percentage points. Country-specific food commodity prices (column 1) are calculated as weighted averages of the FAO food price indices for cereals, oils, meat, dairy products and sugar, using trade weights. The trade weights were calculated for the period 1998-2005.

Figure 2.12. Increases in headline and food inflation rates between 2007 and 2008

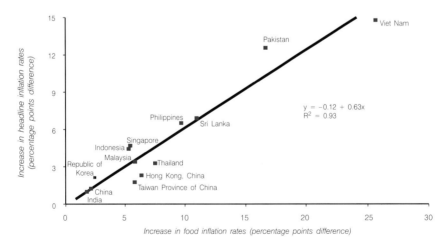

Sources: ESCAP, based on data from national statistical offices websites.

Notes: The increases in inflation rates are calculated as the average year-on-year inflation rates for January-December 2008 minus those for January-December 2007. For India the differences are between for January-November 2007 and January-November 2008.

and in Thailand it fell from 9.2% in July to 0.4% in December. Even in countries where inflation escalated rapidly during 2008, such as Pakistan and Viet Nam, it levelled and started to decrease by August 2008. ESCAP forecasts that this trend will continue during 2009, with the annual average inflation rate dropping to 4.0% for the developing economies of the region, compared with 7.9% in 2008 (figure 2.13). East and North-East Asia is forecast to experience inflation of 0.9% in 2009, down from 5.2% in 2008. Inflation in South-East Asia is forecast to ease to 4.2% in 2009 from 8.8% in 2008. Similarly, inflation in South and South-West Asia is forecast to come down to 9.6% in 2009 from 11.6% in 2008, and in North and Central Asia it will drop to 10.7% in 2009 from 14.3% in 2008.

A major concern about food inflation is its adverse impact on poor households that are net buyers of food. Food insecurity is not a new issue in the Asia-Pacific region. In 2003-2005, the region had 542 million under-nourished people, representing 64% of the world total. It is estimated that higher food prices have increased the number of undernourished people in the region by an additional 41 million as of 2007 (FAO, 2008a). The

additional food price increases in 2008, along with the marked slowdown in economic activity towards the end of the year, is likely to increase the number of undernourished even more. As a result, the Millennium Development Goal of halving the 1990 proportion of undernourished by 2015 seems less likely to be attained.[15]

While these aggregates are worrisome, from a policy point of view it is more important to identify which groups are most affected by the increase in food prices. Two critical distinctions to consider are (1) between poor and non-poor households and (2) between those households that are net sellers of food and those that are net buyers of food. In principle, it might seem like the second distinction is roughly equivalent to that between rural and urban households. However, recent research based on detailed household surveys shows that most rural households are, in fact, net buyers of food (Zezza et al., 2008). Moreover, poor rural households with no land or small landholdings, as well as those who do not use fertilizers and pesticides, are among the most severely affected by the increase in food prices. Poor female-

Figure 2.13. Rates of CPI inflation, by ESCAP subregion, 2007-2009

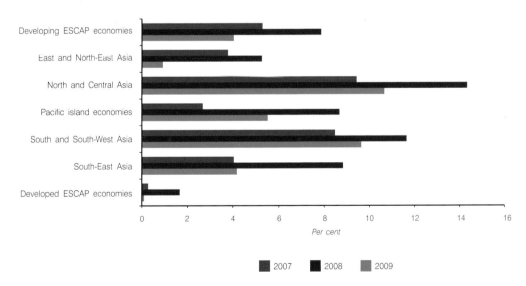

Sources: ESCAP, based on national sources; IMF, *International Financial Statistics* (CD-ROM); ADB, *Key Indicators for Asia and the Pacific 2008*; Interstate Statistical Committee of the Commonwealth of Independent States, www.cisstat.com; and ESCAP forecasts.

Notes: Estimates for 2008 and forecasts for 2009. Subregional rates are weighted averages using 2004 GDP in United States dollars at 2000 prices at weights.

---

[15] The regional rate of undernourishment decreased from 20% in 1990-1992 to 16% in 2003-2005, still high above the 10% target for 2015.

headed households, both rural and urban, suffer the most because their expenses include a larger share of food products and because they are more likely to face constraints in accessing land and credit.

Although food price increases can have serious consequences for the poor in the short-term, most worrisome are the long-term implications for their productivity, their ability to generate income and eventually exit poverty, particularly if their coping mechanisms consist of depleting an already meagre asset base or cutting essential expenditures, such as education, as the following anecdotal examples from the region illustrate.

In Sri Lanka, impact assessments conducted by the International Fund for Agricultural Development (IFAD) revealed that poor rural people have been adopting various strategies to cope with higher food prices, including reducing the number of times and the variety of foods they eat, migrating seasonally and mortgaging or selling properties or other assets (Herath, 2008). The first coping strategy can lead to malnutrition; the third one can make it more difficult for poor people to exit poverty in the future.

In 2007, higher food prices in Fujian Province, China, forced poor rural people to reduce their consumption of meat and oil, cutting their consumption of pork by 15% and eggs by 20% (Sun, 2008). Farmers tended to buy lower-priced food, which is usually poorer in quality and nutritional value. Although food continues to be widely available in China and the grain harvest has been average or above average in the last few years, the problem falls on the poorest members of society, who are unable to afford the price of more expensive food.

In Nepal, food insecurity increased substantially during 2007-2008 not only because of increasing food prices but also because of poor harvests caused by drought in nine western districts of the country. A Rapid Emergency Food Security Assessment for these nine districts conducted by the World Food Programme in June 2008 found a significant increase in coping strategies such as borrowing money, purchasing food on credit and migration (WFP, 2008). A higher proportion of the population was adopting unsustainable coping strategies such as selling land, household belongings and agricultural assets. Other harmful strategies included taking children out of school to work and consuming the next season's seed stocks.

Food price increases may push the poor to reduce the number of times and variety of food they eat, sell their meagre assets, or take children out of school to work, harming their and their children's prospects

Reducing food intake or eating food with lower nutritional content is particularly worrisome, as malnutrition has wider ramifications. Low birth weight, inadequate food intake and maternal anaemia are closely linked. Recent data from India's National Family Health Survey revealed that 42% of children under 3 years in the state of Haryana were clinically underweight in 2005-06, compared with 34% in 1998-99 (Chatterjee, 2007). The data also revealed that 70% of pregnant women in the 15-49 age group were anaemic in 2005-06, up from 56% seven years earlier. (Chatterjee, 2007, p. 1418). Nutritional deficiencies in women in poor rural communities are often associated with food discrimination within the household, by which girls are fed less than boys. Often used as a coping mechanism when there is food insecurity, food discrimination is likely to worsen the nutritional status of both pregnant mothers and newborns, increasing the likelihood of health problems for future generations.

The policy challenge: Managing long-run fuel and food sustainability risks

Figure 2.14 schematizes the analysis of the causes and impacts of the recent episode of fuel and food price increases. Economic growth leads to increases in the demand for both crude oil and food. If supply responds adequately to such demand increases, prices should remain stable and economic growth would be sustainable. If the supply response is not sufficient, crude oil and food prices will increase, putting pressure on domestic inflation rates, the poor, and budget balances. If these pressures are large enough, addressing them becomes a key policy priority, detracting the energies of policymakers from longer-term developmental goals. In that sense, supply-demand imbalances in crude oil and food commodity markets make economic growth unsustainable. Notice that the figure assumes a causal link from crude oil prices to food prices. This is due to the impact of crude oil price increases on both the price of agricultural inputs and the profitability of growing crops for the biofuel industry instead of food crops.

Figure 2.14. Sustainability: balancing the demand and supply of crude oil and food

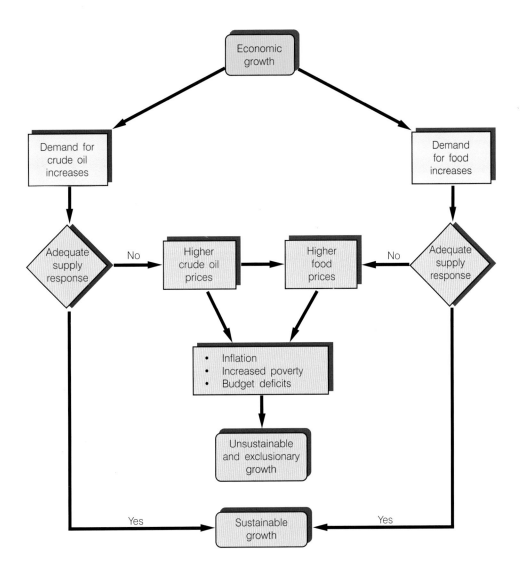

This admittedly simplified scheme suggests that the implementation of policies to ensure an adequate long-term supply to meet future demand in crude oil and food markets is critical to ensure the sustainability of economic growth. That sustainability is, in turn, fundamental to the inclusiveness of the development process and to continuing making progress in eradicating poverty. Three areas where the implementation of long-term sustainability policies is important are energy, food and biofuels.

Although implementing policies to ensure the long-term balance between demand and supply in the energy and food markets is of critical importance, two other sets of policies are necessary complements. First, given the increasing integration between global commodity and financial markets, policies that promote stability in the latter are critical to avoid disruptions in commodity markets arising from excessive degrees of liquidity and speculation. Second, the low coverage of social protection in developing countries of Asia-Pacific makes large segments of the population vulnerable to future crises. To achieve inclusive and sustainable development in the region, the goal of enhancing the coverage of social protection to all the population should be pursued simultaneously with policies to ensure the long-term supply-demand balance in energy and food markets.

Energy

A sluggish supply response to a large increase in demand since 2002 played a critical role in pushing up the price of crude oil from $25 in 2002 to over $100 in 2008. This trend is likely to continue as the global economy recovers from the financial crisis, with fossil fuels dominating the energy mix, emerging economies comprising a growing share of global energy demand, and an inexorable rise in global CO_2 emissions (IEA, 2008). Under this business-as-usual scenario, IEA estimates that the price of crude oil will jump back up to $100 and above in the medium term.[16]

To minimize the risk of such a scenario, two sets of policies should be emphasized (figure 2.15):

- *Continue investing to enhance crude oil and gas production.* As the decline in production from existing oil fields is inexorable, and as oil and gas are expected to account for 80% of the primary

---

[16] IEA estimates that the price of crude oil will average $100 per barrel (at constant 2007 prices) over the period 2008-2015 and rise to $120 by 2030.

energy mix in 2030 under a business-as-usual scenario, it is critical to keep up investments to develop new oil and gas fields to compensate for the declining production of existing fields.

- *Promote energy efficiency and invest in renewable sources of energy.* Securing energy supplies and speeding up the transition to a low-carbon energy system call for decisive action by governments at the national and local levels, and through coordinated international mechanisms. Households, businesses and motorists will have to change the way they use energy, while energy suppliers will need to invest in developing, and commercializing low-carbon technologies. To make this happen, governments have to put in place appropriate financial incentives and regulatory frameworks that support the goals of both energy security and climate policy in an integrated way (IEA, 2008).

The goal of moving towards a new sustainable energy paradigm has been highlighted by ESCAP and was reflected in the adoption by the Commission of resolution 64/3 of 30 April 2008 on promoting renewables for energy security and sustainable development in Asia and the Pacific (ESCAP, 2008b). One key recommendation is to implement tax reforms aimed at internalizing the ecological costs of carbon emissions into energy prices (ESCAP 2008c). Higher fuel taxes deter consumption and encourage the use of more energy efficient technologies. By the same token, removing subsidies on energy consumption, which according to IEA amounted to a staggering $310 billion in the 20

Figure 2.15. Policies to balance demand for and supply of crude oil

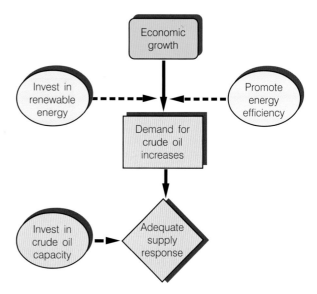

largest non-OECD countries in 2007, could make a major contribution to curbing demand for crude oil and green house gas emissions (IEA, 2008).

Higher fuel taxes deter consumption and encourage the use of more energy efficient technologies; removing subsidies on energy consumption could make a major contribution to curbing demand for crude oil and green house gas emissions

---

An important step in that direction is China's recent reform of its gasoline pricing system. Before the reform, China adjusted gasoline prices infrequently, lagging behind developments in the international crude oil market. Given this lagging pattern of adjustment and the fact that oil prices increased sharply after 2002, gasoline in China was subsidized during most of the period between 2002 and the second half of 2008, encouraging more use of automobiles and other fuel-based vehicles, pushing up China's demand for crude oil. In addition, financial subsidies to keep refiners producing cost the Government tens of billions of yuan (Bangkok Post, 2008). The reform involves two components: (1) relaxing controls over the refined oil prices and letting retailers, wholesalers and refiners jointly determine them in line with market forces; and (2) replacing several administrative fees, including a road maintenance fee, with a fuel tax of 30% to 50%. While the first component eliminates the need to subsidize refiners if the retail price is too low, the second component internalizes the cost of carbon emissions and creates incentives for drivers to switch to less fuel-intensive vehicles.

Another recommendation by ESCAP is to support technological innovations that promote energy efficiency and the development of renewable sources of energy (ESCAP, 2008c). A case in point is India, which has promoted the generation of wind power with an accelerated depreciation of 80%, a 10-year tax holiday for wind farms and exemptions from customs and excise duties (Science and Environment Online, 2008). The diffusion of such innovations within the country is beneficial not just for improving energy security and enhancing growth sustainability. New technologies usually involve a process of learning by both users and producers that, over time, leads to quality improvements and cost reductions. By promoting innovations, a country can acquire a competitive advantage in the new technologies and

export them to other countries. Thus, it is not surprising that as of March 2008, India ranked fourth in the world in installed wind power capacity (Indian Wind Energy Association, 2008).

While the policies mentioned above are important for the goal of sustainable growth, they are also instrumental for achieving climate change mitigation. IEA has considered two climate-policy scenarios corresponding to long-term stabilization of greenhouse gas concentration at 550 and 450 parts per million of CO_2 equivalent (IEA, 2008). The 550 and 450 policy scenarios consider increases is the global temperature of $3^\circ C$ and $2^\circ C$, respectively. To reach either of these outcomes, hundreds of millions of households and businesses around the world would need to change the way they use energy, requiring innovative policies, an appropriate regulatory framework, the rapid development of a global carbon market and increased investment in energy research and development.

To what extent can the ESCAP region reduce the petroleum intensity of its economic growth? Between 1990 and 2005, most ESCAP subregions made progress in reducing their petroleum intensity, measured as barrels per day of petroleum consumption over GDP in millions of 1990 United States dollars (figure 2.16). The Asia-Pacific region as a whole cut petroleum intensity by 18% between 1990 and 2005. The subregion that cut its petroleum intensity the most was North and Central Asia (45%). Only South-East Asia kept its petroleum intensity roughly constant between 1990 and 2005. Still, there is room for more progress. The petroleum intensity of GDP in the developed economies of the region is one third that of the developing economies of the region. Thus, it is critical to foster mechanisms for the transfer of technical expertise in efficient and renewable energy from developed to developing countries.

Food

As in the case of crude oil, lagging investment has been a major reason for the rapid increases in food prices up to mid-2008. Three groups of factors have been holding back agriculture: (1) structural constraints, such as inequality in land ownership, lack of human capital development due to limited access to health and education, and inadequate rural infrastructure; (2) policy constraints, including anti-agricultural macroeconomic policies, limited agricultural credit, and lack of promotion of R&D and extension services; and (3) external factors, such as limited progress in liberalizing agricultural trade, agricultural price instability, and declining official development assistance (ESCAP, 2008a, p. 133). The neglect of agriculture needs to be

Figure 2.16. Petroleum intensity of GDP, by ESCAP subregion, 1990-2005

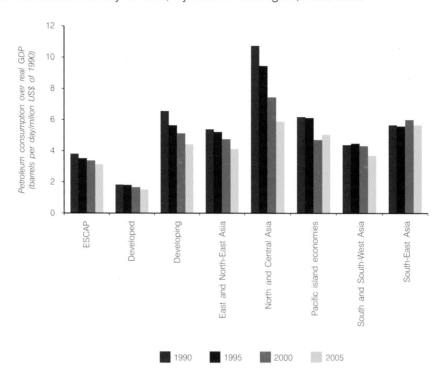

Sources: ESCAP, based on data from the United States Energy Information Administration, http://www.eia.doe.gov/emeu/international/Recent PetroleumConsumptionBarrelsperDay.xls; and ESCAP, Statistical Yearbook for Asia and the Pacific 2007, table 14.1.

urgently redressed if future episodes of soaring prices are to be mitigated. In addition, policies adopted by some grain exporters to protect domestic consumers from the impact of increasing prices, such as export bans and quotas, drove prices up even faster, to the detriment of importing countries. Thus, policies to improve the functioning of the international agricultural trade markets and to promote a mechanism of regional cooperation for emergency access to food need to be boosted. Figure 2.17 schematizes these two sets of policies.

Policies to promote investments in agriculture and rural development should emphasize the following elements:

- *Focus on smallholders*. Despite migration to the cities, 80% of the Asia-Pacific poor reside in rural areas and lack access to enough land, agricultural inputs, finance and markets to benefit from the higher food prices. This state of deprivation needs to be addressed in order to improve the food supply response, reduce poverty and make growth more inclusive. To achieve these objectives, increased public and private investments are needed, investments that will alleviate conditions

for small farmers throughout the supply chain – at the farm level, in production infrastructure, access to markets and processing.

- *Promote opportunities for rural non-farm employment*. A prosperous rural economy depends not only on agriculture but also on non-farm activities, including agro-industries, commerce and other services. Such activities provide additional sources of income for rural households above and beyond agriculture. They also contribute to a more balanced pattern of rural development, which creates both a higher tax base and a constituency that will demand investments in rural infrastructure (roads, electricity) and public goods (schools, health clinics). Finally, a more prosperous rural economy reduces incentives for rural-to-urban migration, easing pressures on urban infrastructure and the provision of public services in cities.

- *Boost R&D investments and disseminate improved technologies*. The International Rice Research Institute (IRRI) has proposed a nine-point programme to boost rice yields and enhance food security. Among its recommendations: (1) reduce gaps in yields across countries and regions through the

Figure 2.17. Policies to balance demand for and supply of food

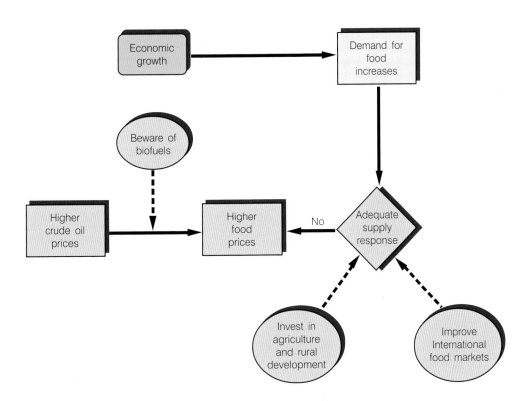

use of better crop management practices; (2) accelerate the delivery of new post-harvest technologies to reduce losses; (3) accelerate the introduction and adoption of higher-yielding varieties; (4) increase funding for the development of new rice varieties; and (5) train a new generation of rice scientists and engineers (Remo, 2008).

- *Promote sustainable agricultural practices.* Increasing food production is a fundamental objective not only for the short- and medium-term but also for the long-term. It is critical to avoid agricultural practices that place stress on natural resources, lead to the depletion of water sources, the nitrification and salination of soils, and the permanent loss of biodiversity and ecosystem services. If agricultural practices damage natural resources, the future food supply response will suffer. A major area of concern is the use of irrigation systems, which are highly inefficient and poorly maintained in most countries of the Asia-Pacific region (ESCAP, 2006).

- *Strengthen producer organizations.* Strong producer organizations facilitate the integration of smallholder farmers into agricultural supply chains. By improving their bargaining power vis-à-vis input

supply and food marketing companies, they can improve the profitability of their production. Finally, producer organizations allow smallholder farmers to pool common resources and learn how best to manage them and save on operational costs.

- *Improve international trade in food.* Countries should avoid actions that meet national needs but make the problem worse for other countries. Therefore, the completion of the Doha Round of trade negotiations, with an enhanced set of agreed rules for a more transparent and fair international trading system, is an important step toward securing more predictable access to food.

- *Strengthen regional mechanisms for emergency access to food.* At the regional level, it is necessary to support mechanisms for improving emergency access to food through stock sharing and fewer restrictions on the release of stocks to other countries under emergency conditions. Policies to build up national food stocks should be pursued with caution because of their high management costs. Finally, the use of market-based risk management instruments can be helpful to both producers and buyers of food products. Instruments such as futures contracts and options allow producers and consumers of food to transfer risks to financial investors. For that purpose, national and regional exchanges could be developed as pilot projects, with the intention of scaling them up in the future. Such programmes, given their inherently complex and risky nature, would need to be complemented by intensive capacity-building programmes and with an appropriate regulatory regime to prevent excessive speculation and volatility.

- *Enhance coherence in multilateral economic governance to smooth out commodity price volatility.* The increased attention on the reform of the international financial architecture provides an opportunity to agree on regulations that prevent excessive speculation on commodity markets. Furthermore, it should be possible to devise a mechanism that provides adequate countercyclical liquidity to soften commodity price shocks (akin to reserve pooling to support sudden drops in currency values as suggested in chapter 1) .

Biofuels

Biofuels provide a renewable source of energy that can help reduce the petroleum intensity of growth. Depending on the production and processing of biofuel feed stocks, the scale of their production and their influence on land use, biofuels also have the potential to reduce the emission of greenhouse gases (FAO, 2008b).[17] In addition, as a major new source of demand for agricultural commodities, they could help revitalize agriculture in developing countries, with potentially positive implications for economic growth, poverty reduction and food security (FAO, 2008b, p. 79). While all of these benefits should be taken into account, it must also be considered that one of the adverse consequences of the expansion of the biofuel industry is its contribution to the merging of the food and fuel markets.

The economics of biofuel production is illustrated in figure 2.18, which shows the breakeven prices for ethanol production in the United States. The upper line shows the break-even prices without subsidies. When the crude oil price is above this line, producers of biofuels make profits. The line is upward-sloping be-

cause increases in maize prices push up the costs of ethanol production. The lower line shows break-even prices with subsidies. The figure includes weekly averages of the international market prices of crude oil and maize from 2005 to 2008. Not surprisingly, prices are clustered mostly along the area between the two break-even price lines because an increase in crude oil prices makes ethanol production more profitable, prompting producers to increase their demand for maize and, in turn, pushing up the price of maize. Similarly, a decrease in the price of crude oil makes ethanol production less profitable and helps pull down the price of maize.

The merging of the food and fuel markets is problematic in the light of the projections of future supply-demand balances in the crude oil market (IEA, 2008). If crude oil prices rebound to $100 or more in the coming years, the incentives to boost biofuel use will increase dramatically, even without government subsidies. As it is easy to adapt motor vehicles to run on biofuels and for gas stations to distribute them, the technological obstacles to the expansion of the industry are relatively easy to overcome. Coinciding with fast-rising crude oil prices, worldwide biofuels production has grown at spectacular average annual rates between 2001 and 2006: 22.7% for ethanol and 43.2% for biodiesel (Gonzales, 2008). Furthermore, projections suggest that these trends will continue, with ethanol substituting for 10% to 20% of the expected global demand for gasoline by 2030 (Walter et al., 2008).

Figure 2.18. Break-even prices for maize and crude oil with and without subsidies

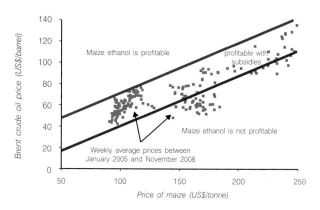

Sources: Data from the Food and Agriculture Organization of the United Nations, http://www.fao.org/es/esc/prices/PricesServlet.jsp?lang=en; and Pacific Exchange Rate Service, http://fx.sauder.ubc.ca/data.htm IFAO.

Notes: The break-even prices for maize and crude oil are taken from FAO (2008b, figure 1.2). The price of maize is for the U.S. No. 2, Yellow, U.S. Gulf (Friday).

---

[17] As discussed in chapter 3, when tropical forests are converted into cropland to grow biofuel feed stocks, greenhouse gases (GHG) are released into the atmosphere for decades, as coarse roots and branches decay and as wood products decay or burn. See Fagione et al. (2008).

Another concern about expanding the biofuel industry is its impact on water resources. As of 2005, 71% of the freshwater withdrawn in the Asia-Pacific region was used for agricultural purposes (ESCAP, 2009). In many countries, water for agriculture is becoming more scarce as a result of increased domestic or industrial uses. In addition, the expected impacts of climate change – reduced rainfall in some producer regions, for example – will place further pressure on already scarce resources. While biofuel production currently accounts for only about 2% of all irrigation water withdrawals worldwide, even these withdrawals constitute an additional demand on an already scarce resource. Finally, a further expansion of the biofuels industry through the conversion of pastures or woodlands may exacerbate soil erosion, sedimentation, excess nutrient run-off into surface water, and infiltration of fertilizer into groundwater (FAO, 2008b, pp. 63-64).

If crude oil prices rebound to $100 or more in the coming years, the incentives to boost biofuel use will increase dramatically, even without government subsidies

---

In sum, there are reasons to re-examine policies that promote the biofuel industry, both on environmental grounds and because its expansion facilitates the transmission of crude oil price increases to food price increases, but it will be difficult to "put the genie back in the bottle". Many governments in the Asia-Pacific region have already implemented policies to support the development of the biofuel industry. Nevertheless, in pursuing the long-term goal of sustainable and inclusive development it is not enough to evaluate policies exclusively according to their impact in reducing the demand for crude oil. Their impact on land, water and the atmosphere are equally important. In other words, a systemic approach to policy evaluation is needed. The following are suggested guidelines for biofuel policy:

- *Re-examine current policies, including subsidy schemes.* Biofuel policies should advance sustainability objectives, particularly those linked to the protection of the agricultural base, forest areas, water resources, watersheds and biodiversity, while also ensuring that food production is not compromised.

- Support the development of second generation biofuels, particularly if use is made of degraded and abandoned agricultural lands to grow native perennials. Second generation biofuels offer better

prospects for balancing food security objectives because they are based on non-food feed stocks – for example, cellulosic ethanol, which is produced from the lignocellulosic parts of woody biomass, grass and other non-edible parts of a plant.

- *At the global level, develop biofuel guidelines and safeguard measures that minimize adverse impacts on global food security and the environment.* Such guidelines can form the basis for an internationally negotiated code of conduct.[18]

- *Take into account the substitutability between fossil fuels and biofuels when undertaking tax reforms.* Reforms to the pricing of gasoline, such as those proposed above, would eventually lead to increases in the price of fuel once the price of crude oil recovers from its current lows. In the absence of coordination among the tax regimes for fuels and biofuels, such a development would create an implicit subsidy for the use of biofuels, with possibly undesirable consequences. Thus, apart from taking steps to regulate the biofuel industry, it is also necessary to harmonize its tax regime with that of the ordinary fuels industry.

Social protection

This chapter has dealt so far with long-term aspects of development which need to be taken into account in the present if the likelihood of future commodity price crises is to be reduced. The policies suggested above, if successful, will help make economic growth compatible with stable commodity prices and enough production of energy and food to meet both present and future needs without depleting invaluable natural resources. If growth could proceed without major disruptions to energy and food prices, and without major financial crises, eradicating poverty and the fulfillment of the Millennium Development Goals would be more feasible, though not by any means automatic. The coexistence in the Asia-Pacific region of 583 million undernourished people with the world's fastest rates of economic growth attest to this claim.

---

[18] The Food Security Summit held in Rome in June 2008 recommended forging an international consensus in the following five areas: (1) safeguard mechanisms for food security; (2) sustainable principles; (3) research and development, knowledge exchange and capacity-building; (4) trade measures and financing options; and (5) methodologies for measuring and monitoring biofuel impacts. See FAO (2008c).

While fast economic growth does not automatically translate into growing prosperity for all members of society, it creates resources that can be tapped to make the region's societies more responsive to the needs of the poor and vulnerable. Those resources are making it increasingly feasible for countries in the region to achieve the goal of providing social security to all members of society, which is enshrined by Article 22 of the Universal Declaration of Human Rights:

> "Everyone, as a member of society, has the right to social security and is entitled to realization, through national effort and international cooperation and in accordance with the organization and resources of each State, of the economic, social and cultural rights indispensable for his dignity and the free development of his personality".

However, the coverage of basic social protection programmes is very low in developing economies of Asia-Pacific. It is estimated that only 20% of the population has access to health care assistance; 30% of the elderly receive pensions; and 20% of the unemployed and underemployed have access to labour market programmes such as unemployment benefits, training, or public works programmes, including food for work programmes. On the other hand, the coverage of child protection and social assistance to the poor is high, 83% for the region as a whole, but that number is influenced by the weight on the regional averages of China and India, where coverage is virtually universal.[19] For close to half of the 30 countries considered by Wood (2009), the coverage of these programmes is less than 50%. Deficiencies in coverage of social protection are particularly noticeable for workers employed in the informal economy (Mehrotra, 2009).

Enhancing the coveraging of social protection is not only a moral imperative but also good economics. In times of crisis and uncertainty about the future people tend to increase their savings to protect themselves from the risk of losing their jobs or suffering a loss of income. When millions of individuals react in the same way, they cause the crisis to deepen by affecting aggregate domestic demand. Thus a behaviour that is natural and rational at the individual level is detrimental to the economy at the aggregate level. To reduce this adverse macroeconomic implication, it is necessary to induce a change of behaviour at the individual level. It is in this context that enhancing the coverage of social

protection could help. By providing a basic level of income support, social protection schemes make individuals feel more secure and less inclined to increase their savings to protect themselves from possible income losses in times of crisis, contributing to domestic demand and macroeconomic stability.

To be sure, there is no lack of social protection programmes in the Asia-Pacific region, and during the food price crisis of the first half of 2008 many additional emergency responses were instituted. Some countries sold rice at subsidized prices; others provided cash assistance to poor households. Subsidies to water and electricity consumption to small users, fuel subsidies, free transportation in selected buses and trains, rice distribution to children attending elementary school, and raises of minimum wages were among the many ad hoc measures implemented to protect the poor from the impact of rising food prices. These measures have been effective in tackling the emergency and minimizing the likelihood of social upheaval, but they were improvised, relatively costly, and temporary.

Social protection schemes make individuals feel more secure and less inclined to increase their savings to protect themselves from possible income losses in times of crisis, contributing to domestic demand and macroeconomic stability

---

Because episodes of soaring commodity prices are likely to recur in future, a better and longer-term policy response to protect the poor and vulnerable must be put in place. What is needed is the development of comprehensive social protection systems that will be in place before new crises strike. Their details are likely to vary across countries depending on their specific needs, social infrastructure and vulnerability patterns, as well as their technical and fiscal capacity to administer different types of programmes (HLTF, 2008). Developing such social protection systems is akin to investing in projects to enhance the long-term sustainability of economic growth. Both types of investments aim at minimizing future developmental risks. They are thus important building blocks for a more inclusive and sustainable pattern of economic development in the region.

A desirable goal for social protection systems in the region should be to capture all the people who fall under socially vulnerable categories and provide them with minimum grant levels. A minimum floor of social security benefits for all citizens should include:

---

[19] Regional averages are computed from national data provided by Wood (2009) for 30 Asia-Pacific countries using 2007 populations as weights.

- a universal guarantee of access to basic health services,

- guaranteed income security for all children through family and/or child benefits,

- guaranteed access to basic means-tested or self-targeted social assistance for the poor and the unemployed, and

- guaranteed income security for people in old age and invalidity through basic pensions.

In recent years, there has been much interest in boosting social safety nets in the Asia-Pacific region, addressing the third bullet point from the list above. Safety nets consist of cash or in-kind government transfers to the poor. Both kinds can be conditional or unconditional. Conditional transfers provide transfers to families or individuals as a reward for actions such as attending school, participating in public works, or doing a medical checkup. Unconditional transfers do not depend upon recipient's behaviour. Two selected examples of safety net programmes in the Asia-Pacific are described below.

India's National Rural Employment Guarantee Act (NREGA) provides a legal guarantee for one hundred days of employment in every financial year to adult members of any rural household willing to do unskilled manual work at the statutory minimum wage. The central government funds the cost of wages, 75% of the cost of materials, and part of the administrative expenses; the remaining costs are funded by state governments. Participants in NREGA work in projects such as water conservation, flood control, irrigation, and land development, among others. The programme has many benefits, including the reduction of distress migration, employment generation in the most distressed areas, and improvements in the natural resource base of livelihoods in poor communities.

Philippine's Pantawid Pamilyang Pilipino Program (4Ps) provides poor households P500 a month for their health needs and a P300 educational subsidy for each child up to age 14. Poor families can get the educational subsidy for a maximum of three children. In return, beneficiaries are required to comply with the following conditions: (i) Pregnant women must get pre-natal care, child birth must be attended by a skilled or trained person, and mothers must get post-natal care; (ii) Children 0-5 years must get regular health check ups and vaccinations; and (iii) Children 6-14 must attend school at least 85 per cent of the time. Failure to comply with these conditions could mean losing the subsidy. School principals and the municipal health officers are tasked to monitor compliance. The rationale for the conditions is to create incentives for the

recipients to invest in their own human capital. Such investments will give them, especially the children, a better chance to exit poverty permanently in the long-term.

Both programmes combine a safety net component with the generation of assets, land improvements in the case of NREGA and human capital in the case of the 4Ps, which can help recipients and the communities where they live to reduce their poverty in the longer-term. However, the two programmes differ in the way they target the poor. NREGA is an example of a self-targeted programme, characterized by low administration costs and high accuracy in reaching the targeted population. By guaranteeing income support to anyone willing to participate in unskilled manual labour at low wages, and only for 100 days in a year, the programmme' ensures that only the neediest will apply. In contrast, conditional cash transfer programmes such the 4Ps require the implementation of a targeting mechanism to ensure that its benefits reach the desired recipients. Ensuring the accuracy of such targeting mechanisms could be expensive, administratively complicated, and time-consuming.

The region's fast economic growth over the last decades is creating the means to make definitive progress in eradicating poverty and hunger, but reaching such goals calls for the implementation of effective social protection systems

---

In any event, the Asia-Pacific region has already a rich experience in the implementation of various types of social protection programmes, and much more experimentation is under way. Although countries in the region differ in their needs and in their technical and fiscal capabilities, there is much to be gained by exchanging information about various experiences and by forging mechanisms for technical cooperation in the design and implementation of social protection programmes. Such programmes should not be seen as mere palliatives. The region's fast economic growth over the last decades is creating the means to make definitive progress in eradicating poverty and hunger, but reaching such goals calls for the implementation of effective social protection systems. Such systems can contribute to make the region not only prosperous but also more socially inclusive, and they can also contribute to macroeconomic stability in future times of crisis.

References

Abbott, Philip C., Christopher Hurt, and Wallace E. Tyner (2008). "What's driving food prices?", Farm Foundation issue report, July.

Bangkok Post (2008). "China's next reform in the pipeline", 13 December 2008.

Burkhard, James (2008). "The price of oil: A reflection of the world", testimony before the Committee on Energy and Natural Resources, United States Senate, 3 April (Cambridge Energy Research Associates, Washington, D.C.).

Chatterjee, Patralekha (2007). "Child malnutrition rises in India despite the economic boom", *The Lancet*, vol. 369, issue 9571, 28 April, pp. 1417-1418.

Crespo Cuaresma, Jesus, and Andreas Breitenfellner (2008). "Crude oil prices and the Euro-Dollar exchange rate: A forecasting exercise", University of Innsbruck, Working Papers in Economics and Statistics 2008-8.

Davidson, Paul (2008). "Crude oil prices: 'Market fundamentals' or speculation?", *Challenge*, vol. 51, issue 4, pp. 110-118.

ESCAP (2006). *The State of the Environment in Asia and the Pacific 2005* (United Nations publication, Sales No. E.06.II.F.30).

_____ (2007). *Economic and Social Survey of Asia and the Pacific 2007* (United Nations publication, Sales No. E.07.II.F.4).

_____ (2008a). *Economic and Social Survey of Asia and the Pacific 2008* (United Nations publication, Sales No. E.08.II.F.7).

_____ (2008b). *Annual Report, 24 May 2007-30 April 2008, Official Records of the Economic and Social Council, 2008, Supplement* No. 19 (E/2008/39-E/ESCAP/64/39), chap. IV, resolution 64/3, www.unescap.org/EDC/English/Annual Reports/2008(64).pdf.

_____ (2008c). *Energy Security and Sustainable Development in Asia and the Pacific* (United Nations publication, Sales No. E.08.II.F.13).

_____ (2009). *Towards Sustainable Agriculture and Food Security in the Asia-Pacific Region* (United Nations publication, Sales No. E.09.II.F.12).

Fagione, Joseph, Jason Hill, David Tilman, Stephen Polasky, and Peter Hawthorne (2008). "Land clearing and the biofuel carbon debt", *Science*, vol. 319, issue 5867, 20 February, pp. 1235-1238.

FAO (2008a). "Briefing paper: Hunger on the rise – Soaring food prices add 75 million people to global hunger rolls", 17 September, www.fao.org/newsroom/common/ecg/1000923/en/hungerfigs.pdf.

_____ . (2008b). *State of Food and Agriculture 2008 – Biofuels: Prospects, Risks and Opportunities*.

_____ . (2008c). "Bioenergy, food security and sustainability – Towards an international framework", HLC/08/INF/3, ftp://ftp.fao.org/docrep/fao/meeting/013/k2498e.pdf.

Gately, Dermot, and Hillary G. Huntington (2002). "The asymmetric effects of changes in price and income on energy and oil demand", *Energy Journal*, vol. 23, issue 1, pp. 19-55.

Gonzales, Alan Dale C. (2008). "Overall stocktaking of biofuel development in Asia-Pacific: Benefits and challenges", background paper for *Policy Dialogue on Biofuels in Asia: Benefits and Challenges*, Beijing, China, 24-26 September 2008.

Hamilton, James D. (2008). "Understanding crude oil prices", mimeo (revised) (San Diego: Department of Economics, University of California at San Diego).

Herath, Anura (2008). "Higher food prices, fewer meals in Sri Lanka" in IFAD, *Making a Difference in Asia and the Pacific*, issue 21, June-July.

HLTF (High Level Task Force on the Global Food Security Crisis) (2008). "Comprehensive framework for action", July, http://www.ifad.org/operations/food/documents/cfa/cfa_draft.pdf.

Hossain, Mahabub (2007). "A balancing act", *Rice Today*, April-June.

IEA (International Energy Agency) (2008). *World Energy Outlook 2008*.

IFPRI (International Food Policy Research Institute) (2008). "Speculation and world food markets", *IFPRI Forum*, July.

IMF (various issues). *World Economic Outlook*, Statistical Appendix.

IMF (2006). *World Economic Outlook* (Washington, D.C.).

Indian Wind Energy Association (2008), www.inwea. org.

Krugman, Paul (2008). "Running out of planet to exploit", *New York Times*, 21 April 2008.

Mehrotra, Santosh (2009). "The poor in East and South East Asia in the time of financial crisis", paper presented at the Conference on the Impact of the Economic Crisis on Children, National University of Singapore, 6-7 January.

Mitchell, Donald (2008). "A note on rising food prices", World Bank Policy Research Working Paper No. 4682.

Remo, Amy R. (2008). "IRRI proposes ways to increase worldwide rice production", *Philippine Daily Inquirer*, 3 May 2008.

Science and Environment Online (2008). "Fanning an alternative", 15 August 2008, www.downtoearth. org.in/cover.asp?foldername=20080815& filename=news&sid =41&page=.

Smith, Yves (2008). "Is the commodity boom driven by speculation?", Naked Capitalism, 19 May, www.nakedcapitalism.com/2008/05/is-commodities-boom-driven-by.html.

Sun, Yinhong (2008). "Poor Chinese farmers sell and buy less in response to rising food prices" in IFAD, *Making a Difference in Asia and the Pacific*, issue 21, June-July.

Trostle, Ronald (2008). "Global agricultural supply and demand: Factors contributing to the recent increase in food commodity prices", 9 July revised (United States Department of Agriculture).

UNCTAD (2007). "The development role of commodity exchanges", TD/B/COM.1/EM.33/2 (Geneva).

United Kingdom, Renewable Fuels Agency (2008). *The Gallagher Review of the Indirect Effects of Biofuels Production*.

Vidal, John (2008). "Soaring fertilizer prices threaten poor farmers", *The Guardian*, 12 August 2008.

von Braun, Joachim (2008). "Food prices, biofuels, and climate change" (International Food Policy Research Institute), www.ifpri.org/presentations/200802jvbbiofuels.pdf.

Walter, Arnaldo, Frank Rosillo-Calle, Paulo Dolzan, Erik Piacente, and Kamyla Borges da Cunha (2008). "Perspectives on fuel ethanol consumption and trade", *Biomass and Bioenergy*, vol. 32, issue 8, pp. 730-748.

Webb, Sara (2008). "Golf courses, developers nibble at Asia's rice paddies", *Vancouver Sun*, 1 May 2008.

WFP (2008). Food Security Bulletin – 20, Food Security Monitoring and Analysis System, August.

Wood, Joe (2009), "A social protection index for Asia", paper presented at the Conference on Asia Social Protection in Comparative Perspective, National University of Singapore, 7-9 January.

World Bank (2007). *World Development Report 2008: Agriculture for Development* (Washington, D.C.).

Yergin, Daniel (2008), "Oil at the break point", testimony before the United States Congress Joint Economic Committee, 25 June (Cambridge Energy Research Associates, Washington, D.C.).

Zezza, Alberto, Benjamin Davis, Carlo Azzarri, Katia Covarrubias, Luca Tasciotti, and Gustavo Anriquez (2008). "The impact of rising food prices on the poor", mimeo (FAO).

ESCAP photo

"Green growth is not a matter of choice, but a requirement that we must fulfill by all means for our future survival. What matters is whether we can take the lead based on our own original technology, or whether we have to lag behind other countries.

Lee Myung-bak
President of the Republic of Korea

CHAPTER 3. THE CLIMATE CHANGE CHALLENGE: REORIENTING DEVELOPMENT TOWARDS GREENER AND SUSTAINABLE GROWTH

The present turbulent and uncertain financial and economic conditions present a window of opportunity for the climate change agenda. Just as countries have coordinated their response to the financial crisis, so should they work together to galvanize the response to climate change. In particular the formulation of their fiscal stimulus packages should be coordinated so that they not only raise short-term domestic demand but also promote truly sustainable development. The Global Green New Deal promoted by Secretary-General of the United Nations (Jaura, 2008) provides a way forward towards a low-carbon development path in which ESCAP has taken the lead in the region. Developing countries, in particular, should be proactive in adopting similar initiatives to stay competitive while mitigating climate change. At the multilateral level, as discussed in chapter 1, the region should play an increasingly influential role in framing regional cooperation. Shaping the post-2012 climate change agenda (UNFCCC, 2007) is a key priority on the region's international policy agenda. It is also an opportune time to advocate a concept of "human responsibility to nature" wherein every individual, firm and Government has a right to a clean and safe environment and a responsibility to protect the environment. At a time of crisis, there is a tendency for Governments to postpone some of their long-term investment initiatives, such as mitigating the impact of climate change. In this context, the Secretary-General of the United Nations, Ban Ki-moon, emphasized that:

> "Investing in the green economy is not an optional expense. It is a smart investment for a more equitable and prosperous future".

This issue has assumed an increased urgency. The global climate has changed dramatically in recent decades and continues to do so at a rapid pace. Surface temperatures have been rising, mountain glaciers and ice caps have been declining and sea levels have been rising. Widespread changes in extreme temperatures are causing longer droughts, warmer winters and colder days and nights – and floods, storms and cyclones have become more frequent and intense.

Climate change is having a severe impact on the Asia-Pacific region, particularly on the agricultural and water sectors. It brings with it serious implications for people's health and affects the lives of women and girls who spend most of their time fetching water. It will also entail immense economic costs – ranging from 5% to 20% of gross domestic product (GDP) per annum (Stern, 2006). Even some small islands in the Pacific and the Maldives could disappear due to the rise in sea level if the worst scenario of climate change becomes reality.

A drastic change in the "grow first and clean up later" attitude towards the environment is urgently required

---

Countries across the region now need to move on from the "grow first and clean up later" attitude towards the environment – and instead pay urgent attention to both mitigation and adaptation, and make preparations to reduce the impact of disasters. These efforts will also need to involve the private sector, for which climate change activity should represent a business opportunity.

This chapter analyses the socio-economic impact of climate change and then proposes three strategies for the region to consider: utilizing the window of opportunity for climate change created by the financial crisis; promoting a shift in the attitude towards climate change; and playing a critical role in the global climate change agenda. It concludes that, in order to address climate change, a major shift in the way goods and services are produced and consumed is critical – towards greener and sustainable development. Promoting eco-efficiency, developing sustainable infrastructure and investing in research and development in technological advancements are some of the priority areas for which resources from fiscal stimulus packages designed to fight the financial crisis would need to be allocated. Such fiscal stimuli could be combined with fiscal reforms, such as the introduction of green taxes, in order to secure financial resources.

Climate change and related vulnerabilities

Environmental impacts

Asia and the Pacific has experienced a continuous change in meteorological and hydrological conditions – sea level rise, changing patterns and amounts of rainfall and flows of river water, severe floods and droughts, heavier and more frequent storms, and possibly an increase in the frequency and intensity of the El Niño Southern Oscillation.[1]

The increase in the surface temperature in Asia and the Pacific is much higher than the global average...so is the impact

---

In the last century, the average global surface temperature has increased by 0.74 °C. In the last 50 years, surface warming has doubled and the mean temperature increase in Asia and the Pacific has far exceeded the global trend. Recent estimates indicate that the global average temperature by the end of the century could rise 2 °C or 3 °C, or even as much as 6 °C.

This has critical implications for mountain glaciers, which feed Asia's seven major rivers – the Brahmaputra, the Ganges, the Indus, the Salween, the Mekong, the Huanghe and the Yangtze – which constitute a lifeline for over 1 billion people (IPCC, 2007a). Himalayan glaciers are shrinking at an average of 10-60 metres annually; some are retreating by 74 metres a year and many could melt entirely by 2035.

The region has also experienced significant temporal and spatial variations in rainfall. Decreasing trends have been observed in the Russian Federation, north-eastern and northern China, the coastal belts and arid plains of Pakistan, parts of north-east India, Indonesia, the Philippines and some areas in Japan. On the other hand, annual mean rainfall is increasing in western China, the Changjiang Valley and the south-eastern coast of China, the Arabian Peninsula, and Bangladesh and along the western coasts of the Philippines. Though in

aggregate across the region the volume of yearly precipitation might remain relatively stable, the changes in different places could result in a serious mismatch between water supply and demand.

There are also extensive implications for sea levels. Since 1993, the sea level has been rising at a rate of about 3 millimetres annually – a major threat to coastal areas and many Pacific island countries, affecting coastal erosion, freshwater supply and fish stocks. The increased frequency of El Niño episodes since the 1970s has already raised sea temperatures, and coral reefs, which even now are close to their threshold temperature tolerance, could suffer irreversible damage (FAO, 2008).

Then there are the risks of extreme meteorological events. Cyclones originating in the Pacific and the Bay of Bengal, for example, have become more intense, and more intense precipitation events are likely to occur in many parts of the region.

Socio-economic impacts

Climate change will have a profound effect on many people in the region, particularly the poorest in the least developed countries who depend on climate-sensitive activities, such as agriculture, forestry and fishing, and who lack the resources and options for mitigation and adaptation.

Heightened livelihood insecurities

Water resources

The region is facing a growing discrepancy between the demand for and availability of freshwater. Many countries are already experiencing stress, even at the current levels of rainfall, but climate change will make things much worse – and pose a major threat to the achievement of the Millennium Development Goals. Currently, about 650 million people in Asia and the Pacific lack access to clean water (ESCAP, ADB, UNDP, 2007).

Higher temperatures will reduce the capacity of natural systems to store water in the form of snow and glaciers. They will also cause more evaporation of surface water and intensify rainfall, further increasing the risk of flash floods. Changes in the pattern and amount of precipitation also increase the severity of prolonged drought – affecting 185 million to 1 billion people in South and

---

[1]   The El-Niño Southern Oscillation is the result of a cyclic warming and cooling of the surface ocean of the central and eastern Pacific. See http://www.john-daly.com/elnino.htm for details.

South-East Asia (IPCC, 2007b). In addition, water scarcity will constrain food production and could lead to conflicts, not only within but also between countries, while also accelerating migration to cities, aggravating urban poverty and increasing slum populations.

A billion people in the region could be affected by water stress

---

Between 13 million and 94 million people in low-lying areas of South, South-East and East Asia face the prospect of flooding and disruption to drinking water supplies. The countries most affected would be Bangladesh, China, India and Viet Nam (IPCC, 2007b). Small Pacific island States are also at particular risk. By 2050, some of their freshwater lenses[2] could shrink by as much as 20%.

Just as significant will be the effect on water quality. If the sea level rises by as much as 40 centimetres by the end of this century, the ingress of seawater in many coastal areas could make the subsurface water saline, compounding the damage done by direct pollution of water through the discharge of chemical effluents, e-waste and untreated wastewater. Bangladesh, China and India are especially vulnerable.

Agriculture and food security

Agriculture provides employment for 60% of the region's working population, and the region is a net exporter of agricultural products. But in recent years agricultural productivity has not increased fast enough to meet the rising demand from an increasing population and economic growth – a consequence of the lack of investment in agricultural infrastructure, along with soil erosion, salinization and water stress. In the future, agriculture could suffer even more from uneven weather patterns. Excessive rainfall during the harvest season damages crops, and monsoon torrents can wash away irrigation canals and deposit sand and gravel in rice fields.

By altering soil temperature and moisture, climate change can also alter growing seasons. This may boost agricultural output in countries in the middle to higher latitudes but reduce output in lower latitudes. Many developing countries, including those in Asia and the Pacific, are in equatorial regions and thus are

likely to be net losers. Overall, by 2050, compared with the 1990 baseline, agricultural productivity in Asia is expected to decrease by 5% to 30%, particularly in Central Asia and South Asia, as a consequence of rising temperatures, declines in humidity and growing pest populations. Every 1 °C increase in minimum temperature during the growing season can result in a 10% decline in rice yields (IPCC, 2007a).

---

30 million people in the region could become environmental refugees

---

In coastal areas, a higher sea level would increase soil salinity – submerging land and causing other environmental hazards – and so reduce the quantity of land available for agricultural production, with severe consequences for many island States in the Pacific as well as Bangladesh and the Maldives. In Bangladesh, a rise in sea level of 1 metre would lead to the inundation of 15% to 18% of the country's land mass, and, by the year 2050, a total of 30 million people could become environmental refugees (UNDP, 2007).

Fisheries

The Asia-Pacific region produces more than half of the world's captured fish and 90% of aquaculture fish (FAO, 2006), and millions of people across the region rely on fish for their protein intake and livelihoods. Of the estimated 41 million people working as fishers and fish farmers in 2007, the great majority, many on a small scale, are in developing Asia (FAO, 2007).

The actual impact of climate change on fisheries is very difficult to predict, given the complexity of the many interacting factors, but rising sea temperatures and ocean currents could alter the breeding habitats and food supply of fish, including predator species, such as tuna – posing a direct economic threat to Pacific island countries that depend on revenues from fishing licences. There will also be damage to coral reefs and associated inshore fisheries.

Coastal areas

In the next 30 years, higher temperatures could lead to the disappearance of 30% of Asia's coral reefs. The rising sea level will also cause coastal erosion and inundation of low-lying areas. It may also induce lagoon flushing, the loss of coastal marshes and wetlands and the increasing salination of rivers, bays and aquifers. Coastal regions would also be subject to increased wind and flood damage due to storm surges (IPCC, 2007a).

---

[2] This refers to the strip of underground water also known as an aquifer.

Most at risk are countries such as the Maldives and the atolls and coral islands of the Pacific where people will be forced to adapt or to abandon their habitats. Many depend upon the Pacific Ocean for their subsistence, and in some cases rely heavily on tourism. But a number of other countries with large coastal populations are also vulnerable, such as Bangladesh, parts of China (Shanghai), India and Viet Nam. Many major cities in the region could also be at risk from coastal surges, including Tokyo, Shanghai, Mumbai, Kolkata, Karachi and Hong Kong, China.

Health threats

Climate change will certainly affect human health. Environmental risk factors contribute to 85 of the 102 categories of major diseases and injuries (WHO, 2004). Moreover, on a global level, an estimated 24% of the disease burden and an estimated 23% of all premature deaths are attributable to environmental factors. Children are particularly vulnerable – to diarrhoea, lower respiratory infections and malaria (Prüss-Üstün and Corvalán, 2006).

Climate-sensitive diseases could be a major threat, particularly on the poor

---

Climate-sensitive diseases include: (a) vector-borne diseases, which could increase as a result of rising temperatures; (b) respiratory disorders exacerbated by the use of fossil fuels; (c) water- and food-borne diseases from compromised freshwater supplies; and (d) malnutrition as a result of disruptions in food production due to higher temperatures and variable precipitation (WHO, 2008). There is also the risk of heatstroke and injury, disability and drowning. The rapidly growing elderly population is particularly vulnerable to increasing heat.[3] The displacement of communities could also trigger mental health disorders.

---

[3] For example, hundreds of people were killed in Andra Pradesh, India, in a 2002 heat wave (see http://www.wsws.org/articles/2002/may2002/indi-m22.shtml). A heat wave in 2005 across South Asia claimed more than 200 lives in India alone. Deaths were also reported in Bangladesh, Nepal and Pakistan (see http://earthobservatory.nasa.gov/IOTD/view.php?id=5603). Heat waves are also common in several areas of China (see http://www.china.org.cn/english/China/37074.htm).

In parts of the Asia-Pacific region, temperature increases have already contributed to a rise in the incidence of dengue fever. In Singapore, for example, the mean annual temperature from 1978 to 1998 increased from 26.9 °C to 28.4 °C, and over the same period the number of cases of dengue fever and dengue haemorrhagic fever rose more than tenfold, from 384 to 5,258 (Omi, 2007). In Cambodia, the situation is particularly severe. In 2007, 40,000 dengue patients, most of them children, were admitted to hospitals, and 407 people died, the highest number of fatalities in nearly a decade (*International Herald Tribune*, 2008). The contribution of environmental factors to various diseases varies considerably from place to place. For instance, 25% of all deaths in developing regions are attributable to environmental causes, while in developed regions the figure is only 17% (Prüss-Üstün and Corvalán, 2006).

Threats to food security and health will expose the vulnerable, especially women and girls. Young girls are more likely to suffer from malnutrition and lack of schooling than boys. Women also carry the burden of dealing with any kind of devastation and destruction since they are invariably responsible for caring for members of the family and holding families together. Yet, it is women and girls who will suffer as a result of eating less food or food of poorer nutritional quality.

Increased destruction of infrastructure

Transport-related infrastructure

Climate change will also take its toll on transport and infrastructure. Some of the direct and indirect consequences are:

- *Temperature*: Overheating of vehicles, tyre deterioration and increased use of air conditioning. Thermal expansion can lead to buckling on bridge expansion joints, paved surfaces and railway lines.

- *Rainfall*: Flooding leads to the disruption of construction and maintenance activities, causes weather-related delays and reduces safety. On the other hand, decreased rainfall will reduce water levels in vital inland waterways.

- *Storms*: Frequent and intense storms will increase debris on roads and railway lines and damage to overhead electric railway lines.

- *Storm surges*: These can temporarily inundate transport infrastructure.

- *Sea level rise*: This can lead to inundation of transport infrastructure.

These direct and indirect consequences affect the poor the most due to their low level of mobility.

While data are limited and methodologies to assess the economic cost of these events are still being developed, examples indicate that the costs are very high. Reinsurance companies, such as Munich Reinsurance Group and Swiss Reinsurance along with the Regional Disaster Information Management System (REDAT), have made some estimates.[4] Various aid agencies and development banks have also prepared reports on specific disasters, such as the 2004 tsunami and major floods and storms. Table 3.1 lists examples of damage and losses to infrastructure in Asia from 2006 to 2008. Total damages and losses ranged from $210 million to $4.1 billion, damage to infrastructure (mainly transport) ranged from 4% to 35%. The data not shown here are the damage and losses to housing, which amounted to $105 million as a result of the Aceh flood and $647 as a result of Cyclone Nargis.

Table 3.1. Selected examples of infrastructural damage and losses resulting from climatic events in Asia, 2006-2008

Country	Climatic event	Year	Damages and losses (millions of United States dollars)		
			Total	Infrastructure	Percentage
Bangladesh	Flood	2007	1 067	370	35
Bangladesh	Cyclone Sidr	2007	1 675	230	14
Indonesia	Aceh Flood	2006	210	35	17
Myanmar	Cyclone Nargis	2008	4 134	168	4

Sources: Compiled from World Bank, *Ache Flood – Damage and Loss Assessment* (Washington, D.C., World Bank, Kecamatan Development Programme Indonesia, 2007); Bangladesh, "Consolidated damage and loss assessment, lessons learnt from the flood 2007 and future action plan: executive summary" (Dhaka, Disaster Management Bureau, Ministry of Food and Disaster Management and Comprehensive Disaster Management Programme (CDMP), 2007); Tripartite Core Group (TCG), *Post-Nargis Joint Assessment*, July (Jakarta, TCG, 2008); Bangladesh, "Cyclone Sidr in Bangladesh: Damage, loss and needs assessment for disaster recovery and reconstruction" (Dhaka, Government of Bangladesh, 2008).

---

[4] Since 1988, the WHO Collaborating Centre for Research on the Epidemiology of Disasters (CRED) has been maintaining the Emergency Events Database (EM-DAT). The EM-DAT was created with the initial support of WHO and the Government of Belgium. USAID/OFDA also supports the project by making available specialized validated databases on natural and technological disasters.

Policy responses to climate change

In December 2007, the 13th Conference of Parties to the United Nations Framework Convention on Climate Change (UNFCCC) adopted the Bali Action Plan, under which key post-2012 issues on climate change are to be negotiated by the end of 2009. As UNFCCC spells out, developed and developing countries have common but differentiated responsibilities and capabilities and it confirms that developing countries should be supported and enabled through technology, financing and capacity-building. Nevertheless, developing countries, too, have a vital part to play, by using resources more efficiently and helping stabilize GHGs in the atmosphere.

The cost of inaction is too high to be neglected

Mitigating climate change might seem expensive, but the cost of inaction will be even greater. The *Stern Review on the Economics of Climate Change* estimates that, if no action is taken, the overall costs and risks of climate change will be equivalent to losing at least 5% of global GDP each year, now and forever. If a wider range of risks and impacts are taken into account, the estimates of damage could rise to 20% of GDP, or more. A comparison of models shows that the expected annual cost of stabilizing greenhouse gas emissions at about 500~550 parts per million (ppm) CO_2e[5] is likely to be about 1% of global GDP by 2050, with a range of +/−3%, reflecting uncertainties over the scale of the mitigation required, the pace of technological innovation and the degree of policy flexibility.

---

[5] CO_2e refers to equivalent carbon dioxide and is the concentration of CO_2 that would cause the same level of radiative forcing as a given type and concentration of greenhouse gas. Examples of such greenhouse gases are methane, perfluorocarbons and nitrous oxide. CO_2e is expressed in parts per million by volume (ppmv). CO_2e is distinct from carbon dioxide equivalency (CO_2-eq), which is the quantity that describes the amount of CO_2 that would have the same global warming potential (GWP) for a given mixture and the amount of GHG measured over a specified timescale, commonly expressed in millions of metric tons of carbon dioxide equivalent (see http://www.ipcc.ch/pdf/glossary/ar4-wg1.pdf).

A review of economic impacts in Asia also shows that inaction will have significant economic costs (IGES, 2008). In China, losses from a 100-year high water tide are estimated to be $4.8 billion, while the cost of action is estimated at $400 million. Paying for preventive action would therefore result in a net benefit of more than $4 billion. In Malaysia, the initial national communication to UNFCCC estimated that a 1 °C rise in temperature would reduce power output by 2%, causing a loss of about $12.4 million per year for an electricity generation capacity of 6,600 megawatts. A study in Indonesia projected that sea level rise would result in the loss of 90,260 square kilometres by 2100 – at an estimated land value of $0.28 million per square kilometre, that would occasion an economic loss of $25.5 billion.

The cost of climate change will be strongly felt in the agriculture sector, which constitutes a significant portion of GDP in developing countries. The contribution of agriculture to the GDP of South Asian countries ranged from 16.8% (Sri Lanka) to 36.8% (Nepal) in 2006 (see Sri Lanka, 2006 and Nepal, 2007). For those countries, even a small loss in agricultural productivity would severely affect the poor in rural areas.

As the *Stern Review* suggests, there are additional costs inherent in actions to mitigate climate change, particularly those aimed at reducing the demand for emission-intensive goods, increasing energy efficiency, switching to lower-carbon technology and taking action on non-energy issues, such as afforestation.   But any delay in action on climate change will only accelerate the damage and bring higher economic and social costs.

While such actions require initial expenditures, the benefits gained from innovation will offset some of these costs by, for example, increasing energy efficiency and the potential for creating greener jobs. An IPCC report estimated that, by 2030, the global average macroeconomic cost of ensuring that GHG levels eventually stabilize at 445-710 ppm ranges from less than 3% of GDP to a gain of 0.6% (IPCC, 2007b). This translates into an annual reduction in the GDP growth rate of less than 0.12% to 0.06%, far smaller than the dividend that could be reaped from the decades of rapid expansion that might be expected after the current economic crisis. The cost of inaction is potentially disastrous.

As the stakes of inaction are very high, urgent action is required to address climate change. A three-pronged strategy is proposed to tackle climate change and move towards greener and sustainable development.

The first strategy is to take advantage of the opportunities created by the current financial crisis to undertake mitigation and adaptation measures. But investment in mitigation measures would not reduce GHG emissions without a behavioural change. Accordingly, the second strategy focuses on how to promote a shift in the attitude towards climate change. The third strategy highlights the region's critical role in the global climate change agenda.

First strategy: Utilizing the window of opportunity created by the financial crisis

The current financial crisis and the global recession may appear to threaten action on climate change, especially if the economic stimulus plans maintain or scale up unsustainable economic practices. But the current economic crisis should not be allowed to overshadow critical long-term issues, such as climate change. Instead, Governments need to redirect investment away from energy-intensive economic activity based on fossil fuels and towards low-carbon, greener technology and industrial activity; they also need to improve access to services that meet the basic needs of the poor. The economic stimulus plans can thus act as catalysts to turn today's crisis into tomorrow's sustainable growth. In this respect, the region could study recent initiatives such as the "Green New Deal" and the Green Growth initiative promoted by ESCAP, in order to devise a regional programme of technical and financial assistance.

A number of countries have taken positive steps through the "Green New Deal" being promoted by the European Union, the United States, and the Republic of Korea, among others. In particular, the European Parliament set legally binding targets in December 2008 to cut GHG emissions by 20%, to establish a 20% share for renewable energy and to improve energy efficiency by 20%, by 2020. The European Commission had proposed a "green new deal" for addressing both the climate crisis and the current economic crisis, thereby enhancing the competitiveness of European Union industry.

The policy of the United States Government's on the green new deal, for example, focuses on: retrofitting buildings to improve energy efficiency; expanding mass transit and freight rail; constructing "smart" electrical grid transmission systems; and expanding greener sources of power, including wind and solar power and next-generation biofuels. Common elements of the green new deal include: investment in sustainable infrastructure; energy efficiency and renewable energy technology; and "green jobs". By adopting low-carbon initiatives in terms of investing in eco-efficient technology, the "Green New Deal" of the Republic of Korea is expected to create about a million jobs by 2012, thereby facilitating long-term low-carbon green growth. Japan is also considering its own "green new deal" to counter the twin threats of climate change and the economic downturn. Under the initiative, Japan is expected to cut CO_2 emissions by 15% from 1990 levels by 2020; the initiative sets the ambitious targets of a 20-fold increase in the use of solar power and a 40% boost in the use of next-generation environmentally friendly cars. All of these initiatives should lead to a low-carbon development path.

The region needs to act now by adopting its own "green new deal" based on a programme of mutual responsibility

One of the advantages of the surge in oil prices was that it encouraged greater investment in renewable energy and energy efficiency. Now that prices have plummeted there is the risk that enthusiasm will wane, especially if the current recession limits financial resources. But oil prices will not stay low: indeed they will probably rebound with vigour once economies recover. By then, however, the world will have lost precious time. This is where Governments and multilateral financial institutions could step in to provide a boost for investments in climate change mitigation and adaptation. The Asia-Pacific region, having accumulated over $4 trillion in foreign exchange reserves, should take the lead – through fiscal incentives, fiscal stimuli and outright public investments.

The region needs to act now by adopting its own "green new deal" and Green Growth approaches if it is to maintain its competitiveness in goods and services, which can lead to greener, more sustainable development. Such a strategy will prepare the ground for the region to pursue a path of sustainable development when the global economy bounces back.[6]

The region will not, of course, be starting from scratch. Major countries, such as China, India, Japan and the Republic of Korea already have action plans aimed at emissions reduction and sustainable development (box 3.1). An effective way forward would be to integrate climate-related action into each country's national development plans and poverty reduction strategy papers (PRSPs). This would not only give political legitimacy to action on climate change but also integrates it into broader development policy frameworks.

Some of the key economic and social policy areas aimed at emissions reduction (mitigation) and adaptation to climate change are summarized below. These would incur financial cost and could be considered under the strategy of the Green New Deal.

Policies towards mitigation

Improving energy efficiency

Improving energy efficiency is one of the most cost-effective mitigation options

---

In Asia, one of the most cost-effective mitigation measures is to boost energy efficiency. By using current technologies more efficiently in existing industrial and power facilities, an energy savings of 20% could be achieved, and increases in GHG emissions between 2000 and 2020 could be halved as a result

(IGES, 2008). During harsh economic times, cost-saving measures assume added importance from the perspective of both household consumption and business operations. With supportive policies, it is clear that the financial crisis will impel the adoption of energy-efficient and cost-effective mitigation measures. China probably has the world's largest potential for emission reduction – approximately 3.5 gigatons of carbon dioxide equivalent by 2020 – and the goal of the 11th Five-Year Plan of China to improve energy efficiency by 20% would be the world's largest CO_2 mitigation action. The Philippines is planning to promote energy efficiency and renewable energy so as to achieve 60% self-sufficiency by 2010, which could prevent 50.9 million tons of CO_2e of GHG emissions over the period 2005 to 2014 (ESCAP, 2005).

Most countries in the region generate power through carbon-intensive infrastructures, using either outdated plants or coal as a major source. They also lose a sizeable portion of the electricity – from 10% to 30% – in transmission. That figure could be reduced if distribution networks were improved; it would be necessary to allocate additional government resources for the purpose. Another option would be to promote off-grid technology, such as microgeneration (i.e. solar and wind power). Countries can also curtail emissions at low cost by applying energy-efficient standards for buildings, electrical appliances and vehicles (UNDP, 2008). Eco-labelling and certification as well as the use of green building codes could also be considered.

Public policy needs to be used to influence both the use of efficient production technologies and a behavioural change in energy use

---

Industrial production and consumer behaviour can be strongly influenced by public policy, including market-based fiscal incentives. The current challenges related to food, fuel, water and climate can be directly attributed to a failure of both *market* and *government* of unprecedented proportions. Under the current system, markets have not reflected the *real* (ecological and social) cost of production into the final prices of goods and services. Moreover, government intervention within the market has not only failed to correct the price discrepancy, but has actually exacerbated the situation by subsidizing research into environmentally harmful products and processes. This has fostered an incentive structure that discriminately favours unsustainable activities such as coal-based energy production over that of renewables. Some policy options could be:

---

[6] ESCAP advocated such policies long before the current economic crisis – promoting green growth both through macro-policy frameworks and micro-policy practices for specific sectors that can lead to national eco-efficiency. This has five major tracks: green tax and budget reform, sustainable consumption, sustainable infrastructure, green markets and business. All five are in line with the approach proposed in the Bali Action Plan and support the efforts of countries to meet their development needs while taking action on climate change and mitigating GHG emissions. ESCAP has also been facilitating regional consultations to share information about policy options for mitigation and adaptation to climate change, and to develop regional perspectives on the post-2012 framework. In particular, ESCAP promotes engaging market mechanisms to scale up global technical and financial supports for climate change mitigation in developing countries.

Box 3.1. National action plans on climate change

China, India, Japan and the Republic of Korea account for over 70% of the CO2 emissions of the Asia-Pacific region – so their actions will have a significant influence on the region's contribution to reducing GHG emissions. All have national action plans for both mitigation and adaptation, based on R&D, and institutional mechanisms. They also have programmes for raising public awareness of climate change.

China. The National Climate Change Programme, launched in 2007, envisages reducing energy consumption per unit of GDP by 20%, having 10% of the primary energy supply come from renewable sources, stabilizing the emission of nitrous oxide from industrial processes, maintaining 20% forest cover, and by 2010 increasing carbon sinks by 50 million tons over the 2005 level.[a] It includes plans to expand the area for improved grassland by 24 million hectares, develop coal-bed methane and coal-mine methane industries, and support the development and utilization of wind, solar, geothermal and tidal energy. A white paper issued by China in 2008 states that China should address climate change within the framework of sustainable development.[b]

India. The National Action Plan on Climate Change promotes the development and use of solar energy for power generation, efficiency in energy and water use, afforestation of 6 million hectares of degraded forest lands and climate adaptation in agriculture. This will involve, for example, retiring inefficient coal-fired power plans and promoting renewable energy.[c]

Japan. The Climate Change Action Plan is aimed at cutting GHG emissions by up to 80% by 2050. It calls for technological innovation, using next-generation vehicles including hybrid and electric cars by 2020, and improving energy efficiency, particularly that of household heat pumps and air conditioners – a 50% improvement by 2030.[d] It also targets carbon trading. Under the Cool Earth 50 initiative, Japan encourages public participation in achieving the Kyoto Protocol's national GHG reduction target of limiting such emissions to 94% of 1990 levels. The initiative also provides financial assistance for developing countries that intend to introduce advanced technologies in energy conservation and low-carbon energies.[e]

Republic of Korea. The Act on Climate Change, calls for achieving by 2012 a 3.2% reduction in 2005 levels of industrial CO_2 pollution.[f] It sets up a voluntary emissions trading agency and a carbon trading market in 2009. An incentive and reward system is in place for businesses, increasing renewable energy use from the present levels of 2.3% to 5% by 2012 and 9% by 2030. It also promotes reductions in residential and vehicular GHG emission and the expansion of carbon sinks, particularly through forestation efforts. The country has also launched a low-carbon, green growth initiative to create a virtuous cycle between economic development, energy security and climate security. Among other things, this envisages investment in climate-friendly technology and incentives for private sector participation in GHG mitigation. The initiative is also aimed at tax reform and a national emission trading system.

Although there are no specific targets for cuts in GHG for developing economies under the Kyoto Protocol, the initiatives by these and other countries are a step forward in addressing global warming. This is encouraging at a time when momentum on climate change is fading at the global level due to the current financial turmoil. According to a survey of leaders of government, business and media prior to the Asia-Pacific leaders Summit in Peru in November 2008, global warming did not even figure among the top priorities to be addressed.[g] In such an environment, political commitment to implement these action plans is necessary for success. Countries need emission reductions that are measurable, reportable and verifiable. In this regard, it may be possible to establish, at the global level, a special registry to recognize such national actions so that their outcomes can be measured and quantified on a global scale.

---

[a] China, "China's National Climate Change Programme" (National Development and Reform Commission, 2007), http://www.ccchina.gov.cn/WebSite/CCChina/UpFile/File188.pdf.

[b] China, "China's Policies and Actions for Addressing Climate Change" (Beijing, Information Office of the State Council, 2008).

[c] Pew Center on Global Climate Change, "Summary: India's National Action Plan on Climate Change" (Arlington, Virginia, United States, 2008), http://www.pewclimate.org/international/country-policies/india-climate-plan-summary/06-2008.

[d] "Japan's climate change action plan targets heat pumps and cars", July 2008, http://www.r744.com/article.view.php?Id=729.

[e] Yasuo Fukuda, Prime Minister of Japan, special address on the occasion of the Annual Meeting of the World Economic Forum Congress Center, Davos, Switzerland, 26 January 2008, accessed from http://www.mofa.go.jp/policy/economy/wef/2008/address-s.html, on 27 February 2009.

[f] G. Hudson, "Korea to Decrease CO_2 Emissions with the 'Act on Climate Change'" *Ecoworldy* (Korea), 24 February 2008, http://ecoworldly.com/2008/02/24/korea-to-decrease-co2-emissions-with-the-act-on-climate-change/.

[g] "Climate Change Momentum Fading: Asia-Pacific Survey", Lima, 19 November 2008, http://www.spacedaily.com/2006/081119171128.moufx8ea.html.

- Providing tax incentives for investments in newer and cleaner technologies for electricity generation, fuel combustion, manufacturing and construction. This could be a key component of fiscal stimuli designed to address falling demand for the development of sustainable infrastructure resulting from the financial crisis as it would generate greener employment.

- Creating an enabling environment for renewable energy through "feed-in" tariffs, inducing electricity utilities to purchase electricity generated from renewable sources at above-market rates.

- Imposing graded user charges on the use of energy, including electricity, while providing incentives for energy conservation.

- Imposing higher taxes on old and inefficient motor vehicles and those with high engine displacement, or auctioning permits for buying and using motor vehicles.

- Providing incentives to adopt energy-efficient technologies for producing goods and providing services.

- Applying building and industry standards in energy use; in particular, promoting active solar-integrated buildings and improved insulation, and the upgrading of old industry infrastructure.

- Managing consumption demand by pricing utilities properly and adopting policies that oblige consumers to be ecologically responsible, by, among other things, regulating the use of inefficient electrical appliances and high-energy-consuming lights.

Many countries in the region subsidize energy products, which has the effect of encouraging the excessive use of energy by the affluent. In 2005, energy subsidies in five countries in the region (Russian Federation, Islamic Republic of Iran, China, India and Indonesia) alone amounted to about $140 billion (IEA, 2007). Instead they could consider market-oriented pricing mechanisms that incorporate the cost of environmental damage, while also offering targeted subsidies.

Reducing vehicle emissions

The transport sector is a major contributor to GHG emissions. A number of models have been devised to address this. They include the Integrated Environmental Strategies (IES) tools and resources developed by the United States Environmental Protection Agency. Countries in the ESCAP region with IES projects include China, India, the Philippines and the Republic of Korea.

The policies available to address climate change are similar to those used to address energy efficiency and air quality. They focus on eight areas: (1) types of energy, including fuel switching; (2) vehicle fuel consumption standards; (3) the age structure of the vehicle fleet; (4) vehicle technology; (5) modal shifts in passenger and freight transport; (6) operational and intermodal efficiencies; (7) vehicle drivers; and (8) transport infrastructure. Some of the measures in selected countries and regions are listed in table 3.2.

Some countries in the region have developed markets in petroleum oil substitutes, including ethanol, biodiesel and gas in the form of compressed natural

Table 3.2. Implementation of policy measures for technical fuel efficiency improvement

	Regulatory standards	Voluntary targets	Vehicle tax differentiation	Consumer information
European Union	PI[a]	Im[a]	PI[b]	Im
Japan	Im		Im	Im
United States	Im		Im	Im
Canada	PI	Im[a]		Im
China	Im		Im	Im
Republic of Korea	Im	Im		Im
Australia		Im		Im

Source: Onoda, T. (2008). "Review of international policies for vehicle fuel efficiency", *International Energy Agency Information Paper,* August.

Notes: Im = implemented

PI = planned or under consideration

[a] Voluntary and regulatory measures in the European Union are on CO_2, not directly on fuel efficiency. Similarly, the voluntary target in Canada is on GHG.

[b] Several European Union member States have already implemented the tax systems and the European Commission is currently calling for harmonization of the systems.

gas (CNG) or liquefied petroleum gas (LPG). Several issues are involved: (1) the trade-off between the use of agricultural land for food or fuel (see box 3.2); (2) the volumes of biofuels that could be produced to substitute for fossil fuels; and (3) the costs of the refuelling infrastructure required for gaseous fuels due to the shift to alternative fuels.

Policies are needed to reverse the trend towards using heavy, energy-inefficient vehicles

Fuel consumption and emissions can be reduced by developing lighter vehicles with better aerodynamics and propulsion. A number of manufacturers have intro-duced hybrid-electric propulsion systems, though since these are more expensive, Governments may need to offer subsidies encouraging the development of fuel cells and hydrogen and electrical propulsion systems. They can also promote mass transit schemes, including bus rapid transit (BRT) coupled with the integration of non-motorized transport in urban areas while shifting freight from road to rail and water transport. To be effective, land use changes for such modal shifts should be carefully planned. Economic hardships during the current financial crisis provide a golden opportunity to promote ecologically balanced transportation systems. The use of heavy gas-guzzling vehicles should be discouraged. The use of light vehicles or public transportation should be encour-aged instead by evoking cost and environmental con-sciousness.

Another important issue that should be addressed is the issue of congestion. Green tax and budget reform

Box 3.2. Trade-offs in biofuel production

Interest in biofuels has increased dramatically in recent years as the price of oil has reached new highs. China, Indonesia and Thailand for example, have introduced targets for biofuels in their energy mix.[a]

Whether biofuels will be environmentally friendly or harmful depends on how they are produced. Biofuels have been blamed for food shortages, rapid price increases, deforestation, soil erosion and impacts on water and the environment. On the other hand, some argue that, because of their so-called carbon neutrality, agricultural crops used as feedstock for biofuels hold great promise for contributing to the reduction of GHG emissions.[b]

Recent studies show that converting rainforests, peatlands, savannas or grasslands to produce food-crop based biofuels may result in a "biofuel carbon debt". Fargione et al (2008) find that converting lowland tropical rainforests in Indonesia and Malaysia to produce palm biodiesel would result in a carbon debt of – 610 megagrams per hectare of CO_2 that would take nearly 86 years to repay.[c] In a similar study, Danielsen et al (2008) reveal that it would take at least 75 years for the carbon emission saved through the use of biofuels to compensate for the carbon lost through forest conversions. And if the original habitat were carbon-rich peatland, achieving the balance would take more than 600 years.[d] Converting tropical rain forests – one of the world's most efficient carbon storage tools – could hasten climate change with irreversible repercussions.

One solution would be to grow biofuel crops on degraded and abandoned lands. Stemming the growing pressure to convert rainforests for biofuel production will require common standards for producing biofuels.

[a]   Gonzales, A.D.C. (2008). "Overall stocktaking of Biofuel Development in Asia-Pacific: Benefits and Challenges", background paper for "Policy Dialogue on Biofuels in Asia: Benefits and Challenges, Beijing, China," 24-26 September.

[b]   Ibid.

[c]   Fargione, J., J. Hill, D. Tilman, S. Polasky, P. Hawthorne (2008). "Land clearing and the biofuel carbon debt", *Science*, vol. 319, No. 5867 pp. 1235-1238.

[d]   Danielsen and others (2008). "Biofuel Plantations on Forested Lands: Double Jeopardy for Biodiversity and Climate", *Conservation Biology*.

in the transport sector offers many policy initiatives that can work to alleviate congestion. They include, for example, parking, congestion, fuel and vehicle taxes. To be effective they should be implemented in coordination with transportation demand management tools such as value capture.

Improving the skills of drivers can also reduce fuel consumption significantly, as can maintaining recommended vehicles tyre pressures. Additional air-quality policies include improved fuel quality, better enforcement of emission control regulations, promotion of good vehicle maintenance and improvement in air pollution data and monitoring systems.

In Asia and the Pacific, considerable progress has been made in reducing emissions and improving air quality through the adoption of similar principles.

Reducing GHG emissions in agriculture

Agricultural and industrial practices for producing and processing food are key sources of GHG emissions, particularly CH_4 and N_2O. Agriculture accounted for an estimated emission of 10~12% of all global GHG emissions in 2005 (IPCC, 2007b). Agriculture has a particularly high share in GHG emissions in Asia as a result of emissions from animal sources, enteric fermentation and manure, as well as the increased use of nitrogenous fertilizers and the conversion of forested area to cultivated or grazing land. As a result, unlike most industrial sectors, agriculture is threatened by its own by-products.

Investment in R&D would pay high dividends in mitigating the impact of climatic conditions on agriculture

---

Many agricultural mitigation opportunities use current technologies and can be taken advantage of immediately. Others will require technological development. They include:

- Developing and promoting low-emission and high-yielding varieties of rice, along with semi-drought rice cultivation.

- Applying modern irrigation and water management practices.

- Applying fertilizers tailored to the condition of the soil.

- Strengthening the management of animal waste, the treatment of solid and liquid waste, and using methane emissions to produce renewable energy.

Managing waste

Although waste contributes only 3% of GHG emissions in the Asia-Pacific region, the potential threat is still high. Many cities in the region have become open dumping grounds for urban liquid and solid wastes which emit methane, which as a GHG is 21 times more potent than CO_2. There are many options. Urban solid waste can be converted into compost and organic fertilizer. ESCAP, for example, has helped cities in Bangladesh, Pakistan, Sri Lanka, and, Viet Nam, in managing solid waste by replicating an initiative of Waste Concern, an NGO in Bangladesh, using decentralized treatment plants. Plans are underway to extend that assistance to cities in several other countries in the Asia-Pacific region and beyond. While only raw compost is produced at present, the system can be transformed to produce organic fertilizer tailored to the needs of local farmers. Other options include recovering methane from landfills, recovering energy during waste incinerations and controlling wastewater treatment. Recycling and waste minimization can be promoted at both the domestic and industrial levels through financial incentives, including tax relief. In addition, landfill taxes, differential tipping fees for waste hauling can help encourage construction and demolition recycling for buildings.

Asia and the Pacific also suffers from cross-boundary dumping, particularly with regard to hazardous waste. This is mainly due to weaknesses in existing agreements, such as the Basel Convention on the Control of Transboundary Movements of Hazardous Wastes and their Disposal, which needs to be reviewed. But Asia-Pacific countries could themselves develop a regional code of conduct.

Adaptation policies

Standards for the discharge of chemical affluent, e-waste and waste disposal are required to address water pollution

---

While a country should take measures to mitigate the anthropogenic impact on climate, it must also adapt to the new environment to minimize the adverse impacts on its economy and the livelihoods of its people.

Addressing issues related to water

With water stress expected to intensify, countries need to enhance their efforts to ensure that water is available; those efforts include expanding rainwater harvesting, investing in water storage, grey-water recycling and conservation techniques, promoting water reuse and improving the efficiency of irrigation. They should also implement standards for the discharge of chemical effluents, e-waste and waste disposal, while improving water treatment. Proper drainage systems reduce the contamination of water. Singapore, which has developed advanced technology for wastewater treatment and adopted conservation methods for attaining water self-sufficiency, provides a good example of best practices in water resources management.

Addressing adverse impacts on agriculture

A warmer climate will require the adjustment of planning dates and crop variety, crop relocation and the improvement of land management. Greater investments in research and development will be needed to create, for example, drought-resistant and heat-resistant seed varieties (ESCAP, 2008). The food and fuel crises also indicated the urgent need for greater investments in the agricultural sector to boost production. Government efforts to facilitate adaptation should, however, go hand in hand with institutional reform, land tenure and land reform, as well as programmes for training and capacity-building. ESCAP member States could make use of the policy research and technical assistance provided by two of the Commis-

sion's regional institutes: (a) the Asian and Pacific Centre for Agricultural Engineering and Machinery (APCAEM), for enhancing environmentally sustainable agricultural and food production and applying green and modern agro-technology; and (b) the Centre for Alleviation of Poverty through Secondary Crops Development in Asia and the Pacific (CAPSA), for increasing agricultural productivity, particularly that of smallholders. Managing financial risk through crop insurance, subsidies and tax credits will provide the financial incentives to undertake adaptation strategies.

Public-private partnerships in environmental management

While climate change poses critical challenges in developing countries, it also offers opportunities for Governments and the private sector. Governments have to play a leading role in addressing climate changes since the environment is a public good. But this should also involve facilitating the involvement of the private sector and civil society, especially in environmental management reforms. Governments can, for example, collaborate with the private sector and civil society in environmental assessments ensuring that major investments are climate-proofed. They can also engage in public-private partnerships to exploit opportunities arising from the CDM, and to manage environmental heritage and eco-tourism. Such activities can be supported by corresponding regional initiatives to strengthen corporate social responsibility on green initiatives and provide business opportunities for environmentally friendly goods and services (box 3.3).

Box 3.3. Adapting to climate change by the private sector: ESCAP-Sida joint action

ESCAP and Sida (Swedish International Development Cooperation Agency) jointly initiated discussions on the role of the private sector in adaptation to climate change by organizing the Asia-Pacific Business Forum 2009 on the theme of Climate Game Change – Innovations and Solutions for Climate Change Adaptation, held in Bangkok on 22 January 2009 with the participation of private sector firms.

Although the private sector is a key emitter of GHG, adaptation has been mostly left to the choice of individual companies. It is therefore important to raise the awareness of the private sector generally about the significance of adaptation action in order to reduce both business risks and the socio-economic vulnerabilities of society as a whole and to promote opportunities.

In the context of climate change, the private sector faces two major tasks. The first is to address physical risks – such as extreme weather events and changing ecosystems. Companies will therefore need to make their operational systems climate-resilient. The second is to adapt to changing socio-economic and market conditions. These include new rule under the post-2012 mechanism, which will be finalized in Copenhagen in December 2009, for lowering carbon footprints. At the same time the private sector can provide the goods and services needed to aid adaptation across society, in some cases through government contracts.

Just as the private sector played a key role in the export-led growth of Asia, Asian entrepreneurs need to seize the opportunities created by the growing interest in climate change. The Asian Development Bank (ADB) estimates that, in 2005, the total global market for environmental goods and services was worth about $607 billion and that, by 2015, it will grow to over $836 billion (ADB, 2005). The region already has many success stories. Suzlon Energy, one of the top five wind energy companies in the world, started in 1994 as a small family business in Gujarat, India. But with its entrepreneurial, technological and managerial capacity, it grew to be a global success by investing in clean energy (Karmali, 2006). Grameen Shakti, established in 1996, is one of the largest and fastest growing rural-based renewable energy companies in the world. It popularizes solar home systems among rural villages by blending market and social forces to provide the rural poor with energy at low cost. Sunlabob is a company in the Lao People's Democratic Republic which stepped in to supply power to remote areas beyond reach of the main electricity grid. Such entrepreneurships not only help address GHG emissions but also help improve socio-economic conditions. However, as the Swedish International Development Cooperation Agency reports, the private sector has so far been slow to react to climate change (Sida, 2009). Governments could promote such ventures by providing a conducive environment for businesses and financial incentives for investment in R&D into greener technologies and adaptation.

Effective social safety nets are critical to protect the most vulnerable from climate change

---

Improving heath services

Preparing to address the health risks of climate change represents one of the key challenges for Governments. The rapidly ageing population in the Asia-Pacific region would compound this challenge. As many developing countries in the region have weak health systems and low health outcomes, countries need to redouble their efforts to improve health systems and the provision of health services. Public investment in the health sector needs to be substantially increased not only for the upgrading of health infrastructure but also for human resource development in the health sector. As the lack of skilled health professionals is a major barrier to addressing climate-related health problems, urgent action is required.

In addition to boosting public health services, Governments need to provide a conducive environment for private health care and health insurance. Community-based health insurance could be an option for vulnerable groups, for whom Governments lack the institutional capacity to provide health services. This would not only improve health outcomes but also place the Government in a fiscally stronger position to face future health challenges related to climate change. These priorities are even more vital in the face of the current global recession, which also threatens the most vulnerable.

Provision of social safety nets

Climatic events could displace people from their homes, prevent the affected from engaging in their usual livelihood activities for survival, orphan children and put women and children at risk of exploitation and abuse. Social protection mechanisms need to be in place to protect the most vulnerable from such events. Mechanisms should be in place to provide alternative shelter and employment opportunities for those who are displaced so that they can be integrated into the new environment. Orphans should be provided with homes, care and education for a better future. Opportunities for exploitation and abuse of women and children when a disaster strikes should be minimized through the effective implementation of the rule of law and public and community participation.

As noted above, climate change could seriously affect people in many Asia-Pacific developing countries in terms of their ability to generate income. People employed in the agricultural sector would be affected the most, and action would be required to put in place social benefit schemes, including targeted cash transfers to the most needy.

Second strategy: Promoting a shift in the attitude towards climate change

The second strategy is to take steps to evoke a shift in the attitude towards climate change. Policies towards mitigation will not be effective without a major shift in the way goods and services are produced and consumed. Both social norms and domestic and international laws could induce a change in people's attitude towards the environment. Good governance principles could strengthen their impacts. While these initiatives require mainly rules, regulations and standards to be in place, they would entail minimal financial cost if any.

Human responsibility to nature

As much as climate change is a global issue, addressing it is a shared responsibility. The very existence of humans depends on nature. Therefore, every individual, firm and Government has a responsibility to protect the environment. One way to ensure that this happens is to introduce the concept of "human responsibility to nature". Such a concept would obligate each individual to be responsible for nature not only as a debt owed but also as a moral obligation. It also emphasizes that, simply because climate change is a long-term issue, fixing it should not be left to future generations.

"Human responsibility to nature" should be a critical element of managing climate change

---

Under the concept of human responsibility to nature, each and every person can protect nature and the environment by exercising the right to challenge actions against the environment in a court of law, possibly forcing others to pay for actions that harm the environment, and take environmentally friendly action in production and consumption. Social norms and action at the national level to promote the concept would be key to its success, as would the enactment of national and international laws. Governments could also consider pricing mechanisms to influence the attitude towards the environment in order to promote conservation. Civil society could play its part by encouraging voluntary engagement in such conservation at the community level.

About a hundred countries in the world currently recognize the right to a clean and healthy environment and/or the State's obligation to prevent environmental harm (Earthjustice, 2004). Constitutions in 53 countries explicitly recognize the right to a clean and healthy environment. But the responsibility to the environment is mostly a neglected one. Only 26 countries in the Asia-Pacific region recognize the responsibility of citizens or residents to protect the environment. But Japan considers that individual action is critical for meeting emission reduction targets under the Kyoto Protocol. Japan also promotes, under its Cool Earth 50 campaign, individual action to achieve "1 person, 1 day, 1 kg of CO_2 reduction".

Promoting carbon-neutral lifestyles

A change of attitude towards the environment at the level of the individual and of the household is impor-

tant in energy conservation. Changing the kind of food people consume could help mitigate emissions substantially. A kilogram of beef produces 16 kilograms of CO_2 equivalent emissions: 10 times higher than chicken (Oberman, 2009). A cow consumes a much greater deal of grain and grass before it matures and produces harmful methane. Given the increasing trend of meat consumption, technology alone will not help reduce GHG emissions. The way in which households use electricity and vehicles, consume other goods and services and farm their lands could be influenced by appropriate pricing mechanisms and regulations as well as social norms. Governments could facilitate such practices by providing alternative renewable energy sources, mass transportation facilities and access to improved farming practices, among others. Car pooling is a common practice throughout the region – even among United Nations staff members. But such practices as well as the use of non-motorized modes of transport need to be promoted.

In developed countries, many businesses are now offering and promoting carbon-neutral products or services. An increasing number of consumers are buying products and services from companies that purchase carbon offsets. A similar movement can be encouraged in Asia and the Pacific, particularly among the growing, globally connected and environmentally aware middle class. This can be done through a partnership between Governments and civil society organizations, particularly international environmental organizations, such as Greenpeace and the World Wildlife Fund. These partnerships could encourage producers in developed countries that sell products in Asia and the Pacific to promote carbon-neutral production and develop demand for CDM projects in the region.

Governments can encourage export-oriented firms to be carbon neutral and capture shares in this growing market by improving their efficiency and investing in carbon offsets locally. These initiatives could be supported by removing distortional national energy subsidies, which will not only save money but reduce primary energy consumption and CO_2 emissions. Such a move could have short-term effects on inflation and growth, but it would ease the fiscal burden on Governments, promote innovation in energy efficiency and help internalize the environmental costs of greenhouse gases. It would also promote long-term growth and stability.

Reversing deforestation

Forests play a critical role in climate change. Land use change and deforestation accounts for 18% of GHG emissions globally, and 27% in Asia (World Resources

Institute 2009). South and South-East Asia are losing over 28,000 square kilometres of forest, or 1% of forest cover, every year. Reversing deforestation is therefore critical for climate change mitigation; it is also a relatively low-cost strategy.

Deforestation accounts for 25% of global CO$_2$ emissions: urgent action is required to reverse it

---

Sustainable forest management in the developing countries will require technical and financial support from developed countries through UNFCCC, in particular the clean development mechanism (CDM) project and the international markets for forest products and services.[7] So far, developing countries hardly receive any benefits from the forest CDM project. They have made more use of the voluntary offset market, but this is still relatively small – $330.8 million in 2007 (Hamilton and others, 2008) compared with total transaction values of nearly $64 billion in the formal markets, including the European Union Emission Trading Scheme (EU ETS) and CDM. But while the forestry sector accounts for only 0.07% of all projects in CDM it has 18% of total offset credits in the voluntary market.

Voluntary markets are likely to expand along with the growing public concern about climate change. Since the projects involved are generally small-scale and community-based they offer opportunities for many developing countries, in particular those that are unable to obtain the benefits of the CDM. Similarly, promoting the voluntary carbon market would also aid mitigation efforts in developing countries, which are not expected to take on any binding emission targets in a post-2012 climate agreement.

Policies to reduce emissions will also involve strong action at the regional level. Two approaches should go hand in hand:

---

[7] CDM is a mechanism under the Kyoto Protocol that allows advanced countries with a commitment to GHG emission to invest in projects that reduce GHG emissions in developing countries at low cost as an alternative approach to reducing HGH in their economies. CDM can function as an incentive mechanism for emission reduction projects in developing countries as it enables them to trade carbon.

- First, action is required to reverse the trend in deforestation. This would require minimal technology. Instead, its success depends on political will and commitment to: (1) enact and implement regulations to stop illegal and excessive logging and deforestation, particularly in rain forests; (2) avoid offering subsidies or permits for the extraction of resources in forests; and (3) conserve land. China provides a good example: from 2000 to 2005, its forest cover increased by 40,580 square kilometres per year. It is important to note, however, that reforestation outside rainforests (secondary forests) will not compensate for the loss in rainforests, for their impacts on climate change differ vastly. Rainforests, while helping to reduce GHG emissions, also play a critical role in maintaining diversity and ecological balance, which the secondary forests lack. The protection of rainforests should be a priority.

Action needed on afforestation to recover the 400,000 square kilometres of forest cover lost since 1990

- Second, countries in the Asia-Pacific region, in particular in South and South-East Asia, should implement afforestation programmes to recover the 400,000 square kilometres of forest cover lost since 1990. Public, private and community partnerships for carbon trading through existing initiatives, such as CDM, could be promoted. Governments could be facilitators while building institutional capacity. The other option for reducing GHG emissions is to promote public-private partnerships and community participation in reforestation programmes. A model project has been implemented by the local government, private sector and community in Jambi, East Sumatra, Indonesia. The recent initiative by the Asian Development Bank to establish the Future Carbon Fund with a view to providing initial capital for related projects is a welcome step (ADB, 2008).

These actions could be supported by promoting conservation agriculture and agroforestry and introducing sustainable forestry certification standards.

Standards for sustainable transport and transport infrastructure

The components of transport systems most vulnerable to climate change are bridges and culverts, causeways and coastal roads, paved surfaces, surface drainage and hillside slopes. Conventionally designed transport infrastructure needs to be adapted to withstand the impact of climate change. Depending on the estimated rise in water level, it may, for example, be necessary to move existing coastal roads to higher locations. Future systems will also need to be appropriately designed and for this purpose environmental impact assessments for transport projects could be extended to take into account the risks and uncertainties. In addition, transport providers should work closely with emergency response agencies so that they can plan appropriate responses in order to safeguard infrastructure, warn the public and facilitate evacuation and emergency response.

Providing technology and finance to undertake green projects would offer both developed and developing countries a win-win situation

---

Third strategy:
Asia and the Pacific playing a critical role in the global climate change agenda

The Asia-Pacific countries need to play a proactive role in the global climate change, agenda. Given that climate change issues are cross-boundary in nature, the Governments of the region need to transcend their national interests (Loh and Tay, 2009). Their spectacular growth over the past few decades has been accompanied by a surge in energy demand, which has grown at an annual rate of about 3%, one third higher than the world average. This will continue to expand the region's share of global GHG emissions, currently 34% (IEA, 2008). This emerging position of the Asia-Pacific region in the global economy compels it to play a duel role.

Leading role in global negotiations

First, the region has to actively engage in global negotiations on climate change and influence the rules of the game. The region can no longer afford to consider itself likely to be affected by climate change as a result of the actions of others and that the duty to reduce future greenhouse impacts therefore rests with the industrialized countries. Leading economies, such as China, India and Japan, could play a pivotal role in those negotiations as they are already among

the top five emitters of GHG in the world (*Bangkok Post*, 2009). While recognizing their own importance in global emission reductions, China and India, in particular, also need to take the lead in representing the interests of the developing countries of the region and avoid the risk of being dictated to by developed countries. Active participation by the countries of the region in the global negotiations on climate change would also enable them to exert pressure on developed countries to do more to rein in GHG emissions. This should go hand in hand with private sector entrepreneurs playing a leading role by developing and adopting green technologies in their businesses.

Regional cooperation in financing and technology transfer

Secondly, the countries of the region can promote regional cooperation for their own benefit in climate change mitigation. Technical assistance and finance for mitigation and adaptation are two key pillars of the post-2012 climate change framework. Developing countries want to address climate change but generally lack the funds or the technology for monitoring, mitigation and adaptation. Although they lack the capital, developing countries possess vast labour resources which can be used in developing a green-job-oriented service economy. They should be able to avail themselves of some of the climate-friendly technologies, which are generally in the domain of the private sector, through the CDM. But only a small number have been able to do so and only in a few sectors. To take greater advantage of these and other opportunities they will need to increase their own readiness and absorptive capacity and improve their procedures.

To raise the necessary finance, they could consider allocating a small percentage of the revenue they receive from windfall gains, such as increased oil revenues and commodity export taxes, to a contingent liability fund. These and other efforts could be strengthened by South-South cooperation within and across regions. Emerging China and India, for example, could help other developing countries in the region to develop more practical and affordable climate-friendly technologies – in energy efficiency, renewable energy and carbon capture and storage. Asia-Pacific countries could also benefit from the Cool Earth 50 initiative of Japan, which provides developing countries with financial assistance in adopting advanced technologies to enhance energy efficiency.

Developed countries should also consider placing climate-related advanced technologies, many of which are in the domain of the private sector, in the public domain so that developing countries can apply them in their initiatives. The benefits would then be reaped by all.

References

ADB (2005). "Asian Environment Outlook 2005: Making Profits, Protecting our Planet", Asian Development Bank, Manila.

_____(2008). "ADB Commences Future Carbon Fund", ADB News Release, 13 December, http://www.adb.org/Media/Articles/2008/12752-asian-carbon-funds/.

Ban Ki-Moon and Al Gore, "Let the new mantra be 'growing green'", *Bangkok Post*, 20 February 2009.

Bangkok Post (2009). "Expert: Asia risks being left out in the cold over climate policy", Global Warming, 21 February, p. 7.

EarthJustice (2004). "Issue Paper: Human rights and the environment", a paper prepared for the sixtieth session of the United Nations Commission on Human Rights, Geneva, 15 March-23 April (Oakland, California, EarthJustice), available online at http://www.earthjustice.org/library/references/2004UNreport.pdf.

ESCAP (2005). *Electricity and Sustainable Development in Asia and the Pacific 2003-2005* (ST/ESCAP/2471).

_____(2008). *Economic and Social Survey of Asia and the Pacific 2008* (United Nations publication, Sales No. E.08.II.F.7).

ESCAP, ADB, UNDP (2007). *The Millennium Development Goals: Progress in Asia and the Pacific 2007* (ST/ESCAP/2465).

FAO (2006). *Yearbook of Fishery Statistics*, ftp://ftp.fao.org/fi/stat/summary/default.htm.

_____(2007). *State of World Fishery and Aquaculture 2006* (Rome).

_____(2008). *Climate Change and Food Security in Pacific Island Countries*, Secretariat of the Pacific Regional Environment Programme and University of the South Pacific, in cooperation with the FAO Sub-Regional Office for the South Pacific (Samoa).

Hamilton, K., M. Sjardin, T. Marcello and G. Xu (2008). "Forging a Frontier: State of the Voluntary Carbon Markets 2008" (Ecosystem Marketplace and New Carbon Finance).

IEA (2007). *World Energy Outlook 2007* (Paris).

_____(2008). *Key World Energy Statistics 2008* (Paris).

IGES (2008). *Climate Change Policies in the Asia and the Pacific: Re-uniting Climate Change and Sustainable Development* (Kanagawa).

International Herald Tribune (2008). "Dengue fever killed 407 people in Cambodia last year", Asia-Pacific, 4 January 2008, http://www.iht.com/articles/ap/2008/01/04/asia/AS-MED-Cambodia-Dengue.php.

IPCC (2007a). *Fourth Assessment Report* (Geneva).

_____(2007b). *Climate Change 2007: Mitigation of Climate Change*, Working Group III contribution to the Intergovernmental Panel on Climate Change Fourth Assessment Report, accessed from http://www.ipcc.ch/ipccreports/ar4-wg3.htm.

Jaura, R. (2008). "Climate change: And now a New Green Deal?", Inter Press Service, accessed from http://ipsnews.net/news.asp?idnews=45082 on 27 February 2009.

Karmali, N. (2006). "India's 'wind man' is blowing strong", Forbes.com, 14 June.

Loh, Christine and S. Tay (2009). "Marshalling Asia to Act", http://globalasia.org/pdf/issue4/v2n3_loh.pdf.

Nepal (2007). "Economic report 2006/07" (Kathmandu, Nepal Rastra Bank).

Oberman, M. (2009). "Hamburgers are the Hummers of food in global warming: scientists", 17 February, accessed from http://www.theprovince.com/story_print.html?id=1298363&sponsor= on 23 February 2009.

Omi, S. (2007). Speech given at the Side Event on Health Protection from Climate Change by World Health Organization Regional Director for the Western Pacific, Geneva, 21 May, http://www.wpro.who.int/regional_director/speeches/speech_20070521.htm.

Prüss-Üstün, A. and C. Corvalán (2006). *Preventing Disease through Healthy Environments: Towards an estimate of the environmental burden of disease* (Geneva, WHO).

Sida   (2009). *Making Climate Your Business* (Stockholm, Sida).

Stern, N. (2006). *Stern Review on the Economics of Climate Change* (London, HM Treasury, Government of the United Kingdom).

Sri Lanka (2006). "Annual Report 2006" (Colombo, Central Bank of Sri Lanka).

UNDP (2007). "Climate change and the MDGs in Asia Pacific: Challenges and opportunities", *Inside Asia Pacific*, vol. 2, issue 2 (Colombo, UNDP Regional Centre), accessed from http://www.undprcc.lk/rcc_web_bulletin/Issue2/country_Bangladesh,shtml.

_____ (2008). *Human Development Report 2007/2008* (New York).

UNFCCC (2007). "Bali Action Plan", adopted by the 13th Conference of the Parties, Bali, Indonesia, 3-14 December 2007 (FCCC/CP/2007/6/Add.1, decision 1/CP.13.).

WHO (2004). *World Health Report 2004* (Geneva).

_____ (2008). Statement on World Health Day, http://www.searo.who.int/EN/Section260/Section2468.htm.

World Resources Institute (2009). Climate Analysis Indicators Tool, accessed from http://cait.wri.org/cait.php on 11 February 2009.

" *It's one thing in the developed country where the economy is down, well, you may be out of a job. In some parts of the world when the economy is down, you may be without food to eat. And that's a different degree of seriousness.* **"**

Lee Hsien Loong
Prime Minister of Singapore

CHAPTER 4. SUBREGIONAL VARIATIONS: PERFORMANCE AND POLICY RESPONSES

The Great Recession has hit the developed world, and the Asia-Pacific region is not recession proof. In 2008, growth decelerated to 5.8% from 8.8% a year earlier, and with growth expected to decelerate further to 3.6% in 2009, it is clear that rapid economic growth, the hallmark of the region's developing countries over the past decades can no longer be taken for granted – a worrisome challenge, given the hard-won reductions in income poverty achieved over the past decades. This calls for coordinated macroeconomic policies that will see the region move to a more inclusive and sustainable path of economic growth.

...rapid economic growth, the hallmark of the region over the past decades can no longer be taken for granted...

A key issue for the region is how Asia and the Pacific will use fiscal policy in 2009. While most countries will have significant flexibility to undertake expansionary policies due to relatively solid budgetary situations and an easing of monetary policy due to moderating infla-tion, not all countries have this flexibility. Some countries, notably in South Asia, face strained fiscal positions together with inflationary pressures. Others, notably developed countries, continue to struggle with recession – both cyclical and structural – and obstinate deflationary pressures. And some, less affected by the financial crisis, notably small island developing States, face other threats of a stealthier, but potentially more virulent long-term impact. Export-oriented countries, notably those of South-East Asian subregions whose manufacturing sectors account for about 90% of merchandise exports, could see the financial crisis evolve quickly into an industrial crisis if expansionary fiscal and monetary policies do not have the intended effects.

It is clear that averages for a region as vast and diverse as Asia and the Pacific invariably mask subregional variations. Consequently, this chapter assesses the impact of the economic crisis on the subregions and their individual economies. It examines the commonalities and draws out the variations among subregions. It also reviews the various macroeconomic policy responses and lays the groundwork for chapter 5, the *Survey's* concluding chapter which addresses the regional policy gaps arising from the triple threat to development.

East and North-East Asia: Impact of global financial crisis begins to take its toll

East and North-East Asia faced very strong head winds in the latter part of 2008. The impact of the global financial crisis began to take its toll, first in the export sector and then spreading into domestic demand. Inflationary pressure subsided over the course of the year, giving more room for accommodating monetary policy in the face of slackened economic performance.

Impact: Strong head wind slows economic performance

Marked slowdown in GDP growth

Growth in East and North-East Asia declined sharply from 10.0% in 2007 to an estimated 6.1% in 2008 (figure 4.1), the largest percentage point fall in growth of any subregion. China continued to lead the growth in East and North-East Asia, despite experiencing relatively large percentage point fall in growth in 2008 in the subregion.

Figure 4.1. Slackening of economic growth in 2008, selected economies

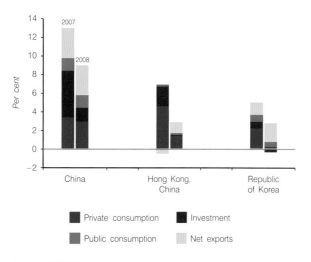

Sources: ESCAP calculations based on national sources, CEIC Data Company Limited and ESCAP estimates.

Note: Figures for 2008 are estimates.

Despite the sharp slowdown in growth, East and North-East Asia remained in 2008, as in 2007, the fastest growing subregion of Asia and the Pacific. Economic growth in East and North-East Asia in 2008, for the year as a whole, remained relatively robust, riding on the back of momentum in the subregion's trademark export performance in the early months of the year. However, the subregion faced a strong head wind in the latter part of 2008, with particularly sharp declines in exports occurring in the last month of 2008 and early 2009. Current account balances deteriorated and are expected to deteriorate further. The impact of the global financial crisis began to take its toll, first in the export sector and then in domestic demand (table 4.1).

Inflation accelerated in 2008 to 5.2% but remained below the average of 7.9% for developing economies of the Asia-Pacific region. However, following the easing of international commodity prices, inflationary pressure began to subside in the latter half of the year. For most of the economies in the subregion, exchange rates against the United States dollar remained largely stable in 2008.

Growth in China slowed in 2008 to 9.0%, its lowest level since 2002, due primarily to a slowing of net exports and export-related investment as well as a decline in real estate investment. The impact on investment has had the most effect on overall growth, given that investment accounts for 40% of the GDP. The slowdown was triggered by the effect of the decelerating real estate sector on domestic investment. Housing sales started to decline in early 2008, and housing prices have moderated, especially in large cities. Real estate investment, the second-largest contributor to urban fixed-asset investment, has been impacted. The amount of floor space of residential housing sold in the first 11 months of 2008 contracted by 18.8% from a year earlier (*China Daily*, 2009a), while urban housing prices declined year-on-year in December for the first time since July 2005 (*China Daily* 2009b). The deceleration was prompted when Government tightened up on lending and other curbs on the sector early in the year. Demand-side measures, such as tighter lending conditions for second houses, were combined with supply-side measures, such as stricter land-supply and credit policies for project developers. The decrease in consumer confidence caused by the global financial crisis in late 2008 contributed to further contraction. The Govern-

Table 4.1. Rates of economic growth and inflation in East and North-East Asia, 2007-2009

(Per cent)

	Real GDP growth			Inflation[a]		
	2007	2008[b]	2009[c]	2007	2008[b]	2009[c]
Subregion total	10.0	6.1	3.8	3.8	5.2	0.9
China	13.0	9.0	7.5	4.8	5.9	0.7
Hong Kong, China	6.4	2.5	−2.5	2.0	4.3	1.5
Mongolia	9.9	8.6	7.0	9.0	25.6	13.0
Republic of Korea	5.0	2.5	−1.5	2.5	4.7	1.6
Taiwan Province of China	5.7	0.1	−2.0	1.8	3.5	0.4

Sources: ESCAP, based on national sources; IMF, *International Financial Statistics* (CD-ROM) (Washington, D.C., November 2008); ADB, *Key Indicators for Asia and the Pacific 2008* (Manila, 2008); and ESCAP estimates.

[a] Changes in the consumer price index.
[b] Estimate.
[c] Forecast (as of 27 February 2009).

ment has responded with measures to support the real estate sector, such as reducing the property deed tax for small houses and the minimum down payment for mortgages, suspending the stamp duty and VAT for individual home sales, and lowering minimum mortgage rates for first homes.

By the end of 2008, the main impact on China's growth had come from a rapid slowdown in net exports and export-related investment due to decreased consumption in developed countries. The share of export-related investment in total investment is 15% to 20%. This impact on investment, coupled with the slowdown in real estate investment, has contributed to the overall decrease in investment growth. Decreasing consumption and investment also slowed the steel and cement sectors.

Consumption in China will be affected by the growth slowdown and by the loss of wealth from declining market assets. The growth slowdown will affect jobs and wages, particularly in enterprises connected to export and real estate. The ongoing slowdown in property prices, combined with sharp falls in equity markets, has led to slower wealth accumulation for the burgeoning middle class and constrained their consumption. However, the wealth impact in China is moderate compared to other countries, because home ownership financed by borrowing has not been as widespread in China, where there are high minimum down payments for mortgages.

Growth in the Republic of Korea also moderated, from 5.0% in 2007 to an estimated 2.5% in 2008. The economy put up a strong performance in the first half of 2008, achieving growth of over 5%, but consump-

tion slackened noticeably in the second half. As the global financial crisis deepened, the economy was inevitably hit due to its heavy dependence on merchandise exports and high exposure to the financial markets.

Consumption in China will be affected by the growth slowdown and by the loss of wealth from declining market assets

The growth of Hong Kong, China slackened significantly in the second half of 2008, as the external sector was dampened by faltering global demand. Concurrently, the impact on domestic demand began to emerge, along with a marked correction in the real estate and financial markets. The setback in private consumption was particularly sharp, dropping from a growth rate of 7.6% in the first quarter to −3.2% in the fourth quarter. For 2008 as a whole, the economy is estimated to have grown by 2.5%, notably slower than the 6.4% in 2007.

The pace of growth in Taiwan Province of China also slowed, from 5.7% in 2007 to an estimated 0.1% in 2008. The noticeably weakened private consumption in the second half of 2008 is attributable to shaken consumer confidence, insecure employment prospects and a sharp correction in asset markets. Investment expenditure fell, owing to liquidity constraints and dimmer profit expectations.

Macao, China continued to experience remarkable economic growth in the first half of 2008, bolstered by strong performance in the gaming industry and buoyant tourism. However, investment sagged upon completion of a number of large construction projects. Reportedly, new investment initiatives were held back because the business outlook was uncertain. To tide the economy over during the economic difficulties, a fiscal stimulus package was introduced in October 2008.

Growth in Mongolia, unlike other countries in the subregion, remained robust in 2008 at an estimated 8.6%, after 9.9% growth in 2007. This performance was led by the mining sector, which represents almost one-third of the country's GDP, and benefited from sharp rises in the international prices of copper and gold in the first half of 2008. Construction and financial services benefited from the economic spillover of the mining sector. Following the outbreak of the global financial crisis and significant declines in copper and gold prices, however, growth in the mining sector was constrained in the latter part of the year. High inflation, falling housing prices and share prices further capped consumption growth.

Inflation accelerated with rising food and energy prices

High international oil and food prices pushed inflation in East and North-East Asia to an estimated 5.2% in 2008, up from 3.8%. In tandem with the economic slowdown, however, oil and food prices came down significantly in the second half of 2008, easing the inflationary pressure in the region (figure 4.2).

China saw a rapid slowdown in inflation in the latter part of 2008, but overall inflation for the year was 5.9%, still greater than 2007. While the global slowdown in fuel and food prices contributed to the lessening of inflation, food prices also stabilized due to the fading effects of pig disease in 2007 and snowstorms in February 2008. Consumer price growth slowed as general domestic growth also slowed, while producer prices dropped due to greater competition in the face of curtailed demand and high supply. Inflation in China was affected less in 2008 than in previous years by excess demand, due to the injection of money into the economy to manage currency appreciation.

Inflation peaked in the Republic of Korea in mid-2008 pushed by higher oil and non-oil commodity prices. Sharp depreciation of the currency added further inflationary pressure from imported sources. Yet the inflationary pressure subsided as private consumption weakened and international commodity prices dropped

sharply. The inflation rate stood at 4.7% for 2008 as a whole, still, nearly double the 2.5% in 2007. Similarly, inflation in Hong Kong, China has fallen noticeably since the third quarter of 2008. Along with the easing of food inflation, the one-off relief measures of the government of Hong Kong, China, such as a subsidy of electricity bills and reduced public housing rentals for low-income households, also kicked in. Taken together, the inflation rate accelerated to 4.3% in 2008, up from 2.0% in 2007.

In tandem with the economic slowdown, however, oil and food prices came down significantly in the second half of 2008, easing the inflationary pressure in the region

---

Taiwan Province of China also saw its inflation come down since mid-2008 on the back of falling food and fuel prices. In 2008, consumer prices in Taiwan Province of China recorded an estimated increase of 3.5%, higher than the 1.8% in 2007. Inflationary pressure mounted in Mongolia, running over 30% in August and September 2008 due to rising imported costs of food and fuels. Inflation in Macao, China was on a climb in

Figure 4.2. Acceleration of inflation rate in 2008, selected economies

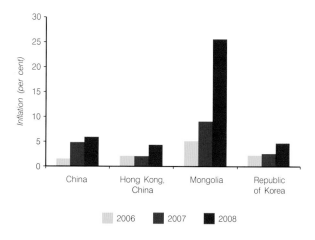

Sources: ESCAP calculations based on national sources; IMF, *International Financial Statistics* (CD-ROM) (Washington, D.C., November 2008).

Notes: Figures for 2008 are estimates. Inflation refers to changes in consumer price index.

the first half of 2008 before easing along with lower food and energy prices. To counteract the burden of inflation on households, the government of Macao, China introduced a number of one-off subsidies and allowances for households.

Mixed exchange rate movements across the subregion

Pressure for appreciation of the Chinese yuan diminished somewhat over the course of 2008, in line with the regional slowdown in exports and capital inflows. Relatively fast appreciation of the yuan until mid-2008 was followed by less upward movement in the latter part of the year, as the effects of the global financial crisis were felt (figure 4.3). Pressure for currency appreciation was reduced because of slowing exports and lower interest rates. Less need for Government intervention in managing currency values contributed to a slower build-up of reserves.

The Korean currency, the won, fell significantly against the United States dollar over the course of 2008 due to capital outflows, as investors withdrew their portfolio investments in the Republic of Korea. Compared to end-2007, the won had lost more than 25% of its value against the United States dollar at end-2008. The exchange rate of the Mongolian tugrik against the United States dollar remained largely stable, before deprecia-

ting abruptly towards the end of 2008. The sharp depreciation was attributable to concerns about the banking sector and deteriorating "twin-deficit" positions of the current account and the fiscal balance. On the other hand, the value of the Hong Kong dollar continued to be closely tied with the United States dollar under the Linked Exchange Rate system. The exchange rate of the New Taiwan dollar against the United States dollar remained largely stable during 2008.

Struggles in the export sector

The export sector remained the key driver of growth of the subregion, providing strong support in the first half of 2008. But along with weaker external demand, export growth began to slacken in the second half of the year, affecting economies' current accounts (figure 4.4).

China's export performance held up reasonably well in the initial months of the export slowdown. Still, export growth was on a downward trend, while import growth decreased faster. By November 2008, there was a contraction in exports of 2.2% year-on-year, the first monthly fall in almost seven years. But the export contraction was accompanied by an even faster import contraction of 18.0%, leading to a larger trade surplus for the month. December 2008 and January 2009, saw a continuation of the trend, with a contraction in exports of 2.8% and 17.5% year-on-year, re-

Figure 4.3. Mixed exchange rate movements: sharp depreciation of the Korean won and Mongolian tugrik, other currencies stable

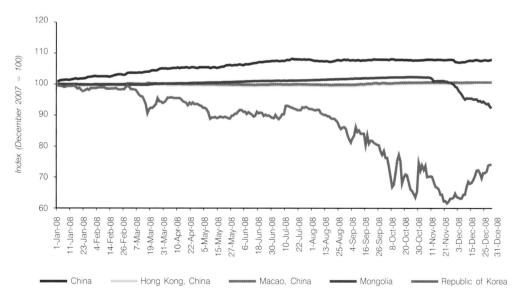

Sources: CEIC Data Company Limited; and Bank of Mongolia.

Figure 4.4. Deterioration of current account balances in 2008, selected economies

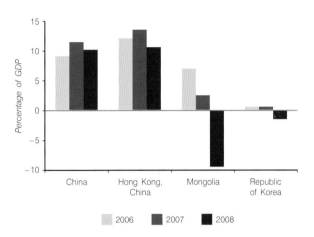

Sources: IMF, *International Financial Statistics* (CD-ROM) (Washington, D.C., 2008); and ESCAP estimates.

Note: Figures for 2008 are estimates.

spectively. More worrisome was an accelerating decrease in imports of 21.3% and 43.1% for the same period, most likely reflecting further downturns in future export performance. The Government has attempted to support exports through various policy measures. Three rounds of export tax rebates were announced, with the latest round in December 2008 affecting 3,770 items accounting for 28% of total exports. Export duties have also been removed on a range of products.

Exports from the Republic of Korea remained strong until the third quarter of 2008, due partly to a much weaker Korean won, which helped enhance the competitiveness of Korean products in overseas markets. As the negative impact of the global financial crisis set in, the export sector began to feel the pinch, and export performance retreated notably in the last quarter of the year, falling 9.9% year-on-year. The current account balance turned into a deficit in 2008.

Hong Kong, China, registered strong growth in merchandise exports in the first half of 2008, before decelerating to modest growth in the third quarter and declining in the fourth quarter by 1.7% year on year. Exports to the United States market posed the greatest drag. Exports to other markets were also gradually affected, owing to the global downturn. Still, exports of services held up relatively well in most of 2008, underpinned by the continued notable growth in offshore trade. Taken together, the current account for Hong Kong, China, continued to register a sizeable surplus.

Exports from Taiwan Province of China were robust in the first half of the year, supported by buoyant exports to China. In the second half of the year, there was a drastic turnaround as the shrinkage in external demand took its toll, with fourth quarter year-on-year exports falling sharply by 24.7%. The merchandise trade surplus went down notably in the third quarter. For 2008 as a whole, the current account still recorded a surplus, though lower than in 2007.

In Mongolia, while export earnings in the mining sector increased sharply, the value of imports escalated even more due to higher food and fuel prices. As a result, the merchandise trade deficit widened in the first nine months of 2008, and the country's current account swung from a surplus in 2007 to a deficit in 2008.

Net capital outflows

Portfolio capital inflows to China moderated during the course of the year because of declining asset values and reduced expectations for currency appreciation. Equity market values fell throughout the year in response to the slowing domestic economy and reduced appetite for global risk. Property markets reversed in late 2008 as the Government took measures to rein in the sector and lower consumer demand. China continued to see FDI growth during the year, though the pace had slowed sharply by the end of the year. The late slowdown in FDI was likely due to the lag in FDI data, reflecting decisions taken months earlier and revealing more circumspect investment because of slowing global and domestic economic conditions.

In the Republic of Korea, net capital outflow was recorded in the first three quarters of 2008. Significant net direct investment outflow and portfolio investment outflows were only partly compensated for by net inflows of other investment. Hong Kong, China registered net capital outflows in the first three quarters of 2008, due mainly to net outflows of portfolio investment and other investment, which were only partially offset by the net inflows of direct investment and financial derivatives. Taiwan Province of China also saw net capital outflows in the first three quarters of 2008. Continued significant investments abroad caused a net direct investment outflow. Additionally, there was massive portfolio outflow, caused by increased portfolio investment outside the economy and reduced portfolio investment in the economy. Mongolia continued to attract substantial FDI, which has been its major source of capital inflows.

Policy responses: Space for expansionary policies

To support their economies in the face of the global financial crisis and to alleviate the burden of inflation on households, Governments introduced various forms of fiscal stimulus packages, bailout plans and relief measures. The Government of China introduced the region's largest fiscal stimulus package ($584 billion) in late 2008, equivalent to around 13% of GDP, led by expenditure in infrastructure, followed by a number of further plans in early 2009. The Government of the Republic of Korea announced a bank bail-out package of $100 billion in the form of Government loan guarantees. In late 2008, the country approved a fiscal support plan equivalent to around 4% of GDP, comprising both fiscal expenditure expansion and tax reduction (table 4.2).

The Government of China has made efforts to counteract the growth slowdown through a fiscal policy package of 4 trillion yuan ($584 billion), announced in November 2008, followed by further plans, announced in early 2009, dedicated to science and technology and the health care system. Though some of the amount in the late-2008 fiscal package includes previously announced spending plans, the size of the package is unprecedented in China. The package is heavily directed toward infrastructure investment – railways, airports, environmental infrastructure, low-cost housing and the reconstruction of areas affected by the Sichuan earthquake of May 2008 (figure 4.5). Real estate investment will be boosted by the support for low-cost housing. The Government's "harmonious society" initiative to reduce the socio-economic gap between regions and sections of the population will be supported by the share of spending to be directed to rural livelihoods.

While such supportive policies by Governments could help stabilize and ride out the prevailing economic downturn, Governments will face increased dilemmas in terms of keeping a prudent budget policy in a sustainable manner. Most economies in the subregion have shown significant improvement in their fiscal balances since the financial crisis of late 1990s. But rising public-sector spending and reduced revenue will add an extra budgetary burden and will weaken the fiscal position of the Governments (figure 4.6). Failure to keep Government budgets in check will lead to concerns about public-sector debt. Overexpansion of the public sector will also crowd out private-sector investment incentives. This will be discussed in more detail in chapter 5.

Figure 4.5. China's fiscal stimulus package focusing on infrastructure investments

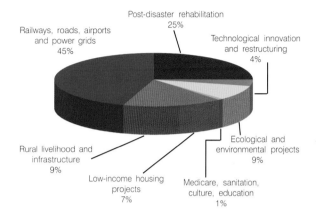

Source: National Development and Reform Commission, China, 27 November 2008.

Figure 4.6. Solid but weakening fiscal positions in 2008, selected economies

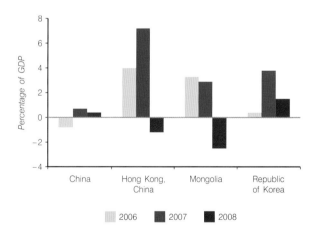

Sources: ESCAP calculations based on national sources; ADB, *Key Indicators for Asia and the Pacific 2008* (Manila, 2008); and ESCAP estimates.

Notes: Figures for 2008 are estimates. In the case of Mongolia, budget balance in includes grants.

Table 4.2. Fiscal stimulus packages in China and the Republic of Korea

	Salient features
China	■ $584 billion (4 trillion yuan) fiscal stimulus plan announced on 9 November 2008 intended to stimulate domestic demand. • 1.8 trillion yuan will go to construction of railways, highways, airports and power grids. • 1 trillion yuan for reconstruction in regions worst hit by the earthquake of 12 May. • 280 billion yuan to speed low-income housing projects. • 370 billion yuan to improve people's living standards and infrastructure in rural areas. • 40 billion yuan for health and education programmes. • 350 billion yuan for ecological and environmental projects. • 160 billion yuan for technological innovation. ■ $88 billion (600 billion yuan) announced on 12 January 2009 dedicated to scientific and technical innovation and upgrades. • Will expedite investment in six major projects closely related to the current economic development situation. • The six plans were among those approved in China's National Medium- and Long-term Science and Technology Development Plan (2006-2020). ■ $123 billion (850 billion yuan) announced on 21 January 2009 to improve the nation's health care system. ■ Authorities would take measures within three years to provide basic medical security to all Chinese in urban and rural areas, improve the quality of medical services, and make medical services more accessible and affordable for ordinary people. • Increase the amount of rural and urban population covered by the basic medical insurance system or the new rural cooperative medical system to at least 90% by 2011. • Each person covered by the systems would receive an annual subsidy of 120 yuan from 2010. • Improve quality of medical services by upgrading grassroots medical institutions, improving health services in rural areas and launching a pilot programme to reform services of public hospitals.
Republic of Korea	■ The National Assembly approved the 2009 Budget and Public Fund Operations Plan to Overcome Economic Difficulties in mid-December. The fiscal support measures, equivalent to around 4% of GDP, promote both fiscal expenditure expansion and tax reduction. In order to provide imminent support to the economy, the Government aims to execute 60% of the budget in the first half of 2009. These fiscal support initiatives include the following objectives: • Create more jobs by providing better job training through expansion of the internship system, vitalization of venture enterprises, and increased numbers of job positions for the underprivileged. • Increase welfare support to stabilize livelihoods of low-income, underprivileged classes and provide aggressive support in reducing childcare costs. • Increase social overhead capital investments with a focus on investments in construction projects, including leading projects for the advancement of the metropolitan economy and provincial traffic network expansion. • Support stabilization of SMEs and the financial markets by increasing SME guarantees. • Provide an additional 1.9 trillion won for regional finances to offset the reduced real estate tax arising from amendments to the comprehensive real estate taxes. ■ The Government announced establishment of the "Green New Deal Job Creation Plan" in early January 2009. The eco-friendly policy initiative is valued at 50 trillion won. It aims to generate of 960,000 jobs in four years, of which 140,000 jobs will be created in 2009. Focus areas of the Green New Deal include: • Energy conservation, recycling, and clean energy development to build an energy-saving economy. • Green transportation networks and clean water supplies to upgrade the quality of life and environment. • Carbon reductions and stable supply of water resources to protect the earth and future generations. • Building of industrial and information infrastructures, and technology development to use energy efficiently in the future.

Turnaround of tight monetary policy

East and North-East Asia experienced a notable change in monetary policy in 2008. Facing high oil and food prices in the first half of the year, central banks focused on containing inflation. When the global financial turbulence hit the region, a liquidity squeeze became a mounting concern. At the same time, the sharp correction in international commodity prices also provided more room for loosening monetary policy.

China reversed its monetary policy over the course of the year as inflation pressures subsided. Until early 2008, the Government attempted to curtail lending to the real estate sector and manage excessive investment through various administrative and market-based banking policies. Since 2007, interest rates have been raised six times; the reserve requirement ratio, 15 times. In response to the slowing of the real estate sector, general consumption and investment, these measures were reversed in the latter half of 2008. The People's Bank of China relaxed credit quotas and cut both interest rates and bank reserve ratios in late 2008. Interest rates were reduced four times, starting in September 2008; the cut of 108 basis points in late November 2008 was the largest reduction since the 1997 Asian crisis. The Government announced in October 2008 that it would not apply the credit quotas that had served to curtail lending since late 2007.

To counteract rising inflation, the Bank of Korea raised its key policy rate by 25 basis points to a seven-year high of 5.25% in August 2008. As the risk of economic slowdown continued to rise, the Bank cut its key policy interest rate by 25 basis points in early October in a coordinated move with other central banks. As the severe credit freeze deepened, the Bank slashed the interest rate again in late October by 75 basis points. That was followed by cuts of another 25 basis points and 100 basis points in November and December, respectively. With all the cuts, the Bank of Korea base rate was reduced to 3.0% at end-2008, compared with 5% at end-2007.

Under the currency board arrangement, Hong Kong, China followed United States monetary policy closely and cut its interest rate aggressively. A total of 525 basis points were slashed during 2008.[1] The discount window base rate was 0.5% at end-2008, compared to 5.75% at end-2007. Taiwan Province of China also followed suit and cut interest rates aggressively. The Central Bank of China brought the discount rate down to 2% by end-2008, compared to 3.375% at end-2007. The Bank of Mongolia followed a tightening monetary policy during most of the year, but, facing the rising risk of economic slowdown and easing inflationary pressure, it cut the interest rate by 50 basis points towards the end of the year, to 9.75% at end-2008.

Outlook: Difficult times ahead as export engine falters

The East and North-East Asia subregion is forecast to grow by 3.8% in 2009, dragged down by recession in its more advanced economies. The main impact on growth will come from the slowing of the critical manufacturing export sector, leading to the subregion being forecast to lose its position as the fastest growing subregion of Asia and the Pacific to other subregions which rely more on relatively insulated domestic demand.

Economic growth in China in 2009 will be dragged down by the impact on the export sector of weaker external demand. Domestic demand, supported by a loosened monetary stance and increased public spending on infrastructure projects, is expected to provide a partial cushion. As a result, the economy of China is forecast to attain 7.5% growth in 2009.

Growth in the Republic of Korea is forecast at −1.5% for 2009, primarily due to weaker export performance. Private consumption and investment will also slow as concerns grow about employment, prices and high consumer debt.

Hong Kong, China, is forecast to see growth of −2.5% in 2009. The export sector will be hit by weaker external demand, whereas domestic demand will be dampened by rising unemployment and dimmer economic prospects. Taiwan Province of China is forecast to shrink by 2.0% in 2009. It is expected that export growth will be limited in 2009.

---

[1] This included the reduction of the spread of 150 basis points above the prevailing United States Fed Funds Target Rate to 50 basis points.

North and Central Asia: Overall a year of mixed results

For the economies in North and Central Asia, 2008 was a year of mixed blessings. All the economies experienced a slowing of economic growth. Aggregate GDP in 2008 was 3.0 percentage points lower than in 2007 (table 4.3), when the subregional countries as a whole posted one of the fastest growth rates since the start of their economic transition. Nevertheless, growth was given a boost by high prices in oil, natural gas, metals as well as cotton and cereals, albeit to a lesser extent, for most of the year. By year's end, as these commodity markets became more volatile, the financial crisis compelled the subregional economies to consider the extent to which Governments should provide insulation from external shocks. The rise in world energy and food prices was rather notable in the subregion as inflation accelerated to 14.3% compared to 9.4% in 2007. The subregion faced limited access to foreign loans and monetary policy was tightened. The global financial crisis also led to scaled-back projections for economic growth in 2009-2010.

Impact: Resilient growth with some deceleration

With the exception of Kazakhstan and Georgia, GDP growth in all the economies of North and Central Asia exceeded 5.0% in 2008 (figure 4.7). Growth in 2008 continued to be driven by domestic private consumption and fixed investment. The key factors underpinning the robust domestic demand were rising real wages, strong FDI inflows, and strong growth in overseas remittances.

GDP growth resilient

Azerbaijan, with growth of 10.8%, was expected to record the highest rates of economic growth in the subregion for a fourth consecutive year.

The GDP of the Russian Federation increased by 5.6% in 2008, owing to robust growth in retail sales and investment in fixed assets. Retail turnover and investment in fixed capital grew by 13.0% and 9.1%, respectively, through 2008. The industrial sector, benefitting from expansion in manufacturing, grew by 2.1% over the same period. Agricultural production rose by 10.8% in 2008. The grain harvest was expected to be 108 million tons for 2008, exceeding the 2007 harvest by more than 25 million tons and permitting exports of grain to neighbouring countries. The country remained the second-largest oil producer in the world in 2008. Despite the sharp decline in oil prices, the hydrocarbon sector continued to play a key role in economic development.

Table 4.3. Rates of economic growth and inflation in North and Central Asian economies, 2007-2009

(Per cent)

	Real GDP growth			Inflation[a]		
	2007	2008[b]	2009[c]	2007	2008[b]	2009[c]
Subregion total	8.6	5.6	3.6	9.4	14.3	10.7
Armenia	13.8	6.8	6.5	4.4	9.0	5.5
Azerbaijan	25.0	10.8	8.0	16.7	20.8	15.0
Georgia	12.4	4.0	4.0	9.3	10.0	9.0
Kazakhstan	8.5	2.4	1.5	10.8	17.0	8.5
Kyrgyzstan	8.2	7.6	4.5	10.2	24.5	10.0
Russian Federation	8.1	5.6	3.5	9.0	14.1	11.0
Tajikistan	7.8	7.9	5.5	21.5	20.4	14.0
Turkmenistan	8.5	5.0	3.0	6.3	13.0	10.0
Uzbekistan	9.5	8.6	7.0	12.3	12.0	6.5

Sources: ESCAP, based on data from the Interstate Statistical Committee of the Commonwealth of Independent States, accessed from www.cisstat.com, 22 October 2008 and *Press Release*, 3 February 2009; and ESCAP estimates.

[a] Changes in the consumer price index.
[b] Estimate.
[c] Forecast (as of 27 February 2009).

Figure 4.7. Real GDP and sectoral growth in North and Central Asian economies, 2007-2008

GDP growth

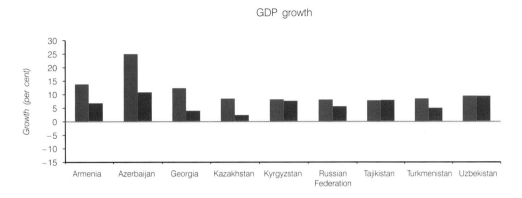

Agricultural production

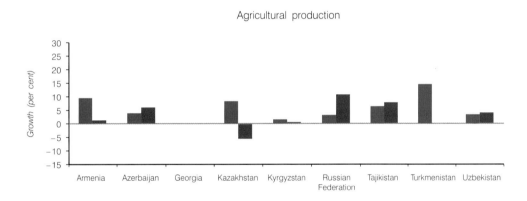

Industrial production

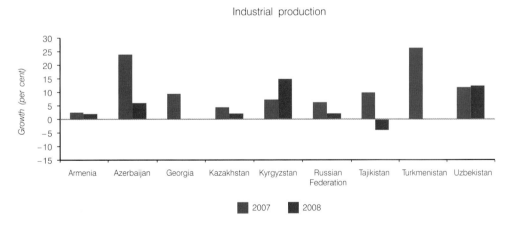

■ 2007   ■ 2008

Sources: ESCAP, based on data from the Interstate Statistical Committee of the Commonwealth of Independent States, accessed from www.cisstat.com, 22 October 2008, and *Press Release*, 3 February 2009; and ESCAP estimates.

Notes: Gross domestic product growth rates for 2008 are estimates for Turkmenistan. Gross domestic product growth rates for 2008 in Georgia and Uzbekistan refers to January-September. Agricultural production growth for 2007 in Turkmenistan refers to January-June; for Uzbekistan, January-September, while growth for 2008 in Uzbekistan refers to January-September. Industrial production growth for 2007 in Georgia refers to January-June, for Turkmenistan, January-October, and for Uzbekistan, January-September while growth for 2008 in Uzbekistan refers to January-September.

After averaging 10% annual growth from 2000 to 2007, the GDP of Kazakhstan grew by 2.4% in 2008, which is much lower than the targeted goal of 6 to 7%. Industrial output grew by 2.1% in 2008, down from the 4.5% recorded in 2007. The mining and utilities sectors were leading drivers of growth in industrial production. The grain harvest of 2008 was not as favourable as in 2007, and overall agricultural production fell by 5.6% in 2008 compared with 2007. Oil and gas condensate production was expected to come to 70 million tons in 2008, 4.4% higher than in 2007.

Weakness in oil output and double-digit inflation continues to impede economic growth in Azerbaijan. The country's GDP grew by 10.8% in 2008, compared with the rate of 25% recorded in 2007. The industrial sector expanded by 6.0%, and retail sales grew by 16.1% in 2008. The construction sector boomed, expanding by 38% in the first nine months of the year, as oil revenues financed public infrastructure projects. The mining sector, including oil and gas, accounted for around 80% of total industrial output and grew by 12.1% in the first nine months of 2008, compared with 33.5% in the corresponding period of 2007. Agricultural output increased by a record of 6.1% in 2008, owing to a good grain harvest.

The economy of Tajikistan grew 7.9% in 2008, but industrial production fell by 4.0% due to the cold weather that caused electricity blackouts at industrial facilities. Agriculture production grew by 7.9% in 2008. Cotton continued to constitute the primary agricultural output for Tajikistan and remained the second-highest source of export earnings for the country, after aluminium. The harvest of cotton fell, however, by 4.4% in 2007 and was expected to fall further in 2008 due to water shortages and a locust attack that damaged thousands of hectares of agricultural crops.

Armenia's GDP increased by 6.8% in 2008 as a result of a boom in construction, financial services and communications. Industrial output grew 2.0% in 2008. The moderate growth rate of industrial production was attributed to falling global prices in non-ferrous metals, Armenia's leading export. But the energy sector helped to drive economic growth, generating one fifth of overall industrial output in the first 10 months of 2008. Financial services grew strongly, owing to robust demand for consumer credit. An increase in fruit harvests contributed to a 1.3% increase in the agriculture output in 2008.

Kyrgyzstan's GDP grew 7.6% in 2008. Gold production boosted overall growth, as the non-gold economy suffered from difficulties in the banking sector. Industrial output grew 14.9% in 2008, primarily due to an increase in textile and metals production. Low water

levels limited electricity deliveries to industrial enterprises. Agricultural production rose 0.6% in 2008, due to an increase in the area under cultivation for grains, vegetables and cotton.

Georgia's GDP grew at a record level of 12.4% in 2007, up from an annual average of 9.5% in 2005/06, due to a rebound in agricultural output and stronger growth in transport and construction. GDP growth slowed to 4.0% in the first nine months of 2008 because of slower agricultural and manufacturing production. Services grew much faster than in 2007, thanks to rising household incomes and an improving financial sector. And privatization of several important industrial enterprises generated additional investment to stimulate economic growth.

Azerbaijan was expected to record the highest rates of economic growth in the subregion for a fourth consecutive year

---

In Turkmenistan, the hydrocarbon industry remained the main driver of the economy and the largest contributor to industrial production in 2008. GDP grew by 7.5% in the first seven months of the year, mainly because of strong growth in industrial output and investment. Degradation of the soil and reduction of grain and cotton harvests weakened agriculture. But with strong demand and high prices for the country's main commodities of cotton, gas and oil, GDP was expected to grow by 5.0% in 2008.

The economy of Uzbekistan was expected to grow at a healthy pace in 2008. GDP growth in the first nine months of 2008 was 9.4%. Industrial output and retail trade grew by 12.4% and 15.0%, respectively, in that period. Gross fixed investment grew more than 20%, and foreign trade turnover benefited from an expansion in exports in the first nine months of the year. Key commodities such as cotton, gas and gold received a boost from strong commodity prices. And the automotive sector raised its sales abroad by taking advantage of strong demand for cars in the Russian Federation.

State budget targets were mostly met

The budget of the Russian Federation, which has recorded a surplus for the last eight years, was expected to have a surplus of 5.5% of GDP, compared with 5.4% in 2007 (figure 4.8). Because oil and gas exports are expected to comprise one third of budget revenue in 2009, the Government took steps in 2008 to diversify the economy and reduce dependence on hydrocarbons. It diverted more oil revenues into the Stabilization Fund, which for years has been absorbing windfall taxes from energy exports to help control inflation. The three-year budget approved by the country's parliament in November 2008 envisaged budget targets for 2009-2011 that take into account a high inflation rate and falling oil prices. The budget surplus is expected to decline to 3.6% of GDP in 2009 and to 2.8% of GDP in 2010. Government expenditures are planned to rise by about 20% in 2009 and by 14% in 2010.

Due to the rapid growth of hydrocarbon production and massive oil revenue, budget performance was strong in Azerbaijan and Kazakhstan. But the State budgets of these economies were expected to record deficits of 1.6% and over 2.2% of GDP, respectively, in 2008. Additional spending on social infrastructure could worsen the budget performances of both countries in 2009. In September 2008, the Government of Azerbaijan increased minimum monthly wages and labour pensions by 25%. To cover additional social spending from the oil sector, Kazakhstan plans to introduce a new export tax on oil production, which will increase the tax burden on companies developing the country's natural resources and mainly target for-

eign energy companies operating on a production-sharing basis.

The State budget deficit of Armenia was expected to increase from 0.7% of GDP in 2007 to 0.8% of GDP in 2008 because of increased expenditures on social programmes and infrastructure and continued reform of the pension system. Spending was expected to rise by 20% for education and by 24% on medical care, much of it as a pay raise for medical personnel. To meet increased expenditures, the Government undertook measures to reduce tax evasion and improve the tax system, tax and customs administration and the business environment.

The three-year budget of the Russian Federation envisaged budget targets for 2009-2011 that take into account a high inflation and falling oil prices

---

The budget performance of Kyrgyzstan in 2008 was solid because of tightening fiscal policy. A VAT makes up almost half of total tax revenue. But due to rapidly rising inflation, the Government cut the rate of VAT on some food products, affecting revenue targets for 2008. In 2009, the overall VAT rate could be reduced from 20% to 12%, and the unified tax on small businesses from 10% to 6%. The country's 2008 budget deficit target was 2.2% of GDP. However, the State budget of Kyrgyzstan was expected to record a deficit of 0.7% of GDP owing to maintaining tight fiscal control.

The Government of Uzbekistan maintained a relatively prudent fiscal stance to keep the State budget in balance in 2008. Fiscal performance has improved in recent years, owing to strong economic growth, high commodity prices and tax reforms. Favourable trends in export revenue could help the Government meet additional social spending on public-sector wages and pensions.

In Tajikistan the 2007 State budget surplus of 1.7% of GDP was expected to revert to a small deficit of 0.3% of GDP in 2008 because of rising demands on Government expenditure, particularly the implementation of the public investment programme. Budget revenues were reduced because of the country's narrow tax base. Aluminium and cotton were the two main contributors to overall revenues. The expected 2008 deficit of Turkmenistan was due to an anticipated increase in public-sector wages and Government investment. The additional spending was expected to be met by in-

Figure 4.8. Budget balance as a percentage of GDP in selected North and Central Asian economies, 2007-2008

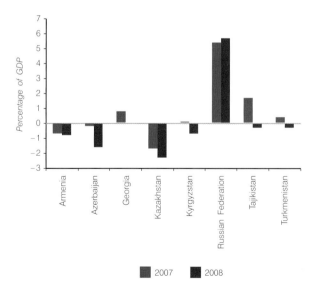

2007   2008

Sources: ADB, *Key Indicators for Asia and the Pacific 2008* (Manila, 2008); and ESCAP estimates.

Notes: Figures for 2008 are estimates. Budget balance of Azerbaijan excludes grants.

creased earnings from the hydrocarbon sector, which has been the main contributor to the budget revenues. Tax revenue was expected to contribute around 20% of total revenue. About 70% of total expenditure is directed towards social spending, including free utilities for the population.

Accommodative monetary policy

The monetary policies of the North and Central Asian countries in 2008 continued to focus on keeping inflation within the targeted range and ensuring stability of national currencies. But inflation started to accelerate in the second half of 2007 and continued in 2008, driven by surging international food and energy prices (figure 4.9). Over the year, consumer price inflation remained in the double digits in most of the subregion's economies. Strong domestic demand and rising real wages added inflationary pressures. The heightened inflation was most pronounced in Tajikistan, Kazakhstan, Kyrgyzstan, and Azerbaijan as consumer prices grew by about or more than 20% in 2008. The main driver of the inflationary surge was food and energy price inflation.

Rising Government expenditures, high prices for imported wheat and mineral products and the rapid expansion of monetary aggregates continued to exert pressure on consumer prices in Armenia. Inflation accelerated to 9.0% in 2008, its highest rate in a dec-

ade, due largely to rising food and energy prices. To combat rising prices, the central bank increased its refinancing rate from 5.75% to 7.75%, but that step had had limited impact. The continued appreciation of the dram, the national currency, negatively affected economic performance and led some to urge more State spending in education and health care. Since 2003, the value of the dram has increased by more than 90% in nominal terms against the United States dollar, owing to both the weakness of the United States dollar and continued robust inflows of overseas remittances. By the end of 2008, however, the dram was expected to weaken against the United States dollar in nominal term (figure 4.10).

> *The monetary policies in 2008 continued to focus on keeping inflation within the targeted range and ensuring stability of national currencies*

In Azerbaijan, large oil export revenues caused an acceleration of consumer price inflation, constraining economic growth and reducing consumers' purchasing power. The inflation rate reached a 12-year high of 20.8% in 2008. Food prices rose almost three times faster than prices of non-food commodities, reflecting

Figure 4.9. Inflation in North and Central Asian economies, 2007-2008

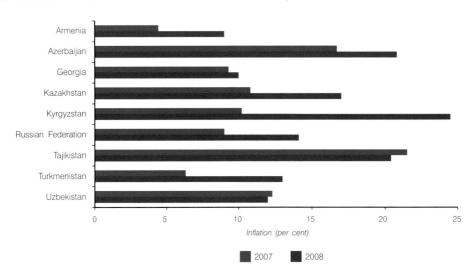

Sources: ESCAP, based on data from the Interstate Statistical Committee of the Commonwealth of Independent States, accessed from www.cisstat.com, 22 October 2008, and *Press Release*, 3 February 2009; IMF, *World Economic Outlook Database* (Washington, D.C., 2008); and ESCAP estimates.

Notes: Inflation rates refer to percentage changes in the consumer price index. Inflation rates for 2008 are estimates for Turkmenistan and Uzbekistan.

Figure 4.10. Exchange rates, against the United States dollar, of selected North and Central Asian economies, 1996-2008

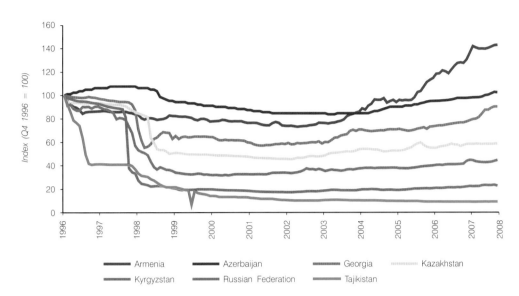

Source: IMF, *International Financial Statistics* (CD-ROM) (Washington, D.C., 2008).

global trends. To bring inflation down, the Government was expected to allow greater nominal appreciation of the manat in 2008. Foreign currency inflows from oil exports strengthened the manat in real terms against the United States dollar by around 35% between the end of 2007 and 2008, and the Government replaced the exchange rate, which was pegged to the United States dollar with a currency basket to combat inflation.

Tight liquidity and high inflation were the key monetary policy concerns for Kazakhstan. Consumer price inflation reached 17.0% in 2008. The national currency, the tenge, was stabilized by drawing on the National Bank's reserves in the second half of 2007, when concerns over liquidity problems in the banking sector sparked higher local demand for foreign currency. In August 2008 the tenge was 4% stronger in nominal terms against the United States dollar than a year earlier. However, the tenge was expected to be devalued in the beginning of 2009.

Consumer price inflation was 24.5% in Kyrgyzstan in 2008. As in other Central Asian countries, inflation was boosted by higher food and fuel prices. The economy was unable to avoid price hikes because of increases in the prices of flour and grain. The Government introduced extraordinary measures to control the prices of these and other staples. To prevent shortages in grain and flour, the Government created a state grain reserve and supplied it at fixed prices. The

Government also reduced prices on diesel fuel for farmers and extended about $3 million in low-interest agricultural credits to farmers. A new law on food security aimed at bolstering emergency measures to ensure minimum food supplies during crises was under preparation. As a result of rising domestic inflation, the national currency, the som, was expected to appreciate in real effective terms against the United States dollar in 2008 after remaining stable in 2006-2007. However, by the end of 2008, the som depreciated by about 13% in nominal term.

Consumer price inflation in Georgia reached 10.0% in 2008, the highest in four years. The price of food rose sharply due to high international food prices and harsh weather. Transport and utility costs also rose rapidly, reflecting high global energy prices. Inflation in the country was fuelled by strong economic activity and growth in monetary aggregates. The national currency of Georgia, the lari, appreciated steadily against the United States dollar in 2006-2007. But in the first seven months of 2008, its real exchange rate against the dollar rose by 23% year due to the weakening of the United States dollar, continued strong inflows of FDI and the successful initial placement of Georgia's Eurobond.

High oil prices, capital inflows and the effects of an earlier fiscal relaxation fed inflationary pressures in the Russian Federation. The Government raised its 2008 inflation projection from 7.5-8.5% to 14%, which would be the highest since 2002. Consumer price inflation was 14.1% in 2008. Food prices, one of the main drivers of consumer price inflation, were expected to moderate by the end of the year as a result of stabilized global food prices and a record grain harvest. The surge in inflation caused the continued appreciation of the ruble in real effective terms – in the first 10 months of 2008, the ruble became 4.7% stronger against the United States dollar. But in November 2008, it fell by 1% against the combined dollar/euro basket of currencies after the Central Bank of the Russian Federation reduced the floor at which it would defend its national currency.

A combination of internal and external factors led to sharp rises in food, fuel and consumer goods prices in Tajikistan. Consumer price inflation accelerated to 21.5% in 2007 and reached 20.4% in 2008. High inflation was expected to cause the national currency of Tajikistan, the somoni, to appreciate in real effective terms against the currencies of the country's main trading partners, the euro and the ruble, in 2008. But remittances from workers living abroad and inflows on the capital account were expected to support the national currency against the United States dollar.

Prices rose in Turkmenistan in 2008 because of large increases in fuel and public-transport prices, and a poor cereal crop led to an increase in food prices. The average rate of consumer price inflation was expected to reach 13% in 2008. In May 2008 the Government tried to control inflation by unifying the official and commercial exchange rates of the manat,

which would reduce the amount of cash in circulation. The unification is expected to be followed by a redenomination of 5,000 "old" to 1 "new" manat in 2009.

Inflation in Uzbekistan was expected to exceed 10% in 2008 due to rising food and fuel prices. To reduce inflationary pressures, monetary policy was tightened in late 2007. But strong export-related inflows and large increases in public-sector wages maintained inflationary pressure in 2008. A moderate nominal appreciation of the national currency, the som, was expected to control inflation in 2009 and reduce reliance on indirect tools of monetary policy.

Current account trends vary

A widening trade deficit was expected to increase the current account deficit of Armenia from 6.4% of GDP in 2007 to 8.6% of GDP in 2008 (table 4.4). The trade deficit widened because of soaring imports and falling export revenue. Import expenditures rose by 43%, to $3.1 billion, and merchandise exports grew by only 0.4%, to $832 million, in the first nine months of 2008 (table 4.5). Building materials, consumer goods and machinery and equipment for new construction projects were among the leading imports. Metallurgy, machine-building and mineral products became important sources of export revenue. But stagnation in the manufacturing sector weakened the export-oriented diamond-processing industry, which had been the country's dominant exporter in recent years.

Table 4.4. External accounts for North and Central Asian economies, 2007-2008

(Per cent)

	Export/GDP		Import[a]/GDP		Current account balance/GDP	
	2007	2008[b]	2007	2008[b]	2007	2008[b]
Armenia	13.0	10.2	30.4	30.1	−6.4	−8.6
Azerbaijan	68.2	71.9	19.2	14.1	30.7	40.6
Georgia	20.5	21.1	48.9	55.0	−12.5	−20.8
Kazakhstan	46.1	47.2	31.7	26.6	−7.1	4.7
Kyrgyzstan	35.7	33.2	70.3	68.8	−7.0	−12.0
Russian Federation	27.6	27.2	17.3	17.6	5.9	6.0
Tajikistan	41.9	35.0	83.9	79.3	−11.2	−8.5
Turkmenistan	82.8	116.3	49.7	62.2	15.4	26.5
Uzbekistan	36.0	37.4	25.7	24.4	19.1	21.7

Sources: IMF, *International Financial Statistics* (CD-ROM) (Washington, D.C., 2008), and *World Economic Outlook Database* (Washington, D.C., 2008); Economist Intelligence Unit, *Country Reports* (London, EIU, 2008), various issues; and ESCAP estimates.

[a] Import value in f.o.b.
[b] Estimates.

Table 4.5. Export and import growth in North and Central Asian economies, 2006-2008

(Per cent)

| | Growth rates | | | | | |
| | Exports | | | Imports | | |
	2006	2007	2008ᵃ	2006	2007	2008ᵃ
Armenia	1.1	17.0	0.4	21.6	49.1	43.0
Azerbaijan	46.6	−4.9	803.0	25.1	8.4	33.8
Georgia	8.2	32.5	42.1	47.7	41.8	31.8
Kazakhstan	37.3	24.8	66.1	36.5	38.3	18.3
Kyrgyzstan	18.2	42.8	27.1	56.0	40.7	52.4
Russian Federation	24.8	17.0	52.5	39.6	44.9	47.6
Tajikistan	53.9	4.9	4.8	29.7	42.3	35.9
Turkmenistanᵇ	17.6	31.2	29.8	13.2	11.1	15.6
Uzbekistanᵇ	18.0	42.9	24.1	16.0	49.2	13.4

Sources: Website of the Interstate Statistical Committee of the Commonwealth of Independent States, accessed from www.cisstat.com, 11 December 2008; and Economist Intelligence Unit, *Country Reports* (London, EIU, 2008), various issues.

[a] All figures refer to January-September, except for Turkmenistan and Uzbekistan, which are whole-year estimates.
[b] Import value in f.o.b.

Azerbaijan was expected to record a current account surplus of 40.6% of GDP in 2008 because of rising oil exports and high global oil prices in the first half of 2008. Oil and gas products accounted for around 60% of total export revenue of the economy in this period. Rising oil production and oil exports enabled Azerbaijan to run a merchandise trade surplus of about $33 billion in the first nine months of 2008. Exports rose more than eightfold, to about $39 billion, and imports grew by 33.8% to $5.2 billion in that period. The country continued to rely on imports of food products, consumer goods and machinery and equipment to complete its hydrocarbon projects and improve infrastructure. An appreciating currency and rising wages boosted expenditures on imported consumer goods.

The current account deficit of Kyrgyzstan was expected to increase from 7.0% of GDP in 2007 to 12% of GDP in 2008, largely because of a widening trade deficit. In the first nine months of 2008, exports grew by 27.1% and imports rose by more than 52%, increasing the trade gap from $1.1 billion in the first nine months of 2007 to $1.8 billion in the corresponding period of 2008. The major imports were wheat and fuel from the Russian Federation and Kazakhstan. But strong growth in remittances from migrant labour abroad and successful negotiation with the Paris Club regarding debt restructuring increased current transfers to the current account of the country in 2008.

The current account deficit of Georgia in 2008 was expected to increase from 12.5% of GDP in 2007 to more than 20.0% of GDP due to a large trade deficit.

Imports rose by 31.8% to $4.7 billion, and exports grew by 42.1% to $1.2 billion in the first nine months of 2008. As a result, the trade deficit of the country increased from $2.7 billion in the first nine months of 2007 to $3.4 billion in the corresponding period of 2008. Ferrous metals and fertilizers continued to dominate the exports of the country, providing more than half of the growth in exports. Among the largest imports were gas, crude oil, petroleum and automobiles.

A foreign trade surplus was expected to cause the current account surplus of the Russian Federation to grow from 5.9% of GDP in 2007 to 6.0% in 2008. Exports grew by 52.5%, and imports rose by 47.6% in the first nine months of 2008. The trade surplus increased from $106 billion in the first nine months of 2007 to $169 billion in the same period of 2008. Hydrocarbon exports accounted for about 70% of the total export earnings in the first nine months of 2008. Machinery and equipment for new construction projects and consumer goods were the largest imports.

The current account deficit of Tajikistan was expected to narrow from 11.2% in 2007 to 8.5% in 2008. Merchandise exports of Tajikistan increased by 4.8% to $1.1 billion, and imports grew by 35.9% to $2.4 billion in the first nine months of 2008. As a result, the trade deficit of the country was more than double the deficit in the corresponding period of 2007. Rising global energy and food prices had a negative impact on the trade balance. Aluminium, cotton and electrical energy remained the country's primary exports; the largest imports were food and consumer goods, and the needs of the economy for wheat and flour were met at a higher than usual cost. Large inflows of remittances could offset the impact of the widening trade imbalance on the current account. The remittances of about one million labour migrants, working mostly in the Russian Federation and Kazakhstan, accounted for 36% of GDP in 2007.

The current account surplus of Turkmenistan was expected to rise from 15.4% of GDP in 2007 to more than 26% of GDP in 2008, due mainly to rising natural gas exports. Export revenue was expected to grow by about 30% and import expenditure by 15.6% in 2008. The merchandise trade surplus was expected to rise in 2008 because of strong demand for the country's gas exports in the Russian Federation. The machinery and equipment for gas exploitation, construction and agriculture continued to dominate the country's import structure.

The current account of Uzbekistan was expected to have a surplus of 21.7% of GDP because of a large trade surplus and increased remittances from citizens working abroad. Rising global prices on the country's principal export commodities – gold, gas and cotton – were expected to increase export revenues by more than 24% in 2008, and hydrocarbons became a more important source of income than in the past. Growing remittances were expected to ensure a surplus of current transfers.

Kazakhstan's 2007 current account deficit was expected to revert to a surplus of 4.7% of GDP in 2008. The merchandise trade surplus was expected to rise in response to strong demand for the country's oil exports. High oil prices increased the trade surplus from $10 billion in the first nine months of 2007 to $28 billion in the corresponding period of 2008. In the first three quarters of 2008, exports from Kazakhstan rose by 66.1% to $56 billion, and imports grew by 18.3% to $28 billion. The Russian Federation remained the largest trading partner of Kazakhstan; China is an important supplier of consumer goods.

Policy responses: Solid fiscal positions, but concerns loom

As in other subregions, policy responses were geared towards dealing with the main challenges that threatened the development of the subregion. Inflation in food prices and continuing wheat shortages, which sparked record high prices for bread and other food products, dominated in the first half of the year as policymakers scrambled to contain the potential social fallout from rising food insecurity. Tajikistan, which imports more than 50% of its food supply enacted a food-security

programme aimed at reducing food shortages and providing food self-sufficiency by 2010. A new legislation and new loan mechanism were introduced by the Government in 2007 and 2008, respectively, to improve the situation in the agricultural sector and make it efficient and profitable. Similarly, in Kyrgyzstan, rising food prices and a shortage of local agricultural products in 2007 and 2008 forced the Government to take urgent steps to increase grain production by raising purchase prices and expanding arable land and yield. Azerbaijan adopted the Reliable Provision of the Population with Foodstuffs programme, to run from 2008 to 2015. The programme – which aims to increase the output of food by domestic producers, reduce the country's food imports and meet its demand for grain, a strategic product for the economy – will allow Azerbaijan to double agricultural output by 2015. It envisages measures to increase investment to the sector and procurement prices for grain and food products, and improve harvesting methods.

By year's end many Governments introduced financial stimulus packages aimed at helping their economies withstand the global financial crisis. Although high commodity prices had brought about significant increases in Government revenues, the worsening economic slowdown compelled many Governments in the subregion to consider the extent to which they had the space to provide full insulation from external shocks.

By way of example, the Government of the Russian Federation has undertaken measures to boost domestic liquidity, repay its external debt, and help the real economy to grow. The Government will continue to implement reforms by lowering the VAT and reducing the tax burden on small businesses. Profit taxes are expected to be cut from 24% to 20% in January 2009 to help businesses withstand the current economic crisis, while unemployment benefits will expand. The Government is also expected to continue to develop sectors of strategic importance, such as oil and gas industries, grain exports, engineering and metals, and banking (table 4.6).

Outlook: Signs of weakening

Overall, expectations of lower export receipts for the subregion reduce the forecast growth in 2009 to 3.6%. Manufacturing exports will continue to remain sluggish due to reduction in international demand. Furthermore, the global liquidity squeeze will continue to pose challenges for the banking sector of the subregion. Some economies of North and Central Asia are at heightened risk of a marked slowdown in 2009 due to decreasing energy prices and exposure to external financing.

Table 4.6. Fiscal stimulus packages in North and Central Asia

	Salient features
Armenia	In December 2008 the parliament of the country approved a package of amendments to the laws regulating taxation. Among them are new mechanisms for calculation of taxes levied from small and medium-sized enterprises, delayed payment of VAT on imports of some types of equipment, and extension of the list of imported capital goods exempted from VAT.
Georgia	Within a tax reform implemented in the country, the Government was expected to reduce personal income tax from 25% to 20% and dividend income tax from 10% to 5% in January 2009.
Kazakhstan	In November 2008 the Government announced a $17 billion action plan for 2009-2010 to stabilize the economy. The plan includes measures for financial sector stabilization, development of the real sector, support for small and medium-sized enterprises, development of the agro-industrial sector, and realization of industrial and infrastructural projects. A new tax code introduced in January 2009 envisaged the increase of the tax burden on companies developing the natural resources sector, with the aim of reducing taxes for companies operating in other sectors, and cut the rate of corporate profit tax.
Kyrgyzstan	A new tax code, introduced in January 2009, reduced the rate of VAT from 20% to 12% and unified taxes for small businesses from 10% to 6%.
Russian Federation	In November 2008 the Government announced a $20 billion package of fiscal stimulus that includes cuts in corporate tax and regional tax by 4 percentage points, and tax on business income from 15% to 5%. The Government will also support the real economy through faster amortization schedules, Government guaranties, restructuring of debts, excise policy and tariffs.
Turkmenistan	In October 2008 the Government announced the establishment of a stabilization fund to protect the country from the global financial crisis. The fund is expected to allocate financial resources for socioeconomic projects and for investment in low-risk assets.

Source: Economist Intelligence Unit, Country Reports (London, EIU, January-February 2009).

Growth in the subregion will depend to a large extent on trends in global commodity prices and levels of growth in the Russian Federation, the largest trading partner and investor for other subregional economies. Domestic demand and increased oil and gas production will enable the Russian Federation to continue its expansion in 2009-2011, but GDP growth rate is expected to slow to 3.5% in 2009, compared with the 5.6% expected in 2008. Inflationary pressures could accelerate from an increase in fiscal expenditure, greater foreign-exchange inflows and domestic demand.

Growth of demand in the Russian Federation is particularly important in supporting economic growth in Kyrgyzstan and Tajikistan. These two economies are expected to develop their energy resources and infrastructure and increase energy self-sufficiency with technical and financial assistance from the Russian Federation. Kyrgyzstan plans to improve its investment climate, reduce inflationary pressure and stabilize prices as a foundation for sustainable development. But the country's GDP growth is expected to slow from 7.6% in 2008 to 4.5% in 2009. Average annual GDP growth in Tajikistan in 2009-2010 is also expected to be lower than in 2008, due to the effects that weakening global growth will have on the country's exports and difficulties in the energy and food sectors. The country will need additional international assist-

ance to solve problems of food supplies, infrastructure repair and capacity-building.

> *Growth in the subregion will depend to a large extent on trends in global commodity prices and levels of growth in the Russian Federation*

Armenia and Uzbekistan have significantly accelerated their economic growth and strengthened their fiscal position over the past five years. GDP is expected to grow 6.5% and 7.0% respectively in 2009. Armenia is expected to improve its business climate by strengthening tax and revenue administration. However, the deterioration in global trade and reduction of domestic demand could have a negative impact on the country's economic prospects in 2009-2010. Benefitting from sound fiscal and monetary policies, Uzbekistan is expected to continue its tax and banking reforms, liberalize its trade and payments systems and adopt a more flexible exchange-rate policy. The country's 2009 budget is expansionary, envisaging a further increase in public-sector wages, benefits, pensions and student grants.

Pacific island developing countries: Global economic slowdown clouds long-term prospects

The global financial crisis indirectly affected economic performance in countries of the Pacific in 2008 as economic growth in their major trading partners slowed. Aggregate GDP growth in the Pacific was still expected to rise from 2.4% recorded in 2007 to 4.8% in 2008 (table 4.7) growing largely due to continued economic expansion in Papua New Guinea as a result of the commodity boom in early 2008. The fall in global commodity prices in late 2008, however, was expected to slow activity in countries with commodity-based economies, such as Papua New Guinea and Solomon Islands. The recession in the United States and New Zealand and the economic slowdown in Australia are expected to lead to a fall in the number of tourists to Fiji, Samoa, Vanuatu, Palau and the Cook Islands. Meanwhile, smaller countries with trust funds were adversely affected by stock market falls. The sharp appreciation of the United States dollar and consequent depreciation of the Australian and New Zealand dollars owing to the financial crises was furthermore expected to affect the terms of trade in many of their economies. In the long term, impacts of climate change and sea level rise, however, continued to be a key concern for countries and territories in the Pacific (box 4.1).

Inflation was a pressing concern in most economies of the Pacific. Since petroleum imports represent a significant part of the import bill, the spikes in fuel prices in early 2008 had an adverse impact, not only on their balance of payments, but also on the Government budgets in countries which provided subsidies on electricity. The ensuing fall in fuel prices therefore was expected to lead to a marked decrease in inflation in 2009.

The financial crisis initially had limited impact on countries in the Pacific since their financial sectors are relatively insulated from global financial markets. The banking system remains small and domestic credit is limited, consisting to a large extent of short-term consumer loans, with heavy reliance on high interest personal loans. In 2008, a number of Governments instituted programmes to encourage commercial banks and Government lending agencies to reduce interest rates on loans and to emphasize lending for business development. If the financial crisis has a prolonged effect on commodity prices, financial institutions in some of these economies may be forced to monitor credit quality more closely. According to the central banks of Fiji, Samoa and Vanuatu, banking

Table 4.7. Rates of economic growth and inflation in selected Pacific island economies, 2007-2009

(Per cent)

	Real GDP growth			Inflation[a]		
	2007	2008[b]	2009[c]	2007	2008[b]	2009[c]
Subregion total[d]	2.4	4.8	4.3	2.7	8.7	5.5
Cook Islands	0.4	..	..	2.4	..	..
Fiji	−6.6	1.2	2.4	4.3	7.5	4.5
Papua New Guinea	6.7	7.3	6.0	0.9	10.6	6.1
Samoa	6.1	3.3	3.0	5.6	6.5	5.2
Solomon Islands	10.3	7.0	4.0	7.7	15.1	9.0
Tonga	−0.3	1.0	1.3	5.1	10.0	5.6
Vanuatu	6.6	5.7	2.9	3.9	4.5	3.6

Sources: ESCAP, based on national sources; IMF, *International Financial Statistics* (CD-ROM) (Washington, D.C., November 2008); and *World Economic Outlook Database* (Washington, D.C., October 2008); and ADB, *Key Indicators for Asia and the Pacific 2008* (Manila, 2008).

[a] Changes in the consumer price index.
[b] Estimate.
[c] Forecast (as of 27 February 2009).
[d] 2008 estimates and 2009 forecasts are available for selected economies.

Box 4.1. Responding to climate change in the Pacific: The Pacific Plan 2005

A steadily warming Earth is predicted to lead to a 40-centimetre rise in the sea level by the end of this century. Significant changes to the Earth's climate and weather patterns are already taking place, and plants and animal life have begun adjusting to the damaging impacts of climate change. Leaders of the Pacific Island Forum, which includes all the independent and self-governing island countries in the Pacific together with Australia and New Zealand have acknowledged the growing threat of climate change to national development and security affecting the social and economic interests of all Forum member countries. They responded by crafting the Pacific Plan, a comprehensive subregional programme, to support national efforts that address the harmful impacts of climate change.

Climate change objectives of the Pacific Plan

• Develop and implement national sustainable development strategies, using appropriate cross-cutting and Pacific relevant indicators;

• Improve natural resources and environmental management by implementing the Pacific Island Energy Policy and associated strategic action plans to provide affordable and environmentally sound energy for the sustainable development of all Pacific island communities;

• Develop adaptation and mitigation proposals linked to the Pacific Climate Change Framework 2006-2015 and the Pacific Disaster Risk Reduction and Disaster Management Framework for Action 2006-2015, including public awareness raising, capacity-building and improving governance, risk and vulnerability assessments and considering measures to address population dislocation;

• Facilitate international finance for sustainable development, biodiversity and environmental protection and climate change in the Pacific, including through the Global Environment Facility.

Pacific Plan performance

The region continues to intensify the implementation of adaptation and mitigation measures to respond to the threats posed by climate change. Supported by the South Pacific Regional Environment Programme, the Pacific Islands Applied Geoscience Commission, ESCAP, United Nations specialized agencies and bilateral sources, efforts continue to focus on both policy and implementation, with a strong emphasis on mainstreaming climate change into national development planning in areas such as disaster risk reduction and management. The second semi-annual report of the Pacific Plan noted in 2008 that:

• Training workshops to mainstream environmental issues, including the integration of climate change into national development planning, were completed in early 2008, and the Council of Regional Organizations in the Pacific is developing a guideline for mainstreaming environmental and climate change issues into national planning in the Pacific;

• National action plans for mainstreaming disaster risk management have been developed for Vanuatu and the Marshall Islands. Also in place are the national adaptation programmes of action for Kiribati, Samoa, Tuvalu and Vanuatu, developed under the Least Developed Country Fund of the Global Environment Facility. The plan for the Solomon Islands, the remaining least developed country in the Pacific, will be completed by 2009, and other Pacific island countries have also requested similar plans;

• Climate change data is collected and analysed through a number of subregional and national projects coordinated by the South Pacific Regional Environment Programme, and a Pacific Climate Change Roundtable will be set up to monitor climate change;

• The Global Environment Fund is offering countries in the Pacific $100 million over the next four years to work on climate change adaptation and mitigation;

• The cumbersome approval process of the Global Environment Fund has been a source of concern to Pacific countries.

supervision has been strengthened and their financial systems remained strong, resilient and adequately capitalized.

Impact: Growth modest in most economies

In Fiji, the economy was projected to grow by 1.2% in 2008 after a 6.6% contraction in 2007 (figure 4.11). The agriculture sector, which typically comprises 15% of total output, declined in 2007 owing to the non-renewal of land leases for sugar cane production and a drop in the price of sugar exported to the European Union. Production of gold, which had ceased in 2007 when the Vatukoula mine was temporarily closed and its ownership transferred, recommenced in 2008, while production of mineral water also increased in 2008. Private sector investment projects and construction also declined sharply in 2007, owing to lower private sector confidence and public sector capital spending. The decline in tourism revenues in 2007 caused a fall in retail and wholesale trade as well as in transport. Although the number of tourists and tourist revenue increased in 2008, heavy discounting was expected to keep industry profits low. While a number of new resorts were expected to open in 2009, the weakening of the Australian, New Zealand and United States economies could place pressure on tourism, which is

Fiji's main source of foreign exchange. Economic growth of 2.4% was expected in 2009.

The public sector continues to dominate the economic base in the countries of Micronesia. The 3.7% growth in Kiribati in 2008, however, resulted in part from a rise in construction and the retail trade. The Government opened the telecommunications sector to private sector investments and promoted investment in fish processing and tourism on Kiritimati. Economic growth in the Marshall Islands, after rising to 2.3% in 2007 due to growth in construction and tourist arrivals, was expected to moderate to 1.2% in 2008 due to rising energy costs and reduced employment at the United States military base in Kwajalein. Unemployment, especially among youth, remains high. The economy of the Federated States of Micronesia was expected to contract by 1.0% in 2008, after a 3.6% contraction in 2007 that was due largely to downsizing of the public sector in Chuuk and Kosrae. Growth of 0.5% was projected in 2009 as commodity prices fall and Compact of Free Association infrastructure grants are disbursed.

The effects of the global financial crisis in Nauru is expected to be minimal, since its financial system remains non-operational due to an extremely high level of domestic and foreign debt arrears. The key challenges are domestic. The closure of an Australian refugee-processing centre in February 2008 led to a further economic contraction in Nauru, which had al-

Figure 4.11. Real GDP growth in selected Pacific island economies, 2006-2008

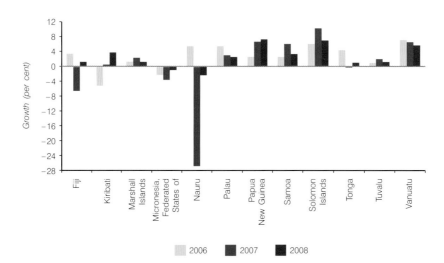

Sources: ESCAP, based on national sources; ADB, *Key Indicators for Asia and the Pacific 2008* (Manila, 2008) and *Asian Development Outlook 2008 Update* (Manila, 2008); IMF, *World Economic Outlook Database* (Washington, D.C., October 2008), *Republic of Marshall Islands: 2008 Article IV Consultation*, Public Information Notice No. 08/69 (Washington, D.C., June 2008), *Federated States of Micronesia: 2008 Article IV Consultation* (Washington, D.C., November 2008) and *Republic of Palau: 2008 Article IV Consultation*, Public Information Notice No. 08/54 (Washington, D.C., May 2008).

Note: Growth rates for 2008 are estimates.

ready started in 2007 as major infrastructure projects were completed, private sector investment slowed and consumer demand weakened. The phosphate industry, which is being rebuilt, will be affected by movements in the phosphate price and the Australian dollar. Economic growth in Palau slowed to 3.0% in 2007, as major infrastructure projects were completed, private-sector investment slowed and consumer demand weakened. Trade, public administration and construction accounted for more than half of Palau's total output in 2007.   Growth was expected to further moderate to 2.5% in 2008 as the global economic downturn was expected to weaken tourism and jeopardize the financing of planned resorts.

The global financial crisis indirectly affected economic performance in countries of the Pacific in 2008

Papua New Guinea's growth rate rose from 6.7% in 2007 to an estimated 7.3% in 2008 as mining expanded and the prices of commodity exports rose, promoting growth in non-mining sectors. Agriculture was expected to grow in 2008 as higher global prices for cocoa and copra raised household incomes. But declining production was expected to lower the contribution from the petroleum sector. The transport sector was expected to grow in 2008 due to the rehabilitation and development of infrastructure while the mining sector fuelled expansion in the building and construction sector. Growth in telecommunications was also expected to exceed projections, as the liberalization of the mobile-phone market led to a substantial increase in the number of subscribers and lower prices for calls in 2008. Liberalization of Papua New Guinea's international air transport market was expected to boost tourism. The tourism industry is constrained, however, by concerns with law and order. The country's economic expansion has been supported in large part by increased Government spending and growth in private sector credit. Although formal private sector employment rose by 8.4% between March 2007 and March 2008, urban unemployment was estimated to remain at around 40%.

Samoa's economy grew by 6.1% in 2007, led by expansion in its agricultural and industrial sectors. Tourism and construction of public sector projects and hotels in preparation for the South Pacific Games in September 2007 boosted growth in the services sector, which accounted for three fifths of total output. Economic growth was expected to slow to 3.3% in 2008, with the slowdown in construction after the Games. The courts and administration complex and a proposed Government complex and convention centre are the only current major construction works. Liberalization of the telecommunications sector was expected to boost growth in the services sector in 2008. A high level of migration and consequent high levels of remittances, allows Samoa to maintain high income growth in per capita terms. Although the labour force increased slightly, the number of employed Samoans as well as the unemployment rate remained unchanged. Given the global economic slowdown, tourist arrivals in 2009 are expected to be lower than forecast, and expansion of tourism-based investment was expected to slow.

Despite falling from 10.3% in 2007 to 7.0% in 2008, the rate of economic growth in the Solomon Islands was the highest among countries in the Pacific. Despite such growth, per capita income in the Solomon Islands remains among the lowest in the Pacific. The earthquake that hit the country in April 2007 had a negligible impact on economic growth, given the dependence on subsistence in large parts of the economy. Two major sources of economic growth are timber exports and tourism. Timber exports accounted for two thirds of total exports in 2007. Because current logging rates are estimated to be five times the sustainable rate, exports could start to decline by 2010. Reliance on this sector therefore presents a risk for the Solomon Islands. The tourism sector grew by nearly 50% between 2003 and 2008 due to recovery from earlier civil unrest and increased political stability. Relaxation of Government controls on international air transport was expected to promote further growth in the services sector. Improved infrastructure and deregulation of island shipping, domestic air services and telecommunications could further ensure development of tourism as well as other sectors of the economy.

The economic contraction in Tonga of 0.3% in 2007 was less than anticipated, despite the slowdown in industry, commerce and tourism. The economy was expected to grow by 1.0% in 2008, as reconstruction of the central business district of Nuku'alofa supports economic recovery. Tourism receipts rose by more than 70% in 2008, while tourist arrivals rose by more than a quarter to an estimated 67,000 visitors, primarily from New Zealand, Australia and the United States, as arrivals by cruise ships increased by two thirds over the figure for 2007. Although the economy was expected to continue growing slowly in the medium term, the expected slowdown in remittances and tourism could adversely affect its prospects. Reconstruction of Nuku'alofa, coupled with construction of a hotel in Vava'u, was expected to boost the construction sector in 2009.

Although growth in Vanuatu slowed from 6.6% in 2007 to 5.7% in 2008, it remained significantly higher than initially expected due to growth in the services sector, which accounts for more than three quarters of GDP. Increased international air services to Australia and New Zealand boosted growth in construction and tourism. The liberalization of the telecommunications sector was expected to further strengthen service sector growth. Economic growth was expected to decline in 2009 as the economic slowdown in Australia and New Zealand and appreciation in the real effective exchange rate affect the tourism sector, which accounts for one third of GDP, and reduce FDI. The number of non-resident visitors to Vanuatu also declined in the second half of 2008, owing to a drop in cruise-ship arrivals. The strong economic growth of recent years, however, provides a cushion against a slowdown. The recent election and formation of a new Government was expected to resolve political uncertainty and promote business and consumer confidence.

Inflation: Pressure from high oil and food prices

Inflation in Fiji rose from 4.3% in 2007 to 7.5% in 2008 as higher import prices imports raised food prices (figure 4.12). Inflation spiked from 5.9% in June 2008, to a 20-year high of 9.8% in September before falling to 8.5% in October. The fall in fuel prices and subsequent decline in transport costs in late 2008 was

expected to moderate price increases for the year. Inflation was projected to fall in 2009 as a result of dropping oil and commodity prices and lower imported inflation. In view of the economic recession worldwide, the inflation rate could fall more quickly than projected, depending on Fiji's exchange rate movements against those of its trading partners. In an effort to keep import prices down, commercial banks have entered into forward foreign exchange contracts with importers of food staples to hedge against price increases.

Inflation was a pressing concern in most economies of the Pacific

---

Higher food and transport costs applied considerable pressure on inflation throughout Micronesia. The Marshall Islands declared a state of economic emergency from 3 July to 1 August 2008 as inflation peaked. The use of the United States dollar in the Marshall Islands and the Federated States of Micronesia provides an anchor for inflationary expectations and a relatively stable real effective exchange rate. Although inflation in Palau declined in the second half of 2008, it remained somewhat higher than in the United States, whose currency Palau uses as legal tender.

Figure 4.12. Inflation in selected Pacific island economies, 2006-2008

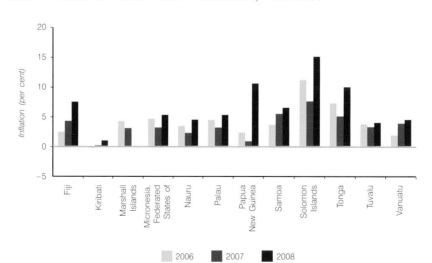

Sources: ESCAP, based on national sources; ADB, *Key Indicators for Asia and the Pacific 2008* (Manila, 2008) and *Asian Development Outlook 2008 Update* (Manila, 2008); and IMF, *World Economic Outlook Database* (Washington, D.C., October 2008).

Note: Figures for 2008 are estimates.

Because of an increase in money supply, private sector growth and a fiscal stimulus, inflation for 2008 in Papua New Guinea was revised upward to 10.6% from an earlier target of 5.2%. The increases in international food and oil prices and the depreciation of the kina against its trading partners' currencies further contributed to higher imported inflation. Although inflation was projected to fall to 6.1% in 2009, large development expenditures and construction of the Government's liquefied natural gas project could apply considerable pressure on domestic prices.

Inflation in the Solomon Islands was expected to rise from 7.7% in 2007 to more than 15% in 2008 as a result of increases in fuel and food prices, growth in private sector credit and expansionary fiscal policy. Inflation was expected to moderate towards the end of 2008 with the stabilization of commodity prices and the tightening of monetary policy.

Inflation in Samoa stood at 6.5% in June 2008 and was projected to remain above the target rate of 3.0% owing to higher food and petroleum prices and an expansionary budget. Growth in inflation in household categories reflects the impact of high oil prices on consumption of household electricity.

High fuel and food prices and dependence on imports raised inflation in Tonga from 5.1% in 2007 to 10% in 2008. Although consumption stimulated by remittances and credit contributed to pricing pressures, inflation was expected to fall in the medium term.

Despite higher civil service wages, a rise in the costs of food and transport and the strengthening of the Australian dollar during the first half of 2008, the Reserve Bank of Vanuatu managed to keep inflation relatively steady at 4.5% in 2008. As a result, inflation remains relatively low compared to other countries in the Pacific.

External sector: Current account deficits widen due to trade deficits

In 2007, exports from Fiji rose slightly while imports declined dramatically. Although exports increased significantly during the first eight months of 2008, a significantly wider trade deficit was expected as imports of intermediate and consumption goods rose. Sugar exports to the European Union have declined in recent years. Given the fall in sugar production, Fiji has had to import sugar to satisfy domestic consumption so that it would be able to meet the European Union sugar export quota in 2008. Exports of mineral water and gold were projected to rise sharply during the year. Tariffs were raised on selected items in 2008 to raise Government revenues and protect local manufacturers. The United States accounted for more than one sixth of Fiji's exports, followed by the United Kingdom and Australia. Imports of petroleum products accounted for nearly one third of imports, followed by imports of consumer goods from Australia and New Zealand.

Fiji's current account deficit declined sharply in 2007 due to the economic slowdown and implementation of exchange controls to protect foreign reserves (table 4.8). Remittances, the largest source of foreign exchange after tourism, have steadily declined over the past two years because fewer Fijians work in security in the Middle East and the United States dollar has lost value relative to the Fiji dollar. Although direct capital investment was expected to be stable in 2008, the global recession is expected to weaken the investment climate in 2009. To encourage investment, Fiji announced incentives, including tax holidays and tax-free zones, in its Government budget.

International reserves in Fiji, equivalent to 4.4 months of imports of goods and services in 2007, were projected to decline to the equivalent of 3.2 months of imports in 2008. Strict exchange controls, a tightening

Table 4.8. Current account balance in selected Pacific island economies, 2005-2008

(Percentage of GDP)

	2005	2006	2007	2008
Fiji	−14.0	−22.6	−15.5	−21.3
Papua New Guinea	4.2	2.9	4.3	3.3
Samoa	−6.6	−10.8	−4.6	−7.8
Solomon Islands	−9.8	−5.6	−2.8	−6.8
Tonga	−2.6	−9.7	−10.4	−10.4
Vanuatu	−7.4	−5.7	−9.9	−11.4

Source: IMF, *World Economic Outlook Database* (Washington, D.C., October 2008).

Note: Figures for 2008 are estimates.

of monetary policy settings and cuts to Government expenditure have kept international reserves within the target range of three to four months of imports. Its international reserves could be exposed, however, given the impact of the financial crisis on its trading partners, a weak outlook for the sugar industry, loss of garment exports and the need to repay in 2011 an offshore bond equivalent to one month's worth of exports.

Although Kiribati's current account deficit equalled 31.1% of GDP in 2007, with revenue from fisheries fluctuating in recent years, the weakening of the Australian dollar against the United States dollar has strengthened earnings. The disbursement of grants, primarily through the Compact of Free Association with the United States, has enabled the Marshall Islands to maintain its balance of payments, while external stability is likewise is not an issue in the Federated States of Micronesia, since external debt remains about 30% of GDP and the country has access to Compact funding. Australia was also expected to sustain high levels of official assistance to Nauru.

A trade surplus was expected in 2008 in Papua New Guinea, where mineral exports comprise more than four fifths of its exports. Australia accounted for two fifths of Papua New Guinea's exports in 2007, followed by Japan, Germany and the Philippines. Exports to China rose in the first half of 2008. This was due to China's increase in demand for raw materials and its strategy of diversifying its sources. Australia also accounted for four fifths of Papua New Guinea's total imports, followed by the United States, Singapore and Japan. Since the kina closely follows the United States dollar, the appreciation of the real exchange rate in late 2008 could reduce Papua New Guinea's international competitiveness and lower its exports. At the same time, the strength of the kina was expected to reduce the costs of imports from Australia as well as inflationary pressures. International reserves, equivalent to 4.7 months worth of imported goods and services at the end of 2007, were projected to rise to the equivalent of 5.2 months of imports by the end of 2008.

Exports from Samoa declined by 19.3% in the first quarter 2008 over the corresponding period a year earlier, led by a significant fall in fish exports. Australia and American Samoa together accounted for three quarters of Samoa's total exports in 2008. Due to increased economic activity and a rise in public sector wages, imports – primarily petroleum and food products from New Zealand, Fiji and Singapore – increased rapidly. In the first quarter of 2008, petroleum imports rose by more than 50% over the corresponding period in 2007. The trade deficit was expected to

widen in 2008. Remittances from Samoans working overseas accounted for more than one fifth of GDP in 2006 and 2007. In the first quarter of 2008, remittances increased by 5.3% over the corresponding period in 2007, largely from overseas workers in the United States. The global economic slowdown, however, could lead to a decline in remittances. International reserves increased from the equivalent of 4.7 months import coverage in June 2007 to 5.2 months import coverage in June 2008, along with a tightening of fiscal and monetary policies.

Effective macroeconomic policies at the disposal of small, open economies in the Pacific are generally limited

Exports from the Solomon Islands continued to rise in 2008. Timber accounted for two thirds of total exports in 2007; this indicates that the Solomon Islands needs greater diversification of exports. After delays owing to land ownership issues, gold production was expected to commence in the next two or three years. Asia accounted for more than four fifths of Solomon Islands' exports. Costs of imports, primarily from Australia and Singapore, continued to rise owing to high fuel prices and growth in domestic demand. The trade deficit was expected to decline to 22.6% of GDP in 2008. International reserves, equivalent to 3.9 months of imports in 2007, was projected to rise to the equivalent of 4.1 months of import cover in 2008 due to receipts from log exports, aid inflows and FDI to the mining sector. Rising import costs due to high fuel prices and sharp credit growth, however, could lower the country's international reserves below projected figures.

Tonga's trade deficit widened in 2008 due to a decline in exports and a growth in imports caused by an increase in remittances and business and household credit. Japan accounted for more than half of the country's exports, followed by the United States and New Zealand. Exports declined due to lower production of root crops, bananas, watermelons and squash. Although fish exports, which had been doing poorly for several years, recovered in 2007, they were expected to fall in 2008. Depletion of fish stocks, harsh weather, shortage of cargo space in airlines and lack of credit for fishermen led to the fall in agriculture and fisheries production. Large inflows of remittances sustain the economy, since more Tongans now live abroad than in Tonga, and their number is increasing. Private transfer receipts rose by 15% annually between

2000 and 2005, and net remittances accounted for 45% of GDP in 2005. A law passed in August 2007 allowing Tongans who have emigrated to retain their Tongan citizenship after becoming citizens of other countries could encourage closer ties between Tongans living abroad and those in their home country. Although foreign exchange regulations were tightened in 2006, international reserves declined from the equivalent of 4.4 months of imports at the end of 2007 to 3.6 months at the end of 2008. Reserves were expected to decline further in the medium term as imports continue to grow more than exports.

In 2008, Vanuatu's exports were expected to continue growing and its imports to slow. Copra, kava and coconut oil accounted for half of the country's merchandise exports. These products, along with beef, cocoa and timber, were exported to the European Union, which accounts for nearly one quarter of Vanuatu's total exports, as well as to New Caledonia and Japan. Nearly one third of Vanuatu's imports came from Australia, followed by New Zealand, Japan and Fiji. The current account deficit remained stable in 2007 and 2008, while the balance of payments deficit rose from 1.2% of GDP in 2007 to an estimated 1.3% of GDP in 2008. Non-debt capital inflows continue to finance the current account deficit. Official international reserves were expected to remain stable at around 8.4 months of merchandise imports at the end of 2008.

Policy responses: Providing macroeconomic stability

Effective macroeconomic policies at the disposal of small, open economies in the Pacific are generally limited. Given the size of their economies, only Fiji, Papua New Guinea, and, to a lesser extent, Samoa, the Solomon Islands, Tonga and Vanuatu are able to implement independent fiscal and monetary policies. Since the Marshall Islands, Federated States of Micronesia and Palau use the United States dollar and Kiribati, Nauru and Tuvalu use the Australian dollar as legal tender, they effectively do not have an independent monetary or exchange rate policy. These countries acutely feel changes in international prices of commodities, since all adjustments to exogenous shocks must be borne by the real sector. Yet such countries, which have only fiscal policies at their disposal, are often highly dependent on aid or revenue from their respective Trust Funds to finance Government expenditures, including fiscal stimulus. As a result, stimulus packages have yet to be launched in countries of the Pacific. American Samoa, Guam and the Northern Mariana Islands, however, benefited from the economic stimulus package of the United States, as indicated in table 4.9.

Table 4.9. Fiscal stimulus package in selected Pacific island economies

	Salient features
Northern Mariana Islands	The $96 million earmarked for the Northern Mariana Islands in the $787 billion economic stimulus package of the United States signed in February 2009 will be spent to improve schools, roads, water systems and infrastructure as well as to create jobs and provide food assistance for low income families.
American Samoa, Guam and Northern Mariana Islands	Tax authorities in American Samoa, Guam and the Northern Mariana Islands issued economic stimulus payments to eligible residents in line with the United States Economic Stimulus Act of 2008.

In Fiji, the Government removed customs duties and VAT on several basic food items, increased the income tax threshold and provided subsidies to bus operators. It also instituted a significant increase in Government spending on education now accounting for one sixth of total current spending, followed by spending on public order, safety and defence, and economic affairs. An increase in expenditure for improving public infrastructure and a reduction in the company tax were expected in 2009, to counteract downward pressures on growth from the financial crisis.

In Kiribati, the market value of the Revenue Equalization Reserve Fund, the country's principal source of budget financing, declined by 20% in 2008 as withdrawals were necessary to cover the country's budget deficit. High fuel prices significantly increased the debt of the electricity utility. Reform of public enterprises might balance the budget and support private sector growth in Kiribati.

An increase in capital funds from the Compact Agreement with the United States reduced the Government deficit in the Marshall Islands to the equivalent of 0.5% of GDP in 2007. Although the country has met its mandatory contributions to the Compact Trust Fund, its gross public and publicly guaranteed external debt equalled 70% of GDP in 2006. The Marshall Islands plans to maintain a fiscal surplus equal to 3% of GDP in the medium term, build reserves in the Compact Trust Fund and prepare for the elimination of Compact grants after 2023.

The Federated States of Micronesia also implemented measures to privatize or shut down loss-making public enterprises and improve the business environment by strengthening the enforcement of contracts in courts, expanding land titling, and liberalizing the investment regime. However, falling global equity prices have reduced the value of the Compact Trust Fund and State investments of the country. The Federated States of Micronesia Development Bank also needs to better support new businesses and improve the functioning of the secured transaction law in order for banks to expand their lending.

In light of dwindling Government revenues in Palau, strengthening of tax administration through the removal of exemptions and a comprehensive overhaul of the tax system was considered. Despite returns on the Compact Trust Fund that are in line with its benchmark, net financial assets remain stagnant due to deficit financing. A sizeable fiscal adjustment would be required even if Compact grants, now scheduled for cessation in 2009, are renewed. Commercialization and privatization of public utilities could strengthen public finances. Although land titling measures have been undertaken, issues of contract enforcement and foreign investment have not been addressed. Amendments to the Financial Institutions Act in February 2008 provided for more-effective bank supervision by allowing the Financial Institutions Commission to issue prudential regulations without legislative approval, require banks to have an annual audit, and grant staff of the Commission legal immunity in carrying out official acts. Although deposits have partly recovered in 2008, credit growth has virtually halted as banks have become more cautious in extending credit and households are highly leveraged.

In Papua New Guinea, high commodity prices and stronger economic growth accounted for total Government revenue, including grants, estimated at one third of the country's GDP. Tax revenue, which accounted for approximately four fifths of estimated revenue in 2008, was expected to rise. More than a third of Government expenditure for 2009 has been allocated to the development budget, with increases in funding for health, education, and roads and road maintenance. Revenue transfers to provincial governments increased by 40% to reach more than 4% of GDP. A key challenge is that such transfers would require a greater ability by the Government to manage large, but temporary, fiscal surpluses while maintaining low inflation. Higher revenues also enabled the Government to reduce taxes on petroleum in 2008 in response to high petroleum prices, which, coupled with high food prices, had a negative impact on both rural and urban households. However, as the global economic slowdown deepens, it may require rationalization of Government initiatives financed by revenue from the commodities boom and careful prioritization of public expenditures. Although Papua New Guinea has direct access to international credit markets, the global credit crunch has raised the cost of borrowing and reduced its financing options for projects in the mining and petroleum sectors. The fall in world commodity prices may compound the country's difficulties in raising financing, since many commodity-based projects may appear less profitable. Lending to the private sector for real estate and construction rose significantly during the first half of 2008 due to strong domestic demand.

Macroeconomic stability requires close coordination of monetary and fiscal policies

---

After several years of surpluses, the Solomon Islands experienced a fiscal deficit in 2007. To improve tax administration and widen the tax base, the reference price of logs was revised to reflect international market prices and ad hoc tax exemptions were narrowed. In addition, the Government considered rationalizing civil service employment, containing the Government wage bill and improving efficiency of State-owned enterprises. Strengthened expenditure-control procedures could also keep spending within budgeted levels and foster budgetary transparency and accountability. Given the expansionary fiscal policies in 2008, the Government recognized the need to control inflation through the tightening of monetary policies. The financial sector in the Solomon Islands has not yet been affected by the global economic slowdown and remains liquid and well capitalized. With the expansion of business lending in recent years, the central bank was expected to monitor developments closely to ensure the soundness of bank assets.

Spending on education increased significantly in 2008 in Samoa, which together with general public services amounts to half of Samoa's Government spending. Parliament recently approved a switch in driving from the current left-hand side of the road to the right-hand side. Importation of left-hand drive vehicles has ceased, and the actual switch will be made in September 2009.

Recurrent revenue in Tonga was expected to increase in 2008, owing partly to a rise in sales and consumption taxes. The largest public expenditures are in education, health and public safety and order. Although expenditure on education has been steady, spending on health and law and order has declined. Tuvalu is dependent on earnings from the Tuvalu Trust Fund, which fell in value in 2008, to finance its budget deficit. New Zealand and Australia agreed to provide funding to the Consolidated Investment Fund, which holds distributions from the Tuvalu Trust Fund until they are drawn down into the Government budget, in response to requests from Tuvalu for assistance to address the expected budget deficit arising from the effects of higher fuel prices and the expected loss of income from the Tuvalu Trust Fund.

Macroeconomic stability in Vanuatu requires close co-ordination of monetary and fiscal policy because its pegged exchange rate limits the effectiveness of monetary policy and places the burden of adjustment on fiscal policy. More than two thirds of Government revenue and grants were derived from tax revenue, namely, import duties and VAT receipts. Grants were expected to decline in the medium term as funds from the Millennium Challenge Account funds are expended. Reduction of Government wage costs through civil service reforms and restructuring of public enterprises could limit pressure on prices and allow an increase in development spending over the medium term. A broadly balanced budget was expected in 2008, following a fiscal deficit equivalent to 0.3% of GDP the previous year. To further promote investment, the Government recognized that land registration and titling needs to be strengthened, operations of public-sector enterprises improved and infrastructural bottlenecks eliminated through greater private sector involvement. Money supply increased in the first half of 2008 due to growth in savings and time deposits by residents in foreign currency. As the tourism, transport, manufacturing and construction sectors raised demand for private sector credit, commercial bank loans almost doubled between 2006 and the first half of 2008. Improved financial sector supervision was expected to minimize risks to the financial system.

Outlook: Slowdown with long term threats looming large

Overall economic growth in the Pacific was forecast to fall from 4.8 % in 2008 to 4.3 % in 2009 as the global economic downturn exerts downward pressure on economic growth. The decline in commodity prices was expected to lower growth in Papua New Guinea while lower tourism receipts affects growth in Samoa and Vanuatu. Since food and fuel comprise a significant proportion of imports in most countries of the Pacific, lower commodity prices could significantly ease pressure on inflation as well as balance of payments. Inflation in the Pacific as a whole was forecast to fall from 8.7 % in 2008 to 5.5 % in 2009.

With the exception of Papua New Guinea, countries in the Pacific are small islands, with population of less than one million and scattered across vast expanses of ocean. As a result of their small domestic markets, these countries have generally not benefited from economies of scale. Distance from major economic centres in Asia and the Pacific has also adversely affected their integration into the regional economy. Since their economies are small and narrowly-based on a few sectors and trading partners, their domestic growth is vulnerable to exogenous factors affecting both supply and demand. The public sector accounts for a large share of employment and overall labour productivity is low. These challenges, coupled with the impacts of climate change and sea level, present greater long-term challenges for these countries.

South and South-West Asia: Downward pressures but steadfast resilience

Economic growth in South and South-West Asia remained strong in 2008 at 5.9% despite some deceleration (table 4.10). Growth was bolstered by relatively high dependence on domestic demand which was less affected by declining external demand amid the economic downturn. India, which had been growing at 9% or more over the past three years, is estimated to grow at 7.1% in 2008, thus providing an anchor of economic stability in the subregion. Bangladesh, Pakistan and Sri Lanka all achieved GDP growth of about 6%, while political stability in Nepal contributed to GDP growth in 2008 of 5.6% – much higher than that of previous years. The economy of the Islamic Republic of Iran, the only net exporter of oil in the subregion, was expected to maintain robust growth, at 6.5% for 2008.

Of more concern was inflation. In comparison to other subregions, inflation was highest in this subregion, on average, driven up by unrelenting pressures from higher international commodity prices, particularly oil, basic metals and particularly sharp rises in the price of food. Food inflation in Pakistan, which was 17.6% in 2008, was much higher than the overall inflation of 12%. As a result, life became more challenging for large segments of the population. The incidence of poverty is still quite high in most countries of the subregion, and persistent high prices for food and

other consumer goods will reverse the recent gains in poverty reduction.

The incidence of poverty is still quite high

In 2008, the fiscal situation deteriorated in most countries in South and South-West Asia. While Government revenues increased in most countries, the increase in expenditures was much larger, mainly for subsidies on fuel oil, food and other commodities. The surge in oil and commodities prices also wreaked havoc on the external balances of some countries, but this was mitigated by the remittances from a large workforce employed in other countries. Workers' remittances are substantial and have been rising in recent years, which thus helped to improve not only the balance of payments position but also contributed to strong growth in several countries of the subregion.

In comparison to other subregions, the impact of the global economic crisis is expected to be medium,

Table 4.10. Rates of economic growth and inflation, South and South-West Asian economies, 2007-2009

(Per cent)

	Real GDP growth			Inflation[a]		
	2007	2008[b]	2009[c]	2007	2008[b]	2009[c]
Subregion total[d]	7.5	5.9	4.3	8.5	11.6	9.6
Bangladesh	6.4	6.2	5.5	7.2	9.9	7.5
Bhutan	21.4	5.0	6.2	5.2	9.0	..
India	9.0	7.1	6.0	6.2	9.0	7.5
Iran (Islamic Republic of)	6.8	6.5	5.0	18.4	25.0	18.0
Maldives	7.2	5.7	4.5	7.4	12.0	..
Nepal	2.6	5.6	5.5	6.4	7.7	7.0
Pakistan	6.8	5.8	2.5	7.8	12.0	20.0
Sri Lanka	6.8	6.0	5.5	15.8	22.6	13.0
Turkey	4.5	2.4	−0.1	8.8	10.4	6.8

Sources: ESCAP, based on national sources; and ESCAP estimates.

[a] Changes in the consumer price index.
[b] Estimate.
[c] Forecast (as of 27 February 2009).
[d] The estimates and forecasts for countries relate to fiscal years defined as follows: fiscal year 2007/08 = 2007 for India and the Islamic Republic of Iran and fiscal year 2006/07 = 2007 for Bangladesh, Nepal and Pakistan.

somewhere between the level of impact felt by more open economies of East and South-East Asia, and that experienced by the geographically isolated Pacific island economies. While financial institutions in the countries of the subregion had little financial exposure to United States securitized assets, the global financial crisis has had its effects, as discussed in chapter 1, particularly with money markets experiencing an unusual tightening of liquidity. A number of countries of the subregion have been experiencing sharp declines in foreign exchange reserves, partly due to outflows of foreign capital. Those particularly affected were India, where during the first two weeks of October 2008 foreign exchange reserves fell by more than $17 billion, and Pakistan, where foreign exchange reserves, which stood at $16.5 billion in October 2007, were down to about $7 billion a year later. Sri Lanka also witnessed a decrease in its reserves towards the latter part of 2008. Both India and Pakistan witnessed a decrease of over 20% in the value of their currencies against the United States dollar during 2008.

Lack of physical infrastructure is a major impediment to business growth in South Asia, most notably shortcomings in electricity service. For example, firms in Bangladesh experience power outages and surges 250 days a year; in Nepal it happens almost every day (World Bank, 2006). About 40% of firms in Bangladesh, India, Maldives, Pakistan and Sri Lanka have their own generators, which add to their cost of production.

Among long-term challenges, poverty remains a major problem for most countries in the subregion, and economic and social inequalities remain widespread. The main challenge is not only to achieve higher growth rates, but to make growth more inclusive. Box 4.2 reviews some inequalities in countries of the subregion and suggests some policy options for a more inclusive growth.

Box 4.2. Inclusive growth to tackle widespread poverty and inequalities in South Asia

Widespread poverty continues to be a major problem in countries of South Asia. Based on a poverty line of one dollar a day per capita, approximately 950 million people living in Asia and the Pacific are considered poor (ESCAP, 2009, forthcoming). A large number of these poor were housed in South Asia. While individual countries show a decline in poverty over time, there is some evidence of an increase in income inequality (measured by the Gini coefficient) over the same period (see figure). Although strict comparisons between countries are not possible due to differences in available data, there are clear linkages between GDP growth rate and poverty reduction. Interestingly, reduction in poverty was achieved despite some worsening in the evenness of distribution. The impact of GDP growth on poverty reduction would have been much higher had income distribution remained unchanged or improved.

Despite rapid urbanization, more than two thirds of the population in many countries of South Asia still live in rural areas. And the incidence of poverty is much higher in rural than in urban areas for all the countries. In Nepal, 35% of the rural population was estimated to be below the national poverty line in 2004, against 10% of the urban population. In India, the ICT boom helped the urban economy, but large parts of the rural economy have been left untouched. Moreover, in most countries there has been a faster reduction in poverty in urban areas, widening the disparities between rural and urban regions. In addition to the rural-urban divide, development is progressing at varying speeds in different regions within countries. India's rapidly growing states in the south and west are well ahead of those in the north and north-east. In Pakistan, Balochistan and the North-West Frontier Province are lagging behind Punjab and Sind. Similar trends are visible in other countries.

In South Asia, widespread social inequalities are a serious problem. South Asia fares little better than sub-Saharan Africa in key social indicators such as education, health and gender equality. South Asian women are among the least likely in the world to have a skilled birth attendant at delivery. In India alone, 14.4 million births per year are not attended by a skilled provider (UNICEF, 2008, p. 21). South Asia also has some of the highest levels of maternal undernutrition in the world, which increases the risk of maternal death. Gender-based discrimination, prevalent in the legal, economic, political and social spheres, affects roughly half of the population. Girls are too often denied an education so their brothers can be educated. Husbands or mothers-in-law often decide whether pregnant women need emergency health care, even when there are complications during labour. And South Asia has both the lowest literacy rates and the largest gap between the rates of male and female literacy.

(Continued on next page)

Box 4.2 *(continued)*

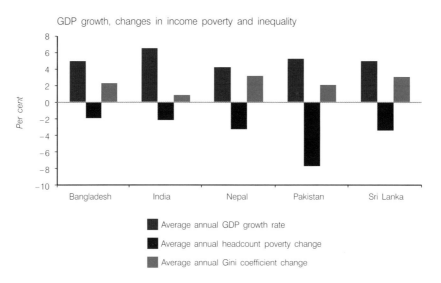

GDP growth, changes in income poverty and inequality

- ■ Average annual GDP growth rate
- ■ Average annual headcount poverty change
- ■ Average annual Gini coefficient change

Sources: National sources and World Bank, PovcalNet, available at http://go.wordbank.org/NT2A1XUWP0.

Notes: Time period covered for Bangladesh is 1992-2000; for India 1994-2005; for Nepal 1996-2004; for Pakistan 2001-2005; and for Sri Lanka, 1996-2007. Headcount poverty estimates are based on national poverty lines and are not comparable across countries.

The main challenge for countries in the subregion, therefore, is not only to improve growth rates on a sustained basis but also to make them more inclusive for a rapid reduction in poverty and inequality. The composition of sectoral growth has important implications for pro-poor growth. Agriculture, construction and small and medium-sized enterprises (SMEs) generate pro-poor growth through employment, and should be supported. Agriculture utilizes substantial labour and takes place in rural areas, where many of the poor live. The experience with agricultural growth suggests a strong correlation with investment in rural infrastructure: irrigation networks, farm-to-market roads and rural electrification. The construction sector is also labour intensive and can absorb a large portion of unskilled labour. Similarly, SMEs provide employment in largely labour-intensive, low-skill activities and are considered to have great growth potential.

To benefit from abundant employment, the development of human resources is essential. In turn, education and health services are key to the development of human resources. Although there have been major advances in extending primary education, the slow progress in reducing the gender divide in secondary education in South Asia remains a matter of great concern. At the national level, secondary schooling should be emphasized and should impart vocational skills for the evolving globalized workplace, which would narrow the income gap between skilled and less-skilled workers. It is particularly important to provide equal access to secondary schooling for girls. Public provision of education and health services is crucial to the poor, as they cannot afford to pay the prices charged by private providers. Print and public media should be used extensively to change people's attitude towards girls' education and other forms of social exclusions and to ensure that the poorest of the poor have access to information on available opportunities.

Social safety nets are also essential for the poor and vulnerable, who are unable to benefit from economic growth directly or indirectly. This support should be strengthened to provide a coping mechanism for the poor, especially in the event of macroeconomic shocks such as the current economic crisis. Without such interventions to address the problem of poverty and inequality, rapid economic growth cannot be sustained over the long term, for there are clear links between inequality and social unrest and violence.

Impact: Moderating but robust growth

Economic growth in South and South-West Asia remained robust in 2008, even though most countries in the subregion experienced some deceleration (figure 4.13).

The economy of India performed relatively well during 2005-2007 by maintaining its growth momentum of previous years along with moderate inflation, resilient capital markets, a manageable current account deficit and favourable foreign exchange reserves. From 2005 to 2007, India achieved an average growth rate of 9.4%, aided by strong performances by industry and services. An investment boom, growth in consumer demand, rising incomes, ample bank credit and robust exports sustained the vibrancy in industry and services. India's economy also benefited from significant inflows of foreign investment and the Government's efforts to contain the fiscal deficit while at the same time stepping up public expenditure for employment generation programmes. Despite the adverse impact of the global recession and high food and energy

prices at home, the Indian economy is estimated to grow at 7.1% in 2008.

Pakistan's economy suffered from political instability, law and order problems, supply shocks, a softening of external demand, turmoil in international financial markets and high prices for oil, food and other commodities. GDP growth slowed to 5.8% in 2008, down from 6.8% in the previous year. The performance of the agriculture sector was dismal, with 1.5% growth compared with 3.7% in 2007. Manufacturing registered modest growth of 5.4% against 8.2% in the previous year. GDP growth in 2008 was principally driven by the services sector, which posted a growth of 8.2% against 7.6% in 2007. On the demand side, economic growth was driven entirely by consumption, especially private consumption. The contribution of investment declined, and net exports remained a drag.

An estimated 2008 GDP growth of 6% in Sri Lanka is encouraging, given the global recession, high and volatile oil prices, sharp increases in food prices and a tight anti-inflationary monetary policy. A significant improvement in the performance of the agriculture sector helped to check an even sharper deceleration in growth from 6.8% in 2007 and a 28-year high of 7.7% in 2006.

Figure 4.13. Economic growth rates and sectoral contributions in selected South and South-West Asian economies, 2007-2008

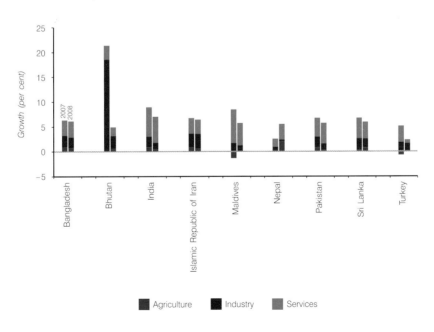

Agriculture   Industry   Services

Sources: ESCAP calculations based on national sources; and ESCAP estimates.

Notes: Figures for 2008 are estimates. GDP growth rates of India, Islamic Republic of Iran and Pakistan refer to real GDP at factor cost.

In the Islamic Republic of Iran, real GDP expanded by 6.8% in 2007, supported by sustained growth in domestic demand. The non-oil sector, driven by strong performance in the manufacturing and service sectors, grew by 7.6%, continuing a streak of high growth since 2006. There was only moderate growth in the oil sector, which was constrained by insufficient foreign investment. Supported by high oil prices during a large part of the year, GDP growth was expected to remain about 6.5% in 2008. Higher oil earnings allowed the Government to continue with its expansionary fiscal policy, which in turn contributed to a high level of private consumption and investment.

Turkey's GDP growth slowed to 4.5% in 2007, down from 6.9% in 2006. Poor weather conditions adversely affected agricultural production, and a strong domestic currency led to deterioration in net exports. Economic growth further moderated to 2.4% in 2008, reflecting higher food and energy prices and difficult external conditions. Turkish banks borrow substantially abroad to finance lending domestically, so the global credit squeeze is having an adverse impact on the Turkish economy.

Bangladesh, one of the least developed countries of the subregion, achieved a robust growth of 6.2% in 2008, down only slightly from 6.4% in 2007, despite back-to-back floods and a devastating cyclone. The Government was able to implement effective rehabilitation programmes and timely policy interventions. The economy recorded 3.6% growth in agriculture in 2008, 6.9% in industry and 6.7% in the services sector. The growth of agriculture was nearly one percentage point lower than the previous year, as almost every subsector in agriculture was affected by natural disaster. The slowed growth in the industrial sector was due to a decline in its two major subsectors, manufacturing and construction. Manufacturing suffered from a loss of business confidence and labour unrest in the export-oriented garment sector. Slower growth in the construction sector growth in 2008 resulted from less private construction because of higher prices of raw materials and a slowdown of public sector construction. The pace of growth in the services sector declined only marginally.

Nepal's GDP grew at 5.6% in 2008, compared with 2.6% in 2007. Despite a weak performance in merchandise exports and manufacturing, the growth was supported by a satisfactory expansion in agriculture, an encouraging increase in tourism and some improvements in services. The agriculture sector expanded by 5.7% as favourable weather conditions led to a strong harvest of key food crops, especially rice. The performance of the manufacturing sector remained dismal at 0.2% as frequent strikes, labour disputes and power shortages continued to curtail

production. Overseas workers' remittances have been growing, and continue to play a major role in the growth of the economy by stimulating domestic consumption.

In Bhutan, completion of the Tala hydropower project in March 2007 provided a boost to economic growth, exports and Government revenues. GDP growth, which peaked at 21.4% in 2007, returned to a more normal level of 5% in 2008. Work on three more hydropower projects will support economic growth in coming years. The tourism industry is also expected to do well.

The Maldives economy contracted in 2005 following the tsunami in December 2004, but it bounced back sharply in 2006 with GDP growth of 18%. Growth in subsequent years was relatively stable and more typical of the pre-tsunami years. GDP expanded by 7.6% in 2007, supported by growth in tourism and construction. Growth moderated in 2008 at an estimated 5.7%, driven again by tourism and construction.

Security in Afghanistan continues to be precarious. Still, the economy experienced strong growth at 11.5% in 2007 as a result of improved weather. A drought in 2008, however, lowered GDP growth to 7.5%, demonstrating how vulnerable the economy is to large fluctuations in weather. Moreover, agriculture is important both for its overall output and as the country's main source of employment. GDP growth in 2008 was mainly supported by private consumption and strong construction investment, much of which was linked to donor-led investment projects. The economy remains heavily dependent on foreign aid, and more effective use of aid can improve its growth. Cost effectiveness in procurement and genuine ownership of development activities by the Government are important in improving aid effectiveness. An agreement by donors to channel a substantial amount of their resources through the national budget will also improve aid effectiveness.

Rapid increase in inflation

Inflation has been driven up in all the countries of the subregion, partly by unrelenting pressures from higher international commodity prices, particularly the prices of oil, basic metals and selected food items. In India, the hardening of international commodity prices forced up consumer prices. To stem inflation, the Government reduced customs and excise duties on raw materials and products and kept a tight monetary policy in place. Despite these measures, the consumer price index for industrial workers rose from 6.2% in 2007 to 9% in 2008 (figure 4.14). Price increases in food and fuel groups were higher than those of other groups.

Figure 4.14. Inflation in South and South-West Asian economies, 2007-2008

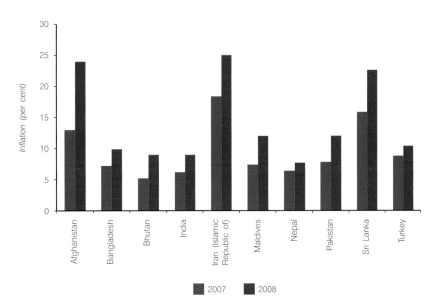

Sources: ESCAP calculations based on national sources; and ESCAP estimates.

Notes: Figures for 2008 are estimates. Inflation refers to changes in the consumer price index. For India it refers to the consumer price index for industrial workers. The inflation calculations and estimates for Sri Lanka and Afghanistan inflation reflect the situation in Colombo and Kabul, respectively.

In Pakistan, inflation rose from 7.8% in 2007 to 12% in 2008. Food inflation was even higher, at 17.6%, driven primarily by an unprecedented rise in global prices of a few items such as wheat, rice and edible oil. The situation was exacerbated by the weakness of the domestic currency, the gradual removal of fuel, food and power subsidies and the monetary overhang of excessive borrowing from the central bank to finance the large fiscal deficit. The same factors are expected to exert pressure on overall prices in 2009. The longer the inflationary pressure persists, the greater the chance for a wage-price spiral to gain hold; tight monetary and fiscal policies are necessary to prevent such a spiral. If the budget deficit is not contained, tight monetary policy alone may not achieve the desired results.

Food inflation was even higher

Inflation in Sri Lanka continued to rise. In 2007 it was 15.8%, and is estimated at 22.6% for 2008. The surging global prices for fuel oil and staple foods, such as milk and wheat flour, drove the high inflation. Expansionary fiscal policy also exerted upward pressure. Inflation began to subside in the middle of 2008 with improvements in domestic supply factors, mod-

eration of international commodity prices and reduced demand due to tight monetary policy.

The increase of already-high inflation has been a serious concern in the Islamic Republic of Iran. Inflation was expected to rise to about 25% in 2008, up from 18.4% in 2007. Such an increase, even after excluding food and energy prices, suggests strong underlying domestic demand pressures. Higher import prices aggravated the cost-push effect. The Government intends to reduce inflation without undermining its programme of short-term growth and employment creation. The country's economy appears to be over-heated, and policies aimed at stimulating domestic demand are less effective in supporting growth and employment. Since an expansionary policy stance, both fiscal and monetary, is largely responsible for the country's high inflation, it is important to tighten those policies to prevent inflationary expectations from becoming entrenched.

In Turkey, higher prices for food, energy and other commodities increased inflationary pressures. Inflation is estimated to have increased to 10.4% in 2008, up from 8.8% in 2007.

Inflation in Bangladesh in 2008 emanated largely from higher food prices caused by global markets. Inflation rose to around 10% in 2008, up from 7.2% in 2007. To curb inflation, the Government's short-term measures included selling food grains at subsidized prices on the open market, withdrawing customs duties on imported food grains and edible oil, increasing food grain imports, lowering interest rates against import credit of food grains, regular monitoring of markets, and fixing the maximum retail price for edible oil.

Because of Nepal's and Bhutan's fixed exchange rate with the Indian rupee, and the fact that India is a major source of imports, inflation in both countries is heavily influenced by price developments in India. In Nepal, inflation accelerated to 7.7% in 2008 from 6.4% in 2007 due to the rise in energy and food prices. In Bhutan, inflation had hovered around 5% in recent years, but it started to rise rapidly in 2008 and stood at about 9%.

In Maldives inflation accelerated to 12% in 2008 from 7.4% in 2007 due to soaring food and oil prices. In Afghanistan rapid increases in fuel and food prices raised inflation to 13% in 2007 from 5.1% in the previous year. Drought in 2008 lowered the production of grains by about one third, partly contributing to the further acceleration in inflation to 24% in 2008.

External balances under pressure

The surge in prices of fuel oil, food and other commodities wreaked havoc on the external balances of some countries in the subregion (table 4.11). India's merchandise trade deficit, led mainly by imports, increased to 7.9% of GDP, and the current account deficit was up to 1.5% of GDP in fiscal 2007. The current account deficit was financed by capital flows, which remained large during the year. As a result, foreign exchange reserves increased by $110 billion in 2007 to $310 billion. The global financial crisis and slowdown brought down exports growth to an estimated 11.5% in 2008. Deceleration in growth in imports was slower, due to strong growth in imports of capital goods, project goods and crude oil. Consequently, the trade deficit and current account deficit as a percentage of GDP were expected to increase in 2008. Management of the current account deficit did not pose difficulties because of the comfortable foreign exchange reserves.

Merchandise exports of Pakistan grew by 16.5% in 2008, compared to 4.4% in 2007. Imports grew by 31.2% with an extraordinary surge in imports of petroleum products as well as food and raw material; the trade deficit was estimated at over $20 billion, more than 12% of GDP, in 2008. Despite a record $6.5 billion in overseas workers' remittances, the external current account deficit grew to $14 billion, equivalent to 8.4% of GDP. This deficit, coupled with a substantial outflow of portfolio investment, resulted in a deficit of

overall balance of payments and reduction in foreign exchange reserves. The Government has taken several measures to contain import growth, and the current account deficit is expected to narrow in 2009.

Reduction in foreign exchange reserves

In 2007 Sri Lanka registered a growth of 11.0% in exports and 10.2% in imports. However, growth in exports decelerated to 6.5% in 2008. While growth in exports of agricultural commodities, particularly tea and rubber, remained strong, growth in exports of industrial products, particularly textiles and garments, was slow. At the same time imports, largely of petroleum products and consumer goods, grew at the high rate of 24.0%. In 2008 the deficit in the trade balance amounted to $5.9 billion, compared to $3.7 billion a year earlier. But private remittances, which amounted to $2.9 billion, helped to narrow the current account deficit, which was estimated at 7% of GDP in 2008. The country's gross official reserves were $2.6 billion by the end of December 2008, down from $3.1 billion in December 2007, and were sufficient to finance more than two months of imports.

The external position of the Islamic Republic of Iran strengthened in 2007 when the current account surplus reached an all-time high of about 12% of GDP because of increased oil earnings. The performance of non-oil exports was also satisfactory, mainly reflecting improved competitiveness. The Government allowed some depreciation in the nominal exchange rate to compensate for the inflation differential vis-à-vis country trading partners and thereby protect the competitiveness of the non-oil sector. Gross official reserves, including those of the Oil Stabilization Fund, rose to the equivalent of 12 months of imports. With a surge in oil prices maintained over a significant part of the year, the current account surplus is estimated to remain high, at about 9%, in 2008.

In Turkey, the current account deficit was widened to 6.0% of GDP in 2008 from 5.7% in 2007. The surge in energy and commodity prices played an important role in the current account deficit.

In Bangladesh, despite an increasing trade deficit propelled by higher imports, the current account balance showed a surplus resulting from robust growth in export earnings and workers' remittances. The foreign exchange market remained mostly stable and the country's currency, the taka, appreciated by 0.4%

Table 4.11. Summary of external accounts for selected South and South-West Asian economies

(Per cent)

	Export/GDP		Import/GDP		Current account balance/GDP	
	2007	2008[a]	2007	2008[a]	2007	2008[a]
Bangladesh	18.0	17.9	25.3	27.4	1.4	0.9
Bhutan	50.6	49.8	49.4	58.5	11.3	..
India	13.9	16.1	21.8	27.2	−1.5	−2.7
Iran (Islamic Republic of)[b]	34.1	28.8	19.8	17.9	11.9	8.8
Maldives[c]	24.6	21.6	89.0	91.2	−39.1	−50.7
Nepal	8.2	7.4	26.8	27.5	−0.1	2.6
Pakistan	11.9	11.6	18.5	20.5	−5.1	−8.4
Sri Lanka	23.9	19.4	34.9	33.4	−4.2	−7.0
Turkey[d]	16.3	17.5	25.8	27.2	−5.7	−6.0

	Growth rates					
	Exports			Imports		
	2006	2007	2008	2006	2007	2008
Bangladesh	21.6	15.7	15.9	12.2	16.3	26.1
Bhutan[a]	47.2	64.4	29.6	−5.6	15.1	56.1
India[a]	21.8	23.7	11.5	21.8	29.9	19.0
Iran (Islamic Republic of)[a,b]	18.2	28.1	10.6	16.1	13.1	18.5
Maldives[c,e]	39.4	1.2	52.6	24.4	18.3	32.3
Nepal[a]	2.2	1.2	11.0	15.8	15.0	26.0
Pakistan	14.3	4.4	16.5	31.6	8.0	31.2
Sri Lanka	8.4	11.0	6.5	15.7	10.2	24.0
Turkey[e]	16.4	25.4	23.1	19.5	21.8	18.7

Sources: Bangladesh Bank website, accessed from www.bangladesh-bank.org, 11 December 2008; Maldives Monetary Authority website, accessed from www.mma.gov.mv/statis.php, 6 October 2008; Nepal Rastra Bank website, accessed from www.nrb.org.np/, 21 October 2008; Central Bank of Sri Lanka website, accessed from www.centralbanklanka.org, 23 February 2009; Central Bank of the Republic of Turkey website, accessed from www.tcmb.gov.tr/yeni/eng/, 11 December 2008; Royal Monetary Authority of Bhutan website, accessed from www.rma.org.bt/, 21 October 2008; State Bank of Pakistan website, accessed from www.sbp.org.pk, 10 December 2008; IMF, *World Economic Outlook Database*, (Washington, D.C., October 2008); CEIC Data Company Limited; and national sources.

Note: Figures are in fiscal year, except those for Maldives, Sri Lanka and Turkey, which are in calendar year.

[a]   2008 data are estimates.
[b]   Import value in f.o.b.
[c]   2007 data are estimates.
[d]   2008 data refers to the first 3 quarters.
[e]   2008 data are projections.

against the dollar during fiscal 2008. But the real effective exchange rate depreciated, and Bangladesh enjoyed some gain in export competitiveness. Earnings from exported merchandise recorded growth of 15.9% in 2008. Several export commodities – knitwear, petroleum by-products, tea, textile fabrics, raw jute, ceramic products, woven garments, home textiles, electronics, terry towels, leather, frozen food and footwear – recorded higher growth than in the previous year. Merchandise imports showed a 26.1% growth in 2008. Imports of consumer goods recorded the highest growth, mainly due to robust import growth in food

grains. While imports of intermediate goods grew at a lower rate, imports of capital machinery declined. The inflow of remittances increased by one third, reaching nearly $8 billion in fiscal 2008. The country's foreign exchange reserves were nearly $6.2 billion at the end of fiscal 2008.

India is the major trading partner of both Bhutan and Nepal, and the two countries maintain a fixed exchange rate with the Indian rupee. Both countries enjoyed a current account surplus in 2008. In Nepal, higher imports and slower growth of exports led to further widening of the merchandise trade deficit in 2008. But workers' remittances increased by more than 50% to roughly $2.2 billion in 2008, helping to move the current account deficit into surplus in 2008. Furthermore, a surge in foreign aid contributed to a rise in the overall balance of payment surplus, which led in turn to an increase in foreign exchange reserves in 2008. In Bhutan, merchandise trade and current accounts moved into surplus in 2007 and 2008, aided by electricity exports to India from the Tala hydropower plant. Despite large revenues from the export of electricity, aid inflows will continue to be an important source of financial support, much of it coming from India.

In Maldives, a huge gap between exports earnings and imports expenditure widened the current account deficit to 39.1% of GDP in 2007, reflecting a surge in construction-related imports and rising commodity prices, and notwithstanding the contribution from strong tourism earnings. The current account deficit is expected to rise to 51% of GDP in 2008. To date, financing such a deficit through external borrowing has not been a problem. But it led to a sharp increase in external debt, which stood at over 70% of GDP in 2008. The Maldives currency remains pegged to the United States dollar.

Fiscal situation deteriorated

The fiscal situation deteriorated in most countries of the subregion. In India, after several years of fiscal

consolidation facilitated by strong economic growth, the budget in 2008 remained under pressure. The deficit of the central Government was brought down to 2.7% of GDP in 2007, and a target of 2.5% was set for 2008 (figure 4.15). However, due to stimulus packages to contain deceleration in economic growth, significant increases in Government salaries and Government subsidies for food, fertilizer and certain fuel products, the budget deficit for 2008 is estimated at 6.0% of GDP.

In Pakistan, the Government's overall revenue increased in 2008, but the increase in expenditure was much larger, due mainly to subsidies on oil, power, fertilizer, wheat and other food items. The fiscal situation deteriorated as the Government absorbed the high price of oil for domestic consumers, while at the same time, it had to import wheat at high prices and sell to domestic consumers at cheaper prices. As a result, the budget deficit rose to 7.4% of GDP in 2008, the highest in the last 10 years.

The Sri Lankan Government took measures to enhance its revenues, mainly by broadening the tax base, changing the tax rates to provide some exemptions to encourage development in specific sectors, and improving tax administration. On the expenditure side, the retail prices of petroleum products continued to adjust to reflect the cost, while administered electricity tariffs were revised upwards in line with increased input costs. The budget deficit was estimated at 7% of GDP in 2008, down from 7.7% of GDP in 2007.

Figure 4.15. Budget deficits as a percentage of GDP in South and South-West Asian economies in 2007-2008

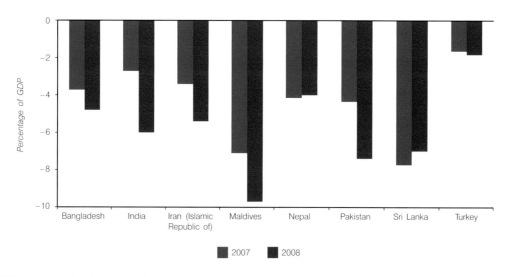

Sources: ESCAP, based on national sources; ADB, *Key Indicators for Asia and the Pacific 2008* (Manila, 2008); and ESCAP estimates.

Notes: Figures for 2008 are estimates. Budget balance excludes grants for Bangladesh, Islamic Republic of Iran, Pakistan and Sri Lanka.

The Islamic Republic of Iran continues to follow an expansionary fiscal policy as it benefits from large oil revenues. But fiscal consolidation will be needed in the medium term to reduce inflationary pressures and prevent an erosion of external competitiveness. The Government is creating a reform package that will phase out explicit and implicit energy subsidies, as well as budgetary non-energy subsidies, and replace them with targeted social assistance.

Fiscal policy in Turkey was relaxed in 2007 to stimulate employment and investment in infrastructure. As a result, the fiscal deficit in 2007 increased to 1.6% of GDP from 0.6% in the prior year, and is estimated at 1.8% for 2008. Fiscal discipline over the past six years helped the Government lower its public debt from 61.5% of GDP in 2001 to around 37% in 2007.

In Bangladesh the fiscal deficit as a percentage of GDP increased from 3.7% in 2007 to 4.8% in 2008 despite healthy growth in Government revenue. The pressure on fiscal balance increased due to large increases in spending on flood and cyclone relief and an expansion of subsidies following the rise in fuel, fertilizer and food grain prices in the international market. Fiscal policy is expected to remain expansionary to promote growth and employment. Subsidies on food and fertilizer are expected to remain in place to contain inflation and boost production of agricultural crops.

The Government of Nepal has had success in raising its revenues over the last two years. Revenue collection increased by 22.6% in 2008 on top of a 21.3% increase in 2007. As a result, the revenue-to-GDP ratio improved to 13.1% in 2008. Expenditures also witnessed a sharp increase, with development expenditure growing at a high rate. The budget deficit stood at 4% of GDP in 2008, almost the same as the previous year. The Government tried to reduce the huge subsidy on fuel oil by increasing oil prices towards the end of fiscal year 2008.

Fiscal deficit has become a serious problem for Maldives. Expenditures have reached extraordinarily high levels, while revenues cannot keep pace. The deficit of 7.9% of GDP in 2007 is estimated to rise to 9.7% in 2008. The Government has been relying on extraordinary revenue measures, such as leasing out islands, to contain the deficit.

Policy responses: Budget deficits under pressure

The global slowdown that has come in the aftermath of the financial crisis will have an adverse impact on the real economies of the subregion. But the adverse impact may not be as strong as in some other, more open subregions. Governments took measures to improve the liquidity of the financial sector. India, Pakistan and Sri Lanka, for example, reduced banks' cash reserve requirements. Policy lending rates were also cut in some countries. Because of large budget deficits and public debt, most countries in this subregion have less flexibility to introduce major fiscal stimulus packages. However, some countries, including India, have introduced fiscal stimulus packages (table 4.12) which should help soften the downturn in the subregion, and further strengthen domestic demand. In some countries of the subregion, the combination of lower Government revenues due to slower economic growth, significant increases in expenditure on Government salaries, and Government subsidies for food, fertilizer and certain fuel products, implemented to boost domestic demand and address immediate economic hardships, will cause budget deficits to rise substantially. In India, the deficit is estimated to rise to 6.0% of GDP in 2008.

Targeted subsidies and special programmes for the poor are needed

Of some concern is what will happen to remittances. If oil prices drop to a very low level and remain there for a long period, accompanied by severe global economic slowdown, workers' remittances are likely to fall. The subregion has a large number of workers in oil-producing countries who could lose their livelihoods. Although past experience shows resilience in outflows of remittances from the Gulf Cooperation Council countries, even when oil prices are volatile, Governments in the subregion are planning to deal with such an eventuality through domestic employment programmes and stronger social safety nets. Some countries may find external imbalances increasingly difficult to handle alone. Financial assistance from multilateral financial institutions can help to overcome immediate problems of balance of payments. The $7.6 billion, 23-month Stand-By Arrangement signed in November 2008 between the International Monetary Fund and the Government of Pakistan, to help the country meet its serious balance of payments difficulties and support the country's economic stabilization programme, holds important pointers for other countries of the region.

Over and above these immediate fire-fighting policy responses, there are long-term policy challenges facing the subregion that will need to receive equal priority. Poverty and rising inequalities remain the key challenge for the region. Targeted subsides and spe-

Table 4.12. Fiscal stimulus package in selected countries in South and South-West Asia

	Salient features
India	The Government of India announced fiscal stimulus packages on 7 December 2008 and 2 January 2009. The packages: (a) provide tax relief to boost domestic demand, including an across-the-board cut of 4% in the ad valorem central value added tax rate, except for petroleum products; (b) include several measures to support exports, the textiles sector, housing, and small and medium enterprises; and (c) aim to increase expenditure on public projects to create employment and public assets.
	The Government has: (a) renewed its efforts to increase infrastructure investment; (b) already accelerated approval for infrastructure projects; and (c) taken an expansionary fiscal stance to boost economic growth, which increased budget deficit from 2.7% of GDP in 2007 to 6.0% in 2008. Budget deficit for 2009 is expected to remain high.
Pakistan	In November 2008, the International Monetary Fund and the Government of Pakistan signed a $7.6 billion, 23-month Stand-By Arrangement to help the country meet its serious balance of payments difficulties and to support the country's economic stabilization programme. The Government plans to reduce budget deficit from 7.4% of GDP in 2008 to below 5% in 2009. GDP growth is expected to decelerate sharply in 2009 due to internal difficulties as well as global slowdown. While the Government lacks financial resources to introduce any fiscal stimulus, through a reprioritization of expenditure, the Benazir Income Support Programme has been launched to help poor families with monthly cash benefits.
Sri Lanka	The Government of Sri Lanka announced a stimulus package in December 2008 to maintain GDP growth around 6% in 2009. The stimulus package, valued at 16 billion rupees ($141 million, 0.3% of GDP), includes cuts in energy prices and incentives for exporters. Exporters in certain sectors (tea, apparel, leather, rubber, among others) who maintain 2008 revenues and do not retrench workers will get a 5% incentive payment on their revenues. Reductions ranging from 5% to 15% in the expenses of Government officials were announced to save resources for the package.

cial programmes for the poor are needed. Many countries have already introduced such programmes, but they need to be strengthened further, as discussed in box 4.2. The fiscal stimulus packages introduced in some countries are clearly aimed at creating employment while addressing public infrastructure bottlenecks that have stymied the dynamic entrepreneurship and cost-effective functioning of the subregion's business sector. Involvement of the private sector through public-private partnerships is the only way to meet the growing needs for physical infrastructure, particularly energy. Along with generating more electricity, it is important to efficiently utilize existing capacity. Transmission and distribution losses are massive, partly due to theft. Rehabilitation and proper maintenance of the distribution system should be a priority to minimize such losses.

Outlook: Moderating growth with downward pressures

The South and South-West Asian subregion is forecast to grow by 4.3 in 2009 (table 4.10). With some moderation in growth, India is forecast to achieve growth of 6.0% in 2009. Economic activity has been moderating in response to earlier monetary tightening, hardening of commodity prices in international markets and continuing financial strains, but the easing of

monetary policy in late 2008 and fiscal stimulus packages should render support to domestic demand.

The 2.5% growth outlook for Pakistan is not promising, mainly because of its internal problems, such as high inflation, large fiscal and current account deficits, severe electricity shortages and precarious law and order. Bangladesh and Sri Lanka are projected to grow between 5% and 6%. Nepal's improved political stability, transition towards stable democracy and more conducive investment climate are expected to pave the way for a more robust economic performance over the medium term. The country's GDP is expected to grow about 5.5% in 2009.

Being the only net exporter of oil in the subregion, the Islamic Republic of Iran is expected to experience slower growth, about 5.0%, due to the sharp decrease in oil prices. Turkey, with a relatively more open economy and a banking sector more closely linked to financial institutions in the developed countries, is expected to register negative growth in 2009.

With falls in oil and other commodity prices, inflation is expected to come down in most countries. Budget balances are expected to remain under pressure. Exports growth for some countries may slow down even faster than reduction in imports growth, causing additional difficulties with the balance of payments.

South-East Asia: International financial crisis evolves into deepening subregional industrial crisis

For South-East Asia, not unlike other subregions, 2008 was a year of many happenings. During the first half of the year, policymakers were preoccupied with inflation, which increased substantially as the commodity price spike was passed on to domestic food prices. The effect of these price increases was mixed, however, as exporters of commodities such as oil and gas, rubber, palm oil, rice and metals benefited from higher export receipts. But by the last quarter of 2008, attention turned to a second and larger shock: the sudden onset of economic crisis. As manufacturing exports from many countries in the subregion experienced double-digit declines, economic growth slowed markedly, darkening the outlook for 2009. Overall, the rate of GDP growth dropped from 6.5% in 2007 to 4.3% in 2008, but it is expected to plummet further to 1.5% in 2009, the slowest among the developing ESCAP subregions. On the downside, there is a marked risk that the global recession driven by the financial crisis will turn into an industrial crisis for the entire subregion, given its integrated industrial production base and a linkage to the global supply chain, thus deepening unemployment and further hurting the poor. On the brighter side, while banking sector vulnerabilities must remain on the radar screen, the improvements in banking supervision and prudential macroeconomic policies implemented after the financial crisis of 1997, which had its origins in this subregion, have strengthened the financial sector and increased its resilience to crises.

Impact: Dramatic drops in GDP and exports

While the slowdown in export demand was pervasive across South-East Asia, its effect on the rate of growth of GDP during 2008 varied across countries according to their trade composition. Countries that relied most heavily on manufacturing exports to industrial countries, such as Cambodia, the Philippines and Singapore, were the most affected by the slowdown. Singapore's growth rate experienced the deepest cut, from 7.7% in 2007 to 1.2% in 2008. In contrast, Indonesia, the Lao People's Democratic Republic and, to a lesser extent, Malaysia benefited from high commodity prices during the first half of 2008 and managed to sustain growth rates only slightly below those of 2007.

As a result of the spike in commodity prices, inflation increased substantially in the economies of South-East Asia in 2008, more than doubling in all countries except Indonesia and the Lao People's Democratic Republic, where it was nevertheless substantially higher than in 2007. The largest increase in inflation occurred in Cambodia, the Philippines, and Singapore, where inflation rates more than tripled between 2007 and 2008.

Exports dropped dramatically at the end of 2008

Data from the last few months of 2008 show a marked deceleration in manufacturing exports from the subregion. In October, Singapore's non-oil domestic exports fell by 15% year-on-year. While exports to the United States contracted the most that month, Singapore exports to other markets, such as the European Union, China, Malaysia and Japan also declined. This trend worsened, and by January 2009 total non-oil exports plummeted 35% from a year earlier. Similarly, exports from the Philippines dropped as much as 40% in December, year-on-year, the worst performance in more than two decades, with electronics exports plunging 48%. Similar year-on-year drops in exports have occurred in other South-East Asian countries, such as Thailand (27% in January 2009), Indonesia (21% in December 2008) and Malaysia (16% in December 2008).

The brunt of the impact of the dramatic fall in exports will be reflected in the 2009 growth rates

The dramatic drops in exports towards the end of 2008 are starting to impact on employment in export-oriented industries. For instance, Cambodia's garment industry sells 70% of its products to the United States, where retail sales have fallen during the second half of 2008. As a result, 10% of the country's garment factories closed operations, leaving 20,000 workers without jobs. In Thailand, the seasonally adjusted GDP fell 6.1% in the last quarter of 2008 compared to the previous quarter, the worst performance in decades.

Because the dramatic fall of exports took place at the end of 2008, it is not fully reflected in that year's rates of GDP growth. The brunt of its impact will be reflected in the 2009 growth rates. Figure 4.16 shows that GDP growth fell for all countries in the subregion between 2007 and 2008, and that deeper cuts in growth are forecast for 2009. These forecasts, however, should be taken with caution. Since the crisis started, forecasts have been continuously revised downward, most recently for Singapore and Thailand. The downward risks are high for all countries and suggest that the worst is still to come.

Domestic demand did not compensate for falls in exports in 2008

As pointed out in last year's *Survey* (ESCAP, 2008), growth in domestic demand in 2007, especially in private consumption, helped smooth out the adverse impact that a deceleration in exports had on the subregion's GDP growth that year. Unfortunately, this was not the case in 2008. As shown in figure 4.17, domestic demand grew slower in 2008 than in 2007 in all the South-East Asian countries. While in Cambodia, the Philippines and Viet Nam, the drop in domestic demand exacerbated the adverse effect of the deceleration of exports, weaker domestic demand countered the expansionary effect of exports in Malaysia.

Figure 4.16. GDP growth dropped in 2008, but the worst is still to come

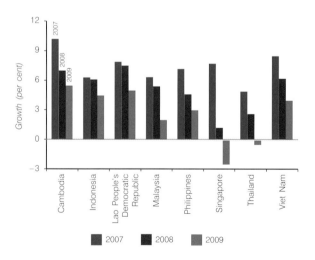

Sources: ESCAP, based on national sources; ADB, *Key Indicators for Asia and the Pacific 2008*; IMF, *International Financial Statistics*; and ESCAP estimates.

Note: 2008 rates are estimates and 2009 rates are forecasts (as of 27 February 2009).

Why has domestic demand failed to compensate for the fall in exports in 2008? In open economies, domestic demand – especially private consumption and investment – is highly dependent on export demand and export prices. For instance, rising prices of coal, palm oil, coffee and rubber in the first half of 2008 increased the income of farmers and miners in Indonesia, boosting sales of motorcycles and cars to record levels. Conversely, the dramatic drop in commodity prices in the second half of 2008 had a dampening effect on private consumption.

Private investment is another component of domestic demand that started to contract significantly toward the end of 2008. The global liquidity crunch made access to project financing more difficult, especially for those funded by FDI. And the large export orientation of investment projects in South-East Asia made investment less profitable. With little access to credit and poor short-term profitability prospects, many firms postponed or cancelled investment projects in the subregion, adding to the recessionary effect of the drop in exports. Foreign investors' financial difficulties have affected not only export-oriented projects but also projects in infrastructure and construction, thus further dampening FDI flows from both outside and within the region. Least developed countries have not been immune. For example, a project to construct seven skyscrapers in the capital of Cambodia financed by a company from the Republic of Korea is reported to have been scaled down to only three skyscrapers, and construction was postponed to 2010.

Idiosyncratic shocks and circumstances affected growth in some countries

In addition to events in the international economy, idiosyncratic shocks had an important effect on the rate of GDP growth of some countries in the subregion. In Myanmar, Cyclone Nargis hit the Ayeyarwady Delta in May 2008, killing over 80,000 people. A joint report of the Government of Myanmar, ASEAN and the United Nations calculated the damage and losses as comparable to those caused by the Indian Ocean tsunami in Indonesia in 2004 (Tripartite Core Group, 2008). The report estimates that the total economic losses caused by the cyclone amount to 2.7% of Myanmar's projected GDP for 2008.

In Thailand political demonstrations late in 2008 were estimated to have caused losses exceeding 100 billion baht ($3 billion), not only to the tourism and aviation industries but also to exporters who were unable to ship their products on time when the airports were shut down (Pitsuwan, 2008). The prospect of damage to the tourism industry is particularly worrisome for

Figure 4.17. Domestic demand growth did not help smooth out the impact of dropping exports during 2008

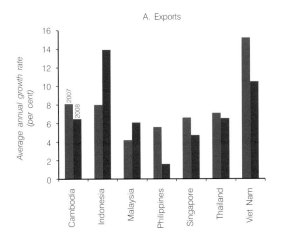

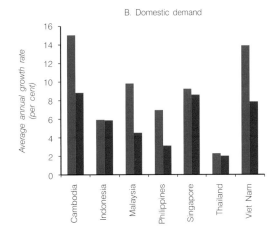

Sources: ESCAP, based on data from Economist Intelligence Unit, *Country Reports;* and ESCAP estimates.

Note: Domestic demand defined as the sum of private consumption, public consumption and gross fixed investment.

Thailand, where it accounts for around 6% of GDP. A report of the National Economic and Social Development Board released just before the airport closures had already raised concerns about tourism slowing, initially because of the high cost of fuel and air travel, then because of the international financial crisis. Revised Board forecasts for 2009 prepared after the airport closures warned that the events could cut GDP growth by as much as 1% compared to the previous forecast (Theparat, 2008).

In open economies, domestic demand – especially private consumption and investment – is highly dependent on export demand and export prices

---

In Viet Nam, economic authorities established a stabilization package in March 2008 to cool an overheating economy, slow inflation and control a deteriorating current account. The package included a large increase in interest rates, and low-priority public investments were cancelled or delayed, saving 1.2% of GDP. The tighter monetary policy induced a slowdown in private investment, mainly in construction. And high inflation, which began to slow toward the end of the year, caused a significant slowdown in private consumption compared to 2007.

Inflation was a big concern in the first half of 2008

Before the impact from the global recession shocked South-East Asia in the last quarter of the year, rising inflation was the most urgent concern of the subregion's policy makers. Consumer price inflation soared in the first half of 2008 as a result of the dramatic increase in international commodity prices (analysed in chapter 2). The transmission from international commodity price inflation to domestic inflation was largely due to food, because of its high weight in the consumer price index of countries in the subregion, which range from 23.4% in Singapore to 47.9% in Viet Nam. While the crude oil price increased even more than food prices, its impact on domestic inflation rates was smaller because energy prices are regulated by most Governments in the subregion and are adjusted infrequently.

Inflation rates increased significantly in South-East Asian countries, reaching a peak between June and August of 2008 before beginning to fall (figure 4.18). The drop in inflation rates reflects an astonishing reversal of the price trends described in chapter 2. In Thailand, inflation dropped from 9.2% in July to 0.4% in December and may drop further in 2009. Viet Nam, which in 2008 experienced its worst bout of inflation since 1992, saw the inflation rate moderate from a peak of 28.3% in August to 19.9% in December. Similarly, Cambodia's inflation rate dropped to 13.5% in December from 22.5% in August. These trends are

Figure 4.18. Inflation trends reverted in the second half of 2008

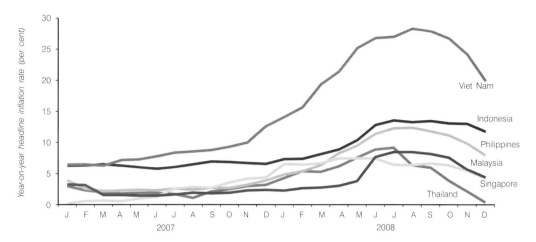

Sources: ESCAP, based on data from national statistical office websites (accessed on 20 February 2009).

expected to continue into 2009. As shown in figure 4.19, inflation rates in 2009 are expected to drop back to levels similar to those of 2007.

Current accounts deteriorated but remain in surplus in most countries

Although the high price of commodities during the first half of the year benefited some countries, the generalized slowdown in exports as a result of the deepening international financial crisis in the second half prevailed, and current account balances deteriorated across South-East Asia (figure 4.20). Nevertheless, most countries continued enjoying current account surpluses. The main exceptions were Cambodia, where the current account deficit increased from 3% of GDP in 2007 to 7.7% in 2008, and Viet Nam, where it increased from 9.9% to 14.1% in the same period. In the Philippines the small current account deficit of 0.9% of GDP would be substantially larger if it were not offset by the remittances the country receives from overseas workers, which represented 11.6% of the country's GDP in 2007. Data for the first nine months of 2008 indicate that remittances increased 17.1% compared to the first nine months of 2007. A reversal in remittances is not expected in 2009, but a slowdown is foreseen because many of the country's overseas workers are based in recession-hit economies. In Viet Nam, the current account deficit deteriorated compared to the year before, most of the decline coming during the first half of the year. Since July, as the stabilization package started to affect domestic demand, imports contracted every month, reducing the current account deficit.

Policy responses: As recessionary pressures mount, urgency of further expansionary policies intensifies

As inflation soared, monetary policy changed from mostly neutral to contractionary by mid-2008. But as the impact of the global financial crisis on economic growth became more evident by the fourth quarter of 2008, monetary policy started to ease. Cuts in policy rates can be expected to continue in 2009. Consistent with monetary easing and the deterioration in current account balances mentioned above, South-East Asian currencies depreciated, especially towards the end of 2008 and into 2009. Nevertheless, with reasonably high levels of foreign exchange reserves, and save for a short bumpy ride for the Indonesian rupiah in November, no major disruption in foreign exchange markets has occurred in the subregion at the time of writing. As for fiscal policy, in most countries during 2008, budget deficits were small and balances remained stable or improved slightly. Thus, the subregion has fiscal space for an expansionary and coordinated response to the global financial crisis. Some of the recently announced fiscal stimulus packages by South-East Asian countries are discussed below.

Monetary policy has been tracking inflation with a lag

Figure 4.21 shows the evolution of selected policy interest rates in the subregion between January 2008

Figure 4.19. 2009 inflation rates expected to drop back to levels similar to 2007

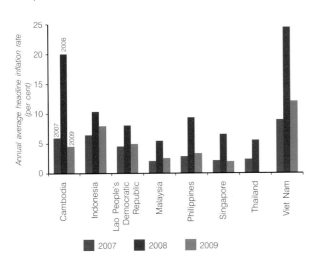

Figure 4.20. Current account balances deteriorated during 2008

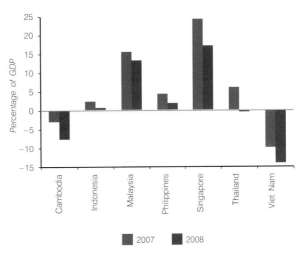

Sources: ESCAP, based on national sources; IMF, *International Financial Statistics*; and ESCAP estimates.

Notes: 2008 rates are estimates and 2009 rates are forecasts (as of 27 February 2009).

Sources: ESCAP, based on data from IMF, *International Financial Statistics and World Economic Outlook Database*; and ESCAP estimates.

Figure 4.21. Monetary policy easing since late 2008

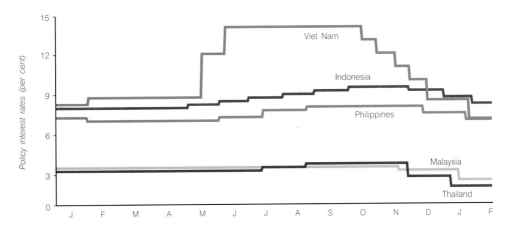

Sources: ESCAP, based on central bank websites (accessed 23 February 2009).

Notes: Policy interest rates are the one-day repurchase (repo) rate 2008 (Thailand), overnight policy rate (Malaysia), Bank of Indonesia rate (Indonesia), overnight lending or repurchase rate (Philippines), and the base (prime) rate (Viet Nam).

and February 2009. It shows that the Bank of Indonesia increased its policy rate by 25 basis points on six occasions, raising it from 8% in May to 9.50% in October, before cutting it to 9.25% in December, 8.75% in January, and 8.25% in February. The Bank of Thailand increased its policy rate more moderately, from 3.25% in July to 3.75% in August, before cutting it by an unprecedented 100 basis points in December, and by another 75 basis points to 2% in January. After keeping its policy rate constant at 3.50% for most of the year, the central bank of Malaysia cut it to 3.25% in November and to 2.50% in January, while the central bank of the Philippines cut its policy rate twice in December and January, from 8% to 7%.

Changes in monetary policy in 2008 were most forceful in Viet Nam, which experienced a dramatic increase in the inflation rate. The State Bank of Viet Nam increased its base rate from 8.75% to 12% in May and to 14% in June and allowed commercial banks to pay interest rates of up to 150% of the base rate for deposits.[2] Since the end of October, the State Bank cut the base rate dramatically, by 100 basis points on four occasions and by 150 basis points in two occasions, lowering it to 7% in February. At the end of 2008, Viet Nam was contemplating a reform of its monetary policy, by which the central bank would set a floor rate and a ceiling rate for intrabank transactions, letting banks set deposit and lending rates (Vietnam Business Finance, 2008).

Exchange rates depreciated, but foreign exchange reserves remain at comfortable levels

Consistent with the deterioration of current account balances, the nominal exchange rate depreciated across South-East Asia. The value of the Philippine peso and the Thai baht dropped steadily over the year, depreciating approximately 15% by February 2009 (figure 4.22). The Indonesian rupiah was stable until early October, when its value dropped nearly 25%. The rupiah recovered partly in December and January, before dropping again in February. The Singapore dollar and the Malaysian ringgit appreciated until May before starting to depreciate, and Viet Nam's dong gradually depreciated over the year, accumulating by February 2009 a fall of 7% from January 2008. Many of the subregion's currencies strengthened a little in December, continuing their downward trends during January and February of 2009.

Despite the weakening of exchange rates, South-East Asian countries appear resistant to major disruptions in the foreign exchange market because of their high level of foreign exchange reserves and low exposure to troubled subprime assets. Yet, the possibility of a future episode of exchange rate volatility should not be ruled out. With continuing uncertainty about how deep and how long the recession will be and how it

Figure 4.22. Currencies depreciated in the second half of 2008

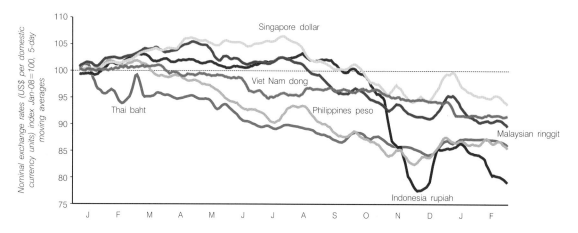

Sources: ESCAP, based on data from the Pacific Exchange Rate Service, accessed on 20 February 2009 from http://fx.sauder.ubc.ca/data.html.

---

2   In the months before this policy change, deposit rates were capped at the base rate. Thus the combination of the increases in base rates plus the increase in the ceiling led to a dramatic hike in deposit rates.

will affect countries in the subregion, stock markets have been especially volatile. Their movements are likely to affect foreign exchange markets, as foreign investors move in and out in search of high returns. As a result, central banks will need to remain vigilant and balance the goal of stimulating domestic demand by cutting interest rates with the need to sustain the stability of their exchange rates.

Budget deficits remained in check in most countries

The subregion's reasonably strong fundamentals can be seen in its fiscal accounts. Fiscal balances remained stable or improved slightly in most South-East Asian countries in 2008 (figure 4.23). The main exceptions were Malaysia and Singapore and, to a lesser extent, the Philippines. The situation was more worrisome in Malaysia; Singapore still had a budget surplus in 2008, while the Philippines had made significant progress in controlling budget deficits and therefore had only a small deficit of 0.9% of GDP. One reason for the increase in Malaysia's budget deficit, especially during the first half of 2008, was the country's fuel subsidies. Although the dramatic drop in crude oil prices in the second half of the year brought much relief to that problem, revenue from oil earnings, which account for a significant share of Government revenue, have been dropping fast along with the price of crude oil. Viet Nam had the second highest deficit in 2008, but has been making some progress in controlling it through its stabilization package.

Figure 4.23. Budget deficits remain under control

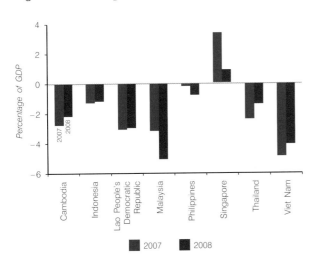

Sources: ESCAP, based on data from ADB, *Key Indicators for Asia and the Pacific 2008*; and ESCAP estimates.

Addressing the food security threat

While the attention of policymakers is currently focused on smoothing out the impacts of the global financial crisis is having on the subregion economies, food inflation was the main threat by mid-2008. As a result, a number of short-term initiatives to support the most vulnerable population groups have been put in place. In addition, longer-term policies to both improve social protection systems and increase agricultural production have been widely discussed. Box 4.3 contains details of both short- and long-term measures to support food security in South-East Asia. While the long-term measures do not seem a priority at the moment, their implementation is as or more important than the short-term measures. According to the analysis in chapter 2, episodes of soaring commodity prices are highly likely to recur after the global economy recovers from the recession. It is very important to be prepared ahead of time, as a systemic response to crises is more effective and less costly than short-term palliative measures.

Outlook

Given the prospect of a sharp fall in growth rates across South-East Asia, most of its countries have announced fiscal stimulus packages to support domestic demand, in an attempt to stop the downward spiral set forth by the dramatic drop in exports at the end of 2008. The details about some of these packages are still sketchy and may be subject to change before being passed into law. Most of the packages announced are relatively small. For Malaysia, Thailand, Viet Nam and Indonesia they represent, respectively, 1%, 1.2%, 1.2%, and 1.4% of GDP. The exceptions are the Philippines (4.6% of GDP) and Singapore (11.5% of GDP). Table 4.13 includes details available at the time of writing.

It is expected that most of these packages will be refined and finalized in coming months. There is widespread agreement that they are the most effective policy tool currently available to fight the recession, for monetary policy has a limited impact when businesses do not have an incentive to invest and consumers are postponing major expenses amid the uncertainty of keeping their jobs. Given the preliminary state of some of these packages, there is still room for further discussion about how they can be made most effective.

In light of the analysis in chapters 2, 3 and 5, there are good grounds for being selective in the use of public funds and taking advantage of the current need to boost fiscal expenditures to enhance the

Box 4.3. Policy responses in supporting food security in South-East Asia

A subregional seminar in Manila in October 2008 examined policy responses to protect the poor from the spike in food prices that had occurred earlier that year. The seminar, which was organized by ESCAP in partnership with the Asian Development Bank and the United Nations in the Philippines, was attended by policymakers from five South-East Asian countries (Cambodia, Indonesia, Philippines, Thailand and Viet Nam), representatives from Philippine NGOs, experts from multilateral organizations and academics.

The programme focused on short-run policies to protect the poor from the impact of increasing food prices, and long-run policies aimed at strengthening social protection systems, increasing agricultural productivity and promoting rural development. The seminar reached several conclusions and recommendations.

Short-term measures to mitigate the impact of food price increases on the poor

Participants exchanged country experiences on a number of short-term programmes and policies:

- Food-for-school programme (Philippines): Providing one kilogram of rice per child that attends class at an elementary school, pre-school programme or day-care centre;

- Selling rice at subsidized prices (Philippines, Cambodia, Indonesia);

- Emergency fiscal measures: (a) reduction in gasoline taxes, subsidies to small users of electricity and water, and free transportation on selected buses and trains (Thailand, for six months only); (b) direct cash assistance to poor households to compensate for the adverse impact of the fuel-price increase (Indonesia, Rp100,000/month, for seven months only);

- Conditional cash programme (Pantawid Pamilyang Pilipino Program, Philippines): P500 per month per household for preventive health checkups and vaccines, and P300 per month per child who attends school (for a maximum of three children per household);

- Increases in minimum wages and Government workers' wages (Cambodia and Thailand);

- Self-help community empowerment (Indonesia): Provide Rp3.0 billion per community annually to generate rural economy activities.

Building resilient social protection systems

The current crisis brought the problem of food insecurity to the centre stage of national and international policy debates, providing a unique opportunity to re-examine how social policies work and how they could be improved and expanded to reach a larger population and eventually all vulnerable groups. During the seminar, the following key issues were raised:

- The ability of countries to implement social protection systems depends on their level of development. Targeted transfers and safety nets, such as unemployment insurance schemes, are expensive and require a sufficient tax base, which low-income countries lack;

- For targeting schemes to be effective and sustainable in the long run, criteria should be developed to ensure that poor and non-poor households are correctly identified;

- Social policies are planned and budgeted by the national Government but are delivered by local governments. Partnerships should be established, not just between the public and private sectors but also between the national and local governments;

(Continued on next page)

Box 4.3 *(continued)*

- Building resilient rural communities ameliorates the need for social protection. Empowering farmer organizations, diversifying the rural economy, and improving economic infrastructure in rural areas should receive policymakers' priority attention;

- The ability of the tax system to generate sufficient funding for social policies should be addressed. Equity issues should be considered as well (for example, should children of middle-class and wealthy families received a subsidized university education?);

- The human-rights approach to the universal provision of social services should be further explored. Some countries have already moved in that direction, such as Thailand in health care and Viet Nam in free health care for children under six.

Reinvigorating the agricultural sector to boost food production and fight rural poverty

Investment in agriculture has been downplayed in recent decades, resulting in a sharp drop in the growth rate of yield. In the face of increasing demands on land and water to grow biofuel crops and a growing frequency of prolonged droughts and heavy rainfalls, it is critical to implement policies to reverse this trend. In this regard, several issues were examined during the seminar:

- The crisis in food prices led to the recognition that investment in agriculture and rural infrastructure has been neglected. Policymakers should redress this neglect as a matter of priority, not just to support millions of poor rural families but also to ensure that enough food is available for the urban poor;

- Various countries provided details of their policy responses to improve agricultural production. Most of those policies overlapped with the Philippines' FIELDS program – a comprehensive program to improve agriculture production, with six components: (F) fertilizer and micronutrients; (I) irrigation, facilities rehabilitation and restoration; (E) extension, education and training; (L) loans for inputs and crop insurance; (D) dryers and other post-harvest facilities provision; (S) seed subsidy on quality genetic materials;

- While high food prices are detrimental to urban households, short-term measures to bring them down may remove farmers' incentives to increase production, which would not be helpful in the long run. Policymakers should try to improve the social protection of the urban poor simultaneously with policies to improve agricultural production, as the latter – to be effective – should keep farm gate prices higher than in the past;

- Sustainable agriculture should be considered a valuable option for improving food security and reducing rural poverty, in addition to policies that support conventional agriculture. Successful grass-roots experiences, such as the Infanta Integrated Community Development Assistance in Philippines, are replicable models. Partnerships between Governments and NGOs should be considered for that purpose;

- Efforts to improve and disseminate knowledge about agricultural techniques should be emphasized, especially as climate change puts stress on agricultural systems and increases the frequency of weather-related disasters;

- In many countries, working-age people, particularly males, migrate to the cities or abroad to find better employment, leaving older relatives, spouses and children on the farm. It is thus critical to provide safety nets and disseminate technical knowledge for those left behind.

Table 4.13. Selected fiscal stimulus packages in South-East Asian region

	Size	Salient features
Indonesia	Rp 71.3 trillion ($6.1 billion); 1.4% of 2008 GDP; (budget deficit in 2008: 1.2% of GDP)	Tax breaks for individuals and companies (Rp 43 trillion); waived import duties and taxes (Rp 13.3 trillion); infrastructure spending (Rp 10.2 trillion); diesel subsidy (Rp 2.8 trillion); rural development (Rp 0.6 trillion).
		Announced in January 2009; enhances a previous Rp 27.5 trillion stimulus package.
Malaysia	RM 7 billion ($1.9 billion); 1% of 2008 GDP; (budget deficit in 2008: 5.1% of GDP)	Investment funds to promote strategic industries and high-speed broadband (RM 1.9 billion); small-scale projects such as village roads, school repairs (RM 1.6 billion); affordable housing (RM 1.5 billion); education and skills training programmes (RM 1 billion); public transport and military facilities (RM 1 billion).
		Announced in November 2008; a second stimulus package was expected in February 2009.
Philippines	P 330 billion ($6.5 billion); 4.6% of 2008 GDP; (budget deficit in 2008: 0.8% of GDP)	Increase in expenditures (P 160 billion); infrastructure (P 100 billion); tax relief and reduction of corporate income tax rate (P 40 billion); waiver of penalties on loans from social security institutions (P 30 billion).
		Announced in January 2009; specific details not available at the time of writing.
Singapore	S$20.5 billion ($13.7 billion); 11.5% of 2008 GDP; (budget surplus in 2008: 0.9% of GDP)	*Job credit programme*: cash transfers for employers to cover part of their wage bills and avoid mass lay-offs (S$4.5 billion); *special risk sharing initiative*: Government guarantees to working-capital loans (up to S$5 million) to individual firms to stimulate bank lending; *cut in corporate tax rate* from 18% to 17%; and *personal income tax rebates* of 20% of taxes due (capped at S$2,000).
		Announced January 2009; the Government plans to draw down S$4.9 billion from previously accumulated reserves to finance the job credit and special risk sharing initiative programmes, and will also tap reserves held by the Monetary Authority of Singapore (the central bank) and the Government of Singapore Investment Corporation (a sovereign wealth fund).
Thailand	B 115 billion ($3.3 billion); 1.2% of 2008 GDP; (fiscal deficit in 2008: 1.4% of GDP)	One-time distribution of B 2,000 in cash to people who currently earn monthly salaries of less than B 15,000; support for social security; free education programmes; job creation; and low-interest loans to farmers.
		Approved by the cabinet in January 2009, the initiative extends by six months a package of economic stimulus measures implemented by the previous Government, including such measures as, lower water and electricity charges, free rides on some of Bangkok's public buses and free third-class train rides nationwide.
Viet Nam	D 17 trillion ($1 billion); 1.2% of 2008 GDP; (fiscal deficit in 2008: 4.1% of GDP)	Details not announced at the time of writing. Components include: subsidized loans to farmers at an annual rate of 11.5%; a 4% subsidy on the interest rate enterprises pay for their loans; and credit for small businesses.
		Announced December 2008.

subregion's resilience to future crises. From that point of view, spending on policies that promote the long-term sustainability of energy and food markets and that systematically address the deficiencies of current social protection systems is a valuable investment for the future, and also helps to stimulate domestic demand in the short-term. Regional coordination is needed not only to implement fiscal measures at the same time but also to agree on substantive policies that will benefit the subregion in both the short and long term. There is an opportunity for the ESCAP secretariat, in collaboration with the ASEAN secretariat, to organize joint studies and policy dialogues to discuss such substantive policies.

Developed economies in the ESCAP region: Heightened contagion and deepening recession

The three developed economies in the region remained relatively immune to financial crisis in 2007, as their financial sectors had limited exposures to the subprime loans of the United States. A fall-off in demand from the United States was partly offset by the continued strength of export demand from other major trading partners. However, by 2008, as the crisis struck developed countries of Europe and export demand from Asian countries fell sharply, the impact of the crisis spread to the developed countries of the region. In particular, the latest economic data show that the Japanese economy was the hardest hit among developed economies at the end of 2008. This is a reflection of these countries' deeper and more extensive financial, trade and investment interlinkages with the source of the financial crisis. Credit availability was reduced and costs of credit increased, and business and consumer confidence deteriorated rapidly, exacerbated by sharp falls in export demand. This set off a downward cycle of contagion that eventually engulfed both the developed and developing countries of the region.

Impact: The return of recession

The Japanese economy, which had maintained positive growth of 2.4% in 2007, was unable to sustain any growth in 2008 as export growth (figure 4.24), the main driver of previous growth, continued to decline. The economy went into recession after recording a contraction in the second quarter of 2008 – its first contraction since 2002 (table 4.14). It recorded quarterly contraction of 3.3% in the fourth quarter of 2008, reducing the annual growth rate to –0.7%.

Although solid external demand supported business investment and growth, albeit weak, in much of 2007, the pessimistic business sentiments seen at the end of 2007 worsened in 2008, as indicated in the Tankan survey of business confidence in December 2008 (Bank of Japan, 2008a). The surge of commodity prices, together with falling demand, put further strain on corporate profits, which plunged by an annual rate of 22.4% in the third quarter of 2008 – the largest fall

Figure 4.24. Economic growth in developed ESCAP countries, 2006-2008

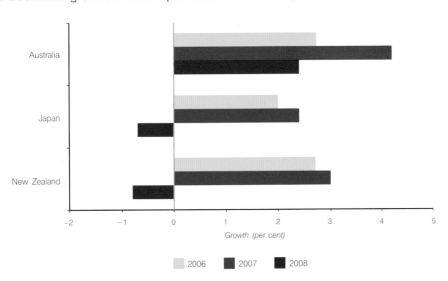

Sources: ESCAP, based on national sources; and ESCAP estimates.

Note: Figures for 2008 are estimates.

Table 4.14. Rates of economic growth and inflation of Australia, Japan and New Zealand, 2007-2009

(Per cent)

	Real GDP growth			Inflation[a]		
	2007	2008[b]	2009[c]	2007	2008[b]	2009[c]
Developed economies	2.6	−0.4	−2.2	0.3	1.7	0.1
Australia	4.2	2.4	0.5	2.3	4.4	3.1
Japan	2.4	−0.7	−2.5	0.1	1.4	−0.2
New Zealand	3.0	−0.8	−1.0	2.4	4.0	2.0

Sources: ESCAP, based on national sources; IMF, *International Financial Statistics* (CD-ROM) (Washington, D.C., 2008); and ESCAP estimates.

[a] Changes in the consumer price index.
[b] Estimate.
[c] Forecast (as of 27 February 2009).

in seven years (Japan, 2008a). Amid falling profits and deteriorating confidence, business investment continued to fall through 2008 in Japan, diving at an annual rate of 13% in the third quarter. Construction, which plunged in the third quarter in 2007 due to the revised building standards law, started to recover during 2008, although it fell again at the end of the year, reflecting the deterioration of consumer confidence. Fears of a credit crunch led corporate managers to rush for bank loans to maintain liquidity while such credit was available. Bank lending grew 3.6% year-on-year in November 2008, following the 16-year high of 2.3% in October (Financial Times, 2008).

Amid falling profits and deteriorating confidence, business investment continued to fall through 2008 in Japan

---

The business slump undermined the modest growth in household consumption seen in 2007, where an increase in business profits had been slowly transmitted to household income through employment growth and dividend payments to shareholders. Consumer confidence has steadily declined since 2007, and household consumption weakened further in 2008, reflecting sluggish wage growth, an increase in unemployment and the erosion of purchasing power due to high oil and food prices.

New Zealand's economy also fell into recession in 2008 after a decade of solid growth, as private consumption dwindled, business investment slowed and import growth exceeded export growth. It recorded negative growth for three consecutive quarters, as of the September quarter of 2008. Australia's economy, in

contrast, sustained moderate growth in 2008, marking the eighteenth year of expansion, although at a moderate pace of 2.4% compared to the strong growth of 4.2% seen in 2007. As in 2007, household consumption and private investment were the main contributors to growth in 2008, while export growth was buoyed by strong commodity prices in the first half of the year.

In Australia and New Zealand the economy was supported by private investment in 2008, although at a moderate pace. In both countries, sizable funding comes from the overseas wholesale market and thus, funding costs have increased, reducing the availability of credit in the domestic market.

Business investment in Australia remained at a high level as a share of GDP in 2008, bolstered by the strength of the mining sector, but reflected a slower pace than in the previous year. Private business investment grew by an annual rate of 12.8% as of September 2008, following record growth of 18.4% in 2007 (Australian Bureau of Statistics, 2008). Nonetheless, business confidence was lower than the long-term average, and firms' intentions for further investment are largely uncertain when ongoing projects are completed. While the mining sector has been largely insulated from the financial crisis so far, tighter credit and the rising cost of equity funding, combined with falling commodity prices, are likely to discourage future investment.

Business investment continued to expand at the beginning of 2008 in New Zealand as well, partly compensating for the weak private consumption growth, although firms were more cautious about further investment. With greater pessimism about profits, business confidence worsened in November, as profit margins decreased in the face of weaker demand and increasing production costs. A softening labour market clearly indicated the loss of business confidence, with the employment intention of firms rapidly dropping in 2008 (New Zealand, 2008). According to the National Bank Business Outlook in November 2008, a net 21% of firms expected to reduce staff during the next 12 months.

Household consumption moderated in Australia in 2008 as households started to rebalance their consumption and debt repayment and growth of disposable income remained weak. Falling stock market and house prices reduced household wealth, while rising interest rates in the past few years gradually increased the burden on the households. By September 2008, household debt had increased to almost 160% of disposable income, compared to about 80% a decade ago (Reserve Bank of Australia, 2009). Debt servicing amounted to 15% of disposable income by September 2008, and households restrained their consumption to reduce their debt. Still, household consumption was expected to maintain positive growth, as lower interest rates would ease the burden of debt repayment, and the fiscal stimulus packages are expected to help restore consumer confidence.

Similarly, household consumption decelerated in New Zealand in 2008, owing to falling disposable income, accelerating inflation, the increasing burden of mortgage payment as a result of tightening monetary policy in the past few years, and falling household financial wealth caused by the fall in house prices. Household debt had increased to 160% of disposable income (nominal) by the third quarter of 2008 compared to 94% a decade ago, and debt servicing increased from just over 9% to almost 15% of disposable income during the same period (Reserve Bank of New Zealand, 2008a), leaving little room to build up savings. Moreover, deterioration of the housing market weakened consumer confidence, as housing accounted for 75% of the assets of the household sector in New Zealand in 2007 (EIU, 2008a). House prices plunged, sales declined by 35% in the year to October 2008 and residential investments fell sharply.

Labour market: rising unemployment

Labour market conditions eased and the unemployment rate edged up in 2008 in all three economies.

In Japan, the tight labour market during 2007 did not translate into wage growth because demand for labour was largely met by an increase in the number of part-time workers, who earn much less than regular workers. Sluggish wage growth, in turn, suppressed consumption growth. With declining corporate profits and bleak prospects for the global economy in 2008, firms started to cut their labour force, particularly part-time workers, further dampening consumer confidence.

In contrast, in Australia the tight labour market seen until the first quarter of 2008 was accompanied by an increase in both full-time and part-time employment,

most significantly in full-time male employment and part-time female employment. The unemployment rate edged up in October 2008, partly due to an increase in the workforce participation rate, and labour demand would ease as the slowdown of the economy would gradually be translated into the labour market, as already indicated by a fall in employment intentions in the business surveys (Reserve Bank of Australia, 2008).

The unemployment rate edged up in 2008 in all three economies

---

A long, steady decline of unemployment in New Zealand also came to an end in 2008, with the unemployment rate rising to its highest since 2003. In contrast to 2007, when both skilled and unskilled labour was in shortage, the downturn forced firms to cut employment or work hours in 2008. While wage growth continued well into 2008, it was largely owing to the delayed impact of high inflation and the tight labour market in the immediate past.

Accelerated inflation

All three economies saw higher inflation in 2008 (figure 4.25). Higher input costs intensified producer price inflation, and high prices of oil and food pushed up the consumer price inflation.

Figure 4.25. Inflation in developed ESCAP economies, 2006-2008

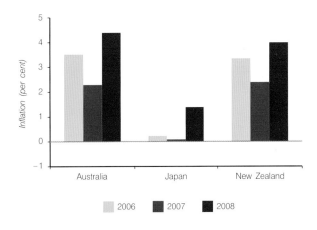

Sources: ESCAP, based on national sources; IMF, *International Financial Statistics* (CD-ROM) (Washington, D.C., 2008); and ESCAP estimates.

Notes: Figures for 2008 are estimates. Inflation rates refer to percentage changes in the consumer price index.

In Japan, the high price of oil and commodities continued to drive up corporate price inflation during 2008, recording a hike in annual inflation of more than 7% in the third quarter 2008. Corporate price inflation put upward pressure on consumer prices, although the impact was partly cushioned as market competition made it difficult for producers to pass on the price increases to consumers. Thus consumer price inflation edged up 1.4% in 2008, reflecting the price increase in oil and oil-related products. However, falling oil prices and the dismal economic outlook since the second half of 2008 brought back concerns about deflation – a key policy challenge for the Japanese economy for over a decade, where consumer price inflation hovered around 0%.

Accelerated consumer price inflation in Australia was broad-based, but especially reflected a surge of non-tradable inflation, while tradable inflation was the main driver in New Zealand. In Australia, broad-based price increases pushed the consumer price index to 4.4% for 2008. Non-tradable inflation jumped to 6.1% during the year ended September 2008 due to an increase in housing-related prices, including rents and costs for building materials, while tradable inflation also continued its upward trend at 3.4% during the same period, reflecting fuel and food price increases. Although the inflation rate excluding fuel and food prices was considered to be just over 1% per year, depreciation of the Australian dollar in the second half of the year put upward pressure on the tradable inflation. By December, the non-tradable inflation slowed to 5.4% while tradable inflation moderated to 1.2%. As for producer prices, the intensified inflation seen in 2008 reflected a broad-based increase in prices of domestic goods. The fall of the Australian dollar reversed the declining trend of import prices in the third quarter of 2008. The wage-price index sustained solid growth in 2008, reflecting the tight labour market, although softening of the labour market is gradually translated into subdued labour cost inflation.

In New Zealand, the rise of commodity prices in 2008 drove inflation to a record level, with costs of non-labour inputs up by 13.6% on an annual basis in the September quarter. Depreciation of the New Zealand dollar insulated the country from the plunge of commodity prices in the global market later in the year and kept the domestic price of commodities high. Output prices also increased by a wide margin, although to a lesser extent than the increase in production costs, as firms found it difficult to pass on the price increase amid the low demand. Nonetheless, pressure on consumer prices was building, and the CPI recorded a 5.1% increase in the third quarter of 2008, the highest since 1990. Tradable inflation exceeded 6% in the third quarter of 2008, up from -0.5%

in mid-2007 (Reserve Bank of New Zealand, 2008b). As in Australia, the high inflation rate is expected to be contained in the coming years, given the weak economy overseas and at home and the consequent easing of capacity constraints.

Developments in the external sector

Japan has recorded an annual trade surplus for over a quarter of century. Destinations of Japanese exports have been increasingly diversified in recent years, cushioning the impact of falling demand from the United States in 2007. Strong export demand from Europe and Asia supported the continued export growth during 2007. But decline of United States demand became a drag on European demand in 2008, followed by the decline of export demand from Asia. Asia has accounted for almost half of Japanese exports in recent years, and the magnitude of the slowdown of Asian demand, most notably of China, had a large impact on the Japanese exports and thus on the health of the ailing economy. Exports started to contract in June 2008 in yen terms[3] and further decelerated during the year, falling by 26.5% in November (Japan, 2008b). Appreciation of the exchange rate in the second half of 2008 placed an overwhelming burden on exporters, as the Japanese yen had appreciated more than 30% since the end of 2007. The surge in fuel prices led to a dramatic increase in the value of imports in the second quarter of 2008. Reflecting the falling exports and increasing imports, the trade surplus shrank as much as 67% in 2008 on annual basis.

...the slowdown of Asian demand...had a large impact on the Japanese exports and thus on the health of the ailing economy

---

On the other hand, Australia's exports benefited from a surge in commodity prices in 2008. The trade balance recorded a surplus in the third quarter of 2008 – the first since 2001. Strong import growth has been surpassed by even stronger export growth, reflecting the growth in value of mining exports, a major export sector in Australia. In response to the surge in commodity prices in 2007, bulk commodity contract prices, such as iron ore and coal, saw a hike in 2008.

---

[3]   The export figures in dollar terms recorded positive growth, as shown in table 4.15, due to the weaker United States dollar against the Japanese yen.

The contract price for thermal coal, for example, more than doubled in 2008. Thus, the value of mining exports increased more than 50% over the year to September, despite the significant fall of commodity prices in the second half of 2008. That figure is expected to moderate as the sharp fall in commodity prices is reflected in future contract prices, while demand from major trading partners such as China is likely to slow down. But depreciation of the Australian dollar would partly insulate the economy from the global downturn. The net income deficit remained high, although it narrowed in 2008, reflecting a decrease in corporate profits remitted to overseas firms as well as an increase in foreign currency assets in Australian dollar terms. The current account deficit was thus reduced from $56.8 billion in 2007 to $37.5 billion in 2008 (EIU, 2008b).

New Zealand's trade deficit widened, as strong export growth was exceeded by even stronger growth of imports in 2008. The growth of imports was partly due to the delayed impact of falling commodity prices as well as still-buoyant capital goods imports. The trade deficit is expected to narrow as depreciation of the New Zealand dollar supports exports and weak domestic demand reduces import demand (table 4.15).

Policy responses

The deepening global downturn led the macroeconomic policies of the three economies in the same direction: supporting domestic demand, particularly household consumption, and ensuring liquidity in the financial sector. The budget balance is expected to worsen in all three economies, as revenue growth decreases and the need for fiscal expenditure, which the three Governments have begun to undertake (table 4.16), grows.

For Japan this means a painful reversal of fiscal policy. Fiscal consolidation has been a major challenge for Japan, which has run a primary deficit for the past 15 years and accumulated public debt equivalent to 170% of GDP (EIU, 2008c). The narrowing budget deficit – from 8% of GDP in 2002 to 3.2% in 2007 – reflected both economic expansion and the Government's effort to cut expenditure. However, the proposed budget for fiscal year 2009 indicates an increase of expenditure by 7%. The Government has effectively postponed its target to achieve a primary balance (excluding social security) by the fiscal year 2011, as the deteriorating economic outlook has led it to make economic recovery a priority over fiscal con-

Table 4.15. Summary of external accounts for ESCAP developed countries

(Per cent)

	Export/GDP		Import/GDP		Current account balance/GDP	
	2007	2008[a]	2007	2008[a]	2007	2008[b]
Australia	16.6	19.4	18.7	20.4	−6.2	−4.7
Japan	15.5	16.2	13.1	15.2	4.8	3.6
New Zealand	21.1	24.4	22.5	25.8	−7.8	−9.0

	Growth rates					
	Exports			Imports		
	2006	2007	2008	2006	2007	2008
Australia[c]	17.6	14.2	37.4	12.6	19.1	25.8
Japan	8.0	9.9	10.0	12.3	7.0	22.9
New Zealand[d]	2.8	20.5	27.1	−0.1	17.9	25.1

Sources: Reserve Bank of Australia website, accessed from www.rba.gov.au, 22 December 2008; Japan External Trade Organization website, accessed from www.jetro.go.jp/en/stats/statistics/, 22 December 2008; Bank of Japan website, accessed from www.boj.or.jp/en/howstat/hs01.htm#st1, 22 December 2008; Statistics New Zealand website, accessed from www.stats.govt.nz, 22 December 2008; IMF, *International Financial Statistics* (CD-ROM) (Washington, D.C., 2008); and ESCAP estimates.

[a] 2008 data refers to the first three quarters.
[b] Estimates.
[c] 2008 data refers to January-October.
[d] 2008 data refers to the first three quarters.

Table 4.16. Fiscal stimulus packages in developed countries in Asia and the Pacific

	Size	Contents	Details
Japan	12 trillion yen fiscal measures; ($125 bn, or about 2% of GDP) (Supplementary budget 2008/09 and budget 2009/10)	Consists of three components: (a) *Assistance toward people's daily lives*, including fixed-sum stipends (2 trillion yen), measures to support employment (1.1 trillion yen), tax reduction on mortgage loans, eco-friendly investment, etc. and the reduction of medical expenses for the elderly; (b) *Assistance to small and medium-sized enterprises*, including tax breaks for the promotion of investment in energy-saving facilities (190 bn yen), and tax cuts (240 bn yen); (c) *Efforts to revive local areas*, including emergency disaster prevention (440 bn yen), subsidies to revitalize local areas (600 bn yen), an increase in allocation of the local government budget for creation of employment and revival of the local economy (2 trillion yen).	Part of a 75 trillion yen package (63 trillion yen allocated for financial measures), distributed within the two supplementary budgets for the fiscal year 2008, 11.5 trillion yen and 27 trillion yen respectively (passed), and for the fiscal year 2009, 37 trillion yen (submitted to the Diet).
Australia	A$10.4 bn economic security strategy, plus A$42 bn (US$26 bn, or about 3.6% of GDP) nation-building and jobs plan	(a) *Economic security strategy* (A$10.4 bn): lump-sum cash payments to pensioners, one-off payment to low- and middle-income families and assistance to first-time home buyers;	Announced in October 2008
	(budget 2008/09)	(b) *Nation-building and jobs plan* (A$42 bn or 3.6% of GDP): (i) A$28.8 bn investment on infrastructure and support to small businesses, including investment in schools infrastructure (A$14.7 bn), housing (A$6.6 bn), energy efficiency (A$3.9 bn), community infrastructure and roads (A$890 mn) and tax breaks for small businesses (A$2.7 bn); (ii) A$12.7 bn immediate stimulus to support growth and jobs.	Announced in February 2009
New Zealand	NZ$500 mn (US$290 mn, or about 0.4% of GDP)	(a) A series of initiatives under jobs and growth plan, including: NZ$483.7 mn of infrastructure spending on education (NZ$216.7 mn), transport (NZ$142.5 mn), and housing (NZ$124.5 mn).	(Announcement by John Key, Prime Minister of New Zealand, 11 February 2009)
	NZ$480 million	(b) Small Business Relief Package (over four years), which consists of: (i) A suite of 11 tax changes; (ii) An expansion to the export credit scheme; (iii) Extended jurisdiction for the Disputes Tribunal; (iv) Expansion of business advice services; (v) A prompt-payment requirement for Government agencies.	(Announcement by the Prime Minister on 4 February 2009)

Sources: Japan, Economic and Fiscal Policy webpage of the Cabinet Office, available at www5.cao.go.jp/keizai/index-e.html; Australia, Budget 2008/09 website, available at www.budget.gov.au/2008-09/index.htm; John Key, speech dated 11 February 2009, available at http://beehive.govt.nz (official website of the Government of New Zealand).

solidation for the time being. The Government announced plans for an economic stimulus package of approximately 75 trillion yen in total, consisting of 12 trillion yen (about 2% of GDP) in fiscal measures and 63 trillion yen in financial measures within the two supplementary budgets for fiscal year 2008 and the budget for fiscal year 2009. The package embraces three components: assistance for consumers, assistance to small and medium-sized enterprises, and the revitalization of regional economies.

The deepening global downturn led the macroeconomic policies of the three economies in the same direction

---

While Australia has enjoyed budget surpluses for over a decade, the surplus narrowed in 2008/2009 budget in the face of the threat of global recession. The initial estimate of a budget surplus of A$21.7 billion was revised down to A$5.4 billion (US$4.7 billion), reflecting a large expenditure on the economic stimulus package and an expected fall in tax revenue due to increasing unemployment and declining corporate profits. To boost domestic consumption amid the worsening global economic and financial outlook, the Government announced its Economic Security Strategy in October 2008, most of which was to be delivered in 2008 and 2009. The package, worth A$10.4 billion, or about 1% of GDP, focuses on household consumption and dwelling investment through lump-sum cash payments to pensioners, a one-off payment to low and middle-income families, and assistance to first-time home buyers. In addition, in February the Government announced a nation-building and jobs plan worth A$42 billion (3.6% of GDP) to help support and sustain up to 90,000 jobs through infrastructure investment, grants and tax cuts.

New Zealand's long record of budget surplus is also likely to suffer in fiscal year 2008, reflecting a fall in tax revenue along with softening GDP growth, while pressure for expansionary fiscal expenditure mounts. In February 2009, the Government announced its plan for economic stimulus packages, aiming to support small and medium-sized enterprises and to invest on infrastructure including education, transport and housing.

Monetary policy was loosened in all three economies, a major turnaround for the policies of Australia and New Zealand. For Japan it meant the first return since 2006 to extremely loose monetary policy. The Bank of Japan cut the target for the overnight call rate in October 2008, from 0.5% to 0.3%. After the United

States Federal Reserve Bank cut its target for the federal funds rate to between 0 and 0.25%, the Bank of Japan cut its target rate to 0.1% in December (Bank of Japan, 2008b).

The past experience of accommodative monetary policy in Japan cast doubt on the effectiveness of the rate cut to prevent a credit crunch, and the Bank of Japan explored other measures to ensure liquidity for the corporate sector, especially small and medium-sized enterprises. An unusual increase in bank lending at the end of 2008 was a clear sign that the business sector feared a credit crunch. To encourage banks to maintain funding for the corporate sector, the Bank of Japan relaxed its requirements for loans to banks so that banks could get loans with lower-rated corporate debts as collateral. It also announced other non-traditional measures, such as the purchase of corporate bonds and commercial paper to reduce corporate financing costs.

As a response to the global financial crisis, Japan agreed in February 2009 to contribute $100 billion (signed in February 2009) of its foreign exchange reserves to the International Monetary Fund (Financial Times, 2009) which may otherwise run out of financial resources if many more large emerging markets need rescue loans.

In Australia and New Zealand, tight monetary policies turned to drastic monetary easing in 2008 in response to the global financial crisis. In Australia, the cash rate target had steadily increased from 4.25% in December 2001 to 7.25% in March 2008; by February 2009, the rate had been cut back to 3.25%. To address threats to the ability of Australian financial institutions to access funding, the Government announced a guarantee of bank deposits and bank wholesale funding of authorized deposit-taking institutions.

In Australia and New Zealand, tight monetary policies turned to drastic monetary easing

---

Similarly, in New Zealand the official cash rate, which was gradually raised over five years from 5% in 2003 to 8.25% in July 2008, was slashed to 3.5% by January 2009. Like other Governments, the Government of New Zealand also took measures to improve access to credit. In October the Treasury offered an insurance scheme that provides a deposit guarantee for retail deposits. Given the heavy reliance of banks in New Zealand on foreign wholesale markets, in November the Treasury announced a temporary guarantee of wholesale borrowing by investment-grade financial institutions that choose to opt into the scheme.

Outlook and key policy priorities

The Japanese economy is expected to contract further in 2009, by −2.5% according to forecasts as export demand continues to contract and domestic demand deteriorates. Inflation is expected to be −0.2%, a worrisome prospect given the deflationary pressures that have come to characterize the Japanese economy. Higher unemployment and declining real wages, combined with uncertainty over the social security system, will further undermine consumer confidence and weaken private consumption. While the global financial crisis placed economic recovery at the forefront of economic policy in Japan in the short term, fiscal consolidation and reform of social welfare systems remain key priorities in the medium term. The huge and growing public debt, combined with a fast-aging population, makes the current social security system unsustainable. The decade-long recession in the 1990s revealed the need for restructuring the social safety net, and the current crisis added the urgency to ensure that the system is resilient to such a large shock and has built in the mechanism to protect vulnerable groups. It is a huge and perplexing task in the face of declining growth.

The Australian economy is expected to weaken to 0.5% growth, and the economy of New Zealand is expected to contract by 1% in 2009 as export demand from the major trading partners remains weak. Depreciation of their currencies would cushion the impact of slower export growth, while weaker domestic demand reduces the import demand. Fiscal and monetary policy measures in both countries are expected to help restore consumer confidence and ease the downward pressure on household consumption. In both economies, the current account deficit is expected to narrow in 2009 while still remaining a key concern in both countries.

Conclusion

Subregions of Asia and the Pacific showed remarkable resilience to the array of crises that hit in 2008, although impacts and coping mechanisms varied among subregions. More worrisome was that developed economies (including Hong Kong, China; Taiwan Province of China, the Republic of Korea and Singapore) entered into recession quickly over the past year and are expected to remain in recession for the whole of 2009, underscoring just how difficult it is to maintain stable and sustained economic growth in mature economies. This, combined with mounting health and social security payouts arising from an ageing society and escalating public debts, has brought a new set of socio-economic challenges for mature economies that will severely test previous assumptions of steady and predictable growth for the region. Resolving these problems will require innovative, untested and possibly unpopular means. More, rather than less, openness to other countries will be needed, built around new avenues of multidirectional and mutually beneficial cooperation between developed and developing countries, as well as among developing countries themselves. In other words, some countries in the region are in a strong position to help not only themselves but also to mitigate the impact of the crisis in other subregions, thus presenting an opportunity for intra- and inter-subregional cooperation to narrow past equity divides and contribute to strengthened regional solidarity.

We return to this in chapter 5.

References

Australian Bureau of Statistics (2008). Australian National Accounts: National Income, Expenditure and Product, 5206.0, September quarter 2008.

Bank of Japan (2008a). Tankan Survey (available at www.boj.or.jp/en/theme/research/stat/tk/index.htm).

_____(2008b). Minutes of the Monetary Policy Meeting of the Bank of Japan Policy Board, Bangkok, 18-19 December 2008 (available at www.boj.or.jp/en/type/release/teiki/giji/g081219.pdf).

China Daily (2009a). "Keeping the housing market humming", 5 January.

_____(2009b). "China's realty prices dip further in December", 12 January.

Economist Intelligence Unit (EIU) (2008a). *Country Report: New Zealand*, December.

_____(2008b). *Country Report: Australia*, December.

_____(2008c). Country data, accessed in December 2008.

ESCAP (2008). *Economic and Social Survey of Asia and the Pacific 2008* (United Nations publication, Sales No. E.08.II.F.7).

_____(2009). *Statistical Yearbook for Asia and the Pacific 2008* (United Nations publication, Sales No. E.09.II.F.1, forthcoming).

Financial Times (2008). "Record loan growth at Japanese banks", 8 December (available at www.ft.com).

Financial Times (2009). "Japan boosts support for trade finance programme", 14 February.

Japan (2008a). Financial Statements Statistics of Corporations by Industry, July-September 2008, Policy Research Institute, Ministry of Finance (available at www.mof.go.jp/english/e1c002.htm).

_____(2008b). Balance of Payments, November, Ministry of Finance (available at www.mof.go.jp/bpoffice/bpdata/pdf/bp0811.pdf).

New Zealand (2008). *Monthly Economic Indicators*, November 2008, New Zealand Treasury (available at www.treasury.govt.nz/economy/mei/archive/pdfs/mei-nov08.pdf).

Pitsuwan, Vichaya (2008). "Industry wants airport remedies: Estimated B137bn in damages from closure", *Bangkok Post*, 10 December.

Reserve Bank of New Zealand (2008a). Key Graph "Household debt" (available at www.rbnz.govt.nz/keygraphs/Fig5.html).

_____(2008b). Statistics (available at www.rbnz.govt.nz/statistics/econind/a3/download.html).

Reserve Bank of Australia (2008). *Statement on Monetary Policy*, November.

_____(2009). "Household Finances – Selected Ratios", Table B21, www.rba. gov.au/Statistics/Bulletin/index.html or www.rba. gov.au/Statistics/Bulletin/B21hist.xls.

Theparat, Chatrudee (2008). "1% dent in growth seen", *Bangkok Post*, 8 December.

Tripartite Core Group (2008). *Post-Nargis Joint Assessment*.

UNICEF (2008). *Progress for Children, A Report Card on Maternal Mortality* (New York).

Vietnam Business Finance (2008). "Vietnam to introduce ceiling, floor rates", 17 December (available at www.vnbusinessnews.com/2008/12/vietnam-to-introduce-ceiling-floor.html).

World Bank (2006). "Can South Asia end poverty in a generation?" (available at http://go.worldbank.org/NF9FFJTM20).

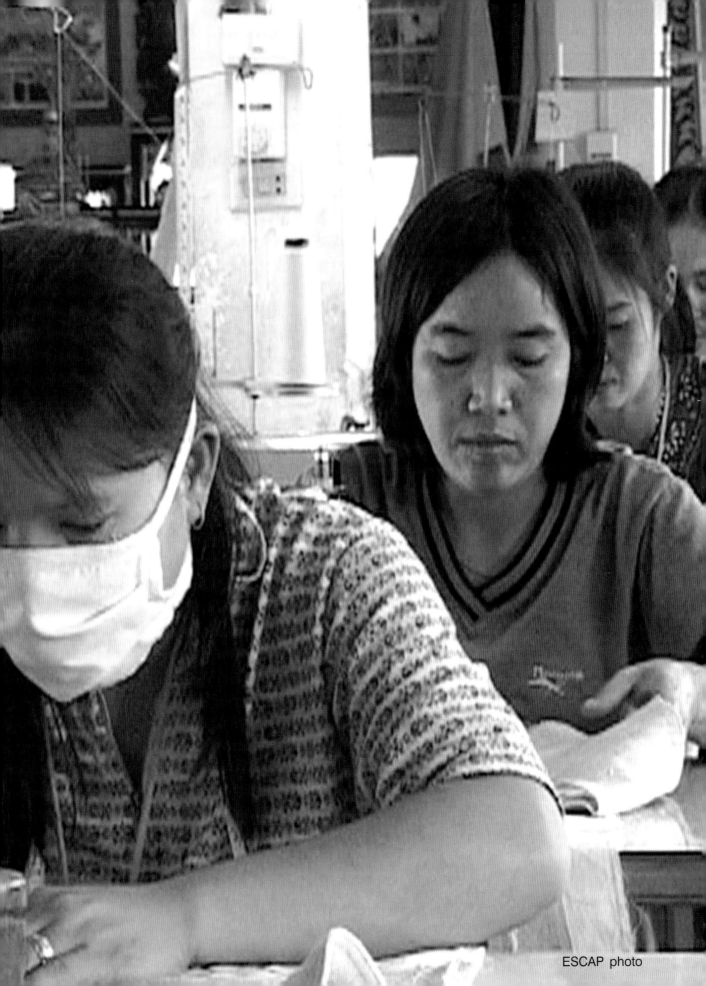

ESCAP photo

The stability of global financial markets is a public good. If governments fail to protect this public good, then those who suffer are the working people of the world whose jobs, whose homes, and standard of living depends on it.

Kevin Rudd
Prime Minister of Australia

CHAPTER 5. CONVERGING CRISES: REDIRECTING POLICIES TO ACHIEVE INCLUSIVE AND SUSTAINABLE DEVELOPMENT

The year 2008 was tumultuous. On the one hand, it continued to deliver impressively on a number of fronts: dynamic trade and investment-led economic growth, continued incisions into poverty and technological advances that opened up treasure troves of prosperity, knowledge and human interconnectedness that may enable us to live longer, healthier and more interconnected lives than we ever thought possible. On the other hand, quite stealthily in the third quarter, 2008 turned out to be a year that shook the world. As the preceding chapters have discussed, the unprecedented occurrence and convergence of three crises left no economy, and very few individuals, unaffected.

How these events will go down in history remains to be seen. Of course, what today appears cataclysmic may with the passage of time become a historical curiosity. This concluding chapter argues that the simultaneous occurrence of the crises will prove to be more significant than a historical footnote. The convergence of the three crises is but a symptom of a larger problem, the enormity of which is still unfolding. It drives home a stark reality that, for all our impressive achievements, the world is under severe stress and more fragile than was thought possible. While in all likelihood the convergence of the multiple threats will not prove catastrophic, we have come frighteningly close to systemic disaster, and such near misses cannot go unaccounted for.

Many questions arise. Have we evolved a global system, with its opaque interplays between financial de-

manders and suppliers that is too complex? For too long, have we allowed excessive greed to prevail? How much market self-correction is socially optimal? Are we ruining the regenerative potential of our ecosystems? Have we created social inequities that can never be corrected? What is the role of government and its partners? Answers to these questions are central to determining the critical threshold of the world's endurance. The convergence of the crises suggests that we have a world teetering on the threshold of its endurance.

The convergence of the crises suggests that we have a world teetering on the threshold of its endurance

---

This chapter addresses the commonalities and policy tensions across the triple threat to development, and proposes a way forward for government and its partners. The stresses are common to more than one crisis, and there are compounding effects that must be taken into account in devising policy responses. The central idea is that the convergence of the crises provides a unique opportunity to address each threat and jump-start a reorientation towards inclusive and sustainable development in which modernized government will form and frame the region's future development.

Commonalities among the crises

One characteristic that runs through the three crises is their global scope. The ever-increasing interdependence of countries, with increasing shares of GDP moving across borders through trade, investments and financial flows, means that no country can remain immune from a crisis. A local infection quickly becomes a systemic disease. The larger the initial point of attack, the faster the contagion and the greater the likelihood of systemic shutdown. The subprime crisis hit the United States and, as it worked its way through the financial and real sectors, it quickly evolved into a full-blown world economic crisis. One country introduced a ban on rice exports, and others soon followed suit, all clamouring to secure self-sufficiency and further exacerbating shortages and price spikes. Crises no longer fit into simplistic developed/developing country classifications. Disaster can strike financial capitals with the same ferocity as emerging markets. Hurricane Katrina and Cyclone Nargis tore apart communities in countries at the opposite ends of the development spectrum. What is certain is that the poor, regardless of their location and regardless of the nature of the crisis that hits, suffer a more severe impact and take longer to recover. They are also those least responsible for causing the crisis.

A second commonality is that all three crises are long-term in character. The current global financial crisis is not just an ordinary downturn in the business cycle. It has roots in macroeconomic and financial vulnerabilities that have been building up for decades. The increases in the prices of crude oil and food commodities between 2002 and mid-2008 reflect a long neglect of investment stemming from declining prices in the 1980s and 1990s. And the threats posed by climate change to food production, water resources and livelihoods in coastal areas are the result of a long period of intense industrial production and human activity.

Hurricane Katrina and Cyclone Nargis tore apart communities in countries at the opposite ends of the development spectrum

---

Third, imbalances are at the root of all the crises. The financial crisis is associated with an imbalance between savings and expenditures, both within countries and across countries. A sluggish supply response to fast-rising demand for crude oil and food commodities, especially cereals, caused inventories to fall and prices to increase. An imbalance between the rich and poor in access to water, sanitation, energy, health and education perpetuates endemic poverty and further environmental degradation across the generations. And imbalances tend to grow. Economic wealth is increasingly concentrated in the hands of fewer people, superimposing wider circles of imbalances that will add compounding and self-perpetuating effects to the crises. When imbalances in financial markets were added to those in energy and food markets, commodity prices soared further, in turn compromising both economic growth and the goal of eliminating poverty and hunger.

Convergence and policy stresses

Given the commonalities across the crises, their convergence brings compounding effects that feed on each other and could result in more stresses and the imposition of new layers of crises. Three pressure points are discussed: a financial crisis that is converging on itself, financial excesses and volatility in commodity prices, and scarce financial resources to address the effects of climate change.

The financial crisis threatens to converge on itself in a deep, downward spiral

The magnitude of the current financial crisis is unprecedented in living memory. Trillions of dollars have evaporated, bringing on a recession in developed countries that will take many months, perhaps years, to turn around decisively. Asia-Pacific countries are experiencing sharp reversals in the growth trend they registered over the period 2002-2007, with the worst yet to come. Setbacks to the region's progress in poverty reduction appear unavoidable as more countries go off track in their quest to attain the Millennium Development Goals by 2015. The prospects for Asia-Pacific less developed countries, which have made remarkable progress in the past few years, are also deteriorating rapidly.

The commodity price collapses that tracked the financial crisis made it clear that commodity and financial markets have become tightly interlinked

Further exacerbating this situation is the distinct possibility that, with expansionary global fiscal and monetary policies proving less effective than hoped for, the developed world will fall into the dreaded "liquidity trap", not unlike the experience of Japan during the 1990s when monetary policy with interest rates close to zero failed to stimulate private consumption and investment. Under these circumstances the financial crisis will converge on itself in a downward spiral. Risk aversion will deepen, and banks will continue to use any liquidity injections to prop up their balance sheets rather than extend loans to households and busi-

nesses. As rescue packages and other fiscal stimulus measures increase, they may eventually lack the credibility needed to restore market confidence. Due to the sheer magnitude of the crisis, fear will deepen that Governments lack sufficient means to finance ever larger bailouts of the financial system. The long-term prospects for recovery will darken considerably as it becomes clear that the enormous increases in public debt will drag down economic recovery in the future.

Views differ widely as to the extent to which the world economy finds itself in this scenario. Whatever the reality, the crisis is deepening, and even if the Asia-Pacific region has shown remarkable resilience up to now, it cannot afford to be complacent.

Financial excesses and commodity price volatility

In the wake of the intensifying financial crisis, the unprecedented volatility in the prices of oil and non-oil primary commodities in 2008 – with oil prices soaring 50% in the first half of the year only to plummet by more than 70% by January 2009, and other commodity prices tracking closely – led to economic losses and huge uncertainties about how to plan for the future. The commodity price collapses that tracked the financial crisis made it clear that commodity and financial markets have become tightly interlinked, that the crises were converging and that they were having compounding effects. The global financial crisis of 2008 was preceded by a period of high international liquidity and low real interest rates, which increased the amounts of risks and leverage that borrowers, investors and intermediaries were willing to take on (Financial Stability Forum, 2008, p. 5). With the bursting of the United States real estate bubble that ignited the subprime crisis, investors tried to reallocate funds to other markets, including commodity markets. In the case of crude oil, the resulting increases in prices, along with the very low real interest rates, created an incentive for producers to save oil for the future instead of selling it today and investing the proceeds in the money market (Frankel, 2008). But with mounting problems in global financial markets and growth projections turning sour, speculative capital rapidly exited from commodity markets, leading to sharp and sustained falls in prices. Looking forward, a key concern is that a massive liquidity injection arising from bailouts may find its way into commodity futures once again, causing another sharp increase in commodity prices, an event for which the region may find itself unprepared.

Looking forward, a key concern is that a massive liquidity injection arising from bailouts may find its way into commodity futures once again

---

Such unpredictable volatility brings with it a number of challenges for Asia and the Pacific. Most worrisome, it increases the risks for long-term investments in the agriculture sector, thus deepening the neglect that has characterized agriculture for decades and compounding pessimism in an already risk-averse environment (ESCAP, 2008a). Unless corrective action is taken, it could perpetuate the immiserization of farmers for some time to come, while also deepening concerns about food insecurity and the possibility of social unrest across wide swathes of the region's population. Furthermore, continued sharp drops in demand from developed countries will worsen the foreign exchange earnings of major commodity exporters who had earlier benefited from the price booms and strong demand – further deepening the economic downturn for this region for a longer period than initially thought.

Financial resources are scarce, and the costs of addressing climate change challenges are high

A third compounding effect of the triple crisis is the increasing fiscal deficits and public debt. With the list of distressed institutions and people growing every day – be it ailing banks, strategic industries hurt by the downturn and price volatilities, farmers who were unprepared for the collapse in commodity prices, urban poor struggling with higher food prices or the increasing ranks of unemployed – Governments may come under severe pressure to spend their funds on immediate emergencies and the need to maintain social stability and order. They may be hesitant to dedicate scarce resources to long-term objectives, such as climate change, where the returns are not immediately obvious. As economic growth continues to decelerate, automatic stabilizers will trigger a significant revenue decrease, giving Governments even less fiscal space. Governments will be tempted to shift costs to future generations.

It is clear that, given all these huge pressures, aid budgets could come under greater pressure and especially affect low-income countries that rely on official development assistance not only for their poverty alleviation strategies and long-term development but also as a cushion against external shocks. The least developed countries that are experiencing large and growing fiscal deficits will be particularly vulnerable.

The future of Asia and the Pacific: Investing in inclusive and sustainable development

What do the triple threat to development and the policy tensions to which it has given rise mean for the future policy design of the Asia-Pacific region? Solutions are to be found by addressing the commonalities and policy tensions across the three crises.

Future policies must be built around a rebalancing of economic, social and environmental systems, and between Governments and their partners. Putting these solutions to work is a process that reaches beyond market dynamics. It stretches across continents, linking people and societies to each other and, across time, linking generations.

The nerve centres for reorienting policies are Governments – their institutions, and how they collaborate with their partners domestically and with each other regionally and in the international arena

---

How can this be done? The nerve centres for reorienting policies are Governments – their institutions, and how they collaborate with their partners domestically and with each other regionally and in the international arena to support long-term visions and keep systems in equilibrium. The sheer magnitude of the financial crisis combined with the food and environmental crises have fundamentally changed the macroeconomic landscape with policies on public spending being a key policy gap. Mitigating climate change and reducing future episodes of soaring crude oil prices entail promoting energy efficiency and the use of renewable energy. But an overemphasis on the need to attain energy security could also worsen food security and climate-change challenges if arable lands meant for the cultivation of food crops disappear or if deforestation takes place.

Yet, this is not enough. Calibrating financial instruments for economic growth and sharing economic wealth for inclusive growth must also be featured more prominently than in the recent past, when allocations were left largely to market mechanisms and their perceived

tendency to self-correct. The costs and the risks inherent in market failures and the relative neglect of government's traditional capabilities for correcting such inefficiencies have proven too brutal.

Public spending: Size matters

Given the scale of the global financial crisis, policies commensurate with the challenge are needed. Public spending of a much larger magnitude than in the past, leading to fiscal deficits that could rise above what sound macroeconomic management would prescribe under normal circumstances.

Public spending should also be expedient so that the depth of the trough is contained expeditiously. With about $4 trillion in foreign exchange reserves, large current-account surpluses and low inflation, many major Asian countries are well placed to expand public spending. Supporting economic growth is a fundamental responsibility, and many developing countries of the region will need real economic growth that is well above 4% to meet employment and poverty goals. Social expenditures must, in addition, make the development process inclusive and sustainable. Faster growth makes this goal feasible by generating job opportunities and revenues to fund the extension of coverage for health, education and other social services until they reach the entire population.

Even more important, perhaps, than the size of the investments that Governments will make is what Governments will spend on and how they will decide.

Quality matters more: The importance of forward planning

Public expenditures should be carefully targeted. Fiscal resources are limited, and today's increases in budget deficits will eventually need to be cut. Ensuring that current fiscal expenditures have the highest social rates of return is crucial for Governments to be able to make sound investment decisions. The composition of the package will depend on country-specific situations, particularly the point at which a country finds itself on the development spectrum. No one-size-fits-all. Nevertheless, certain principles are common to all situations.

Public investments in Asia-Pacific developing countries generally have contributed significantly to economic growth, poverty reduction and development. Typically, the first phase of development spending has been focused on reducing widespread poverty through broad-based economic growth that reaches rural areas. In subsequent phases, more attention has focused on reducing inequalities by focusing on lagging sectors and areas of persistent poverty within countries by targeting specific communities and households. More recently, because Asia and the Pacific is the region with the fastest urbanization and the most acute need for pollution control, widespread environmental degradation has resulted in increasing shares being allocated to clean-up operations.

In this reorientation, government spending should be forward-looking

The convergence of the crises has added novel dimensions to the traditional approach. The challenges emerging from the triple threat offer the basis for a major reorientation of the development process: aligning fiscal stimulus packages with a long-term goal for inclusive and sustainable development. In this reorientation, government spending should be forward-looking.

Investing for inclusive growth and human progress

The importance of investing in the region's richest resource – its peoples in all their diversities and all the wealth in historical heritage, culture and values they represent – cannot be overstated. Spending not only on social infrastructure (hospitals, schools, housing and sanitation) but also on improving the delivery of education and health systems is key to the quality of future economic growth and development in the region. China has recognized the need to invest $120 billion in the reform of its health-care system in the next three years, indicating the priority given to raising standards in public hospitals and on providing basic health insurance for all by 2011.

A related issue is the need to expand social protection systems. Over 80% of the region's population lacks access to social protection of any form, forcing millions to reduce meals, eat less nutritiously, take children out of school, sell livestock and other assets or borrow money to feed their families. Although domestic food price inflation rates are gradually

coming down across the region, there is no guarantee that another episode of fast-rising prices will not be repeated when the global economy resumes growth. It is important to provide all vulnerable individuals with minimum grants to support their food security, especially in countries that are unable to move towards universal coverage of the population.

Forward planning also requires Governments to make provisions for an ageing society. The population of Asia is ageing fast: 17% of its developing-country population is expected to be over 65 years of age by 2025, compared with 6% today. This increase in the aged is twice as fast as that of developed countries. Even more worrying is the narrow coverage of social pensions and a poverty rate among older people that is about double the population as a whole, denying them dignity and security. It prevents older persons from contributing to society as sources of experience, wisdom and heritage or as workers. Investing in pensions will have significant multiplier effects that are immediate – better care of the children whom the older citizens look after, for example, thus making development more inclusive and sustainable while also making societies more cohesive and stable.

If the downturn is prolonged, longer-lasting public spending may be more valuable than fast-acting expenditures

In the current debate about fiscal stimulus packages, some countries have opted for providing tax cuts or transfers to boost private consumption. Such policies are normally viewed as acting faster than public spending for physical or social infrastructure. But that may not be the case in the present circumstances. Given the overall pessimism and uncertainty, many households may opt for saving rather than spending most of these benefits. If the downturn is prolonged, longer-lasting public spending may be more valuable than fast-acting expenditures. Tax reductions, when utilized, should be directed to the poorest members of society, both to meet social goals and because the poor are most likely to spend any extra income, ensuring greater pass-through of tax reductions to national consumption and aggregate growth.

Government should support the development of technological innovations that have yet to reach their peak. Such a policy is not restricted to the more advanced countries of the region; there are numerous examples of less-well-off countries successfully investing in such innovations. These technologies can provide leapfrogging opportunities in many facets of human endeavour. Innovation feeds on itself, and powerful applications of new technologies will emerge in informatics, biotechnology, and robotic engineering that will see the region transform itself into a global source of renewal and growth. Of course, this will bring new ethical and governance challenges, but Asia and the Pacific has the human skills to contribute to human progress and transformative development.

Investing in environmentally sustainable development and innovation

An important application of new technologies will be related to clean technologies for mitigating the effects of climate change and environmental degradation. A major boost to investments in clean energy and energy efficiency will facilitate the diffusion of such technologies, helping to reduce their costs of production and to create technical capabilities among users and producers. A dramatic increase in the production and use of such technologies will not only contribute to easing pressures on the price of crude oil but also create the possibility of making major progress in the reduction of greenhouse gas emissions. Given the vulnerability of Asia and the Pacific to climate change and the rapid increase of greenhouse gas emissions in the region, it is imperative to forge a low-carbon development path. As discussed in chapter 3, inaction today will prove more costly in the future, when ecological trends may be irreversible. In some countries, the costs of dealing with the effects of climate change could rise above 20% of GDP.

Government should support the development of technological innovations that have yet to reach their peak

---

It is heartening to note that G20 Governments are proposing $2 trillion in additional spending over the next one to two years to revive the world economy, and this could prove a unique opportunity for the world community to achieve, through a coordinated effort, a Global Green New Deal: expediting economic recovery and creating jobs while being consistent with the medium-term objectives of reducing carbon dependency, environmental deterioration and extreme world poverty.

Investment in infrastructure is another important component of a forward-looking planning approach, and has already received a fair amount of attention in many countries, as discussed in box 5.1.

How? Government as the people's partner

Times have changed. Government's re-entry in the economy will need to be built around the concept of government as a partner of its people. In large part due to the transformative impact of information technologies, society is organized today around fluid and creative systems of decision-making. Initiative is shifting to people who have detailed knowledge of what is needed or desired, who in turn are linked to each other through a dense overlay of networks. Traditional hierarchies in the workplace or in government can no longer impose specific outcomes or methods and see them implemented according to instructions sent from above. Instead, such plans evolve in the context of shared missions and commonly evolved procedures, with the possibility left open that the dynamism and creativity of individuals will lead to further innovations and improvements. Often, authority shifts according to the nature of the task rather than being predetermined by a structure of hierarchical authority. This diffused organization of creativity is not without its risks: it requires exacting conditions for accountability, transparency and integrity. When such conditions are not in place, or when there is a disconnect between the two, systems overshoot or undershoot and break down, the financial sector being a most extreme example. The key is to find a model of government that blends individual creativity and collective aspirations and harmonizes bottom-up with top-down approaches (OECD, 2001).

With the global downturn deepening in a synchronized manner, public spending needs to assume a key macroeconomic purpose, not seen in many decades. A more directive management of the economy by Governments should therefore not mean a return to old forms of governance, reminiscent of the 1960s and 1970s, when Governments owned, regulated and managed large swathes of productive resources. Evidence abounds of the worst excesses inherent in this model.

The private sector is a key player in this process because businesses create employment, support aggregate demand and build wealth. The convergence

Box 5.1. Infrastructure investment during economic downturns

The rapid economic growth of Asia and the Pacific over recent decades has been facilitated by – and placed increasing demands on – the development of economic infrastructure, including power supply, water supply and wastewater treatment, telecommunications and transport (airports, inland waterways, seaports, railways, roads, and inland ports). At the same time, greater emphasis on social development has increased demand for such social infrastructure as hospitals, schools, housing and sanitation. A major criticism of infrastructure investment programmes is that they are characterized by considerable time lags: (1) the time to recognize the need for a policy intervention (the recognition lag); (2) the time to decide upon and commence implementing the intervention (the lag between decision and action); and (3) the time for the intervention to take effect (the effect lag).

But the lag between decision and action can be shortened in a number of ways. First, annual budgets are based upon long-term plans that identify strategic investments. For example, studies for mass-transit schemes in Thailand have already been completed and the British Chancellor of the Exchequer mentioned the "fast-tracking" of construction projects in the United Kingdom "using money now that had been earmarked for future years". Second, there is a strong case for streamlining all of the elements in the project cycle, including prefeasibility studies, environmental impact assessments, detailed design, land acquisition, competitive bidding, awarding of contracts, mobilization for construction and project management. Unfortunately, cases of corruption have brought large infrastructure projects into disrepute. However, recent developments in information technology, for example e-procurement, can assist in this streamlining process and in improving transparency.

For public works, the effect lag has two main components: the immediate employment benefits and the longer-term developmental effects. While the developmental effects will materialize after the completion of the project, the employment generation effects can be significant and take place as soon as the project begins. In India, for example, the National Rural Employment Guarantee Act and its predecessor Universal Food for Work Programme provided between 750 million and 900 million work-days per year from 2002-03 to 2006-07, principally in rural infrastructure projects.

Despite their time lags, public investments often have high social rates of return. There are complementarities between public-sector capital and private capital in the production and distribution of private goods and services (Aschauer, 1989). For example, investment in public infrastructure serves to support the key housing sector, which contributes a major portion of GDP, employment and growth for many countries and has also been hit hard by the current crisis.

A study undertaken by the United States Federal Highway Administration found that the net social rate of return on highway capital was substantial, about 35%, in the 1950s and 1960s, before declining to about 10% in the 1980s (Mamuneas and Nadiri, 1996). Although the rate of return on highway capital significantly exceeded that of private capital initially, over time, as the economy continued developing, both rates converged to a level similar to the long-term interest rate. As most countries in the ESCAP region are at early stages of infrastructure development and rehabilitation, their social rates of return are likely to be high, realizing the positive long-term development effects of such investments.

In sum, during economic downturns, taking advantage of the need to increase expenditures to promote much-needed investments *in social and economic infrastructure is* critical for development and a better idea than just to "spend our way out of the recession". Even if the immediate effect of these projects on employment and consumption is small, its future benefits will more than compensate for that deficiency. In this respect, countries may wish to consider retaining and perhaps intensifying ongoing initiatives, bringing forward projects that have been through the evaluation process, streamlining the processes in the project cycle and improving public confidence in infrastructure development by increasing transparency.

of the crises has shown that business shares with government common aspirations to achieve a more inclusive and sustainable path of development, opening the possibility of new alliances in which it will be possible for businesses to be profitable while being socially and environmentally responsible. As the Secretary-General of the United Nations has said:

> "We live in a new era. Its challenges can all be solved by cooperation – and only by cooperation. Our times demand a new constellation of international cooperation – governments, civil society and the private sector, working together for a collective global good" (Ban, 2009).

In this regard, the Executive Secretary of ESCAP has stated:

"Businesses are partners in development. The financial crisis provides an opportunity to move towards responsible investment, where there is an incentive for a long-term vision rather than short-term gains. Decisions on investment are not just about returns, but are also about ensuring healthy, productive and sustainable economies and societies … and weaving this principle into the intrinsic fabric of every company" (Heyzer, 2008).

Civil society organizations are also key partners in the new alliances that are forming. Besides monitoring and tracking the performance of Governments, they add transparency and provide checks on potential government failures and excesses. Evolving a clearer system of accountability for civil society organizations will add further legitimacy to their role.

Towards an Asia-Pacific framework for inclusive and sustainable growth and development

Asia and the Pacific has been the fastest-growing region in the world for over 20 years and has made substantial progress in reducing poverty and hunger. Today, the sustainability of such growth is in jeopardy.

The convergence of the crises has changed the macroeconomic landscape in fundamental ways that will see government re-enter the economic sphere. The role of government as planner will need to be given a new priority, as will the need for regional cooperation to guide and support national policies and the development process.

The role of government as planner will need to be given a new priority, as will the need for regional cooperation

---

Building on previous regional processes facilitated by the ESCAP secretariat, members and associate members of the Commission could work on a framework of principles that will guide the region towards a commonly shared future development paradigm. This earlier work includes the "Bali Outcome Document" adopted by the High-level Regional Policy Dialogue (ESCAP, 2008b) and the Regional Implementation Plan for Sustainable Development in Asia and the Pacific, 2006-2010 (ESCAP, 2005).

Making growth and development sustainable in the long run is a necessary condition for poverty alleviation. In the ESCAP region, substantial unmet basic needs coexist with rapidly growing demand for resources, giving rise to scarcities, environmental pressures, climate change disasters and increased food insecurity. Without any change in the pattern of economic growth, new crises such as those we experienced in 2008 loom in the horizon.

However, more than sustainability is needed to make growth and development more inclusive and to attain the Millennium Development Goals and other internationally agreed development goals.

Without addressing the inclusiveness and sustainability of economic growth, the objective of reducing poverty will be substantially more difficult to reach.

But should these investments be the priority when a deep economic crisis is engulfing the global economy? Should policymakers instead devote all their energies to short-term measures aimed at recovering from the recession? The answer to both questions is "yes" because there is no contradiction between counter-cyclical fiscal policies and much-needed investments for the medium to long run. If the only objective of a stimulus package is to counteract the recessionary forces coming from the international economy, almost any measure aimed at increasing domestic spending would suffice. But given the scarcity of public funds available in developing countries and the critical importance of making the Asia-Pacific economies less prone – and more resilient – to future crises, the decision on how to spend these funds should be carefully weighed.

To protect the Asia-Pacific economies from the risk of a major recession, the intergovernmental coordination of monetary and fiscal policies is essential

---

To protect the Asia-Pacific economies from the risk of a major recession, the intergovernmental coordination of monetary and fiscal policies is essential to boost credibility, help shore up confidence and enhance region-wide and global multiplier effects. But the same is true regarding the medium- to long-term objective of making growth and development more inclusive and sustainable. Just as isolated fiscal stimulus packages are not as effective as coordinated fiscal efforts by Governments, initiatives to boost inclusiveness and sustainability that are isolated in time will not take root, and ultimately they will be less likely to lead to societal transformation.

What is needed at the regional level, then, is a way to coordinate national initiatives to make growth and development more inclusive and sustainable and to impart to these policies a planning horizon that is long term and durable. For that purpose, the secretariat proposes that a process be started in which policymakers of the region, in partnership with interested stakeholders, discuss and adopt an Asia-Pacific framework for inclusive and sustainable development. Such a framework would define the region's collective approach to inclusive and sustainable development, express commitments to specific goals and establish mechanisms for technical cooperation with particular attention to assisting the least developed countries in the region. The framework would also stipulate the creation of a regional forum to track progress in the attainment of the objectives proposed, facilitate the exchange of knowledge about technical and policy issues and catalyse new initiatives.

The contents of the framework should evolve and be determined in a consultative process among members and associate members of ESCAP. The secretariat suggests, as a starting point, that the framework should have three pillars as outlined below.

Resuming economic growth and preserving macroeconomic stability

To protect Asia-Pacific economies from present and future risks associated with financial instability and recession, reforming the global and regional financial and economic systems of governance assumes importance.

Enhance the role of Asia and the Pacific in designing a more inclusive and accountable global system of regulating financial markets: At the global level, the political momentum generated by the G-20 leaders ensures that this issue will remain at the top of the international policy agenda for some time to come, and the Asia-Pacific region should have an increasingly influential voice in shaping the future multilateral system of governance in view of its rising contribution to global economic prosperity. Financial regulation and liquidity support, despite the existence of forums and instruments such as the IMF, the Financial Stability Forum and the Basel Framework, have remained to a large extent nationalized, even though financial markets have become increasingly integrated and subject to crises of increased frequency and intensity. Future reforms should centre around a set of key principles that balance the benefits of openness with the need for regulatory strengthening, enhance the accountability of financial institutions, investors and regulators, and revise the provisions contained in international financial standards to increase stability. Financial markets are linked to all markets, and the costs of the excessiveness to which financial markets are prone have come too close to a global systemic breakdown to go unaccounted for.

A world finance mechanism, either through reform of the current architecture, or through the creation of a new organization that balances efficient decision-making with global representation, through a variable geometry configuration of decision-making and consensus building, is certainly needed. The time to act is now. Through a more effective use of existing regional platforms, Governments and their partners in Asia-Pacific countries can debate the policy options, sharpen their focus and build political consensus around the multilateral reforms needed. It is clear that, in the coming years, much more work will be needed towards creating a more stable, inclusive and sustainable system of economic governance at the multilateral level. At the G-20 London Summit on 2 April 2009, meaningful progress on coordinated global policy responses as well as the provision of additional financial sector capacity-building work, is crucial.

> *A world finance mechanism, either through reform of the current architecture, or through the creation of a new organization that balances efficient decision-making with global representation, through a variable geometry configuration of decision-making and consensus building, is certainly needed*

Conclude the Doha Round so that trade can work for development and overall global prosperity: On the trade front, there is a need to ensure that the rules and principles embodied in the multilateral trade system are upheld in the service of development. Furthermore, as recession-hit economies scramble to support ailing domestic industries, the conditions of market entry for exports from this region may become disadvantageous. The conclusion of the Doha Round in accordance with its development mandate should therefore be pursued with renewed commitment. In times of deepening recession and heightened protectionist sentiments, a strengthened multilateral trading system offers the most stable, predictable and transparent environment to conduct both global and regional trade for development.

Strengthen the regional coordination of monetary and fiscal policies: At the regional level, coordination of monetary and fiscal policies has become essential. Conventional monetary policy may not be an option when interest rates are moving towards zero, but recessionary and deflationary pressures remain high, while the coordination in the design, scale, phasing-in and financing of fiscal stimulus packages could have synergistic multiplier effects at the regional level. Furthermore, actions taken at the regional level can enhance coherence in multilateral economic governance and serve as building blocks for a truly inclusive multilateral system of economic governance.

Actions taken at the regional level can enhance coherence in multilateral economic governance and serve as building blocks for a truly inclusive multilateral system of economic governance

---

Strengthen regional contingency and surveillance: The need for Asia and the Pacific to establish a regional contingency plan that would have sufficient resources to respond quickly to the liquidity and capitalization problems of domestic banks is well recognized. An accelerated establishment of a regional surveillance system that focuses on emerging risks should also be given equal priority. The Finance Ministers of ASEAN+3, in their Action Plan to Restore Economic and Financial Stability of the Asian Region, adopted on 22 February 2009, made progress by increasing the total size of the Multilateralized Chiang Mai Initiative from $80 billion to $120 billion, and by agreeing to establish an independent regional surveillance unit to promote objective economic monitoring. More needs to be done at the regional level in terms of expanding the membership, size and purpose of the pool.

Establish more durable regional currency arrangements: The region should also consider establishing coordinated and durable regional currency arrangements. Uncoordinated national management can lead to further competitive devaluations with unnecessary foreign exchange losses, higher debt-servicing costs and balance of payments pressures. Related to this is the need to examine further the challenge of managing vulnerability to reversals in short-term capital flows and evolve regional approaches that will stymie current vulnerabilities. In addition to increasing the regional availability of contingency funds, other measures that could be considered involve managing the quantum of such flows, through, for example, deposit requirements on capital inflows or financial transaction taxes.

Establish a regional trade financing mechanism: The precarious situation of Asia-Pacific exporters has been further exacerbated by the drying up of international credit. More attention needs to be paid to the establishment of a regional trade financing mechanisms specifically dedicated to the provision of export credits and export credit guarantee schemes. Somewhat anomalously for this trade-oriented region, it remains the only one without an institution specifically dedicated to this task. The announcement by the Government of Japan that a $1 billion fund would be provided through the Japan Bank for International Cooperation (JBIC) in collaboration with the ADB Trade Finance Facilitation Programme, is an important step in the right direction.

Improve international trade in food: Building on the key principle of promoting coordination among countries to avoid actions that meet national needs but make the problem worse for other countries, the conclusion of the Doha Round of trade negotiations, with an enhanced set of agreed rules for a more transparent and development-oriented international trading system, is an important step in securing more predictable access to food. At the regional level, it is necessary to support mechanisms for improving emergency access to food through stock-sharing and reduced restrictions on the release of stocks to other countries under emergency conditions, including humanitarian crises. Policies to build up national food stocks should be pursued carefully, as they can drive up prices, and care should be taken to keep the costs of managing those stocks under control. Finally, the use of market-based risk management instruments could be helpful to both producers and buyers of food products. Instruments such as futures contracts and options allow producers and consumers of food to transfer risks to financial investors. For that purpose, national exchanges, where they exist, could be developed further as pilot projects, with the idea of scaling them up and regionalizing them in future. As is well known, however, such programmes are complex and risky in nature. They would need to be complemented with intensive capacity-building programmes and the evolution of an appropriate regulatory regime to prevent excessive speculation and volatility.

Strengthening the social foundation of inclusive development

Comprehensive national, regional and global strategies to promote growth and macroeconomic stability through sound fiscal and monetary policies are essential. They create resources that can be tapped to make the region's societies more responsive to the needs of the poor and vulnerable, thus making it increasingly feasible for countries in the region to achieve the goal, enshrined in Article 22 of the Universal Declaration of Human Rights (United Nations, 1948), of providing all members of society with social security. But increased resources alone are not enough to achieve inclusive and sustainable development.

Strengthen the social foundation through more effective social protection systems: While an in-depth discussion of this issue is beyond the scope of this *Survey*, it is certain that, as the economic crisis weaves its way through the fabric of society, the need for more effective social protection systems will feature prominently on the future policy agenda of the region. Social protection systems should be designed in a way that builds societies with stronger social foundations and contributes to macroeconomic stability in times of economic downturn, present and future. For example, income and consumption transfers – in kind or cash – to the poor boosts domestic aggregate demand, thus shoring up domestic production and employment levels. These systems should be put in place, however, as part of an overall long-term strategy of building resilient social foundations rather than being ad hoc crisis-driven initiatives. The objective of enhancing social protection as a means of strengthening the social foundation for a more inclusive society should thus be included as part of the framework of a new development paradigm for the region.

As the economic crisis weaves its way through the fabric of society, the need for more effective social protection systems will feature prominently on the future policy agenda of the region

---

Among some of the elements that could be considered are the provision of a minimum floor of social security benefits for all citizens, including (1) a universal guarantee of access to basic health insurance and services, (2) guaranteed income security for all children through family benefits, (3) guaranteed access to means-tested or self-targeted social assistance for the poor, the vulnerable and unemployed, and (4) guaranteed income security for people in old age and invalidity though basic pensions.

Building a crisis-resistant society with strong social foundations is crucially dependent on how agricultural policies evolve because, despite the continuous of migrants flows to cities in search of better opportuni-

ties, 80% of the Asia-Pacific poor reside in rural areas and lack access to enough land, agricultural inputs, finance and markets to benefit from the higher food prices. The host of policy challenges that recent food price hikes have brought to the fore is but one example of the long-term planning needed in this sector.

Focus on rural smallholders: Smallholders are in need of special attention, both to improve the food supply response and as a means to reduce poverty and make growth more inclusive. To achieve these objectives, increased public and private investments are needed – investments that will alleviate conditions for small farmers throughout the supply chain – at the farm level and in production infrastructure, access to markets and processing.

Promote opportunities for rural non-farm employment: A prosperous rural economy depends not only on agriculture but also on other, non-farm activities, including agro-industries, commerce and a range of basic social services. The localization of such activities in rural areas should be promoted to provide additional sources of income for rural households above and beyond agriculture. Those activities also help boost the local market for food and other agricultural products. In addition, a more integrated pattern of rural development creates both a higher tax base and a constituency that will demand investment in rural infrastructure (roads, electricity) and public goods (schools, health clinics), further contributing to its development and increasing its appeal for private investment. Finally, a more prosperous rural economy reduces incentives for rural-urban migration, relieving pressures on urban infrastructure and the provision of public services in cities.

Engage business as a partner of government in strengthening inclusive development: Public trust and confidence in business, particularly those operating in financial markets, has been seriously eroded. At the core of this crisis is a collapse of trust in the capital markets. There is a need to reorient business-government partnerships by designing incentives and other innovative mechanisms that will build a greater ethical dimension into profit-making decisions. There is a need, therefore, to refocus from short-term profit considerations to long-term sustainable value creation, built around the integration of economic, social, environmental and governance issues into corporate management and operations. With this crisis comes an opportunity to move towards responsible investment, where decisions on investment are not just about returns but are based on a long-term vision of ensuring health, productivity and a sustainable economy and society. The business sector should therefore be a key partner of government in the design of social protection systems for long-term inclusiveness and sustainability.

Promoting sustainable development

Environmental responsibility and its medium-term objectives of reducing carbon dependency and environmental deterioration is an important component of a new development paradigm reoriented to sustainable and inclusive growth.

Implement fiscal reforms for a sustainable energy paradigm: In this regard, ESCAP (2008c) proposes a new sustainable energy paradigm, elements of which are reflected in Commission resolution 64/3 of 30 April 2008 (ESCAP, 2008c). Governments of the region should consider implementing tax reforms aimed at internalizing the ecological costs of carbon emissions into energy prices. Higher fuel taxes deter consumption and encourage the use of more efficient demand-side technologies. By the same token, the removal of subsidies on energy consumption, which according to IEA (2008) amounted to a staggering $310 billion in the 20 largest non-OECD countries in 2007, could make a major contribution to curbing demand and emissions growth.

Promote energy efficiency and invest in renewable sources of energy: Securing energy supplies and speeding up the transition to a low-carbon energy system both call for radical action by governments – at the national and local levels and through participation in coordinated international mechanisms. Households, businesses and motorists will have to change the way they use energy, while energy suppliers will need to invest in developing and commercializing low-carbon technologies. To make this happen, Governments will need to put in place appropriate financial incentives and regulatory frameworks that support both energy-security and climate-policy goals in an integrated way (IEA, 2008). At the same time, Governments should continue to support the development of new oil and gas fields to compensate for the decline in production from existing oil fields.

Re-examine current biofuel policies and support the development of second generation biofuels, particularly if use is made of degraded and abandoned agricultural lands to grow native perennials: Second generation biofuels offer better prospects for balancing food security objectives because they are based on non-food feed stocks; an example is cellulosic ethanol, which is produced from woody biomass, grass and other non-edible parts of a plant. Furthermore, at the global level, biofuel guidelines and safeguard measures that minimize adverse impacts on global food security and the environment can form the basis for an internationally negotiated code of conduct.

Promote sustainable agricultural practices: Increasing food production is a fundamental objective not only for the short and medium run but also for the long run. Thus, it is critical to promote agricultural practices that avoid undue stress on natural resources, for such stress would lead to the depletion of water sources, nitrification and salination of soils, and permanent loss of biodiversity and ecosystem services. If agricultural practices damage natural resources, the future food supply response will suffer. A major area of concern is the use of irrigation systems, which are highly inefficient and poorly maintained in most countries in the Asia-Pacific region (ESCAP, 2006).

Increasing food production is a fundamental objective not only for the short and medium run but also for the long run

---

Utilize the financial crisis as a window of opportunity for addressing climate change: Climate change is having a severe impact on the Asia-Pacific region; the threats are real and increasing. Just as countries are coordinating their responses to the current financial turmoil, they also need to work together to galvanize support for action on climate change. The stimulus packages for addressing the financial crisis and economic downturn could incorporate action on climate change for sustainable development. In this regard, the region could consider recent initiatives, such as the "Green New Deal" promoted by the Secretary-General of the United Nations and the ESCAP Green Growth initiative, as a way forward. Actions on mitigation and adaptation as well as provision of social safety nets will feature prominently in such initiatives. Technology alone will not solve the issues surrounding climate change.

Shift attitudes towards climate change: A major shift in the way goods are produced and consumed is necessary to stabilize the effects of climate change. Promoting human responsibility to nature and a carbon neutral lifestyle will be critical in this regard.

Enhance the Asia-Pacific role in the global climate change agenda: The region also needs to actively engage in global negotiations on climate change. In view of the cross-boundary nature of climate change issues, the Governments of the region need to transcend their national interests. Regional cooperation, particularly in financing and technical assistance, is as important as ever for a truly global approach to addressing climate change.

A major shift in the way goods are produced and consumed is necessary to stabilize the effects of climate change

---

Guiding principles

The following principles are proposed to guide the process:

- *Comprehensiveness*. Addressing partial aspects of sustainability can create potential inconsistencies if the pursuit of one goal is detrimental to other goals. To avoid this problem, the various dimensions of inclusiveness and sustainability should be considered jointly.

- *Flexibility*. Sufficient flexibility should be built into the architecture of the framework to facilitate future enhancements or amendments as circumstances and needs change.

- *Sufficient details to increase pragmatic relevance*. While agreeing on general goals is a step forward, the urgency with which measures must be taken requires that the framework include, as much as possible, references to specific policy actions and time frames.

- *Coordinated mechanisms for technical cooperation across countries with special emphasis on supporting the least developed countries*. The challenges of implementing a comprehensive reform agenda to foster inclusive and sustainable growth are many, both because of the novelty of some of its components and because it requires building capacity and fostering technical knowledge across government agencies. But advanced countries already have much expertise in these areas, so North-South technical cooperation should be fostered. It is also important to consider the contribution of South-South cooperation to the diffusion of technical expertise within the region.

Conclusion

We need to understand how the three crises are connected and the policy tensions their convergence has given rise to. And it is here by addressing these policy tensions through the principles of sustainability and inclusiveness that the development process of the Asia-Pacific region will take on its full meaning. Rather than playing catch-up with the developed countries, Asia-Pacific countries are now afforded a unique opportunity to work in a collaborative manner with each other and with developed countries to institute a shared paradigm of development that is sustainable over time and inclusive at all levels. Developed countries have as much to gain as developing countries. It may be that 2008 will prove to be a year in which unprecedented crises ushered in an era in which the United Nations vision of creating a world free from want and fear will prevail.

References

Aschauer, David A. (1989). "Is public investment productive?", *Journal of Monetary Economics* 23, pp. 177-200.

Ban, Ki-Moon (2009). "The global compact: Creating sustainable markets", address by the Secretary-General of the United Nations to the World Economic Forum, Davos, Switzerland, 29 January 2009.

ESCAP (2005). "Regional implementation plan for sustainable development in Asia and the Pacific, 2006-2010", *The Fifth Ministerial Conference on Environment and Development in Asia and the Pacific, 2005* (United Nations publication, Sales No. E.05.II.F.31), Annex II.

_____ (2006). *State of the Environment in Asia and the Pacific 2005* (United Nations publication, Sales No. E.06.II.F.30).

_____ (2008a). *Economic and Social Survey of Asia and the Pacific 2008* (United Nations publication, Sales No. E.08.II.F.7).

_____ (2008b). "Bali Outcome Document", adopted by the High-level Regional Policy Dialogue on "The food-fuel crisis and climate change: Reshaping the development agenda", jointly organized by ESCAP and the Government of Indonesia, Bali, Indonesia, 9-10 December 2008 (E/ESCAP/65/15/Add.1), www.unescap.org/unis/press/2008/dec/Bali%20Outcome%20Document.pdf.

_____ (2008c). *Annual Report of the Economic and Social Commission for Asia and the Pacific (Official Records of the Economic and Social Council, 2008, Supplement No. 19 (E/2008/39))*, Chap. IV, resolution 64/3 on promoting renewables for energy security and sustainable development in Asia and the Pacific, pp. 43-44.

Financial Stability Forum (2008). *Report of the Financial Stability Forum on Enhancing Market and Institutional Resilience*, 7 April 2008.

Frankel, Jeffrey (2008). "Monetary policy and commodity prices", OECD Glossary of Statistical Terms, 29 May, www.voxeu.org/index.php?q=node/1178.

Heyzer, Noeleen (2008). "Corporate social responsibility no longer deniable", *Bangkok Post*, Op-ed, 12 December 2008.

IEA (International Energy Agency)(2008). *World Energy Outlook 2008*.

Mamuneas, Theofanis P. and M. Ishaq Nadiri (1996). "Highway capital and productivity growth", in *Economic Returns from Transportation Investment*, Appendix A, p. 56 (Lansdowne, Va.: Eno Transportation Foundation, Inc.), www.fhwa.dot.gov/policy/otps/060320a/060320a.pdf.

OECD (2001). *Governance in the 21st Century* (Paris).

United Nations (1948). Universal Declaration of Human Rights, General Assembly resolution 217 A (III) of 10 December 1948.

Photo: Marc Proksch

" ...crisis, if handled correctly, can be the starting point of change and reform. ... We face hard times ahead. But we still have a choice. Hope or despair. Opportunity or failure. I trust that you will make the right choice. **"**

H. Susilo Bambang Yudhoyono
President of the Republic of Indonesia

STATISTICAL ANNEX

List of tables

Table 1. Real GDP growth rates

(Per cent)

	1997	1998	1999	2000	2001	2002	2003	2004	2005	2006	2007	2008
Developing ESCAP economies	6.2	1.7	6.0	7.4	4.4	6.5	7.0	7.8	7.8	8.4	8.8	5.8
East and North-East Asia	7.7	3.4	7.5	8.2	5.6	7.5	7.3	8.4	8.1	9.1	10.0	6.1
China	9.3	7.8	7.6	8.4	8.3	9.1	10.0	10.1	10.4	11.6	13.0	9.0
Hong Kong, China	5.1	-6.0	2.6	8.0	0.5	1.8	3.0	8.5	7.1	7.0	6.4	2.5
Macao, China	-0.3	-4.6	-2.4	5.8	2.9	10.1	14.2	28.4	6.9	17.1	27.3	..
Mongolia	4.0	3.5	3.2	1.1	1.0	3.8	6.1	10.6	7.3	8.6	9.9	8.6
Republic of Korea	4.7	-6.9	9.5	8.5	3.8	7.0	3.1	4.7	4.2	5.1	5.0	2.5
North and Central Asia	1.7	-4.0	6.1	9.6	5.8	5.2	7.5	7.4	7.1	7.6	8.6	5.6
Armenia	3.3	7.3	3.3	5.9	9.6	13.2	14.0	10.5	13.9	13.3	13.8	6.8
Azerbaijan	5.8	10.0	7.4	11.1	9.9	10.6	11.2	10.2	26.4	34.5	25.0	10.8
Georgia	10.5	3.1	2.9	1.8	4.8	5.5	11.1	5.9	9.6	9.4	12.4	4.0
Kazakhstan	1.7	-1.9	2.7	9.9	13.5	9.8	9.3	9.6	9.7	10.6	8.5	2.4
Kyrgyzstan	9.9	2.1	3.7	5.4	5.3	0.0	7.0	7.0	-0.2	2.7	8.2	7.6
Russian Federation	1.4	-5.3	6.4	10.1	5.1	4.7	7.4	7.2	6.4	6.7	8.1	5.6
Tajikistan	1.7	5.3	3.7	8.3	9.6	10.8	11.0	10.3	6.7	7.0	7.8	7.9
Turkmenistan	-11.4	7.1	16.5	5.5	4.3	-0.6	3.3	5.0	9.0	9.0	8.5	5.0
Uzbekistan	5.2	4.3	4.3	3.8	4.2	4.0	4.4	7.7	7.0	7.3	9.5	8.6
Pacific island economies	-4.0	3.3	8.0	-0.3	2.0	1.9	2.7	3.7	2.7	3.0	2.4	4.8
Cook Islands	-2.4	-0.8	2.7	13.9	4.9	2.6	8.2	4.3	0.2	1.4	0.4	..
Fiji	-2.2	1.3	8.8	-1.6	1.9	3.2	0.9	5.5	0.6	3.4	-6.6	1.2
Kiribati	8.8	15.8	8.2	-0.1	1.5	5.3	-1.1	-1.7	1.6	-5.2	0.5	3.7
Marshall Islands	-5.2	-3.6	-2.9	5.1	2.7	3.8	3.5	5.6	1.7	1.3	2.3	1.2
Micronesia (Federated States of)	-10.6	5.5	-2.1	4.7	0.1	0.9	2.9	-3.3	-0.6	-2.3	-3.6	-1.0
Palau	2.3	2.0	-5.4	0.3	1.3	-3.5	-1.3	4.9	5.9	5.5	3.0	2.5
Papua New Guinea	-6.3	4.7	1.9	-2.5	-0.1	-0.2	2.2	2.7	3.7	2.6	6.7	7.3
Samoa	0.8	2.4	3.1	7.1	8.1	1.8	3.1	3.4	5.2	2.6	6.1	3.3
Solomon Islands	-1.7	3.2	-1.6	-14.2	-8.2	-2.8	6.5	8.0	5.0	6.1	10.3	7.0
Tonga	-3.2	3.5	2.3	5.4	7.2	1.4	3.4	1.1	-3.3	4.4	-0.3	1.0
Tuvalu	3.5	14.9	3.0	3.0	5.9	1.3	4.0	4.0	2.0	1.0	2.0	1.2
Vanuatu	8.6	4.3	-3.2	2.7	-2.6	-7.4	3.2	5.5	6.5	7.2	6.6	5.7
South and South-West Asia	5.0	4.9	3.3	5.2	2.3	5.2	7.1	7.5	8.5	8.1	7.5	5.9
Afghanistan							14.3	9.4	14.5	7.4	11.5	7.5
Bangladesh	5.4	5.2	4.9	5.9	5.3	4.4	5.3	6.3	6.0	6.6	6.4	6.2
Bhutan	4.2	5.8	7.7	7.2	6.8	10.9	7.2	6.8	7.1	8.5	21.4	5.0
India	4.3	6.7	6.4	4.4	5.8	3.8	8.5	7.5	9.4	9.6	9.0	7.1
Iran (Islamic Republic of)	3.4	1.6	2.8	5.1	3.3	7.5	6.7	4.8	5.7	6.2	6.8	6.5
Maldives	11.5	9.3	7.2	4.8	3.4	6.5	8.5	9.5	-4.6	18.0	7.2	5.7
Nepal	4.9	3.5	4.3	5.9	4.7	0.2	3.8	4.4	2.9	4.1	2.6	5.6
Pakistan	1.7	3.5	4.2	3.9	2.0	3.1	4.7	7.5	9.0	5.8	6.8	5.8
Sri Lanka	6.4	4.8	4.3	6.1	-1.5	4.0	5.9	5.4	6.2	7.7	6.8	6.0
Turkey	7.5	3.1	-3.4	6.8	-5.7	6.2	5.3	9.4	8.4	6.9	4.5	2.4
South-East Asia	4.6	-6.9	4.0	6.4	2.1	5.0	5.5	6.6	5.8	6.1	6.5	4.3
Brunei Darussalam	-1.5	-0.6	3.1	2.8	2.7	3.9	2.9	0.5	0.4	5.1	0.6	-0.5
Cambodia	5.6	5.0	12.6	8.4	7.7	7.0	8.5	10.3	13.3	10.8	10.2	7.0
Indonesia	4.7	-13.1	0.8	4.9	3.8	4.3	4.8	5.0	5.7	5.5	6.3	6.1
Lao People's Democratic Republic	6.9	4.0	7.3	5.8	5.7	5.9	5.8	6.9	7.3	8.3	7.9	7.5
Malaysia	7.3	-7.4	6.1	8.9	0.5	5.4	5.8	6.8	5.3	5.8	6.3	5.4
Myanmar	5.7	5.8	11.0	13.8	11.3	12.0	13.8	13.6	13.6	12.7	5.5	2.0
Philippines	5.2	-0.6	3.4	4.4	1.8	4.5	4.9	6.4	5.0	5.4	7.2	4.6
Singapore	8.3	-1.4	7.2	10.1	-2.4	4.2	3.5	9.0	7.3	8.2	7.7	1.2
Thailand	-1.4	-10.5	4.5	4.8	2.2	5.3	7.1	6.3	4.5	5.1	4.9	2.6
Timor-Leste	4.1	-2.1	-35.5	13.7	16.5	-6.7	-6.2	0.4	2.3	-3.4	16.2	4.7
Viet Nam	8.2	5.8	4.8	6.8	6.9	7.1	7.3	7.8	8.4	8.2	8.5	6.2
Developed ESCAP economies	1.6	-1.4	0.3	2.9	0.4	0.7	1.6	2.8	2.0	2.1	2.6	-0.4
Australia	4.0	5.1	4.4	3.4	2.1	4.2	3.0	3.8	2.8	2.7	4.2	2.4
Japan	1.6	-2.1	-0.1	2.9	0.2	0.3	1.4	2.7	1.9	2.0	2.4	-0.7
New Zealand	2.9	0.8	4.7	3.8	2.4	4.7	4.4	4.4	2.7	2.7	3.0	-0.8

Sources: Based on United Nations Statistics Division, National Accounts Main Aggregates Database (online database, September 2008), at website http://unstats.un.org/unsd with updates and estimates from national and local sources; ADB, *Key Indicators for Asia and the Pacific 2008* (Washington, D.C., 2008) website of the Interstate Statistical Committee of the Commonwealth of Independent States, www.cisstat.com, 22 October 2008 and 3 February 2009; national sources and ESCAP estimates.

Notes: Figures for 2008 are estimates. The data and estimates for countries relate to fiscal years defined as follows: fiscal year 2007/08 = 2007 for India and the Islamic Republic of Iran; and fiscal year 2006/07 = 2007 for Bangladesh, Nepal and Pakistan.

Table 2. Gross domestic savings rates

(Percentage of GDP)

	1997	1998	1999	2000	2001	2002	2003	2004	2005	2006	2007	2008
Developing ESCAP economies												
East and North-East Asia												
China	39.0	38.9	38.0	38.0	39.0	40.4	43.0	45.6	47.3	47.8	48.6	49.9
Hong Kong, China	30.7	29.4	30.1	32.0	29.8	31.1	31.2	30.7	33.0	33.1	32.2	31.5
Mongolia	25.8	14.3	14.6	10.4	5.7	3.4	12.2	19.5	32.0	39.8	..	..
Republic of Korea	35.8	37.9	35.8	33.9	31.9	31.4	33.0	35.0	33.2	31.5	30.8	29.4
North and Central Asia												
Armenia	−18.9	−14.7	−10.7	−8.5	−0.9	4.9	6.4	10.1	17.3	19.2	18.7	..
Azerbaijan	19.1	4.8	8.6	20.4	24.9	24.7	27.6	31.3	47.5	54.4	58.2	54.8
Georgia	−8.7	6.5	7.4	9.9	13.9	12.3	13.1	11.6	10.8	2.5	2.8	..
Kazakhstan	17.1	15.9	16.0	26.0	28.7	33.8	34.3	34.9	38.9	44.1	43.4	44.1
Kyrgyzstan	13.8	−6.1	3.2	14.3	17.7	13.8	5.3	5.8	−2.1	−13.1	−18.9	..
Russian Federation	24.2	21.6	31.9	38.7	34.6	30.8	32.1	33.1	33.7	34.0	33.0	33.4
Tajikistan	13.0	6.3	15.9	9.6	−0.3	3.3	3.0	3.2	−12.6	−19.9	−22.6	..
Turkmenistan	12.8	7.3	12.3	49.3	36.2	43.2	31.1	25.2	40.2	32.3	..	..
Uzbekistan	18.7	19.9	17.3	19.4	20.0	21.8	26.9	31.9	32.7	33.9	30.3	..
Pacific island economies												
Cook Islands	13.1	14.8	20.2	21.8	26.7	24.0	21.4	18.1	25.0	21.5	..	..
Fiji	11.6	13.4	10.7	5.0	9.7	17.3	13.6	2.5	1.5	..	..	..
Kiribati	−10.2	4.2	−0.6	2.8	2.1	1.4	2.1	1.9	1.8	1.9	..	..
Papua New Guinea	22.4	22.6	13.2	23.7	12.6	11.7	24.7	26.2	25.7	25.0	..	..
Samoa	−11.9	−6.5	−13.0	−9.2	−14.1	−14.5	−14.0	−14.1	−14.0	−13.9	..	..
Solomon Islands	20.4	19.2	19.5	19.7	19.5	19.6	19.6	19.6	19.6	19.6	..	..
Tonga	−13.1	−17.2	−10.2	−9.4	−22.6	−25.5	−24.3	−20.8	−27.0	−27.6	−31.6	..
Tuvalu	..	..	..	..	..	..	..	..	..	..	..	..
Vanuatu	20.3	22.4	19.2	19.3	17.9	9.4	12.7	16.4	20.2	23.8	..	..
South and South-West Asia												
Bangladesh	15.9	17.4	17.7	17.9	18.0	18.2	18.6	19.5	20.0	20.2	20.5	18.1
Bhutan	23.5	22.9	22.5	23.3	40.9	39.7	39.1	36.0	27.7	37.4	37.2	50.0
India	23.8	22.3	24.8	23.7	23.5	26.4	29.8	31.8	34.3	34.8	35.5	34.5
Iran (Islamic Republic of)	20.7	25.5	25.4	26.8	38.4	38.5	38.6	39.6	40.6	41.6	40.7	43.8
Maldives	45.9	42.9	40.7	40.6	44.9	46.3	49.1	46.2	..	..	..	..
Nepal	13.0	12.8	12.6	14.1	11.7	9.5	8.6	11.7	11.6	9.0	9.7	11.5
Pakistan	13.2	16.7	14.0	16.0	15.9	18.7	17.3	17.6	15.2	16.3	16.0	11.7
Sri Lanka	18.8	19.6	18.0	15.2	16.1	15.5	15.6	15.9	17.2	16.4	16.9	17.6
Turkey	21.8	23.3	19.3	17.8	19.2	19.2	16.6	16.8	16.5	17.1	17.1	15.8
South-East Asia												
Brunei Darussalam	35.5	29.9	36.9	49.4	44.3	47.2	48.6	51.4	59.1	62.1	59.1	..
Cambodia	6.4	2.3	7.6	8.1	11.6	8.5	9.1	8.5	9.9	13.8	16.1	..
Indonesia	31.5	26.5	19.5	31.8	31.5	25.1	23.7	24.9	27.5	28.7	28.2	30.5
Lao People's Democratic Republic	9.4	14.8	16.4	15.1	15.4	17.9	17.0	18.2	17.3	18.7	22.3	27.0
Malaysia	43.9	48.7	47.4	46.1	41.8	42.0	42.5	43.4	42.8	43.2	42.2	41.8
Myanmar	11.8	11.8	13.0	12.3	11.5	10.2	11.0	12.1	..	..	..	..
Philippines	14.2	12.4	14.3	17.3	17.1	19.1	19.7	21.2	21.0	20.1	20.9	19.2
Singapore	52.1	53.0	49.0	47.4	44.2	40.5	43.6	47.1	48.6	49.9	51.4	46.3
Thailand	35.3	34.8	32.5	32.5	31.4	31.7	32.0	31.7	31.0	32.3	33.9	33.3
Viet Nam	20.1	21.5	24.6	27.1	28.8	28.7	27.4	28.5	30.3	30.6	29.1	31.8
Developed ESCAP Economies												
Australia	23.4	23.2	22.6	23.1	22.4	23.1	23.0	23.5	23.9	25.5	26.1	26.3
Japan	29.5	28.1	26.4	26.9	25.4	24.4	24.5	25.0	25.0	25.2	25.5	25.3
New Zealand	22.3	20.6	21.5	23.2	24.7	23.9	23.8	24.0	22.6	22.3	22.6	20.6

Sources: ESCAP, based on Asian Development Bank, *Key Indicators for Asia and the Pacific 2008* (Manila, 2008) with updates and estimates from national sources.

Notes: Figures for 2008 are estimates. Data for Brunei Darussalam refer to gross national savings rates. Data for Islamic Republic of Iran, Lao People's Democratic Republic, Nepal and Turkey are based on national sources. Data for Maldives, Armenia, Georgia, Russian Federation, Tajikistan, Turkmenistan, Australia, Japan and New Zealand are based on World Bank, *World Development Indicators*. Data for Cook Islands, Kiribati, Samoa and Solomon Islands are based on United Nations Statistics Division databases.

Table 3. Gross domestic investment rates

(Percentage of GDP)

	1997	1998	1999	2000	2001	2002	2003	2004	2005	2006	2007	2008
Developing ESCAP economies												
East and North-East Asia												
China	37.9	37.1	36.7	35.1	36.3	37.9	41.2	43.3	43.3	44.5	44.2	41.8
Hong Kong, China	34.0	28.9	24.8	27.5	25.3	22.8	21.9	21.8	20.6	21.7	21.3	20.4
Mongolia	28.1	35.2	37.0	36.2	36.1	39.6	35.5	34.5	37.0	35.1	..	..
Republic of Korea	36.0	25.0	29.1	31.0	29.3	29.1	30.0	30.4	30.1	29.8	29.4	28.3
North and Central Asia												
Armenia	19.1	19.1	18.4	18.6	19.8	21.7	24.3	24.9	30.5	33.6	34.8	..
Azerbaijan	34.2	33.4	26.5	20.7	20.7	34.6	53.2	58.0	41.5	29.9	21.3	21.1
Georgia	17.8	27.2	26.5	26.6	28.3	25.5	27.7	28.3	28.6	26.7	29.0	
Kazakhstan	15.6	15.8	17.8	18.1	26.9	27.3	25.7	26.3	31.0	33.9	35.9	32.3
Kyrgyzstan	21.7	15.4	18.0	20.0	18.0	17.6	11.8	14.5	16.4	24.2	26.3	..
Russian Federation	22.0	15.0	14.8	18.7	21.9	20.0	20.8	20.9	20.1	21.3	24.5	23.3
Tajikistan	19.7	15.4	17.3	11.5	9.8	13.8	13.1	14.9	14.3	14.5	22.8	..
Turkmenistan	38.7	45.5	39.7	34.7	31.7	27.6	25.4	23.1	22.9	..	..	..
Uzbekistan	18.9	20.9	17.1	19.6	21.1	21.2	20.8	23.9	23.0	22.3	19.9	..
Pacific island economies												
Cook Islands	12.2	11.9	11.2	10.9	10.3	10.6	11.0	11.5	10.5	11.0	..	
Fiji	11.6	15.9	14.3	12.4	14.7	19.7	22.0	19.1	19.2	..	..	..
Kiribati	48.7	42.5	44.9	43.2	43.5	43.9	43.5	43.6	43.7	43.6	..	
Papua New Guinea	21.1	17.9	16.1	21.3	21.8	19.8	19.9	20.0	19.8	19.8	..	..
Samoa	8.8	14.0	14.1	14.2	14.3	13.1	12.3	11.2	10.4	9.8	..	..
Solomon Islands	..	..	..	..	..	..	..	..	..	..	..	..
Tonga	19.5	19.0	20.2	19.4	18.0	19.7	18.4	17.9	18.1	16.7	15.4	..
Tuvalu	51.2	54.9	57.9	54.7	55.8	56.1	55.6	55.8	55.8	55.7	..	..
Vanuatu	18.8	17.7	20.3	22.2	20.0	21.1	19.4	21.2	21.5	23.9	..	..
South and South-West Asia												
Bangladesh	20.7	21.6	22.2	23.0	23.1	23.2	23.4	24.0	24.5	24.7	24.3	24.3
Bhutan	33.0	35.7	39.7	47.4	58.8	59.6	57.0	59.7	56.0	51.1	52.8	
India	25.3	23.3	25.9	24.3	22.8	25.2	28.2	32.2	35.5	35.9	37.0	37.7
Iran (Islamic Republic of)	16.2	24.7	26.0	27.1	32.6	33.9	35.1	35.7	36.2	37.5	39.2	38.3
Maldives	33.2	27.6	30.9	24.2	28.1	25.5	27.1	35.0	..	..	..	..
Nepal	23.6	23.1	19.0	22.6	22.3	20.2	21.4	24.5	26.5	26.8	28.0	32.0
Pakistan	17.9	17.7	15.6	17.2	17.0	16.6	16.8	16.6	19.1	21.8	23.0	21.6
Sri Lanka	25.8	25.4	25.6	25.4	22.2	22.0	21.6	24.7	26.1	27.4	27.2	28.3
Turkey	..	22.1	19.1	20.8	15.1	17.6	17.6	19.4	20.0	22.1	22.2	20.3
South-East Asia												
Brunei Darussalam	35.5	33.8	21.4	13.1	14.4	21.3	15.1	13.5	11.4	10.4	12.9	..
Cambodia	14.8	11.8	16.7	16.9	18.5	18.1	20.1	16.2	18.5	20.6	20.8	..
Indonesia	31.8	16.8	11.4	22.2	22.0	21.4	25.6	22.4	25.1	25.4	24.9	25.2
Lao People's Democratic Republic	26.2	24.9	22.7	20.5	21.0	24.0	21.4	21.1	17.5	21.4	22.0	24.0
Malaysia	43.0	26.7	22.4	26.9	24.4	24.8	22.8	23.0	20.0	20.9	21.9	21.8
Myanmar	12.5	12.4	13.4	12.4	11.6	10.1	11.0	12.0	..	..	..	..
Philippines	24.8	20.3	18.8	21.2	19.0	17.7	16.8	16.8	14.6	14.5	15.3	16.9
Singapore	39.2	32.3	32.0	32.5	26.0	23.7	16.0	21.7	19.9	20.0	22.6	28.7
Thailand	33.7	20.4	20.5	22.8	24.1	23.8	25.0	26.8	31.4	28.5	26.8	29.6
Viet Nam	28.3	29.0	27.6	29.6	31.2	33.2	35.4	35.5	35.6	36.8	41.6	42.6
Developed ESCAP economies												
Australia	23.0	23.9	24.8	25.1	22.1	22.9	25.0	26.1	26.3	26.7	27.3	28.5
Japan	28.4	26.3	24.8	25.4	24.8	23.1	22.8	23.0	23.6	24.0	23.8	22.6
New Zealand	21.9	20.3	22.3	21.6	22.3	22.2	23.7	24.4	24.5	22.7	24.0	23.6

Sources: ESCAP, based on Asian Development Bank, *Key Indicators for Asia and the Pacific 2008* (Manila, 2008) with updates and estimates from national sources.

Notes: Figures for 2008 are estimates. Data for Cambodia, Islamic Republic of Iran, Lao People's Democratic Republic, are based on national sources. Data for Maldives, Georgia, Russian Federation, Tajikistan, Turkmenistan, Australia, Japan and New Zealand are based on World Bank, *World Development Indicators*. Data for Cook Islands, Kiribati, Samoa, Turkey and Tuvalu are based on United Nations Statistics Division databases.

Table 4. Inflation rates

(Per cent)

	1997	1998	1999	2000	2001	2002	2003	2004	2005	2006	2007	2008
Developing ESCAP economies	9.3	11.9	10.5	5.6	6.3	4.8	4.3	4.6	4.4	4.4	5.3	7.9
East and North-East Asia	3.1	1.5	−0.9	0.6	1.2	−0.1	1.2	3.2	2.0	1.6	3.8	5.2
China	2.8	−0.8	−1.4	0.4	0.5	−0.8	1.2	3.9	1.8	1.5	4.8	5.9
Hong Kong, China	5.9	2.8	−4.0	−3.8	−1.6	−3.1	−2.5	−0.4	0.9	2.1	2.0	4.3
Macao, China	3.5	0.2	−3.2	−1.6	−2.0	−2.6	−1.6	1.0	4.4	5.1	5.6	..
Mongolia	36.6	9.4	7.6	11.6	6.2	0.9	5.1	7.9	12.5	5.1	9.0	25.6
Republic of Korea	4.4	7.5	0.8	2.3	4.1	2.8	3.5	3.6	2.8	2.2	2.5	4.7
North and Central Asia	17.9	25.3	73.8	19.6	20.0	15.0	12.7	10.2	12.0	9.7	9.4	14.3
Armenia	14.0	8.7	0.6	−0.8	3.2	1.1	4.7	7.0	0.6	2.9	4.4	9.0
Azerbaijan	3.7	−0.8	−8.5	1.9	1.5	2.8	2.2	6.8	10.0	8.3	16.7	20.8
Georgia	7.1	3.6	19.2	4.1	4.7	5.6	4.8	5.7	8.2	9.2	9.3	10.0
Kazakhstan	17.4	7.2	8.3	13.2	8.3	5.8	6.4	6.9	7.6	8.6	10.8	17.0
Kyrgyzstan	23.4	10.5	37.0	18.7	6.9	2.1	3.0	4.1	4.4	5.6	10.2	24.5
Russian Federation	14.8	27.7	85.7	20.8	21.5	15.8	13.7	10.9	12.7	9.7	9.0	14.1
Tajikistan	72.0	43.0	26.0	24.0	36.5	10.2	17.1	6.8	7.8	11.9	21.5	20.4
Turkmenistan	83.7	16.8	23.5	8.0	11.6	8.8	5.6	5.9	10.7	8.2	6.3	13.0
Uzbekistan	70.9	29.0	29.1	25.0	27.3	27.3	11.6	6.6	10.0	14.2	12.3	12.0
Pacific island economies	3.9	9.9	9.2	9.3	7.2	7.7	10.0	3.3	2.5	3.1	2.7	8.7
Cook Islands	−0.4	0.7	1.4	3.1	8.7	3.4	2.0	0.9	2.5	3.4	2.4	..
Fiji	3.4	5.7	2.0	1.1	4.3	0.8	4.2	2.8	2.4	2.5	4.3	7.5
Kiribati	2.1	3.7	1.8	0.4	6.0	3.2	2.5	−1.9	−0.5	−0.2	0.2	1.0
Marshall Islands	4.8	2.2	1.7	1.6	1.7	0.4	−2.8	2.2	4.4	4.3	3.1	..
Micronesia (Federated States of)	..	..	..	2.2	0.5	−0.1	0.1	2.3	4.2	4.7	3.2	5.3
Nauru	6.1	3.9	6.7	..	..	..	..	..	2.7	3.5	2.3	4.5
Palau	..	..	..	..	−1.8	−1.3	0.9	5.0	3.9	4.5	3.2	5.3
Papua New Guinea	4.0	13.6	14.9	15.6	9.3	11.8	14.7	2.2	1.8	2.4	0.9	10.6
Samoa	6.9	2.2	0.3	1.0	3.8	8.0	0.1	16.3	1.8	3.7	5.6	6.5
Solomon Islands	8.1	12.3	8.0	7.1	7.7	9.4	10.0	7.1	7.3	11.2	7.7	15.1
Tonga	2.0	3.0	3.9	5.3	6.9	10.4	11.1	11.7	9.9	7.3	5.1	10.0
Tuvalu	1.6	0.6	4.0	3.9	1.4	5.0	3.3	2.8	3.2	3.8	3.3	4.0
Vanuatu	2.8	3.3	2.0	2.5	3.7	2.0	3.0	1.4	1.2	2.0	3.9	4.5
South and South-West Asia	24.9	27.8	19.2	15.5	15.2	13.9	9.7	6.3	6.7	8.3	8.5	11.6
Afghanistan	..	..	..	..	..	..	24.1	13.2	12.3	5.1	13.0	24.0
Bangladesh	3.7	9.0	7.0	2.8	1.9	2.8	4.4	5.8	6.5	7.2	7.2	9.9
Bhutan	6.5	10.6	6.8	4.0	3.4	2.5	2.1	4.6	5.3	5.0	5.2	9.0
India	7.2	13.2	4.7	4.0	3.8	4.3	3.8	3.8	4.4	6.7	6.2	9.0
Iran (Islamic Republic of)	17.3	18.1	20.1	12.6	11.4	15.8	15.6	15.2	12.1	13.6	18.4	25.0
Maldives	7.5	−1.4	3.0	−1.2	0.7	0.9	−2.9	6.4	3.3	2.7	7.4	12.0
Nepal	8.1	8.3	11.4	3.4	2.4	2.9	4.8	4.0	4.5	8.0	6.4	7.7
Pakistan	11.7	7.9	5.7	3.6	4.4	3.5	3.1	4.6	9.3	7.9	7.8	12.0
Sri Lanka	9.6	9.4	4.7	6.2	14.2	9.6	6.3	7.6	11.0	10.0	15.8	22.6
Turkey	85.7	84.6	64.9	54.9	54.4	45.0	25.3	8.6	8.2	9.6	8.8	10.4
South-East Asia	4.9	21.3	7.9	2.3	5.0	4.7	3.3	4.1	6.1	6.8	4.0	8.8
Brunei Darussalam	1.7	−0.4	−0.1	1.2	0.6	−2.3	0.3	0.9	1.1	0.2	0.3	0.8
Cambodia	7.9	14.8	4.0	−0.8	0.2	3.3	1.2	3.9	5.8	4.7	5.9	20.0
Indonesia	6.2	58.4	20.5	3.7	11.5	11.9	6.6	6.2	10.5	13.1	6.4	10.3
Lao People's Democratic Republic	27.6	90.9	128.4	25.1	7.8	10.6	15.5	10.5	7.2	6.8	4.5	8.0
Malaysia	2.7	5.3	2.7	1.5	1.4	1.8	1.0	1.5	3.0	3.6	2.0	5.4
Myanmar	..	25.3	21.3	−0.2	21.1	57.1	36.6	4.5	9.4	20.0	35.0	27.0
Philippines	5.6	9.3	5.9	4.0	6.8	3.0	3.5	6.0	7.6	6.3	2.8	9.3
Singapore	2.0	−0.3	0.0	1.4	1.0	−0.4	0.5	1.7	0.5	1.0	2.1	6.5
Thailand	5.6	8.1	0.3	1.6	1.6	0.6	1.8	2.8	4.5	4.6	2.2	5.5
Timor-Leste	..	..	..	63.6	3.6	4.8	7.2	3.2	1.8	4.1	8.9	9.0
Viet Nam	3.2	7.3	4.1	−1.7	−0.4	3.8	3.2	7.8	8.3	7.4	8.9	24.4
Developed ESCAP economies	1.7	0.6	−0.1	−0.2	−0.2	−0.5	0.0	0.2	0.0	0.5	0.3	1.7
Australia	0.3	0.8	1.5	4.5	4.4	3.0	2.8	2.3	2.7	3.5	2.3	4.4
Japan	1.8	0.7	−0.3	−0.7	−0.8	−0.9	−0.2	0.0	−0.3	0.2	0.1	1.4
New Zealand	1.2	1.3	−0.1	2.6	2.6	2.7	1.8	2.3	3.0	3.4	2.4	4.0

Sources: Based on International Monetary Fund, *International Financial Statistics* (CD-ROM) (Washington, D.C., 2008), and *World Economic Outlook Database* (Washington, D.C., October 2008); website of the Interstate Statistical Committee of the Commonwealth of Independent States, www.cisstat.com, 22 October 2008 and 3 Feburary 2009; national sources and ESCAP estimates.

Notes: Figures for 2008 are estimates. The data and estimates for countries relate to fiscal years defined as follows: fiscal year 2007/08 = 2007 for India and the Islamic Republic of Iran; and fiscal year 2006/07 = 2007 for Bangladesh, Nepal and Pakistan. Data for the following countries (Brunei Darussalam, Cook Islands, Federated States of Micronesia, Myanmar, Nauru, Palau and Tuvalu) are based on Asian Development Bank, *Key Indicators for Asia and the Pacific 2008.*

Table 5. Budget balance

(Percentage of GDP)

	1997	1998	1999	2000	2001	2002	2003	2004	2005	2006	2007	2008
Developing ESCAP economies												
East and North-East Asia												
China	-1.9	-2.4	-3.0	-2.8	-2.5	-2.6	-2.2	-1.3	-1.2	-0.8	0.7	0.4
Hong Kong, China	6.4	-1.8	0.8	-0.6	-4.9	-4.8	-3.2	1.7	1.0	4.0	7.2	-1.2
Mongolia	-9.1	-14.3	-11.6	-7.7	-4.5	-5.8	-3.7	-1.8	2.6	3.3	2.9	-2.5
Republic of Korea	-1.4	-3.9	-2.5	1.1	1.2	3.3	1.1	0.7	0.4	0.4	3.8	1.5
North and Central Asia												
Armenia	-1.7	-3.8	-5.2	-4.9	-4.3	-2.6	-1.3	-1.7	-2.0	-1.5	-0.7	-0.8
Azerbaijan	-2.4	-1.8	-2.4	-1.0	-0.4	-0.4	-0.2	0.1	-0.7	0.4	-0.2	-1.6
Georgia	-7.7	-7.6	-4.3	-3.9	-2.2	-1.7	-0.6	3.7	2.2	3.4	0.8	..
Kazakhstan	-3.7	-3.9	-3.5	-0.1	-0.4	-0.3	-0.9	-0.3	0.6	0.8	-1.7	-2.2
Kyrgyzstan	-5.2	-3.0	-2.5	-2.0	0.4	-1.0	-0.8	-0.5	0.2	-0.2	0.1	-0.7
Russian Federation	-6.4	-4.8	-1.2	2.4	3.1	1.7	2.4	4.8	7.5	7.5	5.4	5.5
Tajikistan	-4.1	-2.7	-2.4	-0.6	0.1	0.7	1.1	0.2	0.2	0.5	1.7	-0.3
Turkmenistan	-0.2	-2.6	0.0	-0.3	0.6	0.2	-1.4	0.5	0.9	5.9	0.4	-0.3
Uzbekistan	-2.4	-2.0	-1.7	-1.0	0.2	-0.9	-1.3	0.0	-1.0	-1.3	..	..
Pacific island economies												
Cook Islands	1.1	-2.5	-2.4	-1.8	1.3	0.2	-0.8	-1.0	2.1	2.1	3.6	..
Fiji	-6.5	5.0	-0.3	-3.2	-6.5	-5.7	-5.8	-3.1	-3.4	-2.9	-1.3	-1.5
Kiribati	56.0	51.0	11.5	10.0	-42.2	-103.9	-133.6	-146.1	-93.0	-75.4	..	..
Papua New Guinea	0.2	-1.8	-2.4	-1.8	-3.0	-3.3	-1.0	1.6	0.0	3.1	2.5	1.0
Samoa	2.2	2.0	0.3	-0.7	-2.2	-2.0	-1.3	-0.8	0.3	0.3	1.1	-0.3
Solomon Islands	-4.2	-1.6	-3.7	-7.5	-12.3	-10.3	0.2	5.1	2.5	1.5	-1.1	..
Tonga	-4.8	-2.4	-0.2	-0.4	-1.5	-1.4	-3.1	0.9	2.4	1.5	1.5	-1.0
Tuvalu	-31.8	19.1	-3.5	-2.2	-45.7	33.7	-33.3	-14.7	-7.4	18.7	-14.3	..
Vanuatu	-0.5	-9.4	-1.5	-7.0	-3.7	-2.2	-1.8	1.2	2.1	1.2	-0.3	..
South and South-West Asia												
Bangladesh	-3.7	-3.4	-4.6	-6.1	-5.2	-4.7	-4.2	-4.2	-4.4	-3.9	-3.7	-4.8
Bhutan	-2.3	0.9	-1.7	-3.8	-10.6	-4.6	-9.8	1.8	-6.5	-0.8	0.5	..
India	-4.8	-5.1	-5.4	-5.7	-6.2	-5.9	-4.5	-4.0	-4.1	-3.4	-2.7	-6.0
Iran (Islamic Republic of)	-1.0	-2.2	-0.2	-0.2	-0.4	-4.1	-3.4	-3.0	-3.7	-7.2	-3.4	-5.4
Maldives	-1.4	-1.9	-4.1	-4.4	-4.7	-4.9	-3.4	-1.6	-10.9	-7.1	-7.1	-9.7
Nepal	-4.8	-5.5	-4.9	-4.3	-5.5	-5.0	-3.3	-2.9	-3.1	-3.8	-4.1	-4.0
Pakistan	-6.4	-7.6	-6.1	-5.4	-4.3	-4.2	-3.6	-2.4	-4.5	-4.3	-4.3	-7.4
Sri Lanka	-7.9	-8.9	-7.3	-9.7	-10.6	-8.6	-7.7	-7.9	-8.4	-8.0	-7.7	-7.0
Turkey	-6.0	-6.2	-6.4	-5.6	-11.9	-12.0	-8.7	-5.3	-1.5	-0.6	-1.6	-1.8
South-East Asia												
Cambodia	-3.7	-5.4	-3.8	-4.8	-6.3	-7.3	-6.1	-3.8	-2.7	-3.3	-2.8	-2.2
Indonesia	0.5	-1.7	-2.5	-1.1	-2.4	-1.5	-1.8	-1.0	-0.6	-0.9	-1.3	-1.2
Lao People's Democratic Republic	-5.2	-6.6	-2.5	-4.3	-4.2	-3.2	-5.4	-2.4	-4.9	-4.0	-3.1	-3.0
Malaysia	2.4	-1.8	-3.2	-5.5	-5.2	-5.3	-5.0	-4.1	-3.6	-3.3	-3.2	-5.1
Myanmar	-0.9	-5.7	-4.5	-8.4	-5.9	-4.1	-4.5	..	..	..	..	..
Philippines	0.1	-1.9	-3.8	-4.0	-4.0	-5.3	-4.6	-3.8	-2.7	-1.1	-0.2	-0.8
Singapore	3.4	2.5	0.5	2.0	1.6	-1.1	-1.6	-1.1	-0.3	0.6	3.4	0.9
Thailand	-1.5	-2.8	-3.3	-2.2	-2.4	-1.4	0.4	0.1	-0.6	1.1	-2.4	-1.4
Timor-Leste	..	..	..	2.0	1.0	4.0	14.0	83.0	131.0	242.0	297.0	352.0
Viet Nam	-4.1	-2.5	-4.4	-5.0	-4.9	-4.8	-4.9	-4.9	-4.9	-5.0	-4.9	-4.1
Developed ESCAP economies												
Australia	-0.8	-0.3	0.6	1.9	0.9	-0.4	0.7	0.7	1.4	1.7	1.6	1.8
Japan	-4.0	-5.6	-7.4	-7.6	-6.3	-8.0	-8.0	-6.2	-5.0	-3.8	-3.2	-3.4
New Zealand	2.2	2.1	1.5	1.2	1.6	1.7	3.4	4.6	5.7	5.3	2.6	1.4

Sources: ESCAP, based on national sources; Asian Development Bank, *Key Indicators for Asia and the Pacific 2008* (Manila, 2008); International Monetary Fund, *World Economic Outlook Database* (Washington, D.C., October 2008), and IMF Article IV Consultation; and ESCAP estimates.

Notes: Data for 2008 are estimates. Data source for Japan and New Zealand based on International Monetary Fund, *World Economic Outlook Database*. Data for Australia refer to fiscal year and are based on national source.

Table 6. Current account balance

(Percentage of GDP)

	1997	1998	1999	2000	2001	2002	2003	2004	2005	2006	2007	2008
Developing ESCAP economies												
East and North-East Asia												
China	3.8	3.0	1.9	1.7	1.3	2.4	2.8	3.5	7.0	9.1	11.5	10.2
Hong Kong, China	-4.5	1.5	6.3	4.1	5.9	7.6	10.4	9.5	11.4	12.1	13.5	10.6
Mongolia	6.3	-6.8	-5.8	-5.0	-13.0	-8.7	-7.1	1.3	1.1	7.0	2.5	-9.5
Republic of Korea	-1.6	11.7	5.5	2.4	1.7	1.0	2.0	4.1	1.9	0.6	0.6	-1.5
North and Central Asia												
Armenia	-18.7	-22.1	-16.6	-14.6	-9.4	-6.2	-6.7	-0.5	-1.1	-1.8	-6.4	-8.6
Azerbaijan	-23.1	-30.7	-13.1	-3.2	-0.9	-12.3	-27.8	-29.8	1.3	17.7	30.7	40.6
Georgia	-14.6	-7.6	-7.1	-8.8	-6.6	-7.1	-9.8	-8.3	-12.0	-16.2	-12.5	-20.8
Kazakhstan	-3.8	-5.8	-1.0	2.0	-6.5	-4.4	-0.9	0.8	-1.8	-2.5	-7.1	4.7
Kyrgyzstan	-7.8	-25.1	-20.1	-9.0	-3.4	-3.8	-3.2	0.2	-2.4	-10.6	-7.0	-12.0
Russian Federation	0.0	0.1	12.6	18.0	11.1	8.5	8.2	10.1	11.0	9.5	5.9	6.0
Tajikistan	-4.0	-7.3	-0.9	-1.6	-4.9	-3.5	-1.3	-3.9	-2.7	-2.8	-11.2	-8.5
Turkmenistan	-21.6	-32.7	-14.8	8.2	1.7	6.7	2.7	0.6	5.1	15.7	15.4	26.5
Uzbekistan	-4.0	-0.7	-1.0	1.8	-1.0	1.2	8.7	10.1	13.6	17.2	19.1	21.7
Pacific island economies												
Fiji	4.3	4.6	2.2	-6.9	-7.0	-1.2	-6.1	-13.6	-14.0	-22.6	-15.5	-21.3
Kiribati	25.8	40.0	16.5	-1.2	22.2	10.5	12.6	-3.4	-42.2	-27.6	-31.1	-43.7
Papua New Guinea	-5.4	0.9	2.8	8.5	6.5	-1.0	4.5	2.2	4.2	2.9	4.3	3.3
Samoa	7.2	6.6	2.3	4.4	-2.7	1.9	-0.5	-7.1	-6.6	-10.8	-4.6	-7.8
Solomon Islands	-5.3	-1.7	6.9	-10.1	-9.4	-6.5	-9.1	-23.5	-9.8	-5.6	-2.8	-6.8
Tonga	-0.9	-10.9	-0.6	-6.2	-9.5	5.1	-3.1	4.2	-2.6	-9.7	-10.4	-10.4
Vanuatu	-1.0	2.5	-4.9	2.0	2.0	-5.4	-6.6	-5.0	-7.4	-5.7	-9.9	-11.4
South and South-West Asia												
Bangladesh	-1.3	-1.2	-1.1	-1.0	-2.5	0.3	0.3	0.3	-0.9	1.3	1.4	0.9
Bhutan	5.2	10.1	2.2	-9.0	-8.5	-15.8	-23.6	-17.9	-30.4	-4.3	11.3	..
India	-1.4	-1.0	-1.0	-0.6	0.7	1.3	2.4	-0.4	-1.2	-1.1	-1.5	-2.7
Iran (Islamic Republic of)	1.4	-1.1	12.0	17.5	7.1	3.1	0.6	0.9	8.8	9.2	11.9	8.8
Maldives	-6.8	-4.1	-13.4	-8.2	-9.8	-5.6	-4.5	-15.8	-36.4	-33.0	-39.1	-50.7
Nepal	-0.7	-1.0	4.0	2.9	4.5	4.2	2.4	2.7	2.0	2.2	-0.1	2.6
Pakistan	-4.7	-2.2	-2.6	-0.3	0.4	3.9	4.9	1.8	-1.4	-3.4	-5.1	-8.4
Sri Lanka	-2.5	-1.4	-3.5	-6.3	-1.1	-1.4	-0.4	-3.1	-2.7	-5.3	-4.2	-7.0
Turkey	-1.1	0.8	-0.4	-3.7	2.0	-0.3	-2.5	-3.7	-4.6	-6.0	-5.7	-6.0
South-East Asia												
Cambodia	0.6	-5.8	-5.1	-2.8	-1.1	-1.5	-3.7	-2.3	-4.2	-2.0	-3.0	-7.7
Indonesia	-2.3	4.3	4.1	4.8	4.3	4.0	3.5	0.6	0.1	3.0	2.4	0.7
Lao People's Democratic Republic	-17.5	-11.7	-8.3	-0.5	-4.7	0.3	-2.0	-7.7	-5.7	1.4	2.6	..
Malaysia	-5.9	13.2	15.9	9.0	7.9	7.1	12.0	12.0	14.5	16.1	15.6 ·	13.3
Myanmar	0.0	-0.2	-0.1	-0.1	-0.03	0.01	0.00	0.01	0.03	0.03	..	..
Philippines	-5.2	2.3	-3.8	-2.9	-2.4	-0.4	0.4	1.9	2.0	4.5	4.4	1.9
Singapore	15.5	22.2	17.4	11.6	14.0	12.6	23.2	16.7	18.6	21.8	24.3	17.2
Thailand	-2.1	12.8	10.2	7.6	4.4	3.7	3.4	1.7	-4.3	1.1	6.1	-0.1
Timor-Leste	..	..	2.1	-15.0	-19.3	-22.9	-21.4	14.8	61.0	192.2	253.3	230.5
Viet Nam	-5.4	-3.6	4.1	3.5	2.1	-1.7	-4.9	-3.5	-1.1	-0.3	-9.9	-14.1
Developed ESCAP economies												
Australia	-2.8	-4.8	-5.3	-3.8	-2.0	-3.8	-5.4	-6.1	-5.8	-5.3	-6.2	-4.7
Japan	2.3	3.1	2.6	2.6	2.1	2.9	3.2	3.7	3.6	3.9	4.8	3.6
New Zealand	-6.3	-3.8	-6.1	-5.1	-2.7	-3.9	-4.3	-6.3	-8.4	-8.5	-7.8	-9.0

Sources: International Monetary Fund, *International Financial Statistcs* (CD-ROM) (Washington, D.C., 2008) and *World Economic Outlook Database* (Washington, D.C., October 2008) with updates and estimates from national and local sources.

Notes: Data for 2008 are estimates. In the case of Cambodia, current account includes official transfers. Current account balances of Papua New Guinea for 2005-2008 are based on IMF 2007 Article IV Consultation. Current account balances of Samoa and Tonga for 2005-2008 are based on IMF 2008 Article IV Consultation.

Table 7. Change in money supply

(Per cent)

	1997	1998	1999	2000	2001	2002	2003	2004	2005	2006	2007	2008
Developing ESCAP economies												
East and North-East Asia												
China	20.7	14.9	14.7	12.3	15.0	13.1	19.2	14.9	16.7	22.1	16.7	14.0[a]
Hong Kong, China	8.7	11.1	8.3	9.3	−0.3	0.5	6.3	7.3	3.5	16.2	18.8	6.8[b]
Mongolia	42.2	−1.7	31.6	17.6	27.9	42.0	49.6	20.5	37.1	30.8	57.3	2.4[a]
Republic of Korea	14.1	27.0	27.4	25.4	13.2	11.0	6.7	−0.6	3.1	4.4	0.3	10.3[b]
North and Central Asia												
Armenia	29.2	36.7	14.0	38.6	4.3	34.0	10.4	22.3	27.8	32.9	42.3	25.7[a]
Azerbaijan	41.4	−15.2	20.1	73.4	−11.3	14.4	26.8	47.7	23.2	86.9	73.2	48.4[a]
Georgia	42.8	−0.8	20.6	39.2	17.6	17.9	22.8	42.4	26.5	39.7	49.7	0.9[c]
Kazakhstan	24.1	−14.1	84.4	45.0	40.2	30.1	34.2	68.2	26.3	78.1	25.9	30.6[a]
Kyrgyzstan	32.2	17.5	33.7	11.7	11.3	33.9	33.4	32.1	10.0	51.5	33.2	..
Russian Federation	28.8	37.6	56.7	58.0	36.3	33.8	38.5	33.7	36.3	40.6	44.2	21.8[d]
Tajikistan	105.1	28.2	24.6	63.3	35.0	40.5	40.9	9.8	25.9	59.7	169.9	111.0[b]
Turkmenistan	107.2	67.7	75.7	83.3	23.8	1.5	40.9	13.4	27.2	17.7	..	..
Uzbekistan	45.6	27.5	32.7	37.1	54.3	29.7	27.1	47.8	54.2	37.0	30.0	..
Pacific island economies												
Cook Islands	31.2	12.1	16.7	4.8	14.4	3.2	9.9	9.6	−5.2	22.4	−5.8	..
Fiji	−8.7	−0.5	13.6	−1.5	−3.1	7.8	25.0	10.5	15.1	20.2	10.3	4.9[b]
Kiribati	..	..	..	..	..	..	..	..	..	..	..	..
Papua New Guinea	7.7	2.5	9.2	5.0	6.2	7.3	−4.4	14.8	29.5	38.9	27.8	21.6[a]
Samoa	15.2	2.5	15.7	16.3	6.1	10.2	14.0	8.3	15.6	13.7	11.0	6.9[a]
Solomon Islands	6.7	2.5	7.0	0.6	−13.6	6.0	25.4	17.5	38.8	26.0	23.6	9.7[e]
Tonga	6.6	14.8	12.0	18.7	14.3	8.3	14.5	13.9	22.1	5.4	13.5	10.1[e]
Tuvalu	..	..	..	..	..	..	..	..	..	..	..	..
Vanuatu	−0.3	12.6	−9.2	5.5	5.5	−1.6	−0.9	9.9	11.6	7.0	16.0	12.8[a]
South and South-West Asia												
Bangladesh	10.8	10.4	12.8	18.6	16.6	13.1	15.6	13.8	16.7	19.3	17.1	17.6
Bhutan	58.9	13.9	32.0	17.4	7.9	26.9	1.8	19.9	11.9	13.0	13.0	..
India	17.7	18.2	17.1	15.2	14.3	16.8	13.0	16.7	15.6	21.6	22.3	23.6[f]
Iran (Islamic Republic of)	23.7	20.4	21.5	22.4	27.6	24.9	24.5	23.0	22.8	29.1	30.6	25.5[g]
Maldives	23.3	23.0	3.5	4.2	9.1	19.5	14.5	32.8	11.7	20.6	23.7	30.9[a]
Nepal	11.9	21.9	20.8	21.8	15.2	4.4	9.8	12.8	8.3	15.6	13.8	20.9[h]
Pakistan	19.9	7.9	4.3	12.1	11.7	16.8	17.5	20.5	16.5	14.6	19.5	15.5[o]
Sri Lanka	15.6	13.2	13.4	12.9	13.6	13.4	15.5	19.6	19.0	17.9	16.5	10.3[b]
Turkey	97.8	89.3	102.0	40.7	87.4	29.8	14.4	20.8	35.8	22.2	15.2	20.5[d]
South-East Asia												
Cambodia	16.6	15.7	17.3	26.9	20.4	31.1	15.4	28.3	15.8	40.5	61.8	19.9[a]
Indonesia	25.3	62.8	12.2	16.6	11.9	4.8	7.9	8.9	16.4	14.9	19.3	18.2[a]
Lao People's Democratic Republic	65.8	113.3	78.4	46.0	13.7	37.6	20.1	21.6	7.9	26.7	38.7	31.9[h]
Malaysia	22.7	1.5	14.2	5.3	2.3	6.0	11.1	25.2	15.6	17.1	9.5	14.4[c]
Myanmar	28.8	34.2	29.7	42.4	43.9	34.7	1.4	32.4	27.3	27.2	30.0	21.2[e]
Philippines	23.1	8.6	16.9	8.1	3.6	10.4	3.6	9.9	6.4	19.6	5.4	2.9[i]
Singapore	10.3	30.2	8.5	−2.0	5.9	−0.3	8.1	6.2	6.2	19.4	13.4	12.1[a]
Thailand	19.6	10.1	3.8	4.9	5.5	3.8	13.9	5.3	5.6	6.8	2.5	5.3[a]
Timor-Leste	..	..	..	..	..	..	41.1	6.9	18.3	28.2	43.9	29.2[a]
Viet Nam	24.3	23.5	66.5	35.4	27.3	13.3	33.1	31.0	30.9	29.7	49.1	21.0[b]
Developed ESCAP economies												
Australia	7.3	8.4	11.7	3.7	13.2	5.7	12.8	11.4	8.6	15.0	29.9	20.9[a]
Japan	5.8	3.1	2.8	1.3	−17.1	0.9	0.5	0.6	0.5	−0.7	0.8	0.8[b]
New Zealand	5.2	1.8	5.0	2.3	6.8	7.7	10.6	5.2	12.2	13.6	9.8	10.2[a]

Sources: ESCAP, based on national sources; International Monetary Fund, *International Financial Statistics* (CD-ROM) (Washington, D.C., January 2009); and Asian Development Bank, *Key Indicators for Asia and the Pacific 2008* (Manila, 2008) (for Cook Islands, Turkmenistan and Uzbekistan).

[a] October compared with the corresponding period of the previous year.
[b] August compared with the corresponding period of the previous year.
[c] November compared with the corresponding period of the previous year.
[d] September compared with the corresponding period of the previous year.
[e] June compared with the corresponding period of the previous year.
[f] May compared with the corresponding period of the previous year.
[g] March compared with the corresponding period of the previous year.
[h] April compared with the corresponding period of the previous year.
[i] February compared with the corresponding period of the previous year.

Table 8. Merchandise export growth rates

(Per cent)

	1997	1998	1999	2000	2001	2002	2003	2004	2005	2006	2007	2008
Developing ESCAP economies												
East and North-East Asia												
China	21.0	0.5	6.1	27.9	6.7	22.4	34.6	35.4	28.4	27.2	25.7	17.3
Hong Kong, China	4.0	−7.5	−0.1	16.1	−5.9	5.4	11.8	15.9	11.6	9.4	8.8	5.3
Macao, China	7.6	−0.3	2.8	15.4	−9.4	2.4	9.5	9.0	−11.9	3.4	−0.6	−18.6
Mongolia	6.4	−23.5	3.8	30.1	11.9	0.5	17.5	41.2	22.4	44.5	26.3[a]	10.8[b]
Republic of Korea	5.0	−2.8	8.6	19.9	−12.7	8.0	19.3	31.0	12.0	14.4	14.1	13.6
North and Central Asia												
Armenia	−19.3	−2.1	7.9	25.5	13.9	45.6	35.4	6.0	36.2	1.1	17.0	0.4[c]
Azerbaijan	25.5	−16.1	51.2	81.3	11.9	10.9	13.9	42.6	104.4	46.6	−4.9	803.0[c]
Georgia	20.6	−20.2	10.0	39.1	8.1	21:6	37.8	31.4	34.8	8.2	32.5	42.1[c]
Kazakhstan	9.6	−14.9	2.0	55.1	−3.9	12.3	32.0	55.7	37.4	37.3	24.8	66.1[c]
Kyrgyzstan	18.8	−15.2	−13.5	10.4	−6.1	3.8	18.5	24.2	33.3	18.2	42.8	27.1[c]
Russian Federation	−3.1	−14.3	1.5	39.0	−3.0	5.3	26.7	34.8	32.9	24.8	17.0	52.5[c]
Tajikistan	−3.1	−20.0	15.4	13.8	−16.8	13.0	8.1	14.8	15.9	53.9	4.9	4.8[c]
Turkmenistan	−55.1	−19.1	93.3	111.1	4.7	9.1	21.2	11.6	27.6	17.6	31.2	29.8[a]
Uzbekistan	4.6	−21.8	−3.4	5.2	−6.6	−8.4	29.1	31.6	11.6	18.0	42.9	24.1[a]
Pacific island economies												
Fiji	−23.9	−11.6	19.4	−13.7	0.1	3.6	34.5	−0.7	−6.7	−1.6	8.2	34.7[d]
Papua New Guinea	−14.8	−16.1	9.1	7.3	−13.7	−9.5	34.4	15.6	28.4	26.5	12.9	22.5[d]
Samoa[e]	45.5	30.5	..	..	9.7	−8.9	5.2	−18.4	−9.6	−17.0	8.5	8.7
Solomon Islands	7.5	−27.6	4.4	−47.4	−5.0	−21.8	38.6	−4.4	6.0	17.6	39.4	−0.4[d]
Tonga[e]	0.4	−17.8	12.6	−9.9	8.3	50.8	−1.1	−21.6	15.9	−4.0	−13.6	−7.4
Vanuatu	16.9	−4.0	−24.2	5.8	−26.8	1.0	32.3	28.6	0.0	−2.4	−20.2	54.2[d]
South and South-West Asia												
Afghanistan[e]	..	..	..	..	−37.7	82.1	46.7	−13.3	−2.6	7.9	..	..
Bangladesh[e]	13.8	16.8	2.9	8.3	12.4	−7.4	9.4	16.1	13.8	21.6	15.7	15.9
Bhutan[e]	1.7	12.1	−5.9	9.2	−12.9	4.5	8.7	39.7	34.5	47.2	64.4	29.6[a]
India[e]	4.5	−3.9	9.5	21.1	1.5	20.3	23.3	28.5	23.4	21.8	23.7	11.5[a]
Iran (Islamic Republic of)[e]	−17.9	−28.6	60.3	35.3	−16.0	18.1	20.4	29.0	46.8	18.2	28.1	10.6[a]
Maldives	12.3	6.6	−4.3	18.8	1.4	20.1	14.8	19.1	−10.7	39.4	1.2[a]	52.6[b]
Nepal[e]	9.8	12.7	17.4	37.6	4.6	−18.8	4.3	8.9	13.0	2.2	1.2	11.0[a]
Pakistan[e]	−4.4	3.7	−9.8	10.1	7.4	−0.7	22.2	10.3	16.9	14.3	4.4	16.5
Sri Lanka	13.3	1.9	−2.6	19.8	−12.8	−2.4	9.2	12.2	10.2	8.4	11.0	6.5
Turkey	13.1	2.7	−1.4	4.5	12.8	15.1	31.0	33.7	16.3	16.4	25.4	23.1
South-East Asia												
Brunei Darussalam	2.8	−28.7	32.7	54.1	−6.8	1.7	19.4	14.4	23.6	21.7	9.0[b]	8.3[b]
Cambodia	14.4	9.0	40.9	23.6	12.5	12.6	17.9	24.1	12.4	26.9	10.7	11.5[a]
Indonesia	12.5	−10.5	1.7	27.6	−12.3	3.1	8.4	12.6	22.9	19.0	14.0	23.1[b]
Lao People's Democratic Republic	−1.4	7.7	−10.5	9.5	−3.3	−5.9	11.6	8.3	52.2	67.1	5.2	26.0[b]
Malaysia	−27.1	32.7	12.1	16.2	−10.4	6.9	11.3	20.8	11.5	13.4	9.6	15.9
Myanmar	3.9	9.3	5.6	47.7	39.4	24.1	−5.7	8.0	29.4	21.4	35.5[a]	−0.3[a]
Philippines	22.8	16.9	18.8	8.7	−15.6	9.5	2.9	9.8	3.8	14.9	6.4	−2.9
Singapore	0.0	−12.2	4.4	20.3	−11.8	2.8	27.9	24.2	15.7	18.2	10.1	13.0
Thailand	3.8	−6.8	7.4	19.5	−7.1	4.8	18.2	21.6	15.0	16.9	17.2	16.9
Timor-Leste[f]	..	..	..	..	230.8	48.8	21.9	6.4	10.8	0.0	−11.1[b]	37.5[b]
Viet Nam	26.6	1.9	23.3	25.5	3.8	11.2	20.6	31.4	22.5	15.1	16.1	16.3[a]
Developed ESCAP economies												
Australia	6.3	−12.7	0.0	13.1	25.7	−9.0	−24.4	−2.9	14.7	17.6	14.2	37.4[g]
Japan	2.3	−8.5	7.9	14.6	−16.4	2.5	13.3	20.4	6.0	8.0	9.9	10.0
New Zealand	−2.5	−18.0	6.7	3.9	5.8	5.3	15.1	24.6	6.4	2.8	20.5	27.1[c]

Sources: ESCAP, calculated from national sources; International Monetary Fund, Direction of Trade Statistics Database; and Country Reports Series; Economist Intelligence Unit, *Country Reports*; CEIC Data Company Limited; and website of the Interstate Statistical Committee of the Commonwealth of Independent States, www.cisstat.com, 14 January 2009.

[a] Estimate.
[b] Projection.
[c] Refers to first 9 months of 2008.
[d] Refers to first 6 months of 2008.
[e] Fiscal year data.
[f] Excludes oil/gas revenue.
[g] Refers to first 10 months of 2008.

Table 9. Merchandise import growth rates

(Per cent)

	1997	1998	1999	2000	2001	2002	2003	2004	2005	2006	2007	2008
Developing ESCAP economies												
East and North-East Asia												
China	2.5	−1.5	18.2	24.4	12.6	27.1	39.9	36.0	17.6	19.9	20.7	18.4
Hong Kong, China	5.1	−11.6	−2.7	18.5	−5.5	3.3	11.7	16.9	10.5	11.6	10.0	5.7
Macao, China	4.1	−6.1	4.4	10.5	5.9	6.0	8.9	26.3	12.5	16.7	17.5	1.1
Mongolia	3.9	7.5	1.9	19.8	3.8	8.3	16.0	27.5	16.0	23.9	43.1[a]	38.3[b]
Republic of Korea	−3.8	−35.5	28.4	34.0	−12.1	7.8	17.6	25.5	16.4	18.4	15.3	22.0
North and Central Asia												
Armenia	4.3	1.6	−10.5	7.2	0.0	14.2	28.0	5.8	33.2	21.6	49.1	43.0[c]
Azerbaijan	2.8	25.4	−16.9	7.4	−4.8	24.4	49.4	31.5	21.4	25.1	8.4	33.8[c]
Georgia	37.4	−14.5	−13.2	12.4	7.8	4.4	34.5	36.7	33.8	47.7	41.8	31.8[c]
Kazakhstan	8.3	−7.0	−15.4	26.1	11.6	1.2	18.8	44.6	30.1	36.5	38.3	18.3[c]
Kyrgyzstan	−17.5	17.0	−27.1	−8.0	−11.2	27.1	26.6	24.9	98.7	56.0	40.7	52.4[c]
Russian Federation	5.7	−19.4	−31.9	13.5	19.8	13.4	24.8	28.0	28.7	39.6	44.9	47.6[c]
Tajikistan	12.3	−5.2	−6.8	1.8	1.9	4.8	22.2	56.1	97.0	29.7	42.3	35.9[c]
Turkmenistan[d]	−34.5	−213.2	30.0	20.8	23.3	−3.7	18.1	32.7	9.6	13.2	11.1	15.6[a]
Uzbekistan[d]	−11.2	−27.9	−4.8	−5.6	4.6	−14.4	10.0	27.3	8.1	16.0	49.2	13.4[a]
Pacific island economies												
Fiji	−10.1	−19.7	25.3	−7.9	4.8	9.2	39.1	14.6	2.6	12.1	−0.6	32.0[e]
Papua New Guinea	−1.6	−27.0	−0.1	−7.0	−6.4	14.6	10.3	22.4	4.6	30.3	32.0	21.9[e]
Samoa[f]	1.2	1.9	..	..	30.9	12.9	−7.6	23.3	24.3	16.6	15.3	2.0
Solomon Islands	42.4	−40.8	−13.7	−24.5	−13.0	−19.0	36.3	30.1	52.5	27.5	30.8	20.7[e]
Tonga[d, f]	−12.9	18.6	−21.2	12.8	−2.9	0.8	21.0	11.6	27.6	15.8	−11.4	27.5
Vanuatu	−3.5	−5.6	9.3	−7.2	0.8	−4.5	16.4	6.0	16.8	7.5	24.2	39.3[e]
South and South-West Asia												
Afghanistan[f]	..	..	..	..	−8.9	52.5	50.9	2.3	9.0	10.1	..	..
Bangladesh[f]	3.2	5.1	6.5	4.6	11.5	−8.5	13.1	12.9	20.6	12.2	16.3	26.1
Bhutan[f]	18.4	3.7	19.3	14.0	6.1	−5.2	2.2	29.2	75.5	−5.6	15.1	56.1[a]
India[f]	4.6	−7.1	16.5	4.6	12.3	14.5	24.1	48.6	33.8	21.8	29.9	19.0[a]
Iran (Islamic Republic of)[d, f]	−5.8	1.2	−6.0	12.3	20.2	21.6	34.1	29.2	12.8	16.1	13.1	18.5[a]
Maldives	15.6	1.5	13.6	−3.4	−0.3	1.1	20.2	36.3	16.1	24.4	18.3[d]	32.3[b]
Nepal[f]	21.2	−11.8	−11.0	22.1	−0.2	−10.6	13.6	10.6	13.8	15.8	15.0	26.0[a]
Pakistan[f]	0.8	−14.9	−6.8	9.3	4.1	−3.6	18.2	27.6	32.1	31.6	8.0	31.2
Sri Lanka	7.8	0.4	1.5	22.4	−18.4	2.2	9.3	19.9	10.8	15.7	10.2	24.0
Turkey	11.3	−5.4	−11.4	34.0	−24.0	24.5	34.5	40.7	19.7	19.5	21.8	18.7
South-East Asia												
Brunei Darussalam	−14.8	−30.6	−4.9	−16.6	−0.7	37.3	−16.9	6.5	5.8	12.0	6.4[b]	6.8[b]
Cambodia[d]	−0.7	9.6	36.5	21.6	8.2	12.7	13.0	22.5	20.2	20.9	14.2	19.5[a]
Indonesia[d]	4.5	−30.9	−4.2	31.9	−14.1	2.8	10.9	28.0	37.4	6.3	14.9	31.3[b]
Lao People's Democratic Republic	−6.0	−14.7	0.3	−3.4	−4.7	−12.4	3.4	54.2	23.7	25.1	33.0	25.8[b]
Malaysia	−27.2	5.7	9.1	25.1	−10.0	8.2	4.4	26.4	9.2	14.7	12.0	9.5
Myanmar	12.7	16.4	−13.7	2.3	19.5	−19.6	−8.1	4.6	−12.0	34.3	26.5[a]	21.1[a]
Philippines[d]	10.8	−17.5	3.6	12.2	−4.2	18.7	3.1	8.0	8.0	9.2	7.2	−3.9[g]
Singapore	0.8	−23.3	9.4	21.3	−13.9	0.4	17.1	27.4	15.3	19.1	10.2	21.5
Thailand	−13.4	−33.8	16.9	31.3	−3.0	4.6	17.4	25.7	25.9	9.0	8.7	27.6
Timor-Leste	..	..	..	..	13.5	−16.8	−10.8	−16.1	−16.0	−1.6	62.6[b]	54.5[b]
Viet Nam	4.0	−0.8	2.1	33.2	3.7	21.8	27.9	26.6	15.0	22.7	21.9	37.0[a]
Developed ESCAP economies												
Australia	2.6	−2.0	7.3	4.1	13.0	1.6	−15.4	−3.4	7.3	12.6	19.1	25.8[h]
Japan	−3.0	−18.1	11.5	23.3	−8.4	−4.4	13.3	19.1	17.1	12.3	7.0	22.9
New Zealand	−1.4	−13.6	14.3	−2.9	−4.2	12.9	22.4	25.0	13.3	−0.1	17.9	25.1[c]

Sources: ESCAP, calculated from national sources; International Monetary Fund, Direction of Trade Statistics Database; and Country Reports Series; Economist Intelligence Unit, *Country Reports*; CEIC Data Company Limited; and website of the Interstate Statistical Committee of the Commonwealth of Independent States, www.cisstat.com, 14 January 2009.

[a] Estimate.
[b] Projection.
[c] Refers to first 9 months of 2008.
[d] f.o.b. value.
[e] Refers to first 6 months of 2008.
[f] Fiscal year data.
[g] Refers to first 11 months of 2008.
[h] Refers to first 10 months of 2008.

Table 10. Inward foreign direct investment

	FDI inward stock					FDI net inflows				
	Million US dollars	Percentage of GDP				Million US dollars	Percentage of GDP			
	2007	90-95	96-00	01-05	2007	2007	90-95	96-00	01-05	2007
Developing ESCAP economies										
East and North-East Asia										
China	327 087	9.7	16.0	13.5	9.6	83 521	3.6	4.1	3.3	2.5
DPR Korea	1 378	6.4	9.4	10.6	9.3	53	0.1	0.6	0.7	0.4
Hong Kong, China	1 184 471	190.2	188.5	253.8	573.0	59 899	4.4	14.7	13.8	29.0
Macao, China	8 606	55.5	44.5	44.1	45.0	2 115	0.0	0.0	6.2	11.1
Mongolia	1 326	1.4	9.3	27.4	34.1	328	0.5	2.5	6.6	8.4
Republic of Korea	119 630	2.0	4.7	12.0	12.5	2 628	0.2	1.2	0.9	0.3
North and Central Asia										
Armenia	2 448	2.3	18.4	30.2	26.7	661	0.7	5.8	5.0	7.2
Azerbaijan	6 598		62.9	102.3	21.1	-4 817	0.6	13.9	24.4	-15.4
Georgia	5 259	0.3	13.4	34.0	51.7	1 659	0.1	4.8	7.0	16.3
Kazakhstan	43 381		33.8	52.8	41.7	10 259	2.0	6.3	7.7	9.9
Kyrgyzstan	819		21.7	25.3	21.9	208	1.3	3.6	2.8	5.6
Russian Federation	324 065		5.6	21.4	25.1	52 475	0.2	1.1	1.7	4.1
Tajikistan	1 046	0.8	9.3	13.1	28.0	401	0.3	1.8	4.7	10.7
Turkmenistan	3 928	4.2	22.7	34.6	54.2	804	2.6	3.4	5.9	11.1
Uzbekistan	1 648	0.4	3.2	8.8	8.6	262	0.1	0.8	0.9	1.4
Pacific island economies										
American Samoa										
Cook Islands	40	18.9	66.2	25.4	18.8	1	1.0	4.8	0.1	0.5
Fiji	1 464	25.4	26.3	21.4	43.5	269	3.3	2.9	4.7	8.0
French Polynesia	250	3.0	3.6	3.9	4.1	17	0.3	0.2	0.3	0.3
Guam										
Kiribati	159	2.4	72.3	204.3	219.2	11	0.4	28.5	23.6	15.8
Marshall Islands						361	-1.4	38.0	124.5	242.0
Micronesia (Federated States of)							0.0	-7.1	0.0	
Nauru						1	-0.7	1.2	4.5	3.0
New Caledonia	1 360	2.8	3.0	5.3	17.0	288	0.3	0.2	0.8	3.6
Niue	7					0				
Northern Mariana Island	0									
Palau	123		57.4	87.3	72.3	3	0.6	17.0	3.3	2.0
Papua New Guinea	2 337	36.6	43.2	59.7	38.7	96	5.7	6.0	1.3	1.6
Samoa	82	13.4	20.8	16.9	16.0	17	3.1	2.1	0.0	3.2
Solomon Islands	220	37.7	40.5	44.5	45.4	42	4.0	1.3	0.6	8.8
Tonga	74	2.6	6.0	13.0	30.0	24	0.8	0.7	2.9	9.8
Tuvalu	31		1.0	106.4	106.4	2	0.4	-1.2	27.2	5.9
Vanuatu	520	90.0	130.7	143.1	115.2	34	12.9	9.4	5.3	7.5
South and South-West Asia										
Afghanistan	1 116	0.4	0.5	4.5	11.9	288	0.0	0.0	2.3	3.1
Bangladesh	4 404	4.7	6.9	9.1	6.5	666	0.1	1.1	0.9	1.0
Bhutan	106	1.0	1.0	1.7	8.1	78	0.1	0.1	0.5	6.0
India	76 226	0.9	3.0	5.2	6.7	22 950	0.2	0.7	0.9	2.0
Iran (Islamic Republic of)	5 295	2.1	2.2	2.1	1.8	754	0.0	0.0	0.2	0.3
Maldives	209	13.9	17.3	22.4	19.8	15	2.3	2.1	1.8	1.4
Nepal	126	0.3	1.1	1.6	1.1	6	0.0	0.2	0.1	0.0
Pakistan	20 086	4.5	9.8	7.5	12.3	5 333	0.6	0.6	1.0	3.3
Sri Lanka	3 456	9.3	11.5	10.1	10.7	529	1.0	1.4	1.1	1.6
Turkey	145 556	8.4	9.1	14.7	29.9	22 029	0.5	0.4	1.5	4.5
South-East Asia										
Brunei Darussalam	10 045	3.6	52.1	105.1	81.1	184	2.6	12.9	15.7	1.5
Cambodia	3 821	6.0	35.4	41.2	44.2	867	2.2	6.3	3.6	10.0
Indonesia	58 955	8.1	15.9	7.9	13.6	6 928	1.3	0.5	0.6	1.6
Lao People's Democratic Republic	1 180	5.9	28.6	28.1	28.3	324	2.6	4.3	1.0	7.8
Malaysia	76 748	28.2	49.0	35.3	41.1	8 403	7.0	5.2	2.6	4.5
Myanmar	5 433	11.4	41.4	44.8	29.3	428	3.0	7.2	2.3	2.3
Philippines	18 952	12.4	19.2	14.7	13.1	2 928	1.8	2.1	1.2	2.0
Singapore	249 667	77.1	104.5	156.2	154.7	24 137	10.9	14.3	13.8	15.0
Thailand	85 749	10.7	17.3	32.4	34.9	9 575	1.6	3.4	3.8	3.9
Timor-Leste	167	19.0	25.2	46.4	36.8	2	5.2	0.0	5.4	0.3
Viet Nam	40 235	29.8	56.1	66.5	56.5	6 739	7.7	6.4	3.7	9.5
Developed ESCAP economies										
Australia	312 275	25.2	27.1	33.5	33.0	22 266	2.0	1.8	1.2	2.4
Japan	132 851	0.4	0.8	1.9	3.0	22 549	0.0	0.1	0.2	0.5
New Zealand	71 312	33.2	52.3	49.6	54.7	2 768	4.3	3.3	2.1	2.1

Sources: United Nations Conference on Trade and Development, *Foreign Direct Investment* (online database, accessed in June 2008); and United Nations Statistics Division, National Accounts Main Aggregates database (online database, accessed in September 2008).

Table 11. Official development assistance and workers' remittances

| | ODA received | | | | | | Workers' remittances | | | | | | |
| | Million US dollars | | | Percentage of GNI | | | Million US dollars | | | | Percentage of GNI | | |
	1990	2000	2006	1990	2000	2006	1995	2000	2005	2006	1995	2000	2006
Developing ESCAP economies													
East and North-East Asia													
China	2 030.4	1 727.5	1 245.5	0.5	0.1	0.0	350.0	556.2	5 494.7	6 830.5	0.0	0.0	0.3
DPR Korea	7.7	73.3	54.5	0.0	0.7	0.4							
Hong Kong, China	38.2			0.0									
Macao, China	0.2			0.0					54.1				
Mongolia	13.1	217.4	202.6	1.0	20.1	6.4		12.0	177.6	179.8		1.1	5.7
Republic of Korea	52.0			0.0			291.4	62.9	64.1	136.1	0.1	0.0	0.0
North and Central Asia													
Armenia		215.9	213.3		11.4	3.5	12.4	9.3	47.2	76.5	1.0	0.5	1.2
Azerbaijan		139.1	205.7		2.7	1.1		57.1	490.2	662.3		1.1	3.6
Georgia		169.4	360.6		5.3	4.6		94.9	93.8	153.0		3.0	1.9
Kazakhstan		188.7	171.6		1.1	0.2		63.9	55.8	73.0		0.4	0.1
Kyrgyzstan		214.7	311.2		16.7	11.1	1.2	2.2	313.3	730.6	0.1	0.2	26.1
Russian Federation									621.4	766.3			0.1
Tajikistan		123.5	239.8		11.7	6.3			465.2	1 015.0			26.5
Turkmenistan		31.5	26.2		0.8	0.4							
Uzbekistan		185.8	148.6		1.4	0.9							
Pacific island economies													
American Samoa													
Cook Islands	12.1	4.3	32.3	20.7	5.3	17.8							
Fiji	49.6	29.1	55.9	3.7	1.7	1.8		25.7	134.6	126.6		1.5	4.0
French Polynesia	259.7			8.9					11.3	14.4			0.3
Guam													
Kiribati	20.2	17.9	−44.9	46.5	25.8	−48.4							
Marshall Islands		57.2	55.0		39.9	30.6							
Micronesia (Federated States of)		101.5	108.5		43.1	41.3							
Nauru	0.2	4.0	17.4	0.4	15.2	43.7							
New Caledonia	302.4			12.0					5.3	3.7			0.1
Niue	7.2	3.2	9.0										
Northern Mariana Island	63.1												
Palau		39.1	37.3		31.2	23.5							
Papua New Guinea	412.4	275.4	279.0	15.5	8.7	6.7			5.7				
Samoa	47.6	27.4	47.1	28.9	11.8	10.6	39.2					20.3	
Solomon Islands	45.7	68.3	204.5	22.3	20.2	47.8			2.7	9.5			2.2
Tonga	29.8	18.8	21.5	21.5	12.2	8.8			62.2	68.5			28.2
Tuvalu	5.1	4.0	15.3	53.1	32.9	60.3							
Vanuatu	49.5	45.8	48.8	30.2	19.0	13.4	6.1	11.0	0.1	0.1	2.8	4.6	0.0
South and South-West Asia													
Afghanistan	121.7	136.0	2 999.8	3.4	5.0	40.3							
Bangladesh	2 092.8	1 167.8	1 222.7	6.8	2.5	1.9	1 201.7	1 958.1	4 302.4	5 417.7	3.1	4.2	8.4
Bhutan	46.0	53.1	94.1	17.6	11.9	10.2							
India	1 398.9	1 462.7	1 378.9	0.4	0.3	0.2	6 139.0	12 744.9	21 030.3	25 108.9	1.7	2.8	2.8
Iran (Islamic Republic of)	104.8	129.9	121.0	0.1	0.1	0.1							
Maldives	20.9	19.2	38.6	10.2	3.2	4.4							
Nepal	422.8	387.3	514.3	11.8	7.0	6.3	56.8	111.5	1 126.3	1 373.3	1.3	2.0	16.8
Pakistan	1 126.6	692.4	2 147.2	1.9	0.9	1.5	1 712.2	1 075.0	4 277.0	5 113.0	2.1	1.4	3.5
Sri Lanka	728.3	275.7	795.9	9.1	1.7	2.9	789.8	1 142.3	1 968.5	2 325.5	6.0	7.0	8.4
Turkey	1 202.3	326.8	569.9	0.8	0.2	0.1	3 327.0	4 560.0	851.0	1 111.0	1.9	2.3	0.3
South-East Asia													
Brunei Darussalam	3.9			0.1									
Cambodia	41.3	395.9	529.0	3.3	12.6	8.4	10.0	100.0	160.0	180.0	0.3	3.2	2.9
Indonesia	1 715.9	1 654.4	1 404.5	1.6	1.2	0.4	651.0	1 190.2	5 296.3	5 560.3	0.3	0.9	1.6
Lao People's Democratic Republic	149.1	281.6	364.2	17.2	17.0	11.9							
Malaysia	468.5	45.4	240.3	1.1	0.1	0.2							
Myanmar	160.8	105.6	146.6	3.1	1.5	1.1	81.4	76.7	87.0	65.7	1.0	1.1	0.5
Philippines	1 270.6	575.2	562.3	2.9	0.7	0.4	432.0	5 161.0	10 668.0	12481.0	0.6	6.4	9.7
Singapore	−3.1			0.0									
Thailand	795.6	698.2	−215.6	0.9	0.6	−0.1							
Timor-Leste	0.1	231.3	209.7	0.1	71.6	22.0							
Viet Nam	180.6	1 681.4	1 846.4	3.0	5.5	3.1							
Developed ESCAP economies													
Australia													
Japan								504.8	733.4	1026.1		0.0	0.0
New Zealand													

Sources: Organization for Economic Co-operation and Development, Development Database on Aid from DAC Members (online database, accessed in March 2008); and United Nations Statistics Division, National Accounts Main Aggregates database (online database, accessed in September 2008).

Table 12. International migration

	Stock of foreign population						Net migration rate			
	Thousands			% of total population			Per 1 000 population			
	1990	2000	2005	1990	2000	2005	90-95	95-00	00-05	05-10
Developing ESCAP economies										
East and North-East Asia										
China	380	513	596	0.0	0.0	0.0	−0.2	−0.2	−0.3	−0.3
DPR Korea	34	36	37	0.2	0.2	0.2				
Hong Kong, China	2 218	2 701	2 999	38.9	40.5	42.5	10.1	9.3	8.7	8.3
Macao, China	204	240	257	54.9	54.5	54.4	7.8	7.1	10.9	4.2
Mongolia	7	8	9	0.3	0.3	0.4	−5.2	−7.4	−4.0	−2.3
Republic of Korea	572	568	551	1.3	1.2	1.2	−0.5	−0.3	−0.3	−0.1
North and Central Asia										
Armenia	659	314	235	18.6	10.2	7.8	−29.5	−14.3	−6.6	−5.0
Azerbaijan	361	160	182	5.0	2.0	2.2	−3.1	−3.2	−2.4	−1.2
Georgia	338	219	191	6.2	4.6	4.3	−21.3	−14.4	−10.8	−6.8
Kazakhstan	3 619	2 871	2 502	21.9	19.2	16.4	−18.6	−17.1	−2.7	−2.6
Kyrgyzstan	623	372	288	14.2	7.5	5.5	−12.2	−1.1	−3.0	−2.8
Russian Federation	11 525	11 892	12 080	7.8	8.1	8.4	3.0	3.0	1.3	0.4
Tajikistan	426	330	306	8.0	5.4	4.7	−11.3	−11.6	−10.8	−5.9
Turkmenistan	307	241	224	8.4	5.4	4.6	2.5	−2.3	−0.4	−0.4
Uzbekistan	1 653	1 367	1 268	8.1	5.5	4.8	−3.1	−3.4	−2.3	−1.5
Pacific island economies										
American Samoa	21	21	20	45.0	36.2	31.8				
Cook Islands	3	3	3	14.6	18.1	21.8				
Fiji	14	16	17	1.9	2.0	2.1	−9.3	−10.7	−10.3	−8.3
French Polynesia	26	31	34	13.2	13.0	13.1	−0.5	1.4	1.5	
Guam	70	97	113	52.4	62.3	67.3	−4.6	−6.4	1.0	
Kiribati	2	2	3	3.0	2.9	2.8				
Marshall Islands	2	2	2	3.3	3.1	2.9				
Micronesia (Federated States of)	3	3	4	3.2	3.2	3.2	−4.4	−25.4	−17.9	−15.3
Nauru	4	5	5	42.9	45.4	48.7				
New Caledonia	37	41	43	21.4	19.0	18.4	5.8	5.5	4.3	4.5
Niue	0	0	0	10.1	7.5	6.7				
Northern Mariana Island	5	5	5	11.1	7.4	6.5				
Palau	2	3	3	12.9	13.5	15.1				
Papua New Guinea	33	26	25	0.8	0.5	0.4				
Samoa	6	8	9	3.6	4.5	5.0	−15.8	−16.2	−16.6	−10.6
Solomon Islands	4	4	3	1.3	0.8	0.7				
Tonga	3	2	1	3.2	1.6	1.2	−18.0	−19.5	−16.1	−14.9
Tuvalu	0	0	0	3.2	3.1	3.1				
Vanuatu	2	1	1	1.4	0.7	0.5	−1.1	−7.9		
South and South-West Asia										
Afghanistan	29	38	43	0.2	0.2	0.2	42.9	−4.1	9.7	10.1
Bangladesh	882	988	1 032	0.8	0.7	0.7	−0.4	−0.5	−0.7	−0.6
Bhutan	8	9	10	1.5	1.6	1.5	−38.3	0.1	11.7	3.0
India	7 493	6 271	5 700	0.9	0.6	0.5	−0.2	−0.3	−0.2	−0.2
Iran (Islamic Republic of)	3 809	2 321	1 959	6.7	3.5	2.8	−5.3	−1.7	−3.7	−1.4
Maldives	3	3	3	1.2	1.1	1.1				
Nepal	413	718	819	2.2	2.9	3.0	−1.0	−0.9	−0.8	−0.7
Pakistan	6 556	4 243	3 254	5.8	2.9	2.1	−4.3	−0.1	−1.6	−1.7
Sri Lanka	461	397	368	2.7	2.1	1.9	−2.9	−4.3	−4.7	−3.1
Turkey	1 150	1 259	1 328	2.0	1.8	1.8	0.4	0.3	−0.1	0.1
South-East Asia										
Brunei Darussalam	73	104	124	28.5	31.2	33.2	2.6	2.2	2.0	1.8
Cambodia	38	237	304	0.4	1.9	2.2	2.8	1.3	0.2	−0.1
Indonesia	466	330	160	0.3	0.2	0.1	−0.8	−0.9	−0.9	−0.8
Lao People's Democratic Republic	23	24	25	0.6	0.5	0.4	−1.4	−3.5	−4.2	−2.5
Malaysia	1 014	1 392	1 639	5.6	6.0	6.4	3.0	4.5	1.2	0.7
Myanmar	101	115	117	0.3	0.2	0.2	−0.6	0.0	−0.4	0.0
Philippines	164	322	374	0.3	0.4	0.4	−2.8	−2.5	−2.2	−2.0
Singapore	727	1 352	1 843	24.1	33.6	42.6	15.4	19.6	9.6	9.0
Thailand	391	844	1 050	0.7	1.4	1.7	0.6	1.7	0.7	0.5
Timor-Leste	5	5	6	0.7	0.6	0.6		−40.8	21.2	1.7
Viet Nam	28	28	21	0.0	0.0	0.0	−0.7	−0.5	−0.5	−0.5
Developed ESCAP economies										
Australia	3 984	4 072	4 097	23.6	21.3	20.2	5.9	5.0	6.0	4.8
Japan	877	1 620	2 048	0.7	1.3	1.6	0.4	0.4	0.4	0.4
New Zealand	529	708	642	15.5	18.4	15.7	5.3	2.1	5.1	2.4

Sources: United Nations Department of Economics and Social Affairs, *World Migrant Stock: The 2005 Revision Population Database,* http://esa.un.org/migration/ (August 2008); and *World Population Prospects: The 2006 Revision Population Database,* http://esa.un.org/unpp/ (September 2007).

Table 13a. Primary education

	Net enrolment rate		Gender parity index		Completion rate (%)					
	% of primary school-aged children		Ratio		Both sexes		Girls		Boys	
	1991	Latest	Earliest	Latest	Earliest	2006	Earliest	2006	Earliest	2006
Developing ESCAP economies										
East and North-East Asia										
China	99.1				105.2 (91)					
DPR Korea										
Hong Kong, China	93.0 (01)	90.7 (05)	0.96 (01)	0.95 (05)	102.2 (91)	100.2	104.9 (03)	97.9	108.7 (03)	102.6
Macao, China	81.3	92.9 (07)	1.01 (99)	0.97 (07)	96.4 (99)	103.6	96.1 (99)	102.8	96.6 (99)	104.3
Mongolia	95.7	88.8 (07)	1.04 (99)	1.01 (07)	86.6 (99)	108.8	89.4 (99)	110.0	83.8 (99)	107.6
Republic of Korea	99.7	98.2 (06)	0.95 (99)	0.93 (01)	97.9 (91)	101.0	98.3 (91)	95.2	97.6 (91)	106.6
North and Central Asia										
Armenia	90.2 (01)	82.2 (06)	1.02 (01)	1.05 (06)	100.5 (01)	90.8	100.9 (01)	92.9	100.1 (01)	88.9
Azerbaijan	88.8	85.9 (07)	1.01 (99)	0.98 (07)	88.8 (99)	91.9	88.2 (99)	90.0	89.4 (99)	93.7
Georgia	97.1	93.7 (07)	1.00 (99)	0.97 (07)	87.7 (99)	84.7	87.2 (99)	86.3	88.1 (99)	83.1
Kazakhstan	86.7	90.3 (08)	1.01 (00)	1.00 (08)	94.4 (00)	103.6	94.9 (00)	103.8	93.9 (00)	103.4
Kyrgyzstan	92.3	84.5 (07)	0.99 (99)	0.99 (07)	95.1 (99)	99.4	95.0 (99)	99.7	95.3 (99)	99.1
Russian Federation	97.3	90.9 (06)	1.00 (06)	1.00 (06)	95.9 (99)	93.7	94.3 (06)	94.3	93.1 (06)	93.1
Tajikistan	76.7	97.2 (07)	0.93 (00)	0.96 (07)	94.9 (99)	106.1	92.5 (99)	103.7	97.2 (99)	108.3
Turkmenistan										
Uzbekistan	78.2				96.0 (99)	100.2	95.3 (00)	99.3	95.5 (00)	101.2
Pacific island economies										
American Samoa										
Cook Islands	84.8 (99)	74.2 (05)	0.96 (99)	1.03 (05)	87.9 (99)	92.3 (05)	85.9 (99)	91.3 (05)	89.8 (99)	93.2 (05)
Fiji	99.5	86.6 (07)	1.01 (99)	0.99 (07)	100.4 (00)	98.1	99.5 (00)	97.8	101.3 (00)	98.4
French Polynesia										
Guam										
Kiribati	97.0 (99)	97.4 (02)	1.01 (99)	1.01 (99)	107.3 (99)	124.8 (05)	105.0 (99)	126.0 (05)	109.5 (99)	123.7 (05)
Marshall Islands	87.9 (01)	89.6 (03)	1.01 (01)	0.99 (03)	97.5 (99)	125.0 (03)	87.2 (99)	127.5 (03)	107.4 (99)	122.6 (03)
Micronesia (Federated States of)										
Nauru					90.4 (01)	74.8 (03)	93.2 (01)	73.6 (03)	88.1 (01)	75.9 (03)
New Caledonia										
Niue	98.5 (99)		1.00 (99)		85.4 (99)	96.7 (05)	83.3 (99)	86.7 (05)	87.5 (99)	106.7 (05)
Northern Mariana Island										
Palau	96.8 (99)	96.4 (00)	0.94 (99)	0.96 (00)	99.4 (99)	119.1 (04)	88.8 (99)	90.4 (00)	109.2 (99)	106.7 (00)
Papua New Guinea					46.5 (91)		41.9 (91)		50.9 (91)	
Samoa	92.0 (99)	87.0 (07)	0.99 (99)	1.02 (07)	95.5 (99)	96.3 (04)	90.1 (99)	98.4 (04)	100.4 (99)	94.4 (04)
Solomon Islands	63.3 (03)	61.8 (05)	0.97 (03)	0.99 (05)	72.1 (91)					
Tonga	88.1 (99)	95.9 (05)	0.96 (99)	0.97 (05)	101.9 (91)	99.9	98.2 (91)	102.4	105.4 (91)	97.7
Tuvalu					113.3 (99)	105.3	109.3 (99)	118.2	117.0 (99)	93.2
Vanuatu	91.5 (99)	87.8 (06)	0.99 (99)	0.99 (06)	85.2 (99)	86.5 (04)	85.0 (99)	85.9 (04)	85.4 (99)	87.0 (04)
South and South-West Asia										
Afghanistan					37.7 (05)	37.7 (05)	20.8 (05)	20.8 (05)	53.5 (05)	53.5 (05)
Bangladesh	83.1 (99)	88.9 (04)	1.00 (99)	1.04 (04)	78.0 (99)	71.9 (04)	79.6 (99)	74.2 (04)	76.5 (99)	69.7 (04)
Bhutan	56.2 (99)	79.0 (06)	0.89 (99)	1.00 (06)	51.6 (99)	73.2	47.2 (99)	73.1	55.9 (99)	73.3
India	79.2 (00)	88.7 (06)	0.85 (00)	0.96 (06)	63.8 (91)	85.7	51.5 (91)	83.1	75.1 (91)	88.0
Iran (Islamic Republic of)	92.4	93.6 (06)	0.97 (99)	1.10 (05)	92.1 (91)	101.1	85.2 (91)	103.8	96.9 (91)	94.7
Maldives	97.6 (99)	97.4 (06)	1.01 (99)	1.00 (06)	147.3 (03)	128.9	151.6 (03)	127.0	143.2 (03)	130.7
Nepal	64.7 (99)	76.1 (07)	0.79 (99)	0.95 (07)	50.9 (91)	76.0	54.6 (99)	72.3	71.3 (99)	79.6
Pakistan	57.2 (01)	65.6 (06)	0.68 (01)	0.78 (06)	61.5 (05)	61.8	51.0 (05)	52.9	71.4 (05)	70.2
Sri Lanka	99.0 (01)	96.7 (04)	1.01 (01)	1.01 (03)	102.4 (91)	107.5 (05)	102.2 (91)	107.8 (05)	102.6 (91)	107.3 (05)
Turkey	90.4	91.4 (06)	0.93 (02)	0.96 (06)	89.7 (91)	95.9	86.0 (91)	91.1	93.2 (91)	100.6
South-East Asia										
Brunei Darussalam	92.7	92.8 (07)	1.01 (05)	1.00 (07)	100.0 (91)	106.9	123.5 (99)	108.7	124.0 (99)	105.2
Cambodia	75.1	89.4 (07)	0.91 (99)	0.96 (07)	40.9 (99)	86.6	35.3 (99)	86.1	46.3 (99)	87.1
Indonesia	96.7	95.4 (06)	0.97 (00)	0.96 (06)	90.7 (91)	98.8	95.7 (01)	98.9	94.9 (01)	98.7
Lao People's Democratic Republic	61.9	83.7 (06)	0.92 (99)	0.94 (06)	70.2 (99)	75.0	63.7 (99)	69.8	76.5 (99)	80.1
Malaysia	97.7 (99)	99.9 (05)	0.98 (99)	1.00 (05)	91.0 (91)	98.3	90.8 (91)	98.1	91.2 (91)	98.4
Myanmar	95.5 (00)	99.6 (06)	1.00 (00)	1.01 (06)	74.5 (99)	95.3	73.0 (99)	97.8	75.9 (99)	92.8
Philippines	96.3	91.4 (06)	1.00 (99)	1.02 (06)	89.5 (99)	93.8	92.1 (99)	97.5	86.9 (99)	90.3
Singapore										
Thailand		93.9 (07)	0.99 (06)	1.00 (07)	96.0 (99)		95.8 (99)		96.3 (99)	
Timor-Leste	68.1 (05)	63.0 (07)	0.96 (05)	0.96 (07)						
Viet Nam	90.5	93.4 (01)	0.94 (01)		96.1 (99)		93.3 (99)		98.8 (99)	
Developed ESCAP economies										
Australia	99.8	96.4 (06)	1.01 (99)	1.01 (06)						
Japan	99.7	99.8 (06)	1.00 (99)	1.00 (06)	101.4 (91)		101.6 (91)		101.3 (91)	
New Zealand	98.8	99.3 (06)	1.00 (99)	1.00 (06)	100.0 (91)		99.0 (91)		100.9 (91)	

Sources: UNESCO Institute for Statistics, Data Centre (online database, November 2008); United Nations Department of Economics and Social Affairs, *Millennium Development Goals Indicators*, http://mdgs.un.org/unsd/mdg/Default.aspx (online database, January 2009).

Table 13b. Secondary and tertiary education

	Secondary level				Tertiary level			
	Net enrolment rate (%)		Gender parity index (ratio)		Gross enrolment rate (%)		Gender parity index (ratio)	
	Earliest	Latest	Earliest	Latest	1999	2007	Earliest	2007
Developing ESCAP economies								
East and North-East Asia								
China					6.4	21.6 (06)	0.8 (03)	1.0 (06)
DPR Korea								
Hong Kong, China	73.8 (01)	78.6 (07)	1.0 (01)	1.0 (07)	30.6 (03)	33.8	1.0 (03)	1.0
Macao, China	62.1 (99)	77.6 (07)	1.1 (99)	1.0 (07)	27.7	57.0	0.8 (99))	0.9
Mongolia	55.5 (99)	81.1 (07)	1.3 (99)	1.1 (07)	25.7	47.7	1.9 (99)	1.6
Republic of Korea	94.5 (99)	96.0 (06)	1.0 (99)	0.9 (06)	72.6	92.6 (06)	0.6 (99)	0.7 (06)
North and Central Asia								
Armenia	85.9 (01)	85.8 (06)	1.1 (01)	1.0 (06)	23.7 (99)	35.5	1.1 (99)	1.2
Azerbaijan	73.2 (99)	77.8 (06)	1.0 (99)	1.0 (06)	15.4 (99)	14.9	0.6 (99)	0.9
Georgia	76.4 (99)	81.9 (07)	1.0 (99)	1.0 (07)	35.9 (99)	37.3	1.1 (99)	1.1
Kazakhstan	87.0 (00)	85.6 (08)	1.0 (00)	1.0 (08)	24.5 (99)	47.0 (08)	1.2 (99)	1.4 (08)
Kyrgyzstan	82.1 (04)	80.5 (07)	1.0 (04)	1.0 (07)	29.0 (99)	42.8	1.0 (99)	1.3
Russian Federation					65.1 (03)	72.3 (06)	1.4 (03)	1.4 (06)
Tajikistan	62.8 (99)	81.3 (07)	0.9 (99)	0.9 (07)	13.6 (99)	19.8	0.3 (99)	0.4
Turkmenistan								
Uzbekistan					12.9 (99)	9.8	0.8 (99)	0.7
Pacific island economies								
American Samoa								
Cook Islands	59.0 (99)	64.4 (00)	1.1 (99)	1.1 (00)				
Fiji	78.6 (99)	79.1 (06)	1.1 (99)	1.1 (06)	15.5 (03)	15.4 (05)	1.2 (03)	1.2 (05)
French Polynesia								
Guam								
Kiribati	70.4 (03)	68.3 (05)	1.2 (03)	1.1 (05)				
Marshall Islands	74.4 (02)	74.4 (03)	1.1 (02)	1.1 (03)	16.9 (01)	17.0 (03)	1.3 (01)	1.3 (03)
Micronesia (Federated States of)								
Nauru								
New Caledonia								
Niue	93.4 (99)		1.1 (99)					
Northern Mariana Island								
Palau					40.6 (00)		2.4 (00)	
Papua New Guinea					2.0 (99)		0.6 (99)	
Samoa	71.5 (99)	66.0 (04)	1.1 (99)	1.1 (04)	11.5 (99)		1.0 (99)	
Solomon Islands	23.0 (99)	27.3 (03)	0.8 (99)	0.9 (03)				
Tonga	72.2 (99)	60.4 (06)	1.1 (99)	1.2 (06)	3.4 (99)	6.0 (04)	1.3 (99)	1.7 (04)
Tuvalu								
Vanuatu	29.6 (99)	38.1 (04)	0.9 (99)	0.9 (04)	4.0 (99)	4.8 (04)	0.6 (02)	0.6 (04)
South and South-West Asia								
Afghanistan					1.2 (03)	1.3 (04)	0.3 (03)	0.3 (04)
Bangladesh	42.1 (99)	41.0 (04)	1.0 (99)	1.0 (04)	5.4 (99)	6.8 (06)	0.5 (99)	0.6 (06)
Bhutan	16.9 (99)	38.5 (06)	1.0 (99)	1.0 (06)	2.7 (99)	5.5 (06)	0.6 (99)	0.6 (06)
India					9.6 (00)	11.8 (06)	0.7 (00)	0.7 (06)
Iran (Islamic Republic of)	78.5 (04)	77.3 (05)	0.9 (04)	0.9 (05)	18.9 (99)	31.4	0.8 (99)	1.2
Maldives	51.1 (02)	67.1 (06)	1.1 (99)	1.1 (06)			2.4 (03)	2.4 (04)
Nepal					4.1 (00)	5.6 (04)	0.4 (00)	0.4 (04)
Pakistan	22.0 (99)	32.2 (07)	0.7 (99)	0.8 (07)	2.5 (02)	5.1	0.8 (02)	0.9
Sri Lanka								
Turkey	66.0 (05)	68.7 (06)	0.8 (05)	0.9 (06)	21.5 (99)	34.6 (06)	0.7 (99)	0.8 (06)
South-East Asia								
Brunei Darussalam	87.3 (05)	89.1 (07)	1.1 (05)	1.0 (07)	12.3 (99)	15.4	2.0 (99)	1.9
Cambodia	15.4 (99)	30.7 (06)	0.5 (99)	0.9 (06)	2.1 (00)	5.3	0.3 (00)	0.6
Indonesia	48.2 (00)	60.4 (06)	1.0 (00)	1.0 (06)	14.4 (01)	17.0 (06)	0.8 (01)	0.8 (05)
Lao People's Democratic Republic	26.3 (99)	34.9 (06)	0.8 (99)	0.9 (06)	2.4 (99)	9.1 (06)	0.5 (99)	0.7 (06)
Malaysia	65.1 (99)	68.7 (05)	1.1 (99)	1.1 (05)	23.0 (99)	28.6 (05)	1.0 (99)	1.3 (05)
Myanmar	32.1 (99)	45.7 (06)	1.0 (99)	1.0 (06)	7.4 (99)		1.6 (99)	
Philippines	50.7 (99)	60.4 (06)	1.1 (99)	1.2 (06)	28.7 (99)	28.5 (06)	1.3 (99)	1.2 (06)
Singapore								
Thailand	71.0 (06)	76.1 (07)	1.1 (06)	1.1 (07)	33.0 (99)	49.5	1.2 (99)	1.2
Timor-Leste	22.8 (01)				9.6 (02)		1.3 (02)	
Viet Nam	59.1 (99)	61.9 (01)			10.6 (99)		0.8 (99)	
Developed ESCAP economies								
Australia	90.2 (00)	87.2 (06)	1.0 (00)	1.0 (06)	65.4 (99)	72.7 (06)	1.2 (99)	1.3 (06)
Japan	99.4 (99)	98.7 (06)	1.0 (00)	1.0 (06)	45.1 (99)	57.3 (06)	0.8 (99)	0.9 (06)
New Zealand	91.9 (02)		1.0 (02)		64.3 (99)	79.7 (06)	1.5 (99)	1.5 (06)

Source: UNESCO Institute for Statistics, Data Centre (online database, November 2008).

187

Table 14. Poverty and malnutrition

	Share of population below $1.25 (2005 PPP) per day (%)		Share of population below the national poverty line (%)		Gini coefficient of income distribution		Children under 5 moderately or severely underweight (%)	
	Earliest	Latest	Earliest	Latest	Earliest	Latest	Earliest	Latest
Developing ESCAP economies								
East and North-East Asia								
China	60.2 (90)	15.9 (05)	6.0 (96)	4.6 (98)	29.2 (90)	35.4 (05)	19.1 (90)	6.9 (05)
DPR Korea							60.0 (98)	23.4 (04)
Hong Kong, China								
Macao, China								
Mongolia	18.8 (95)	22.4 (05)	36.3 (95)	36.1 (02)	33.2 (95)	33.0 (05)	12.3 (92)	6.3 (05)
Republic of Korea								
North and Central Asia								
Armenia	17.5 (96)	10.6 (03)	55.1 (99)	50.9 (01)	44.4 (96)	33.8 (03)	3.9 (98)	4.0 (05)
Azerbaijan	15.6 (95)	0.0 (05)	68.1 (95)	49.6 (01)	35.0 (95)	16.8 (05)	10.1 (96)	6.8 (01)
Georgia	4.5 (96)	13.4 (05)	52.1 (02)	54.5 (03)	37.1 (96)	40.8 (05)	3.1 (99)	3.1 (99)
Kazakhstan	4.2 (93)	3.1 (03)	34.6 (96)	15.4 (02)	25.7 (88)	33.9 (03)	8.3 (95)	4.0 (06)
Kyrgyzstan	18.6 (93)	21.8 (04)	47.6 (01)	43.1 (05)	47.7 (88)	32.9 (04)	11.0 (97)	3.4 (06)
Russian Federation	2.8 (93)	0.2 (05)	30.9 (94)	19.6 (02)	23.8 (88)	37.5 (05)	3.0 (95)	3.0 (95)
Tajikistan	44.5 (99)	21.5 (04)	74.9 (99)	74.9 (99)	31.5 (99)	33.6 (04)	17.4 (05)	17.4 (05)
Turkmenistan	63.5 (93)	24.8 (98)			26.2 (88)	40.8 (98)	12.0 (00)	11.0 (05)
Uzbekistan	32.1 (98)	46.3 (03)	27.5 (00)	27.5 (00)	25.0 (88)	36.7 (03)	18.8 (96)	5.1 (06)
Pacific island economies								
American Samoa								
Cook Islands								
Fiji							10.0 (97)	10.0 (97)
French Polynesia							7.9 (93)	7.9 (93)
Guam								
Kiribati								
Marshall Islands							13.0 (99)	13.0 (99)
Micronesia (Federated States of)								
Nauru							15.0 (97)	15.0 (97)
New Caledonia								
Niue								
Northern Mariana Island								
Palau								
Papua New Guinea	35.8 (96)	35.8 (96)	37.5 (96)	37.5 (96)	50.9 (96)	50.9 (96)		
Samoa								
Solomon Islands								
Tonga								
Tuvalu								
Vanuatu								
South and South-West Asia								
Afghanistan							48.0 (97)	39.3 (04)
Bangladesh	66.8 (91)	49.6 (05)	58.8 (92)/a	40.0 (05)/a	26.2 (91)	31.0 (05)	67.4 (92)	47.5 (04)
Bhutan	26.2 (03)	26.2 (03)			46.8 (03)	46.8 (03)	18.7 (99)	18.7 (99)
India	51.3 (90)	41.6 (05)	36.0 (94)	27.5 (05)/b	30.9 (90)	32.5 (05)	53.4 (93)	45.9 (05)
Iran (Islamic Republic of)	3.9 (90)	1.5 (05)			47.4 (86)	38.3 (05)	15.7 (95)	10.9 (98)
Maldives							38.9 (94)	30.4 (01)
Nepal	68.4 (95)	55.1 (03)	41.8 (96)	30.9 (04)	37.7 (95)	47.3 (03)	48.7 (95)	38.6 (06)
Pakistan	64.7 (90)	22.6 (04)	28.6 (93)	22.3 (06)/c	33.4 (87)	31.2 (04)	40.4 (91)	37.8 (02)
Sri Lanka	15.0 (90)	14.0 (02)	20.0 (91)	15.2 (07)/d	32.5 (85)	41.1 (02)	37.7 (93)	29.4 (00)
Turkey	2.1 (94)	2.7 (05)	28.3 (94)	27.0 (02)	43.6 (87)	43.2 (05)	10.4 (93)	3.9 (03)
South-East Asia								
Brunei Darussalam								
Cambodia	48.6 (94)	40.2 (04)	47.0 (94)	35.0 (04)	38.3 (94)	41.9 (04)	39.8 (93)	35.6 (05)
Indonesia	54.3 (90)	21.4 (05)	17.5 (96)	16.7 (04)	29.0 (90)	34.5 (05)	34.0 (95)	28.2 (03)
Lao People's Democratic Republic	55.7 (92)	44.0 (02)	45.0 (93)	33.0 (03)	30.4 (92)	32.6 (02)	44.0 (93)	40.0 (00)
Malaysia	1.6 (92)	0.5 (04)			48.6 (84)	37.9 (04)	23.3 (93)	8.1 (05)
Myanmar							32.4 (90)	31.8 (03)
Philippines	30.7 (91)	22.6 (06)	32.1 (94)	25.1 (97)	41.0 (85)	44.0 (06)	33.5 (90)	27.6 (03)
Singapore							3.4 (00)	3.4 (00)
Thailand	5.5 (92)	0.4 (04)	32.5 (92)/e	12.0 (04)/e	45.2 (81)	42.5 (04)	18.6 (93)	9.3 (05)
Timor-Leste	52.9 (01)	52.9 (01)			39.5 (01)	39.5 (01)	42.6 (02)	45.8 (03)
Viet Nam	63.7 (92)	21.5 (06)	37.4 (98)	28.9 (02)	35.7 (92)	37.8 (06)	44.9 (94)	25.2 (05)
Developed ESCAP economies								
Australia								
Japan								
New Zealand								

Sources: World Bank, *PovcalNet,* http://www.worldbank.org/ (November 2008); United Nations Department of Economic and Social Affairs, *Millennium Development Goals Indicators,* http://mdgs.un.org/ (August 2008); and World Bank, *World Development Indicators,* http://www.worldbank.org/ (May 2008).

a Ministry of Finance of Bangladesh.
b Ministry of Finance of India.
c Ministry of Finance of Pakistan.
d Central Bank of Sri Lanka, *Annual Report 2007.*
e National Statistical Office, *Core Economic Indicators of Thailand 2005.*

Table 15. Unemployment by gender and age group

	Unemployment rate						Youth unemployment rate					
	Both sexes			Female			Both sexes			Female		
	Percentage of labour force						Percentage of labour force age 15-24					
	1990	2000	2007	1990	2000	2007	1990	2000	Latest	1990	2000	Latest
Developing ESCAP economies												
East and North-East Asia												
China	2.5	3.1	4.2 (05)									
DPR Korea												
Hong Kong, China	1.3	4.9	4.0	1.3	4.0	3.4	3.4	11.2	10.9 (05)	3.3	10.4	8.0 (05)
Macao, China	3.1	6.7	3.0	4.0	4.6	2.7		9.9	8.2 (05)		6.7	5.8 (05)
Mongolia		17.5	14.2 (03)		16.6	14.1 (03)		22.8	20.0 (03)		23.0	20.7 (03)
Republic of Korea	2.5	4.4	3.2	1.8	3.6	2.6	7.0	10.8	10.2 (05)	5.5	9.0	9.0 (05)
North and Central Asia												
Armenia		11.7	9.6 (04)		15.7	13.8 (04)						
Azerbaijan		16.3 (99)			18.6 (99)							
Georgia		10.8	13.3		10.5	12.6		21.1	28.3 (05)		20.5	30.6 (05)
Kazakhstan		12.8	8.4 (04)			9.8 (04)			14.3 (04)			15.7 (04)
Kyrgyzstan			8.3 (06)			9.0 (06)			15.2 (04)			17.8 (04)
Russian Federation		9.8	6.1		9.4	5.8		24.7 (99)			25.9 (99)	
Tajikistan												
Turkmenistan												
Uzbekistan												
Pacific island economies												
American Samoa	5.0	5.1		4.8	6.0							
Cook Islands	7.2 (91)			9.5 (91)								
Fiji	6.4		4.6 (05)			5.9 (05)						
French Polynesia												
Guam	2.8	11.5			11.5						·	
Kiribati												
Marshall Islands		30.9 (99)			37.3 (99)							
Micronesia (Federated States of)												
Nauru												
New Caledonia		18.6 (96)			22.1 (96)			33.6 (96)			38.5 (96)	
Niue		9.7 (02)			2.1 (01)							
Northern Mariana Island		4.6 (03)			4.3 (03)							
Palau												
Papua New Guinea	7.7	2.8		5.9	1.3			5.3				
Samoa		4.9 (01)			6.2 (01)							
Solomon Islands		31.9 (99)			33.7 (99)							
Tonga	4.1		5.2 (03)			7.4 (03)						
Tuvalu		16.3 (04)			8.6 (02)							
Vanuatu		1.6 (99)										
South and South-West Asia												
Afghanistan		8.5 (05)			9.5 (05)							
Bangladesh		3.3	4.3 (05)		3.3	7.0 (05)		10.7	6.6 (03)		10.3	5.8 (03)
Bhutan			3.2 (05)			3.3 (05))						
India		4.3	5.0 (04)		4.1	5.3 (04)		10.1	10.5 (04)		10.2	10.8 (04)
Iran (Islamic Republic of)			10.5			15.7			23.1 (05)			32.1 (05)
Maldives		2.0	14.4 (06)		2.7	23.7 (06)		4.4			5.1	
Nepal		8.8 (01)			10.7 (01)			3.0 (99)			2.2 (99)	
Pakistan	2.6	7.2	5.3	0.7	15.8	8.4	5.1	13.3	11.7 (04)	1.3	29.2	14.9 (04)
Sri Lanka	14.5	7.6	6.0	23.6	11.1	9.0	33.3	23.6	26.2 (05)	46.9	30.9	37.1 (05)
Turkey	8.0	6.5	9.9	8.5	6.3	10.2	16.0	13.1	19.3 (05)	15.0	11.9	19.3 (05)
South-East Asia												
Brunei Darussalam	4.7 (91)			6.7 (91)								
Cambodia		2.5	1.7 (01)		2.8	2.0 (01)		12.2 (98)			12.0 (98)	
Indonesia		6.1	9.1		6.7	10.8			28.7 (05)			33.8 (05)
Lao People's Democratic Republic			1.4 (05)			1.4 (05)	5.0 (95)			3.9 (95)		
Malaysia	5.1	3.0	3.1		3.1	3.4		8.3			8.3	
Myanmar	6.0			8.8								
Philippines	8.1	10.1	6.3	9.8	9.9	6.0	15.4	21.2	16.4 (05)	19.2	23.6	18.9 (05)
Singapore		6.0	4.0		6.6	4.3			5.2 (05)			6.3 (05)
Thailand	2.2	2.4	1.2	2.4	2.3	1.1	4.3	6.6	4.8 (05)	4.2	6.0	4.6 (05)
Timor-Leste												
Viet Nam		2.3	2.1 (04)		2.1	2.4 (04)		4.8	4.6 (04)		4.6	4.9 (04)
Developed ESCAP economies												
Australia	6.9	6.3	4.4	7.2	6.1	4.8	13.0	12.1	10.8 (05)	12.8	11.3	10.5 (05)
Japan	2.1	4.8	3.9	2.2	4.5	3.7	4.3	9.2	8.7 (05)	4.1	7.9	7.4 (05)
New Zealand	7.8	5.9	3.6	7.3	5.8	3.9	14.1	13.2	9.4 (05)	13.2	12.0	9.8 (05)

Sources: International Labour Organization, *Key Indicators of the Labour Market, Fifth Edition* (online database accessed in May 2008); and United Nations Department of Economics and Social Affairs, *Millennium Development Goals Indicators,* http://mdgs.un.org (August 2008).

Table 16. Energy and water use

	Consumption of electricity for domestic purposes			Energy use per $ 1,000 [2005 PPP] GDP			Water withdrawal					
							Share of total renewable water resources			Withdrawal for domestic purposes		
	kilowatt-hrs. per capita			kgs. of oil equivalent			(%)			cubic metres per capita		
	1990	2000	2005	1990	2000	2006	1992	1997	2002	1992	1997	2002
Developing ESCAP economies												
East and North-East Asia												
China	42	132	215	689	328	318	17.7	18.6	22.3	29.7	20.3	32.2
DPR Korea									11.7			76.9
Hong Kong, China	927	1 344	1 410	84	80	70						
Macao, China	1 534	1 186	1 051									
Mongolia	166	124	236	696	490	386		1.2	1.3		35.0	35.9
Republic of Korea	414	665	1 063	205	230	201			26.7		135.6	140.0
North and Central Asia												
Armenia		506	571	759	293	182	33.3	27.8	28.0	280.5	275.2	288.5
Azerbaijan		1 216	1 467	752	566	273	51.4	41.3	33.3	98.9	27.9	61.1
Georgia		564	662	418	261	194	5.5			136.5		
Kazakhstan		395	322	635	525	421	33.4	30.7	31.9	38.5	37.7	39.5
Kyrgyzstan		475	567	684	331	308	53.4	49.0	49.0	61.4	63.7	63.3
Russian Federation		955	757	469	488	373	1.8	1.7	1.7	98.1	96.2	98.4
Tajikistan		527	478	343	460	351	75.2	74.3	74.8	87.9	69.4	69.6
Turkmenistan		272	277				100.1	96.2	99.7	49.2	80.5	90.7
Uzbekistan		292	269	1 125	1 248	860	124.0	115.2	115.7	95.4	109.0	108.8
Pacific island economies												
American Samoa	509	701	749									
Cook Islands												
Fiji	98	173	226						0.2			12.3
French Polynesia		1 647	1 850									
Guam	2 614	3 478	2 996									
Kiribati			109									
Marshall Islands												
Micronesia (Federated States of)												
Nauru												
New Caledonia												
Niue		1 598	1 838									
Northern Mariana Island												
Palau			1 491									
Papua New Guinea	30	98	185						0.0			7.1
Samoa		225	256									
Solomon Islands	22											
Tonga												
Tuvalu												
Vanuatu			209									
South and South-West Asia												
Afghanistan	22	5	6						35.8			18.9
Bangladesh	12	39	58	163	149	143			6.6	14.4	30.5	17.5
Bhutan	44	54	69						0.4			33.8
India	37	72	91	313	265	213	26.4		34.1	27.9		48.3
Iran (Islamic Republic of)		473	637	202	242	254		60.4	64.4		93.9	66.8
Maldives	70	161	220									
Nepal	12	22	27	433	372	352			4.8		10.8	11.8
Pakistan	83	149	194	240	240	218	69.1		75.2	21.0		21.8
Sri Lanka	30	93	128	165	146	130	19.5		25.2	11.1		15.9
Turkey	158	350	424	166	169	158	14.8		19.7	87.4		91.3
South-East Asia												
Brunei Darussalam	1 720	2 420	2 996	142	159	152	0.9	1.1				
Cambodia		7	8		310	224			0.9			4.5
Indonesia	49	144	182	277	269	240	2.6		2.9	25.1		30.4
Lao People's Democratic Republic		62	88						0.9			24.1
Malaysia	225	487	632	192	212	215	1.7		1.6	42.9	61.9	62.7
Myanmar	16	28	30	786	479				3.2			8.8
Philippines	97	169	190	176	211	163		5.8	6.0		59.6	59.5
Singapore	778	1 425	1 560	187	150	158						
Thailand	149	321	407	195	216	221			21.2	26.9		35.2
Timor-Leste												
Viet Nam	14	139	229	407	300	271	6.1		8.0	28.9		68.0
Developed ESCAP economies												
Australia	2 284	2 548	3 000	211	187	172			4.9			179.6
Japan	1 496	2 030	2 612	139	145	133	21.3		20.6	136.7		136.5
New Zealand	2 880	2 941	3 078	212	211	170			0.6			258.4

Sources: International Energy Agency, http://www.iea.org/ (October 2008); United Nations Department of Economics and Social Affairs, *World Population Prospects: The 2006 Revision Population Database,* http://esa.un.org/unpp/ (July 2008); World Bank, *World Development Indicators,* http://www.worldbank.org/data (July 2008); and Food and Agriculture Organization of the United Nations, *FAO Information system on Water and Agriculture,* http://www.fao.org (November 2008).

Table 17. Pollution and access to water and sanitation

	CO₂ emissions (tons of CO₂ per capita)		Ozone-depleting substances use (kg per 1,000 population)		Share of population with access to improved drinking water sources (%)				Share of population with access to improved sanitation (%)			
					Rural		Urban		Rural		Urban	
	1990	2004	1990	2005	1990	2006	1990	2006	1990	2006	1990	2006
Developing ESCAP economies												
East and North-East Asia												
China	2.1	3.8	51.9	23.9	55	81	97	98	43	59	61	74
DPR Korea	12.2	3.4		12.0		100	100	100				
Hong Kong, China	4.6	5.4										
Macao, China	2.8	4.7										
Mongolia	4.5	3.3		1.7	21	48	97	90		31		64
Republic of Korea	5.6	9.8		111.5			97	97				
North and Central Asia												
Armenia		1.2		28.8		96	99	99		81	94	96
Azerbaijan		3.8		2.6	51	59	82	95		70		90
Georgia		0.9		7.7	58	97	91	100	91	92	96	94
Kazakhstan		13.3	142.5	2.6	91	91	99	99	96	98	97	97
Kyrgyzstan		1.1		3.2		83	97	99		93		94
Russian Federation		10.5	878.6	5.4	86	88	97	100	70	70	93	93
Tajikistan		0.8		0.5		58		93		91		95
Turkmenistan		8.8	39.6	5.6								
Uzbekistan		5.3		0.1	85	82	97	98	91	95	97	97
Pacific island economies												
American Samoa												
Cook Islands	1.2	2.0			87	88	99	98	91	100	100	100
Fiji	1.1	1.3	57.8	7.2	51	51	43	43	55	55	87	87
French Polynesia	3.1	2.7			100	100	100	100	97	97	99	99
Guam					100	100	100	100	98	98	99	99
Kiribati	0.3	0.3			33	53	76	77	20	20	26	46
Marshall Islands				25.4	97			95	51		88	
Micronesia (Federated States of)				4.5	86	94	93	95	20	14	54	61
Nauru	14.4	14.2										
New Caledonia	9.4	11.2										
Niue	1.6	2.2			100	100	100	100	100	100	100	100
Northern Mariana Island					100	97	98	98	78	96	85	94
Palau	15.7	11.9		9.9	98	94	73	79	54	52	76	96
Papua New Guinea	0.6	0.4		3.1	32	32	88	88	41	41	67	67
Samoa	0.8	0.8		1.1	89	87	99	90	98	100	100	100
Solomon Islands	0.5	0.4	6.7	2.3	65	65	94	94	18	18	98	98
Tonga	0.8	1.2			100	100	100	100	96	96	98	98
Tuvalu					89	92	92	94	74	84	83	93
Vanuatu	0.4	0.4			53		93					
South and South-West Asia												
Afghanistan	0.2	0.0		5.8		17		37		25		45
Bangladesh	0.1	0.2	1.8	1.8	76	78	88	85	18	32	56	48
Bhutan	0.2	0.7		0.2		79		98		50		71
India	0.8	1.2		3.8	65	86	90	96	4	18	44	52
Iran (Islamic Republic of)	3.9	6.3	24.6	35.3	84		99	99	78		86	
Maldives	0.7	2.5	20.9	9.1	95	76	100	98		42	100	100
Nepal	0.0	0.1		0.0	70	88	97	94	6	24	36	45
Pakistan	0.6	0.8	12.9	3.8	81	87	96	95	14	40	76	90
Sri Lanka	0.2	0.6	12.7	8.6	62	79	91	98	68	86	85	89
Turkey	2.6	3.1	76.0	10.9	74	95	92	98	69	72	96	96
South-East Asia												
Brunei Darussalam	22.7	24.1		111.3								
Cambodia	0.0	0.0		3.6		61		80		19		62
Indonesia	1.2	1.7		12.1	63	71	92	89	42	37	73	67
Lao People's Democratic Republic	0.1	0.2		3.8		53		86		38		87
Malaysia	3.1	7.0	231.7	26.6	96	96	100	100		93	95	95
Myanmar	0.1	0.2		0.3	47	80	86	80	15	81	47	85
Philippines	0.7	1.0	56.8	14.6	75	88	92	96	46	72	71	81
Singapore	15.0	12.2	1 609.6	34.8			100	100			100	100
Thailand	1.8	4.3	128.6	36.8	94	97	98	99	72	96	92	95
Timor-Leste		0.2				56		77		32		64
Viet Nam	0.3	1.2		5.4	43	90	87	98	21	56	62	88
Developed ESCAP economies												
Australia	16.5	16.3	440.6	8.3	100	100	100	100	100	100	100	100
Japan	8.7	9.8	972.0	8.3	100	100	100	100	100	100	100	100
New Zealand	6.6	7.8	350.5	10.3	82		100	100	88			

Sources: United Nations, *Millennium Development Goals Indicators,* http://mdgs.un.org/ (August 2008); United Nations Department of Economics and Social Affairs, *World Population Prospects: The 2006 Revision Population Database,* http://esa.un.org/unpp/ (September 2008).

Table 18. Natural disasters

| | Deaths | | | | Number of people affected | | | | Economic damages | | | |
| | Cumulative number over the period | | | | Cumulative number, in thousands, over the period | | | | Million US dollars | | | |
	91-95	96-00	01-05	2008	91-95	96-00	01-05	2008	91-95	96-00	01-05	2008
Developing ESCAP economies												
East and North-East Asia												
China	14 045	14 151	5 690	87 679	613 487	563 896	678 155	94 222	48 756	72 736	43 125	29 533
DPR Korea	74	254	344	0	5 703	3 799	204	0	15 110	8 202	30	0
Hong Kong, China	38	83	303	0	7	0	5	0	519	10	0	0
Macao, China	0	0	0	0	1	0	0	0	0	0	0	0
Mongolia	18	97	34	0	100	1 526	846	0	10	1 793	0	0
Republic of Korea	275	751	489	0	25	99	490	0	1 118	2 099	10 414	0
North and Central Asia												
Armenia	0	4	1	0	0	319	0	0	0	141	0	0
Azerbaijan	5	55	0	0	1 503	778	30	0	16	140	55	0
Georgia	10	7	7	0	2	696	21	0	2	230	352	0
Kazakhstan	122	7	54	1	30	611	65	13	40	2	8	130
Kyrgyzstan	220	34	90	0	149	2	1	3	197	4	4	0
Russian Federation	3 366	647	1 488	0	1 102	1 305	1 823	0	540	1 078	1 416	0
Tajikistan	1 606	300	67	0	84	3 257	419	2 000	473	129	127	850
Turkmenistan	0	11	0	0	0	0	0	0	100	0	0	0
Uzbekistan	10	64	0	0	50	600	2	0	0	50	0	0
Pacific island economies												
American Samoa	0	0	6	0	0	0	20	0	0	0	200	0
Cook Islands	0	19	0	0	0	1	1	0	0	0	0	0
Fiji	22	41	34	7	152	267	36	0	361	31	34	0
French Polynesia	0	13	0	0	0	1	0	0	0	0	0	0
Guam	1	0	5	0	0	1	11	0	420	200	131	0
Kiribati	0	0	0	0	0	84	0	0	0	0	0	0
Marshall Islands	0	6	0	0	0	0	0	0	0	0	0	0
Micronesia (Federated States of)	0	19	48	0	0	32	7	0	0	0	1	0
Nauru									0	0	0	0
New Caledonia	0	0	2	0	0	0	0	0	0	0	40	0
Niue	0	1	1	0	0	0	0	0	0	0	40	0
Northern Mariana Island	0	0	0	0	0	0	0	0	0	0	0	0
Palau									0	0	0	0
Papua New Guinea	273	2 433	198	0	245	519	59	0	119	43	0	0
Samoa	13	0	10	0	85	0	0	0	278	0	2	0
Solomon Islands	4	0	0	0	89	0	0	0	0	0	0	0
Tonga	0	0	0	0	0	4	17	0	0	0	51	0
Tuvalu	0	0	0	0	0	0	0	0	0	0	0	0
Vanuatu	6	144	4	0	6	14	68	0	6	0	0	0
South and South-West Asia												
Afghanistan	2 807	8 352	5 305	1 317	241	2 814	548	171	64	20	5	0
Bangladesh	145 422	3 719	3 076	0	53 242	28 216	41 014	0	3 233	5 039	2 700	0
Bhutan	39	200	0	0	66	0	0	0	0	4	0	0
India	20 761	29 486	49 021	130	185 791	222 676	436 885	311	9 014	7 996	15 599	0
Iran (Islamic Republic of)	1 031	3 242	28 393	0	844	37 236	1 890	0	5 383	3 779	1 070	0
Maldives	0	0	102	0	0	0	12	0	30	0	470	0
Nepal	3 609	2 340	1 257	0	660	230	1 162	0	207	35	0	0
Pakistan	4 510	2 237	75 231	0	12 420	4 862	10 274	0	1 102	258	5 477	0
Sri Lanka	118	68	35 648	31	785	1 077	3 056	758	283	3	1 346	0
Turkey	1 353	18 237	452	0	690	3 624	518	0	1 080	22 621	255	0
South-East Asia												
Brunei Darussalam	0	0	0	0	0	0	0	0	0	2	0	0
Cambodia	656	987	108	0	6 059	5 399	4 689	0	250	162	53	0
Indonesia	4 144	3 751	169 340	41	4 734	2 632	1 802	105	545	10 277	4 965	0
Lao People's Democratic Republic	743	89	2	0	1 429	900	603	0	329	1	0	0
Malaysia	385	552	143	0	24	50	140	0	0	356	510	0
Myanmar	96	90	396	133 655	449	104	63	2 400	145	0	501	0
Philippines	9 857	2 114	3 381	667	14 470	20 227	11 081	1 875	2 090	457	321	250
Singapore	0	3	33	0	0	0	2	0	0	0	0	0
Thailand	494	523	8 905	0	10 163	15 031	10 294	0	2 553	317	1 928	3
Timor-Leste	0	0	26	0	0	0	4	0	0	0	0	0
Viet Nam	1 679	6 788	1 242	0	1 352	19 336	6 310	0	559	2 361	945	190
Developed ESCAP economies												
Australia	65	71	40	1	14 969	664	22	3	2 813	4 058	3 091	90
Japan	5 903	223	573	10	465	766	831	0	113 675	18 183	49 671	0
New Zealand	0	4	6	0	0	3	6	0	152	76	531	0

Source: Centre of Research on the Epidemiology of Disasters, Emergency Events Database (EM-DAT) http://www.emdat.be/ (August 2008).

Technical notes

Table 1. Real GDP growth rates

GDP growth rate at constant prices. The real (at constant market prices) annual percentage changes in GDP in national currencies are reported in this table. GDP is defined as the total cost of all finished goods and services produced within the country in a given year. Most countries use constant market price values. The growth rates of some countries are at factor cost, including Fiji, India, the Islamic Republic of Iran and Pakistan, while Nepal is at basic prices. In the case of Timor-Leste, the data refer to real non-oil GDP, including locally paid compensation of United Nations peacekeeping mission staff. The table contains historical data from 1997 to 2007, which are based on United Nations Statistics Division, *National Accounts Main Aggregates Database*, with updates from national and local sources. The data for 2008 are generally ESCAP estimates and calculations, although some projections are in line with the economic programmes/projections of the Governments concerned.

Tables 2 and 3. Gross domestic savings and investment rates

Gross domestic savings (GDS) and investment (GDI). Gross domestic savings are calculated as the difference between GDP and total consumption expenditure in the national accounts statistics. Gross domestic investment (GDI) is the sum of gross fixed capital formation and changes in inventories. Gross fixed capital formation is measured by the total value of a producer's acquisitions minus disposals of fixed assets in a given accounting period. Additions to the value of non-produced assets, such as land, form part of gross fixed capital formation. Inventories are stocks of goods held by institutional units to meet temporary or unexpected fluctuations in production and sales. All figures used in computing the GDS and GDI as a percentage of GDP are in current prices. Historical data are mostly based on Asian Development Bank, *Key Indicators for Asia and the Pacific 2008* and updated with information from national and local sources and inputs provided by national authorities. The 2008 data have been obtained from inputs supplied by national authorities and ESCAP calculations and estimates.

Table 4. Inflation rates

Inflation rates. Rates of inflation in this table refer to changes in the consumer price index (CPI) and reflect changes in the cost of acquiring a fixed basket of goods and services incurred by an average consumer. Historical data are based on International Monetary Fund, *International Financial Statistics* and *World Economic Outlook Database*, October 2008, with updates and estimates from national, local and country sources, statistical publications, secondary publications and documents from IMF. The figures for 2008 are generally estimates and based on ESCAP calculations. The projections/estimates are also provided by country authorities. For India, data refer to the industrial workers index. Consumer price inflation for the following countries is for a given city or group of consumers: for Cambodia, it is Phnom Penh; for Sri Lanka, it is Colombo; and the data for Nepal is for national urban consumers.

Table 5. Budget balance

Government surplus or deficit, as percentage of GDP. The government fiscal balance (surplus/deficit) is the difference between central Government total revenues and total expenditures as a percentage of GDP. This provides a picture of the changes in the Government's financial position each year. When the difference is positive, the fiscal position is in surplus; otherwise, it is in deficit.

Government revenue is the sum of current and capital revenues. Current revenue is the revenue accruing from taxes, as well as all current non-tax revenues, except for transfers received from other (foreign or domestic) governments and international institutions. Major items of non-tax revenue include receipts from government enterprises, rents and royalties, fees and fines, forfeits, private donations and repayments of loans properly defined as components of net lending. Capital revenue is the proceeds from the sale of non-financial capital assets. As for government expenditure, it is the sum of current and capital expenditure. Current expenditure comprises purchases of goods and services by the central Government, transfers to non-central government units and to households, subsidies to producers and the interest on public debt. Capital expenditures, on the other hand, cover outlays for the acquisition or construction of capital assets and for the purchase of land and intangible assets, as well as capital transfers to domestic and foreign recipients. Loans and advances for capital purposes are also included. In most countries, the budget surplus/deficit is the balance and excludes grants. However, for Armenia, Azerbaijan, Bhutan, Cook Islands, Fiji, Georgia, India, Kazakhstan, Kyrgyzstan, the Lao People's Democratic Republic, Maldives, Mongolia, Myanmar (since 1998), Nepal, Papua New Guinea, the Philippines, the Russian Federation, Samoa, Solomon Islands, Tajikistan, Timor-Leste, Tonga, Turkmenistan, Tuvalu, Vanuatu and Viet Nam, the budget balance includes grants. The budget balance as percentage of non-oil GDP is calculated for Timor-Leste. The budget surplus/deficit of Singapore is computed from government operating revenue minus government operating expenditure and minus government development expenditure. The budget balance of Thailand refers to a government cash balance. For developed ESCAP member countries, the budget balance refers to general government fiscal balance. In the case of Australia, budget balance is equal to revenue less expenses less net capital investment and, in the case of New Zealand, the government balance comprises revenue minus expenditure plus the balance of State-owned enterprises, excluding privatization receipts.

Table 6. Current account balance

Current account balance, as share of GDP. The current account balance refers to the sum of the balance on goods, services and income. It also includes current transfers crossing national borders. A positive balance shows that foreign currencies flow into the domestic economy; a negative balance shows that foreign currencies flow out. The figures are reported as a percentage of GDP at current prices (national currency) to allow for cross-country comparisons. Historical data are mainly based on IMF, *International Financial Statistics* and *World Economic Outlook Database*, October 2008, with updates and estimates from national, local and country sources. The 2008 data are derived from projections supplied by national authorities and ESCAP estimates. In the case of Cambodia, current account includes official transfers.

Table 7. Changes in money supply

Growth of money supply. The annual growth rates of the broad money supply (at the end of a given period) as represented by M2. M2 is defined as the sum of currency in circulation plus demand deposits (M1) and quasi-money, which consists of time and savings deposits, including foreign currency deposits. Historical data for M2 are mainly obtained from IMF, *International Financial Statistics*, with updates and estimates from national and local sources. In the case of Cook Islands, Turkmenistan and Uzbekistan, the data are based on ADB, *Key Indicators for Asia and the Pacific 2008*. The data for 2008 are computed by ESCAP on the basis of IMF data and estimates based on national sources.

Tables 8 and 9. Growth rates of merchandise exports and imports

Growth rates of exports and imports. The annual growth rates of exports and imports, in terms of merchandise goods only, are shown in these tables. Data are in millions of United States dollars primarily obtained from the balance-of-payments accounts of each country. Exports in general are reported on a free-on-board (f.o.b.) basis. In this case, exports are valued at the customs frontier of the exporting country plus export duties and the cost of loading the goods onto the carriers unless the latter is borne by the carrier. It excludes the cost of freight and insurance beyond the customs frontier. As for imports, data are reported either on an f.o.b. or c.i.f. (cost, insurance, freight) basis. On a c.i.f. basis, the value of imports includes the cost of international freight and insurance up to the customs frontier of the importing country. It excludes the cost of unloading the goods from the carrier unless it is borne by the carrier.

Historical data on exports and imports are mainly obtained from country sources, statistical publications and secondary publications. The figures for 2008 are generally estimates based on country sources and calculations by ESCAP and are also provided by national consultants.

Table 10. Inward foreign direct investment

FDI inward stock (million US dollars; % of GDP). Inward FDI stock is the value of the share of capital and reserves (including retained profits) attributable to the parent enterprise, plus the net indebtedness of affiliates to the parent enterprise, when the parent enterprise is resident in a different economy.

FDI net inflows (million US dollars; % of GDP). Foreign direct investment inflows comprise capital provided (either directly or through other related enterprises) by a foreign direct investor to an FDI enterprise in the reporting economy.

Table 11. Official development assistance and workers' remittances

ODA received (million US dollars; % of GNI). The amount of official development assistance (ODA) received in grants and loans during the reporting period, expressed in millions of United States dollars and as a percentage of the gross national income (GNI). GNI is GDP less net taxes on production and imports, less compensation of employees and property income payable to the rest of the world plus the corresponding items receivable from the rest of the world.

Workers' remittances (million US dollars; % of GNI). Current transfers from abroad by migrants who are employed or intend to remain employed for more than a year in another economy in which they are considered residents, expressed in millions of United States dollars and as a percentage of gross national income (GNI).

Table 12. International migration

Stock of foreign population (thousand people). Estimated number of international immigrants, male and female, in the middle of the indicated year. Generally represents the number of persons born in a country other than where they live. Where data on the place of birth were unavailable, the number of non-citizens was used as a proxy for the number of international immigrants. In either case, the migrant stock includes refugees, some of whom may not be foreign-born.

Stock of foreign population as share of total population (percentage). The number of international immigrants (see definition for "stock of foreign population") divided by the total population.

Net migration rate (per 1,000 population). The number of international immigrants minus the number of emigrants over a period, divided by the average population of the receiving country over that period.

Table 13(a). Primary education

Net enrolment ratio in primary education (% of primary school-aged children). The number of pupils in the theoretical school-age group for primary education, expressed as a percentage of the total population in that age group.

Gender parity index for net enrolment – Primary and secondary education. Ratio of female to male enrolment ratios for each level of education. A GPI of 1 indicates parity between the sexes.

Completion rate (%). Primary completion measured by the gross intake ratio to last grade of primary education is the total number of new entrants in the last grade of primary education (according to the International Standard Classification of Education or ISCED97), regardless of age, expressed as a percentage of the total population of the theoretical entrance age to the last grade of primary.

Table 13(b). Secondary and tertiary education

Net enrolment ratio in secondary education (% of secondary school-aged children). The number of pupils of the theoretical school-age group for secondary education, expressed as a percentage of the total population in that age group.

Gross enrolment ratio in tertiary education (% of tertiary school-aged children). The number of pupils enrolled in the tertiary level of education, regardless of age, expressed as a percentage of the population in the theoretical age group for the same level of education. For the tertiary level, the population used is the five-year age group following on from the secondary school leaving age.

Table 14. Poverty and malnutrition

Population living below $1.25 (2005 PPP) a day (percentage). The proportion of the population living on less than $1.25 a day at 2005 international prices, adjusted for purchasing power parity (PPP).

Population living below the national poverty line (percentage). The national poverty rate is the proportion of the population living below the national poverty line. The figures are not comparable across countries and may not be comparable over time within a country.

Gini index (index). Gini coefficient multiplied by 100. The extent to which the distribution of income (or consumption expenditure) among individuals or households within an economy deviates from a perfectly equal distribution. An index value of 0 corresponds to perfect equality (all earn the same income) and a value of 100 to perfect inequality (one person receives all the income).

Children under 5 moderately or severely underweight (%). Percentage of children aged 0-59 months who fall below minus 2 standard deviations from the median weight for age of the international reference population as adopted by the World Health Organization (WHO).

Table 15. Unemployment by gender and age group

Unemployment rate; total, women (percentage of labour force). The number of persons of working age who, during the reference period, were without work, currently available for work and seeking work, divided by the total labour force. National definitions and coverage of unemployment may vary. Data are presented for both sexes and for women.

Youth unemployment rate; total and female (percentage of labour force aged 15-24). The number of young persons aged 15-24 who are without work, currently available for work and seeking work, divided by the total labour force in that age group. Data are presented for both sexes and for women.

Table 16. Energy and water use

Household electricity consumption per capita (kilowatt-hours). The annual electricity consumption by households per capita.

Energy supply, apparent consumption per unit of GDP (kilograms of oil equivalent per 1,000 (2005 PPP dollars). The use of energy per 1,000 units of GDP in 2005 constant international PPP dollars. "Energy use" refers to the use of primary energy before transformation to other end-use fuels, which is equal to indigenous production plus imports and stock changes, minus exports and fuels supplied to ships and aircraft engaged in international transport.

Water withdrawal share of total renewable water resources (% of total renewable). The gross amount of water extracted in a day from any source either permanently or temporarily. Water can be withdrawn from surface water or groundwater or it can be produced (non-conventional water sources), such as reused treated wastewater and desalinated water.

Water withdrawal for domestic purposes per capita (cubic metres per year). Drinking water plus water withdrawn for homes, municipalities, commercial establishments and public services, divided by the population.

Table 17. Pollution and access to water and sanitation

Carbon dioxide emissions per capita (tons of carbon dioxide). The quantity of estimated carbon dioxide emissions (tons of carbon dioxide) divided by the total population.

Ozone-depleting substances use (kg per 1,000 population). The sum of the national annual consumption in weighted tons of the individual substances in the group of ozone-depleting substances multiplied by their ozone-depleting potential. Ozone-depleting substances are any substance containing chlorine or bromine that destroys the stratospheric ozone layer.

Share of population with access to improved drinking water sources, urban/rural (percentage). Percentage of the population using improved drinking water sources (including household water connection, public standpipe, borehole, protected dug well, protected spring, rainwater collection and bottled water – if a secondary available source is also improved). Data are disaggregated by urban and rural areas.

Share of population with access to improved sanitation, urban/rural (percentage). Proportion of people using an improved sanitation facility (including flush/pour flush toilet or latrine to: piped sewerage, septic tank or pit; a ventilated improved pit (VIP) latrine; a pit latrine with a slab or a composting toilet/latrine). Data are disaggregated by urban and rural areas.

Table 18. Natural disasters

Deaths caused by natural disasters (number). The number of deaths recorded due to natural disasters, expressed as a cumulative number over five-year periods.

People affected by natural disasters (number). The total number of people affected by natural disasters over a five-year period. "Affected people" are people requiring immediate assistance – such as food, water, shelter, sanitation and medical attention – during a period of emergency. Includes cases of an infectious disease introduced in a region or a population that is usually free from that disease.

Economic damage (million US dollars). The estimated economic impact of disasters consisting of direct (for example, damage to infrastructure, crops, housing) and indirect (for example, loss of revenue, unemployment, market destabilization) consequences on the local economy. For each disaster, the registered figure corresponds to the damage value at the moment of the event (nominal value).

Since the 1957 issue, the *Economic and Social Survey of Asia and the Pacific* has, in addition to a review of the current situation of the region, contained a study or studies of some major aspect or problem of the economies of the Asian and Pacific region, as specified below:

1957: Postwar problems of economic development

1958: Review of postwar industrialization

1959: Foreign trade of ECAFE primary exporting countries

1960: Public finance in the postwar period

1961: Economic growth of ECAFE countries

1962: Asia's trade with western Europe

1963: Imports substitution and export diversification

1964: Economic development and the role of the agricultural sector

1965: Economic development and human resources

1966: Aspects of the finance of development

1967: Policies and planning for export

1968: Economic problems of export-dependent countries. Implications of economic controls and liberalization

1969: Strategies for agricultural development. Intraregional trade as a growth strategy

1970: The role of foreign private investment in economic development and cooperation in the ECAFE region. Problems and prospects of the ECAFE region in the Second Development Decade

1971: Economic growth and social justice. Economic growth and employment. Economic growth and income distribution

1972: First biennial review of social and economic developments in ECAFE developing countries during the Second United Nations Development Decade

1973: Education and employment

1974: Mid-term review and appraisal of the International Development Strategy for the Second United Nations Development Decade in the ESCAP region, 1974

1975: Rural development, the small farmer and institutional reform

1976: Biennial review and appraisal of the International Development Strategy at the regional level for the Second United Nations Development Decade in the ESCAP region, 1976

1977: The international economic crises and developing Asia and the Pacific

1978: Biennial review and appraisal at the regional level of the International Development Strategy for the Second United Nations Development Decade

1979: Regional development strategy for the 1980s

1980: Short-term economic policy aspects of the energy situation in the ESCAP region

1981: Recent economic developments in major subregions of the ESCAP region

1982: Fiscal policy for development in the ESCAP region

1983: Implementing the International Development Strategy: major issues facing the developing ESCAP region

1984: Financing development

1985: Trade, trade policies and development

1986: Human resources development in Asia and the Pacific: problems, policies and perspectives

1987: International trade in primary commodities

1988: Recent economic and social developments

1989: Patterns of economic growth and structural transformation in the least developed and Pacific island countries of the ESCAP region: implications for development policy and planning for the 1990s

1990: Infrastructure development in the developing ESCAP region: needs, issues and policy options

1991: Challenges of macroeconomic management in the developing ESCAP region

1992: Expansion of investment and intraregional trade as a vehicle for enhancing regional economic cooperation and development in Asia and the Pacific

1993: Fiscal reform. Economic transformation and social development. Population dynamics: implications for development

1995: Reform and liberalization of the financial sector. Social security

1996: Enhancing the role of the private sector in development. The role of public expenditure in the provision of social services

1997: External financial and investment flows. Transport and communications

1998: Managing the external sector. Growth and equity

1999: Social impact of the economic crisis. Information technology, globalization, economic security and development

2000: Social security and safety nets. Economic and financial monitoring and surveillance

2001: Socio-economic implications of demographic dynamics. Financing for development

2002: The feasibility of achieving the Millennium Development Goals in Asia and the Pacific. Regional development cooperation in Asia and the Pacific

2003: The role of public expenditure in the provision of education and health. Environment-poverty nexus revisited: linkages and policy options

2004: Poverty reduction strategies: tackling the multidimensional nature of poverty

2005: Dynamics of population ageing: how can Asia and the Pacific respond?

2006: Emerging unemployment issues in Asia and the Pacific: rising to the challenges

2007: Gender inequality continues – at great cost

2008: Unequal benefits of growth – agriculture left behind

This publication may be obtained from bookstores and distributors throughout the world. Please consult your bookstore or write to any of the following:

Sales Section	Tel:	(1) (212) 963-8302
Room DC2-0853	Fax:	(1) (212) 963-4116
United Nations Secretariat	E-mail:	publications@un.org
New York, NY 10017		
USA		

Sales Section	Tel:	(41) (22) 917-1234
United Nations Office at Geneva	Fax:	(41) (22) 917-0123
Palais des Nations	E-mail:	unpubli@unog.ch
CH-1211 Geneva 10		
Switzerland		

Chief	Tel:	(662) 288-1234
Conference Management Unit	Fax:	(662) 288-1000
Conference Services Section	E-mail:	yafei.unescap@un.org
Administrative Services Division		
Economic and Social Commission for		
Asia and the Pacific (ESCAP)		
United Nations Building		
Rajadamnern Nok Avenue		
Bangkok 10200, Thailand		

For further information on publications in this series, please address your enquiries to:

Chief
Macroeconomic Policy and Development Division
Economic and Social Commission for
  Asia and the Pacific (ESCAP)
United Nations Building
Rajadamnern Nok Avenue
Bangkok 10200, Thailand

Tel:	(662) 288-1430
Fax:	(662) 288-1000, 288-3007
E-mail:	escap-mpdd@un.org

READERSHIP SURVEY

The Macroeconomic Policy and Development Division of ESCAP is undertaking an evaluation of this publication, **Economic and Social Survey of Asia and the Pacific 2009,** with a view to making future issues more useful for our readers. We would appreciate it if you could complete this questionnaire and return it, at your earliest convenience, to:

> Chief
> Macroeconomic Policy and Development Division
> ESCAP, United Nations Building
> Rajadamnern Nok Avenue
> Bangkok 10200, THAILAND

QUESTIONNAIRE

	Excellent	Very good	Average	Poor
1. Please indicate your assessment of the *quality* of the publication on:				
• Presentation/format	4	3	2	1
• Readability	4	3	2	1
• Timeliness of information	4	3	2	1
• Coverage of subject matter	4	3	2	1
• Analytical rigour	4	3	2	1
• Overall quality	4	3	2	1
2. How *useful* is the publication for your work?				
• Provision of information	4	3	2	1
• Clarification of issues	4	3	2	1
• Its findings	4	3	2	1
• Policy suggestions	4	3	2	1
• Overall usefulness	4	3	2	1

3. Please give examples of how this publication has contributed to your work:

....

....

....

....

4. Suggestions for improving the publication:

....
....
....
....

5. Your background information, please:

Name: ....

Title/position: ....

Institution: ....

Office address: ....

....

**Please use additional sheets of paper, if required, to answer the questions.
Thank you for your kind cooperation in completing this questionnaire.**